TOKYO GHOUL:re
東京喰種

14 CONTENTS

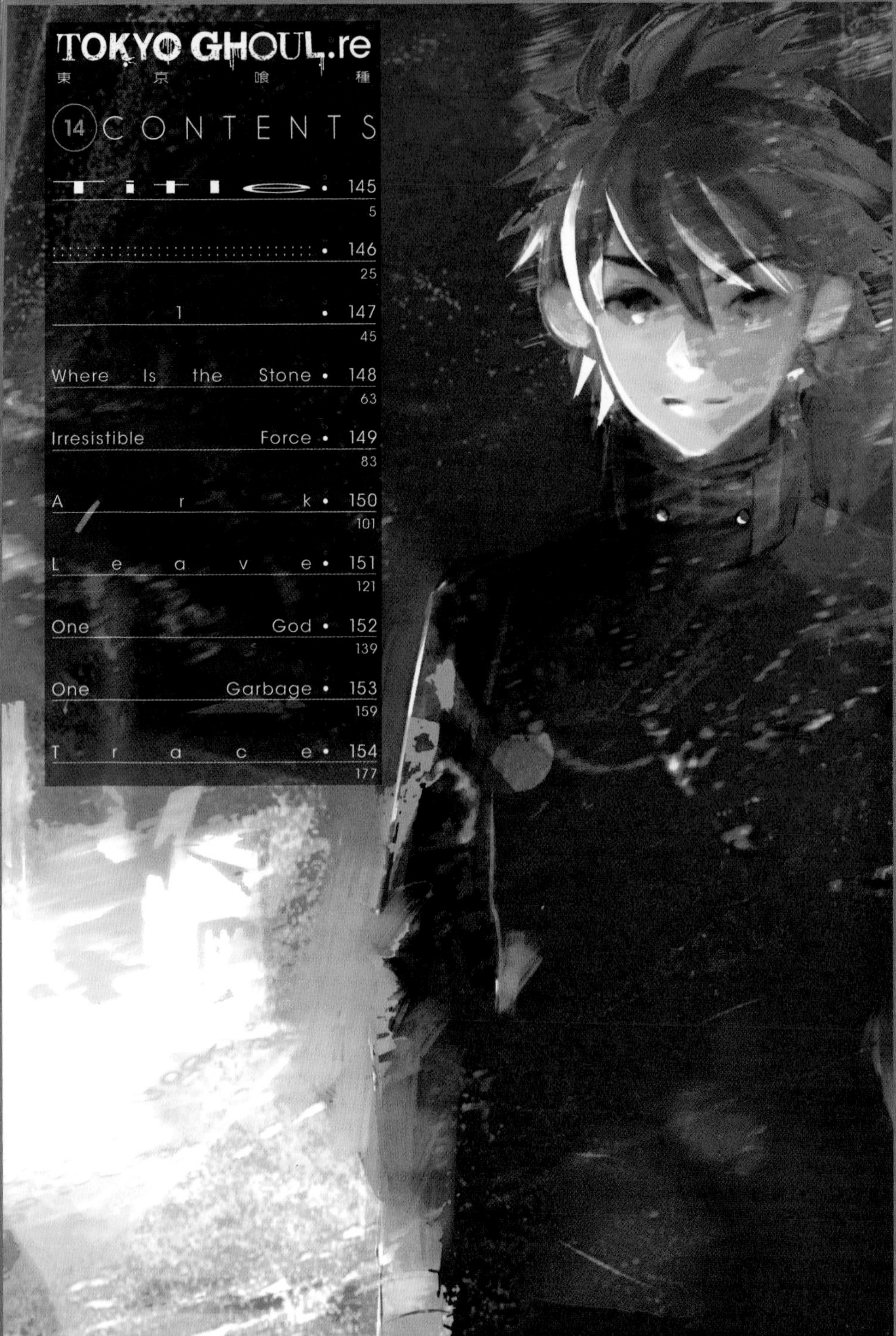

TOKYO GHOUL :re

東京喰種

14

SUI ISHIDA

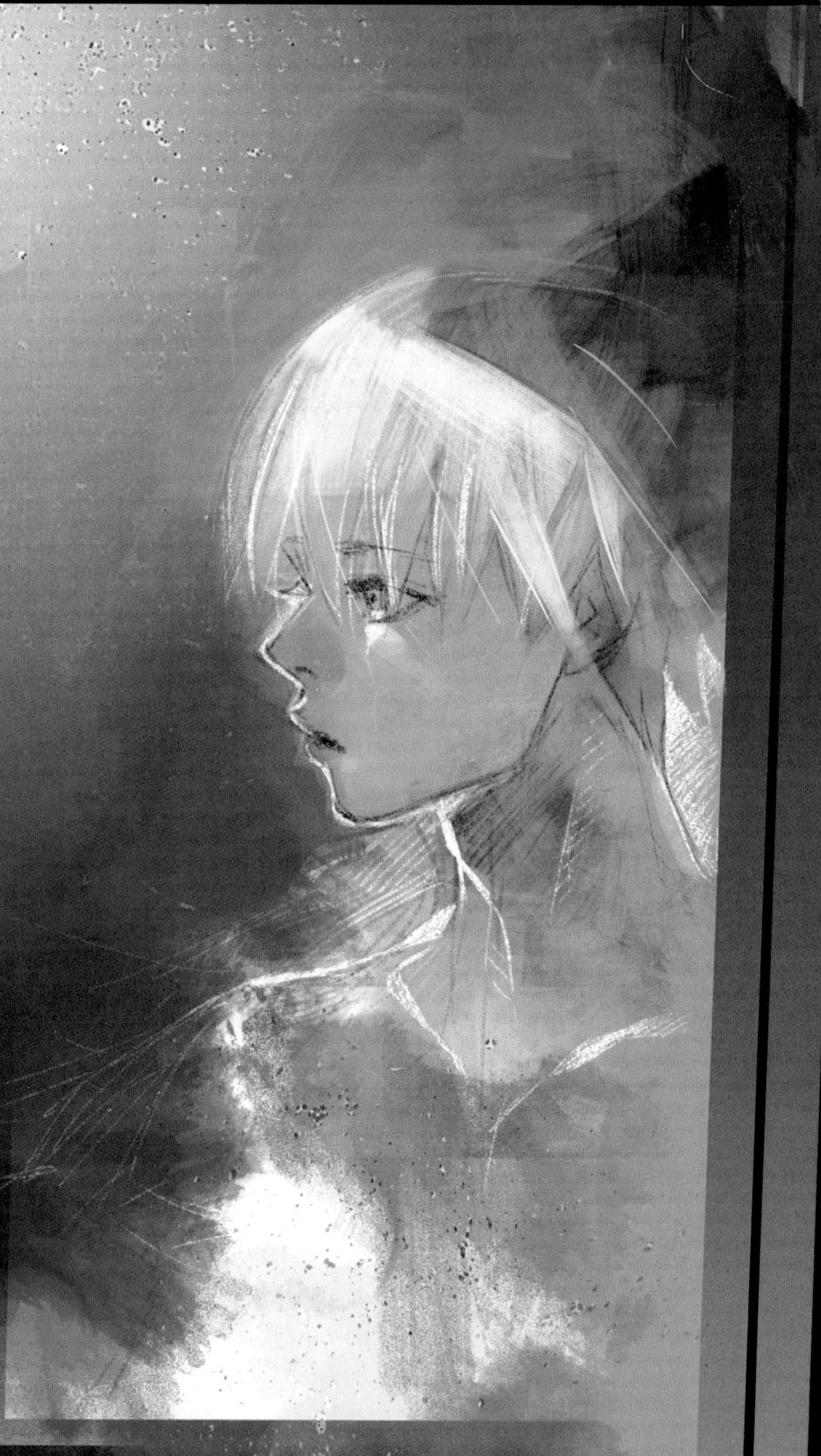

CCG Ghoul Investigators

Tokyo Ghoul :re

The CCG is the only organization in the world that investigates and solves Ghoul-related crimes. Founded by the Washu Family, the CCG developed and evolved Quinques, a type of weapon derived from Ghouls' Kagune. Quinx, an advanced, next-generation technology where humans are implanted with Quinques, is currently under development.

Urie Squad

Qs (Quinx) Investigators implanted with Quinques. They all live together in a house called the Chateau.

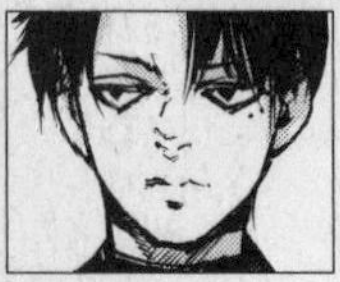

Kuki Urie
瓜江久生
Senior Investigator
New Quinx Squad leader and most talented fighter in the squad. Appointed head of S2 Squad.

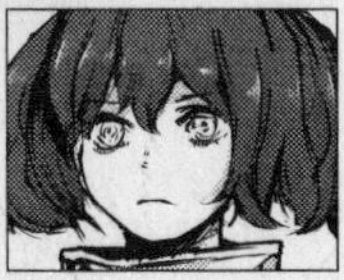

Saiko Yonebayashi
米林才子
Rank 2 Investigator
Supporting Urie as deputy squad leader while playing with her subordinates. Very bad at time management and a sucker for games and snacks.

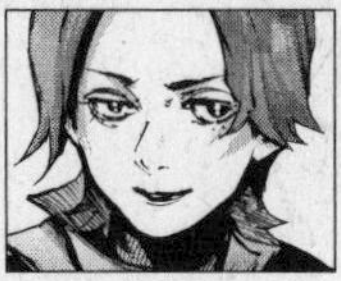

Toma Higemaru
髯丸トウマ
Rank 3 Investigator
Discovered his Quinx aptitude before enrolling in the academy. Looks up to Urie. Comes from a wealthy family.

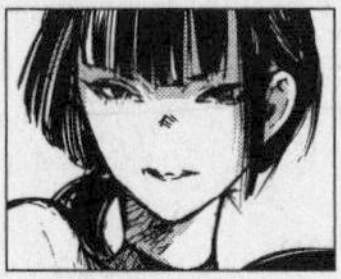

Ching-li Hsiao
小静麗
Rank 1 Investigator
From Hakubi Garden like Hairu Ihei. Skilled in hand-to-hand combat. Came to Japan from Taiwan as a child.

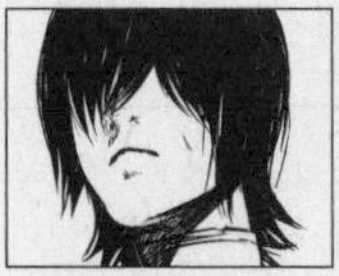

Shinsanpei Aura
安浦晋三平
Rank 2 Investigator
Nephew of Special Investigator Kiyoko Aura. Unlike his aunt, who graduated at the top of her class, his grades were not that great.

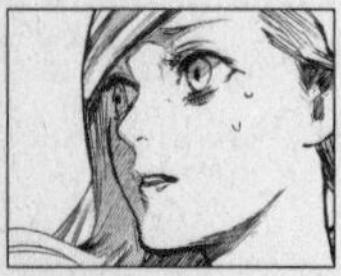

Akira Mado
真戸 暁
Former-Assistant Special Investigator
Mentor to Haise. Determined to eradicate Ghouls. Discharged from the CCG after aiding a Ghoul during the Rushima operation. Working with Amon.

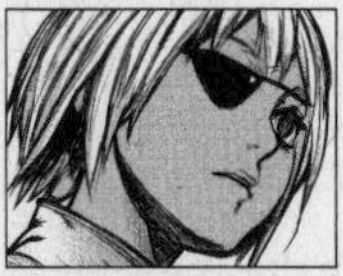

Toru Mutsuki
六月 透
Rank 1 Investigator
Assigned female at birth, he transitioned after the Quinx procedure. Struggling with the lie he has been living with...

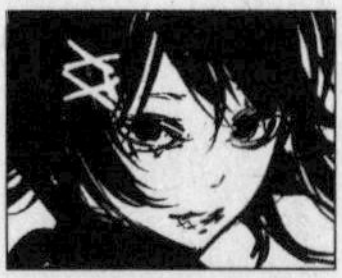

Juzo Suzuya
鈴屋什造
Special Investitgator
Promoted to special investigator at 22, a feat previously only accomplished by Kisho Arima. A maverick who fights with knives hidden in his prosthetic leg. Appointed head of S3 Squad.

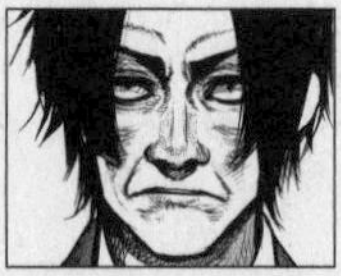

Itsuki Marude
丸手 斎
Special Investitgator
Leads Countermeasure II. Working independently to rebuild the CCG due to his doubts about the Washu family.

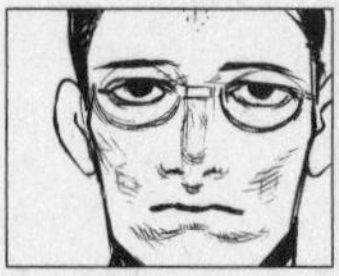

Matsuri Washu
和修 政
Special Investitgator
Yoshitoki's son. A Washu supremacist. Is skeptical of Quinxes. The only surviving member of the Washu family after the Rushima Operation.

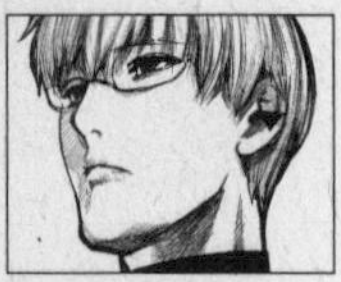

Kisho Arima
有馬貴将
Special Investigator
An undefeated investigator respected by many at the CCG. Killed at Cochlea by the One-Eyed King.

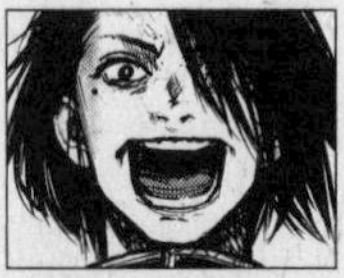

Kichimura Washu
和修吉福
CCG Bureau Chief
Mysterious investigator related to the Washu family. Developed the Oggai for Tokyo Dissolution, a plan to eradicate all Ghouls.

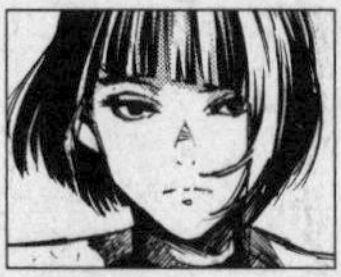

Kori Ui
宇井 郡
Special Investigator
Formerly with the Arima Squad. Became a special investigator at a young age. Assistant to the new bureau chief.

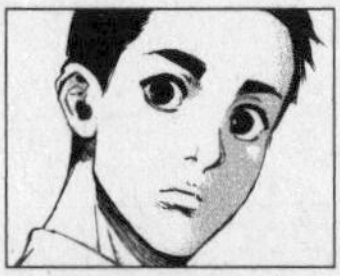

Takeomi Kuroiwa
黒磐武臣
Rank 1 Investigator
Son of Special Investigator Iwao Kuroiwa. Has a strong sense of justice and has restrained Ghouls with his bare hands.

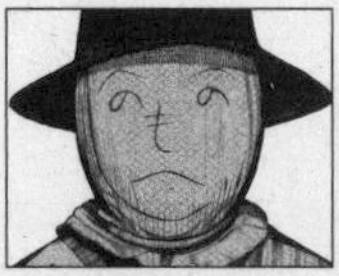

Scarecrow
スケアクロウ
Kaneki's friend Hideyoshi Nagachika.
The man working behind the scenes.

T ● K Y ● G H ● U L

Tokyo Ghoul :re ● Ghouls

They appear human, but have a unique predation organ called Kagune and can only survive by feeding on human flesh. They are the nemesis of humanity. Besides human flesh, the only other thing they can ingest is coffee. Ghouls can only be wounded by a Kagune or a Quinque made from a Kagune.

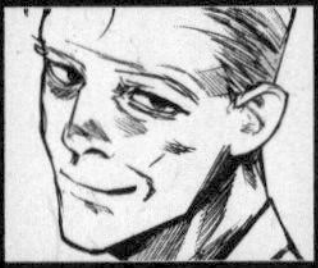

● Akihiro Kano
嘉納明博
Medical examiner for the Aogiri Tree. Researching transplanting Kakuho into humans to create artificial half-Ghouls. Transplanted Rize's Kakuho into Kaneki.

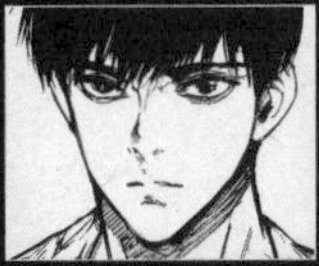

● Kotaro Amon
亜門鋼太朗
Known as Floppy after a Kakuho transplant. Makes a miraculous recovery with Rc Suppressants. Reunited with his former colleague Akira Mado.

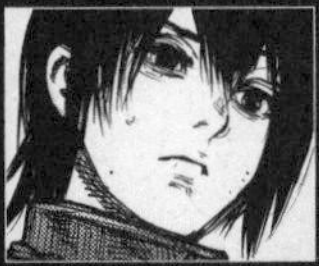

● Ayato Kirishima
霧嶋絢都
Touka's younger brother. A Rate SS Ghoul known as the Rabbit. Exploring the 24th Ward's lowest level.

Goat

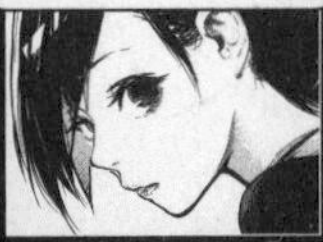

● Touka Kirishima
霧嶋董香
Former manager of Café :re, founded in order to carry on the traditions of Anteiku. Pregnant with Kaneki's child.

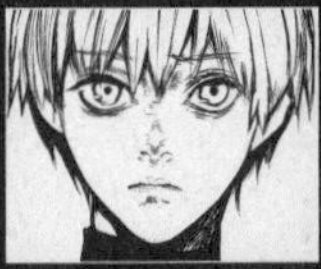

● Ken Kaneki
金木 研
Served as the Qs Squad mentor as Haise Sasaki. A half-Ghoul who has succeeded Kisho Arima as the One-Eyed King. Leader of the Goat, an anti-human organization based in the underground 24th Ward of Tokyo. Working to feed noncombatant Ghouls and stealing Quiques to render the CCG powerless. Recently married Touka Kirishima but then transformed into the Dragon after ingesting the Oggai.

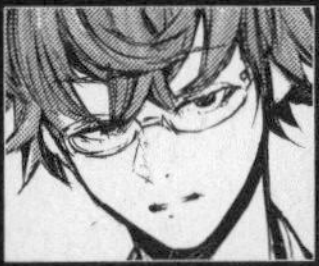

● Nishiki Nishio
西尾 錦
The Ghoul known as Orochi. Tracking the Aogiri Tree.

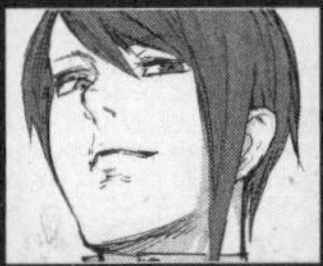

● Shu Tsukiyama
月山 習
Continues to follow Ken Kaneki after the dissolution of his family's conglomerate.

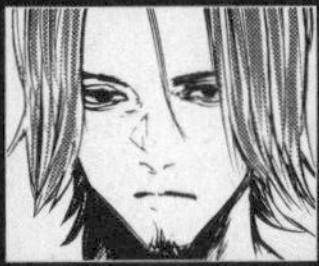

● Renji Yomo
四方蓮示
Cafe :re barista. Touka and Ayato's uncle.

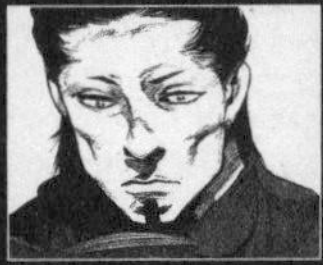

● Banjo
万丈数壱
Ayato's lieutenant during his Aogiri Tree days.

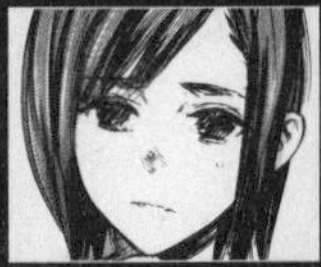

● Hinami Fueguchi
笛口雛実
Freed from Cochlea by Kaneki.

Clown Masks

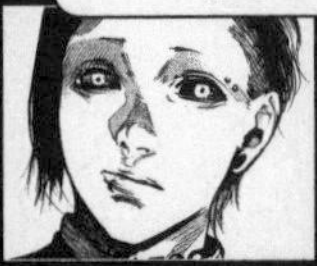

● Uta
ウタ
Owner of HySy Artmask Studio. Made masks for Kaneki and the Qs.

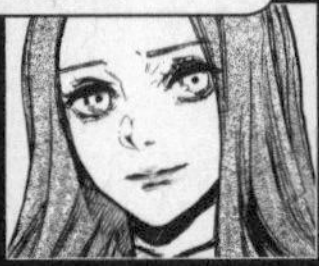

● Itori
イトリ
Owner of the bar Helter Skelter. Values information.

So far in :re

T ● K Y ● G H ● U L

Ken Kaneki succeeded Kisho Arima as the One-Eyed King and formed the anti-human organization Goat after the conflicts at Cochlea and Rushima, hoping to create a world where Ghouls and humans can coexist peacefully. Meanwhile, the Washu family's dark side has been made public and Nimura Furuta, now known as Kichimura Washu, has been appointed new Bureau Chief of the CCG. He hopes to completely eradicate and displace all Ghouls from Tokyo with the Oggai. At the Goat's 24th Ward hideout, Kaneki and Touka's wedding celebration abruptly ends when the Oggai, under orders from Furuta, crash the party. When Kaneki returns after getting a bad feeling, the Suzuya Squad is waiting for him. Narrowly defeated, Kaneki consumes the Oggai, triggering his transformation into the Dragon. Swallowing everything in its path, it rises to the surface...

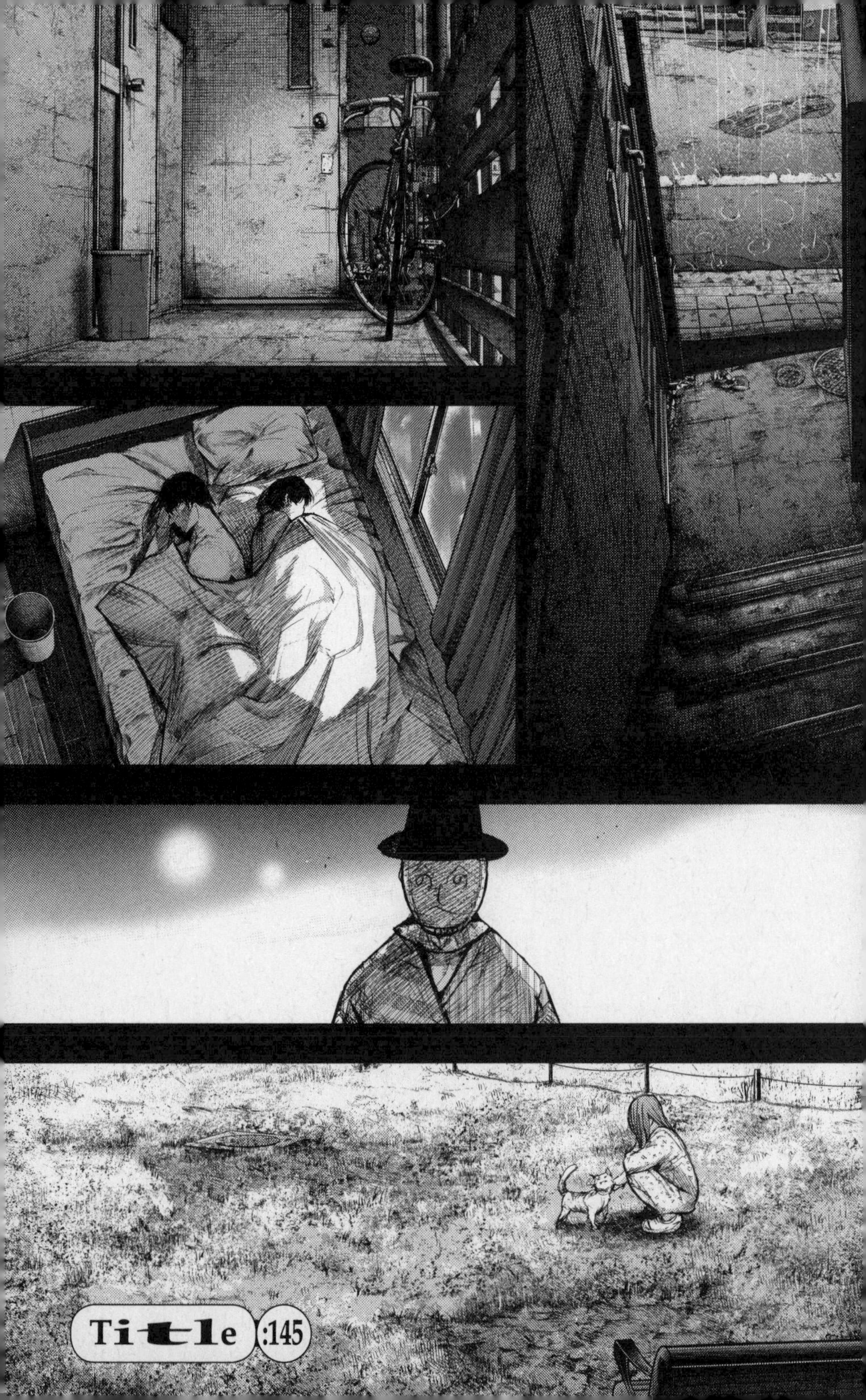
Title :145

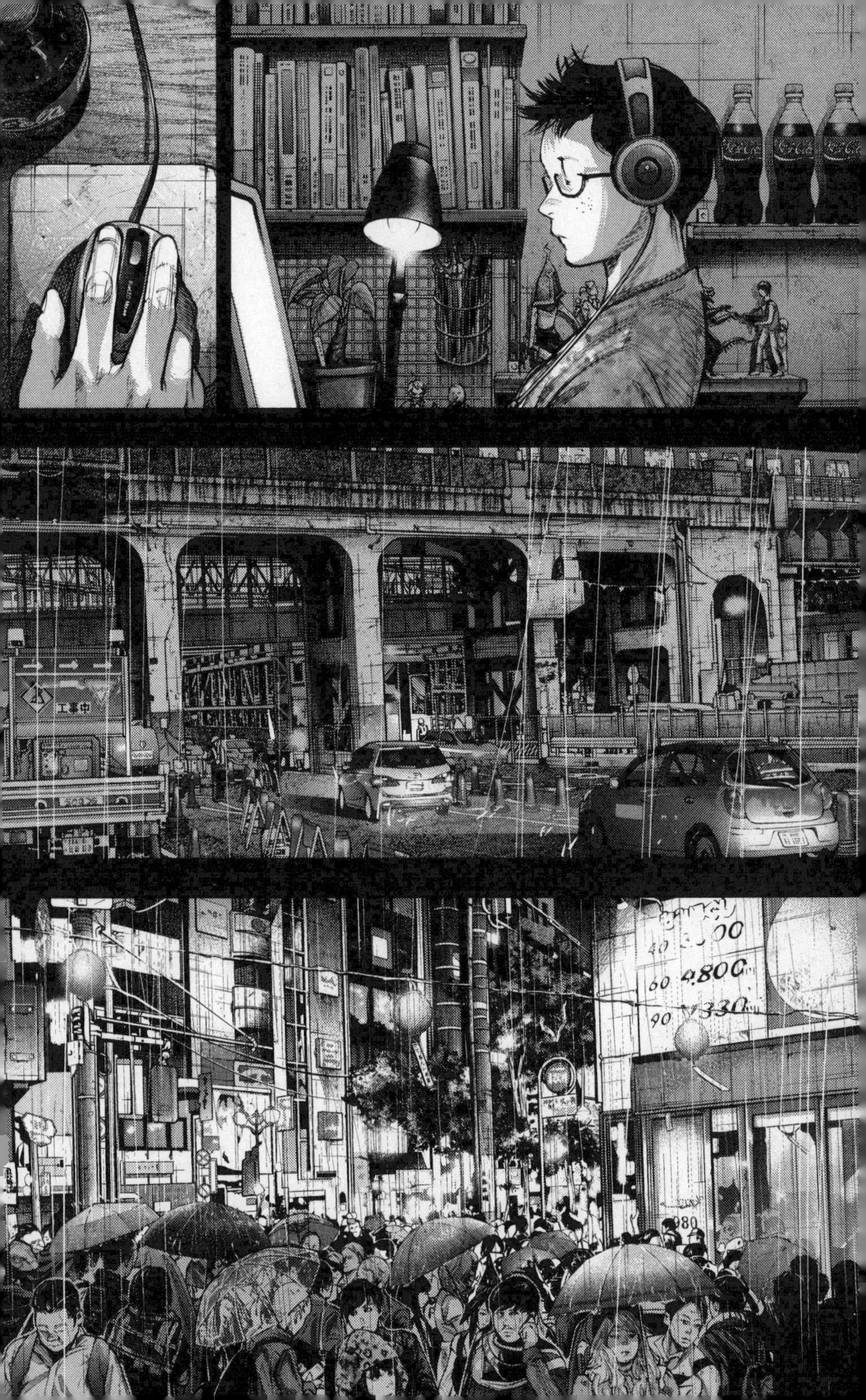
工事中

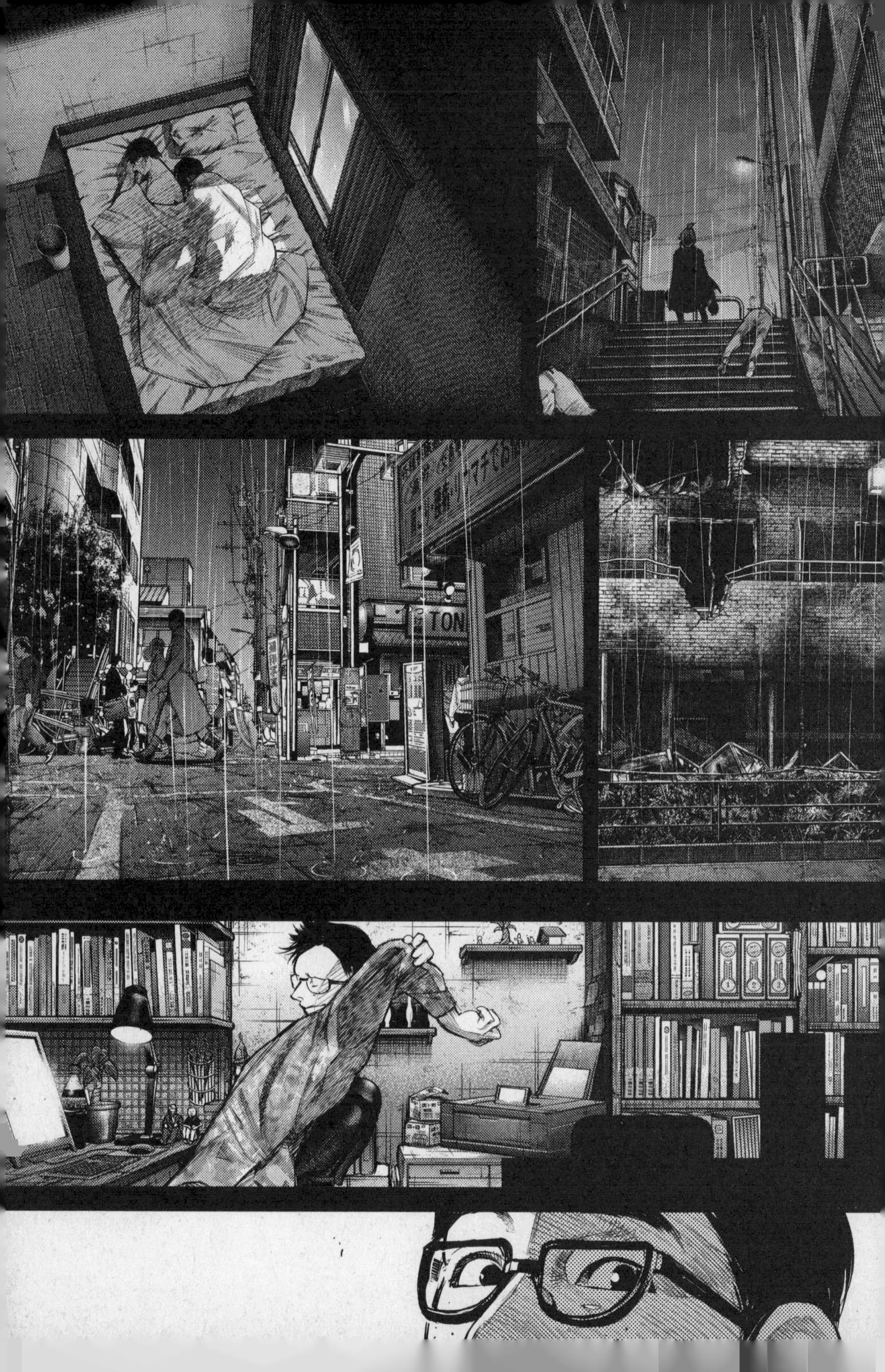
TON

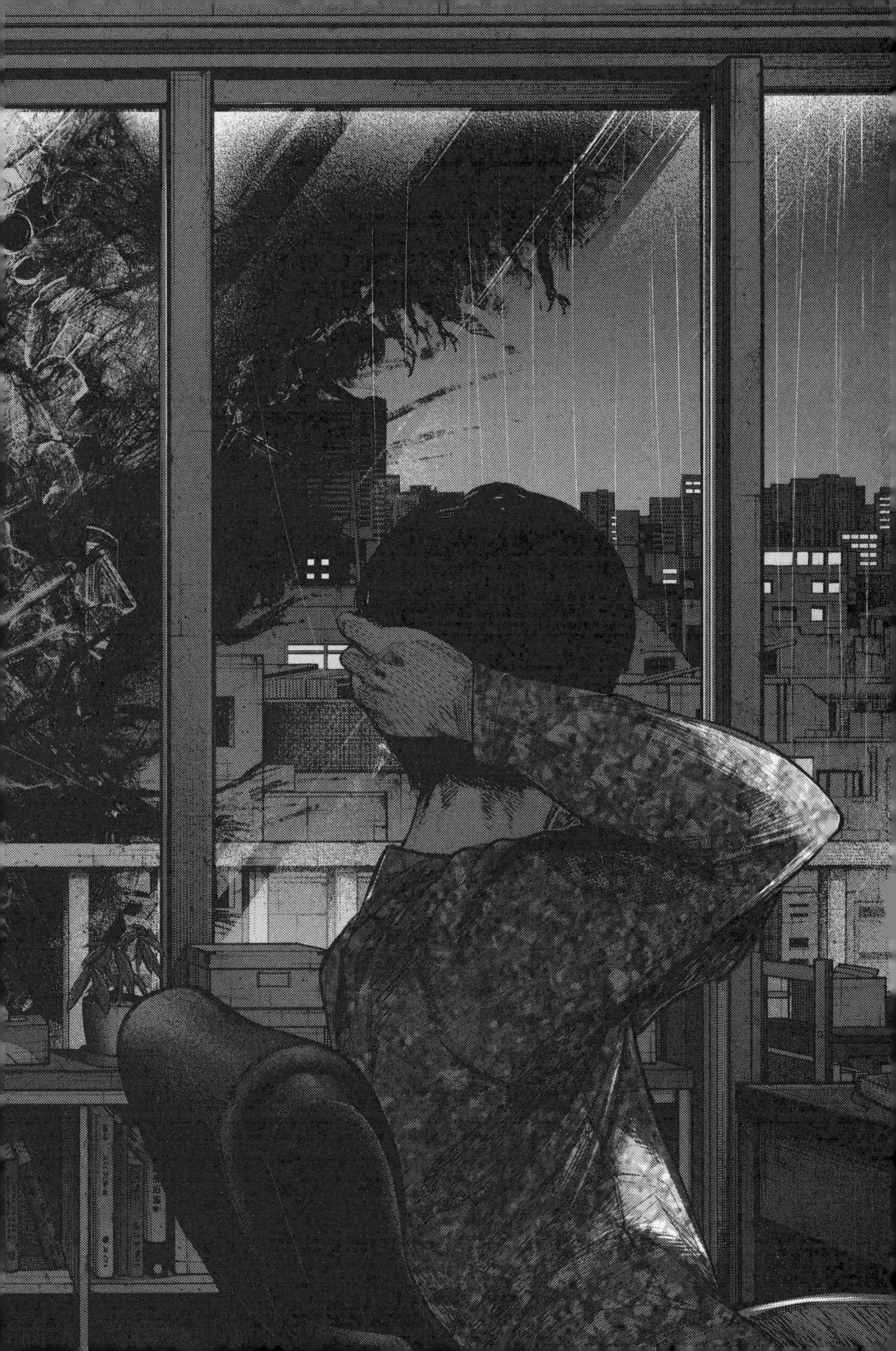

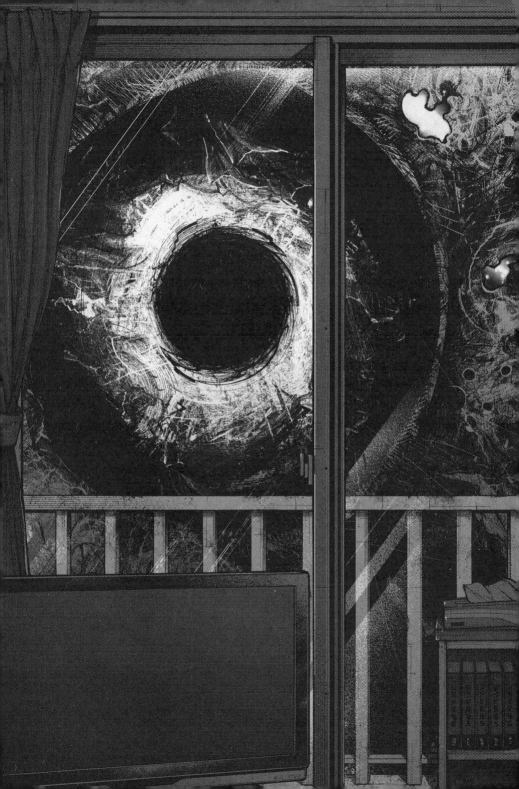

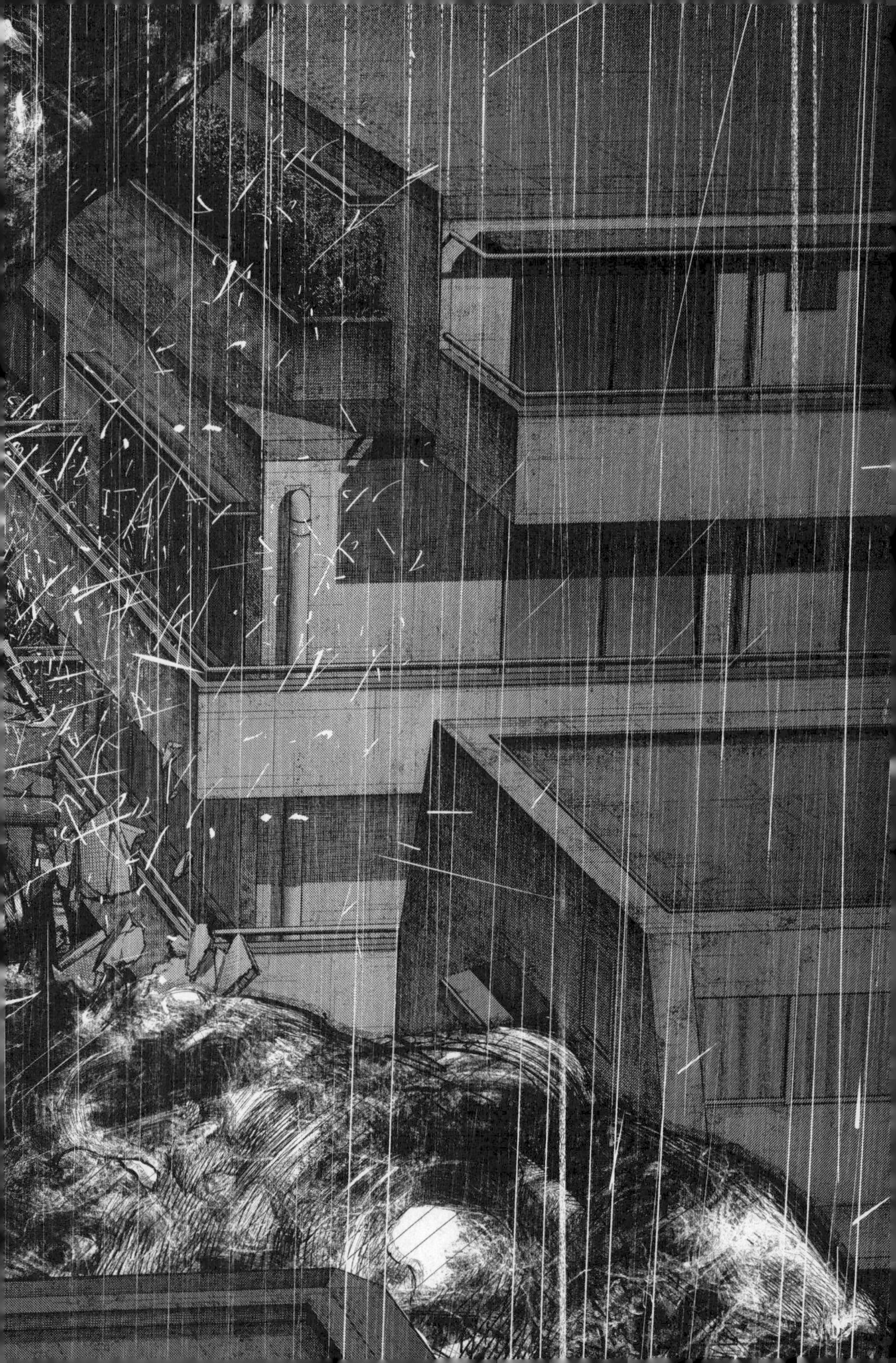

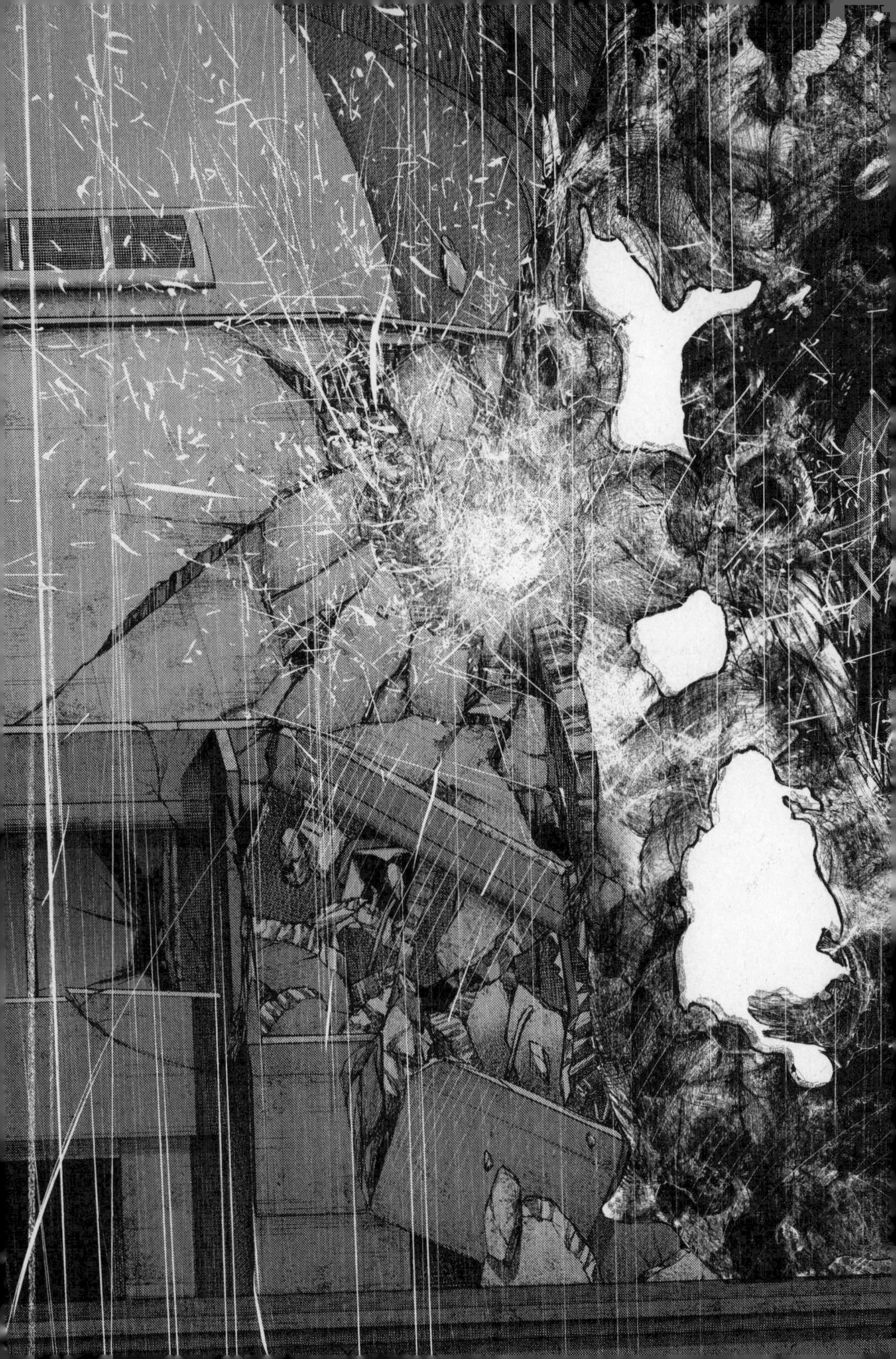

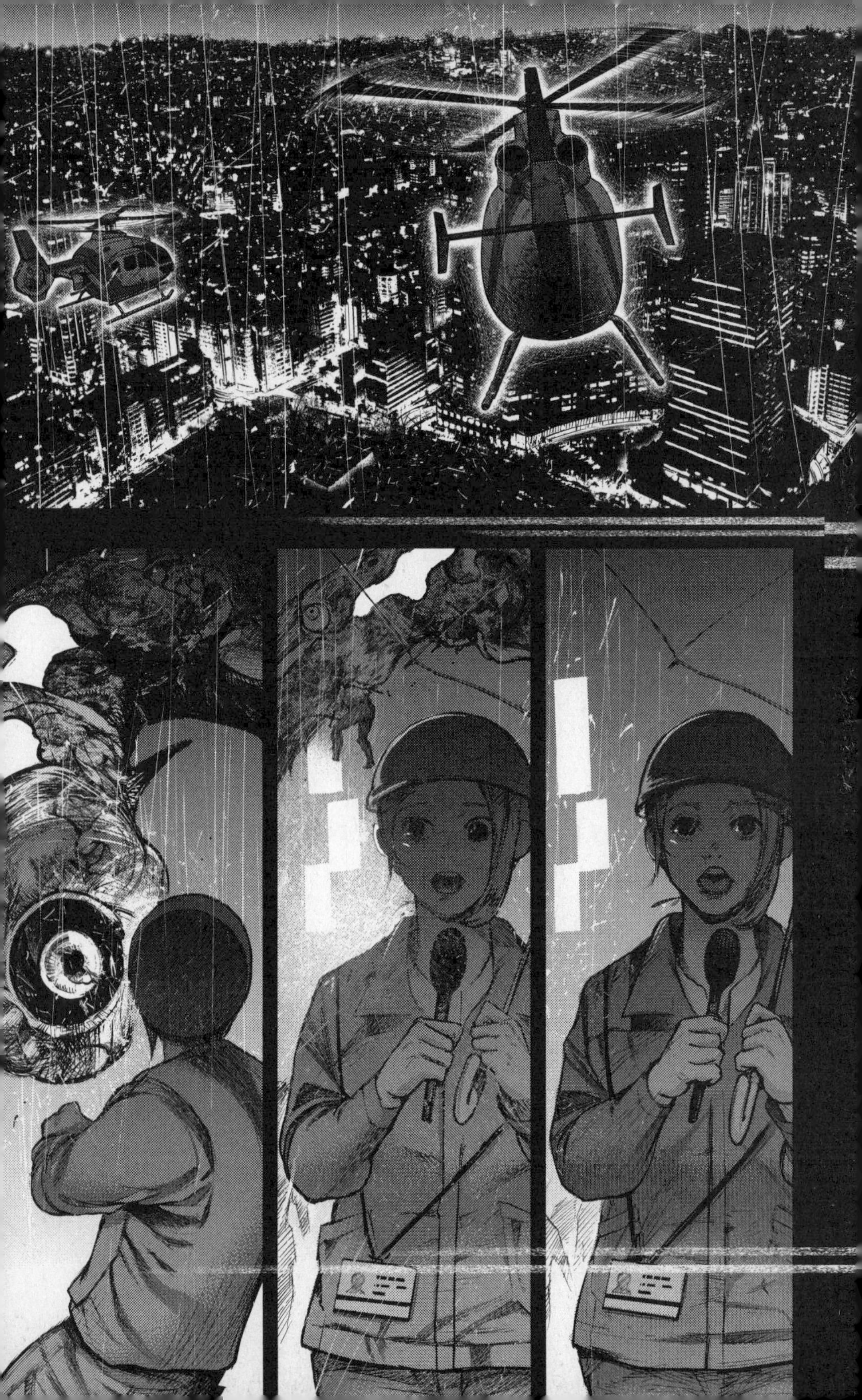

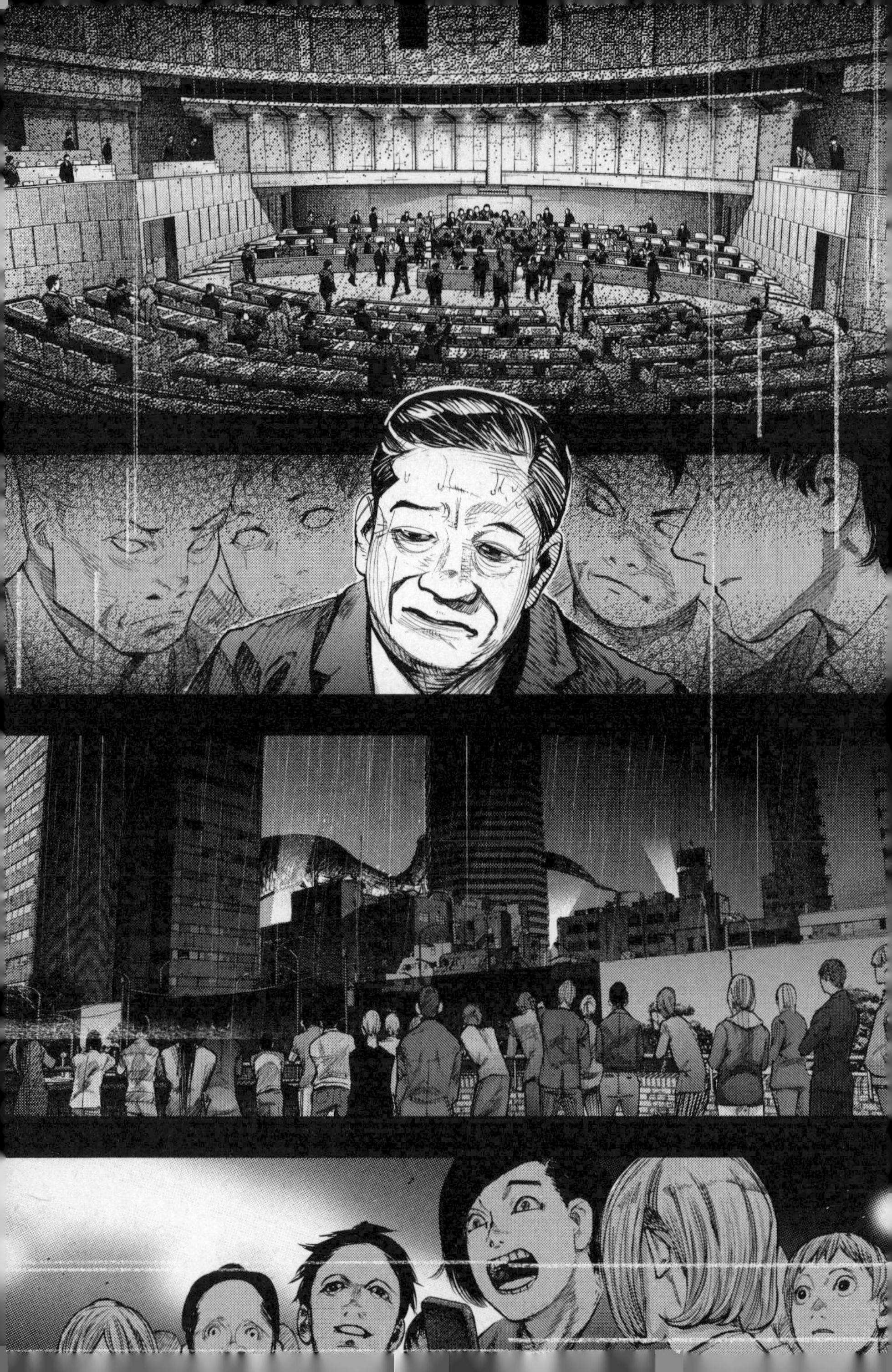

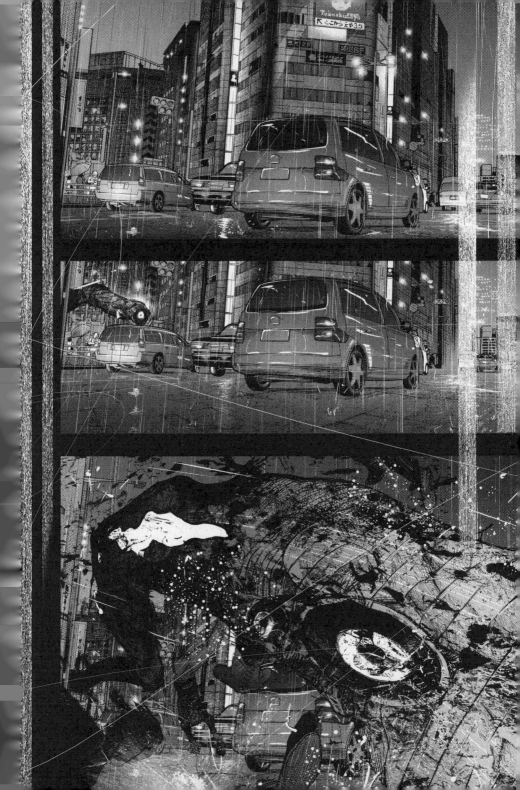

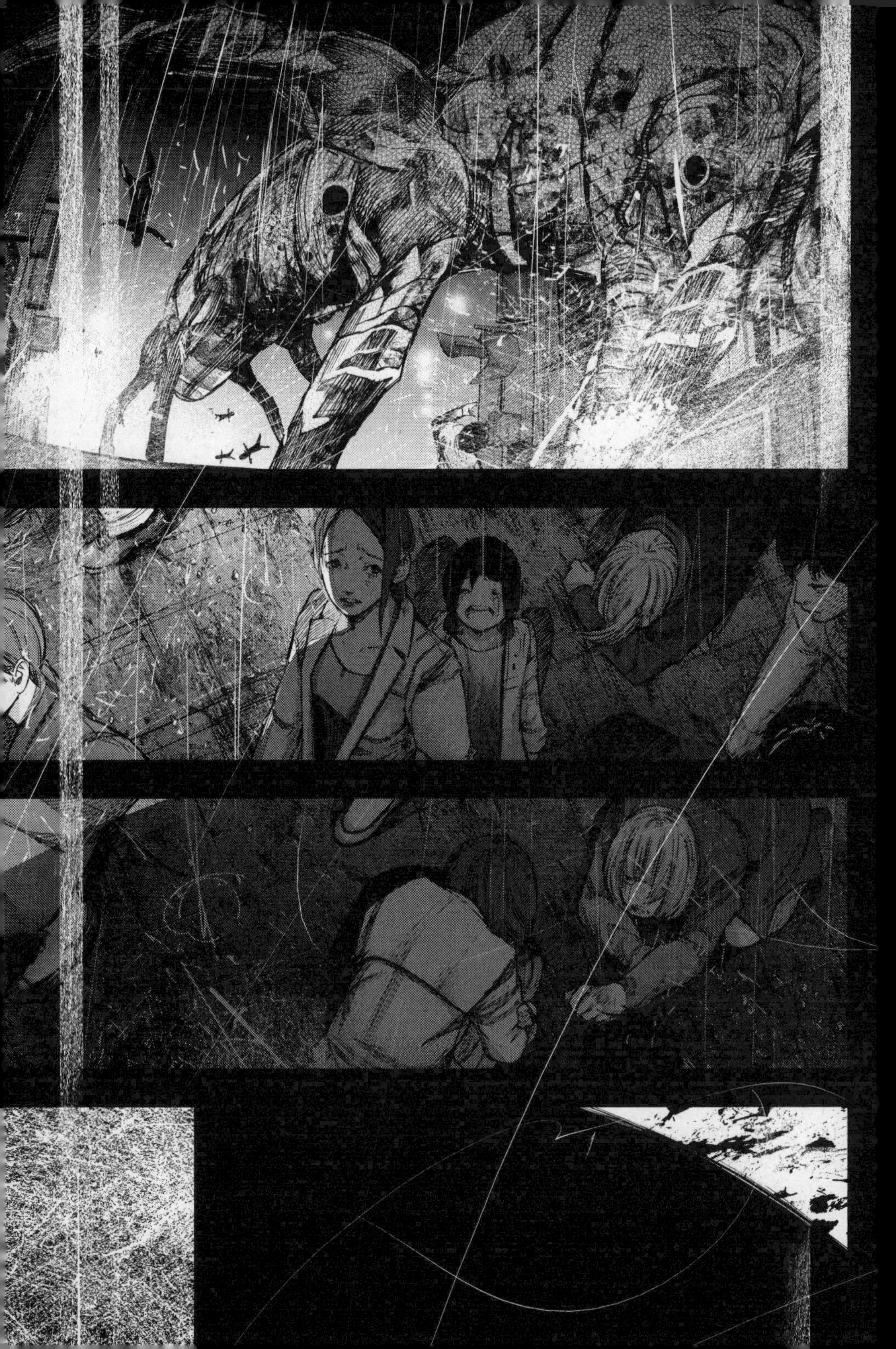

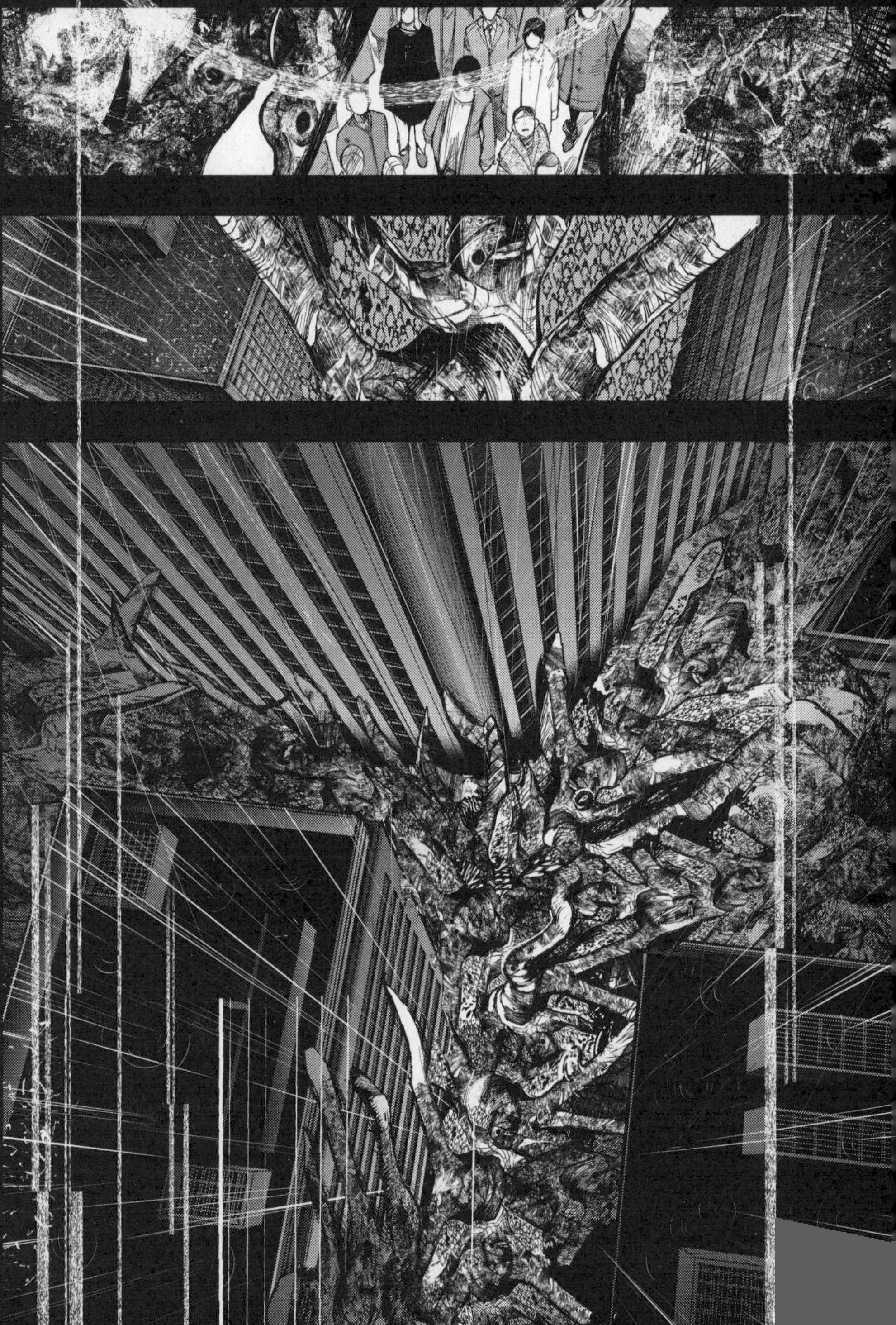

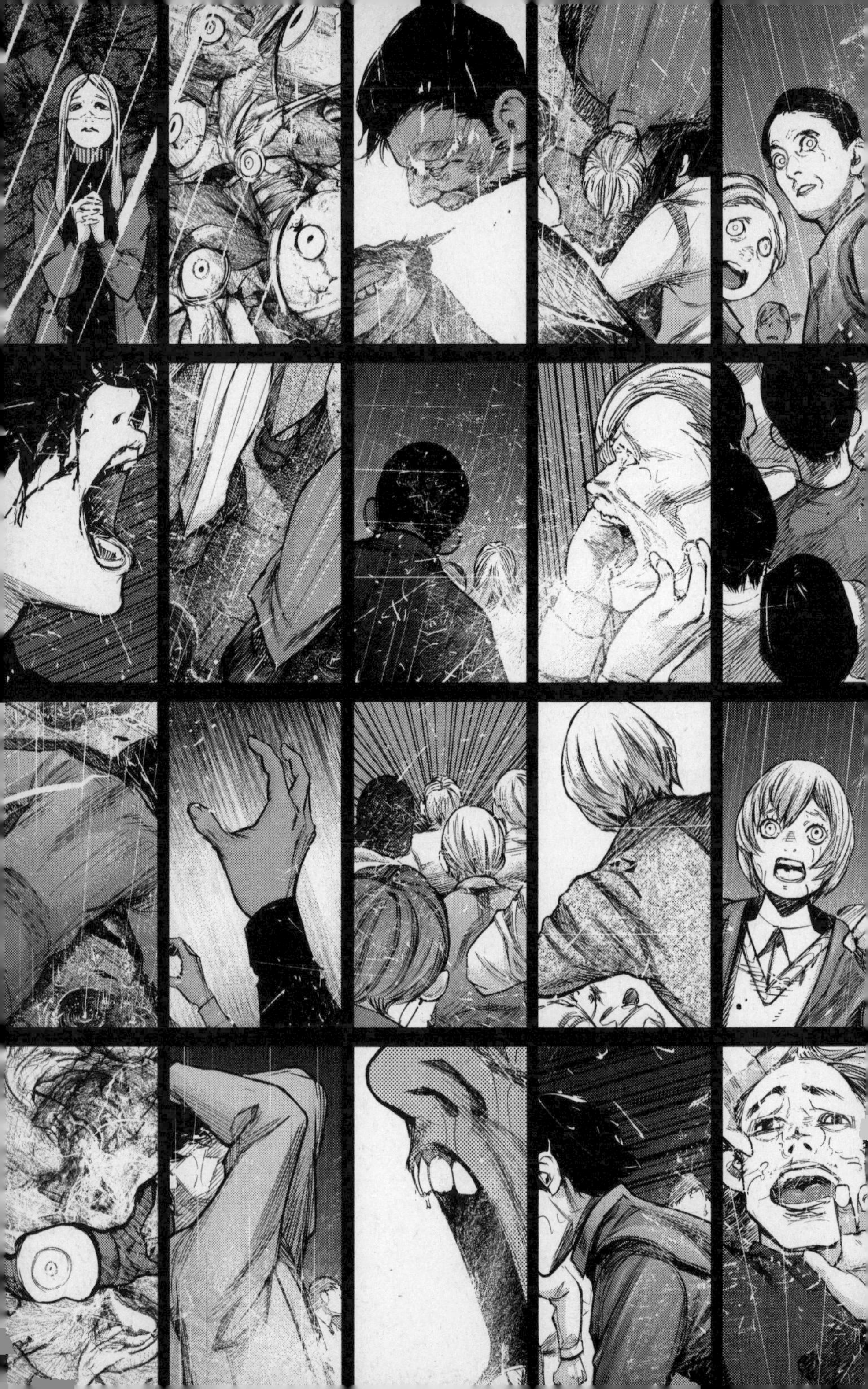

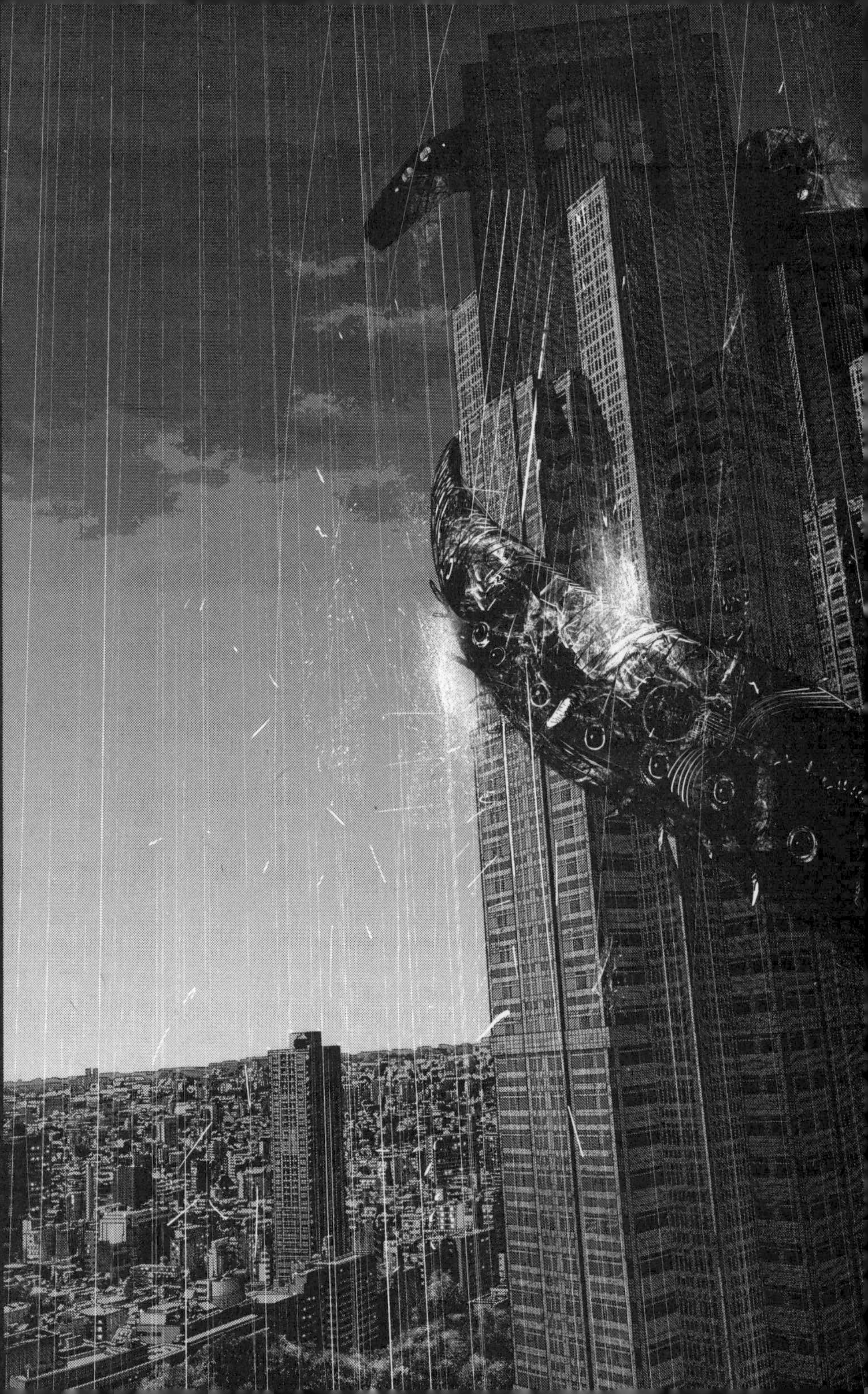

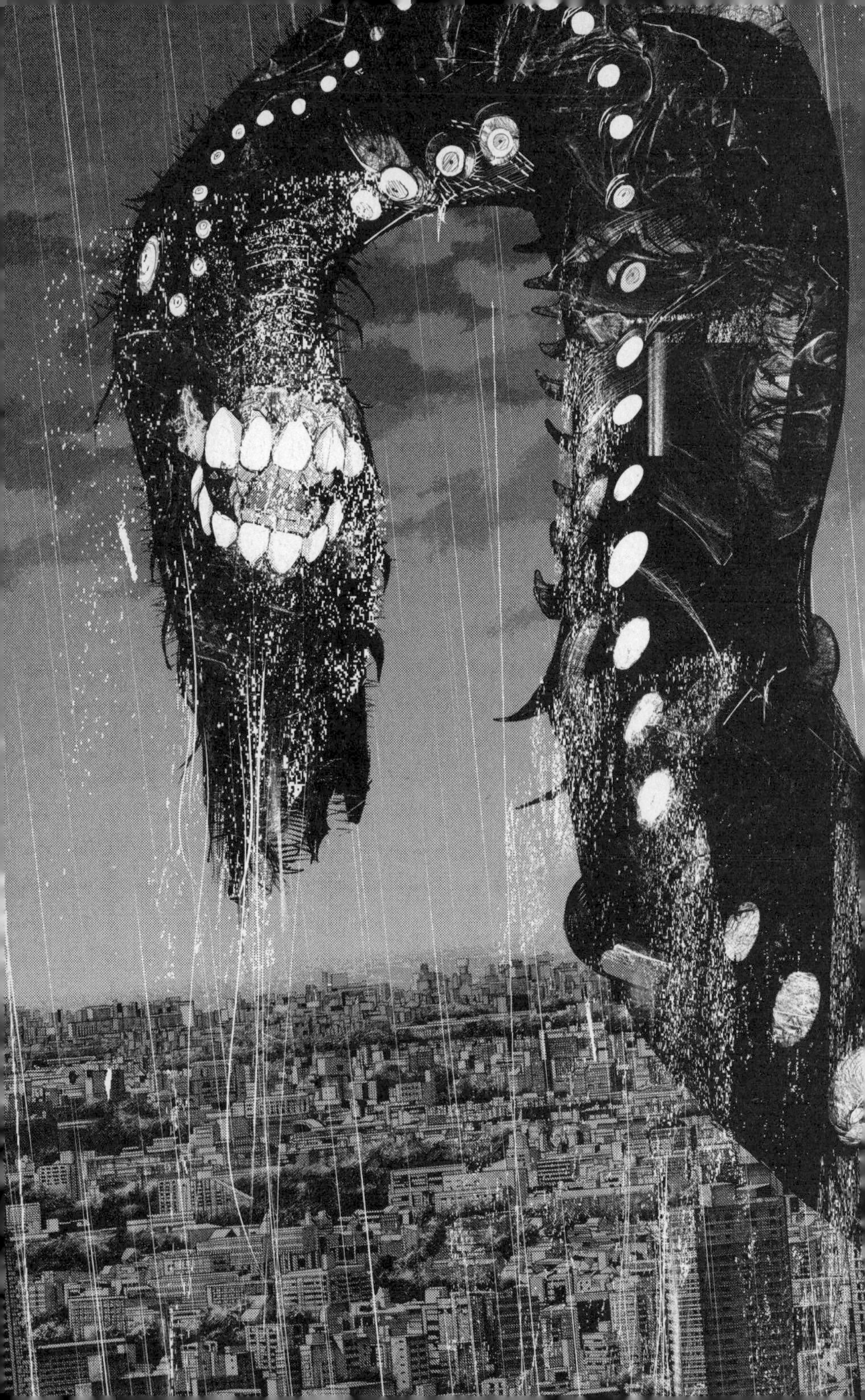

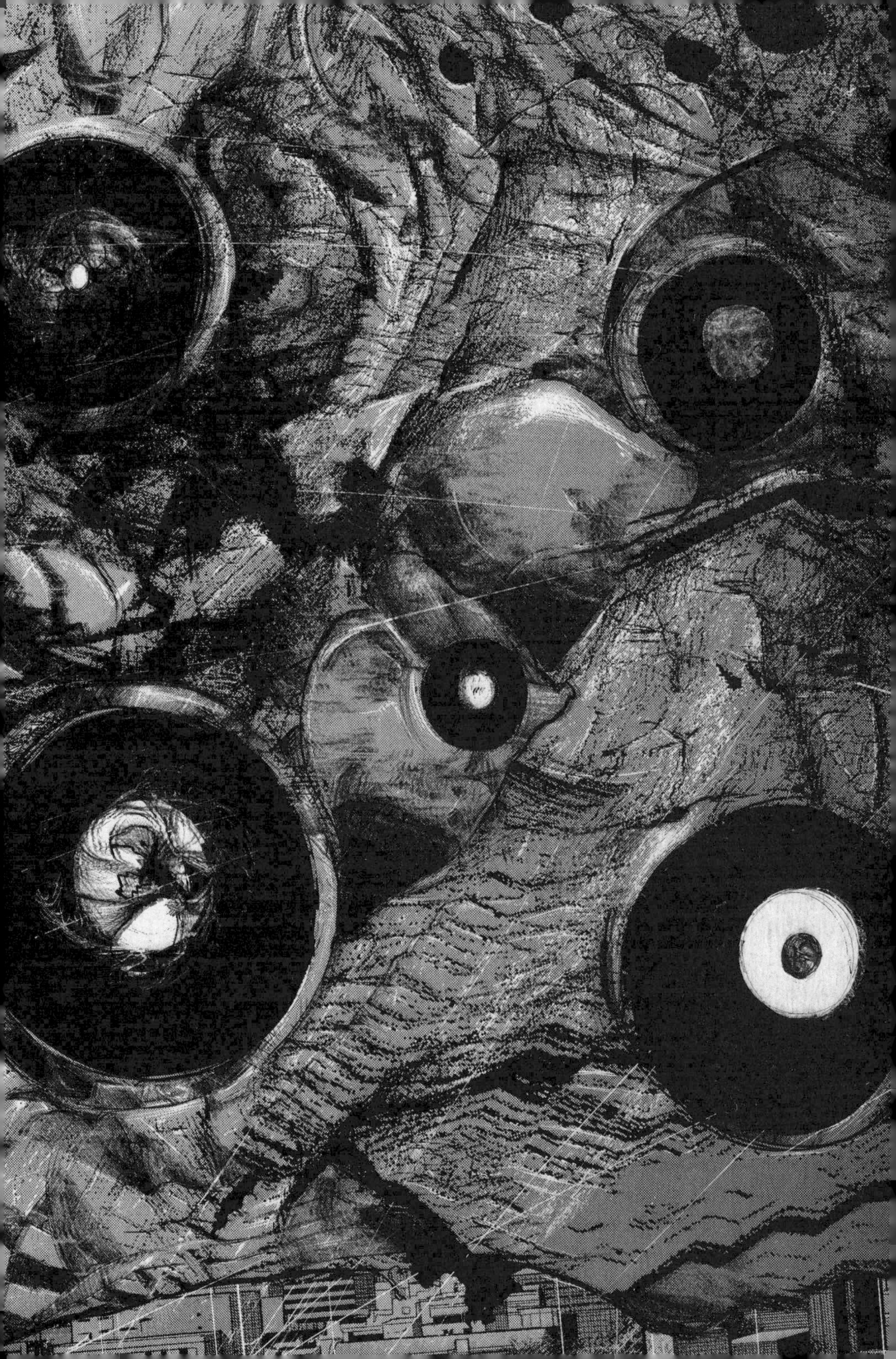

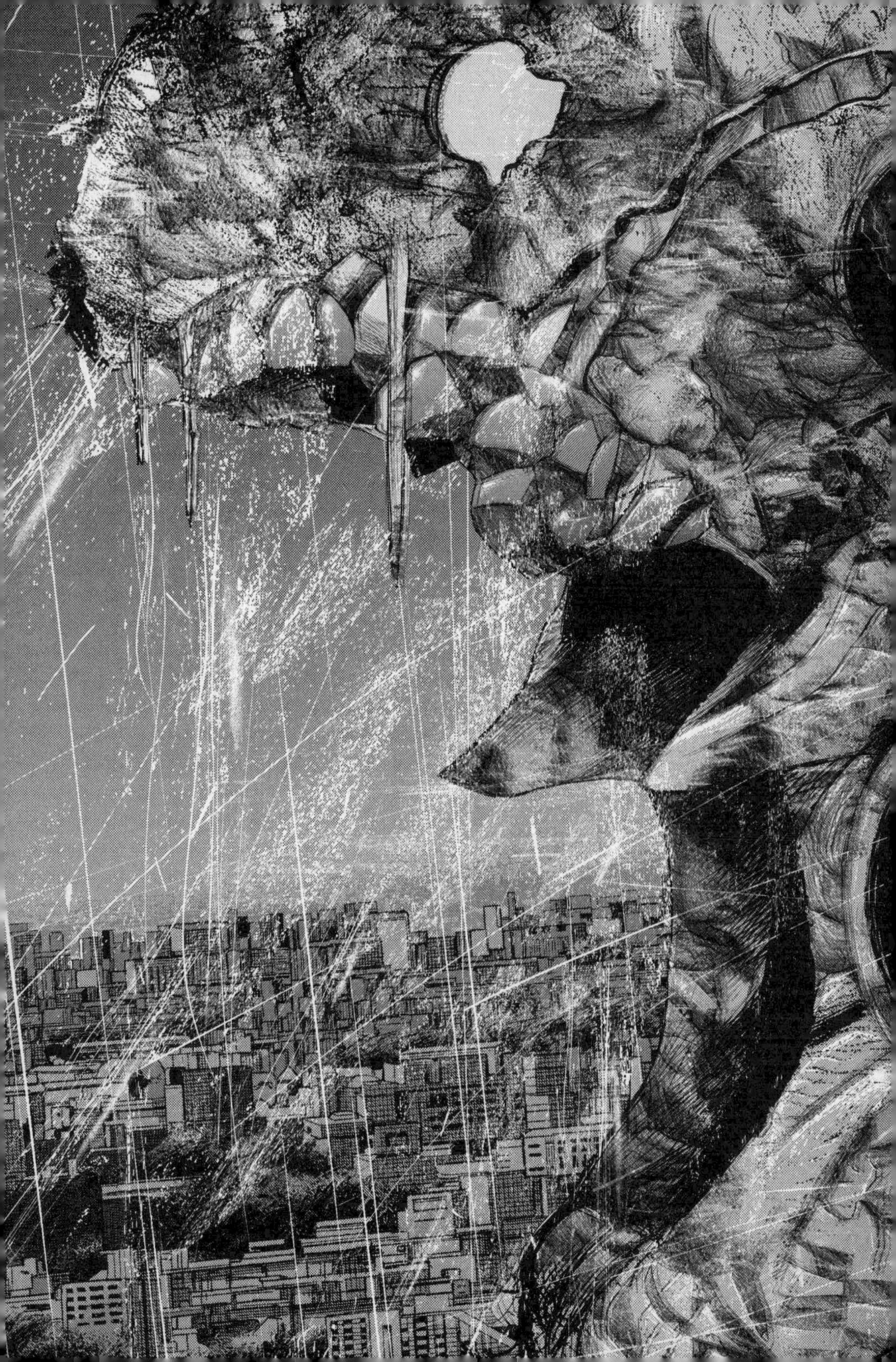

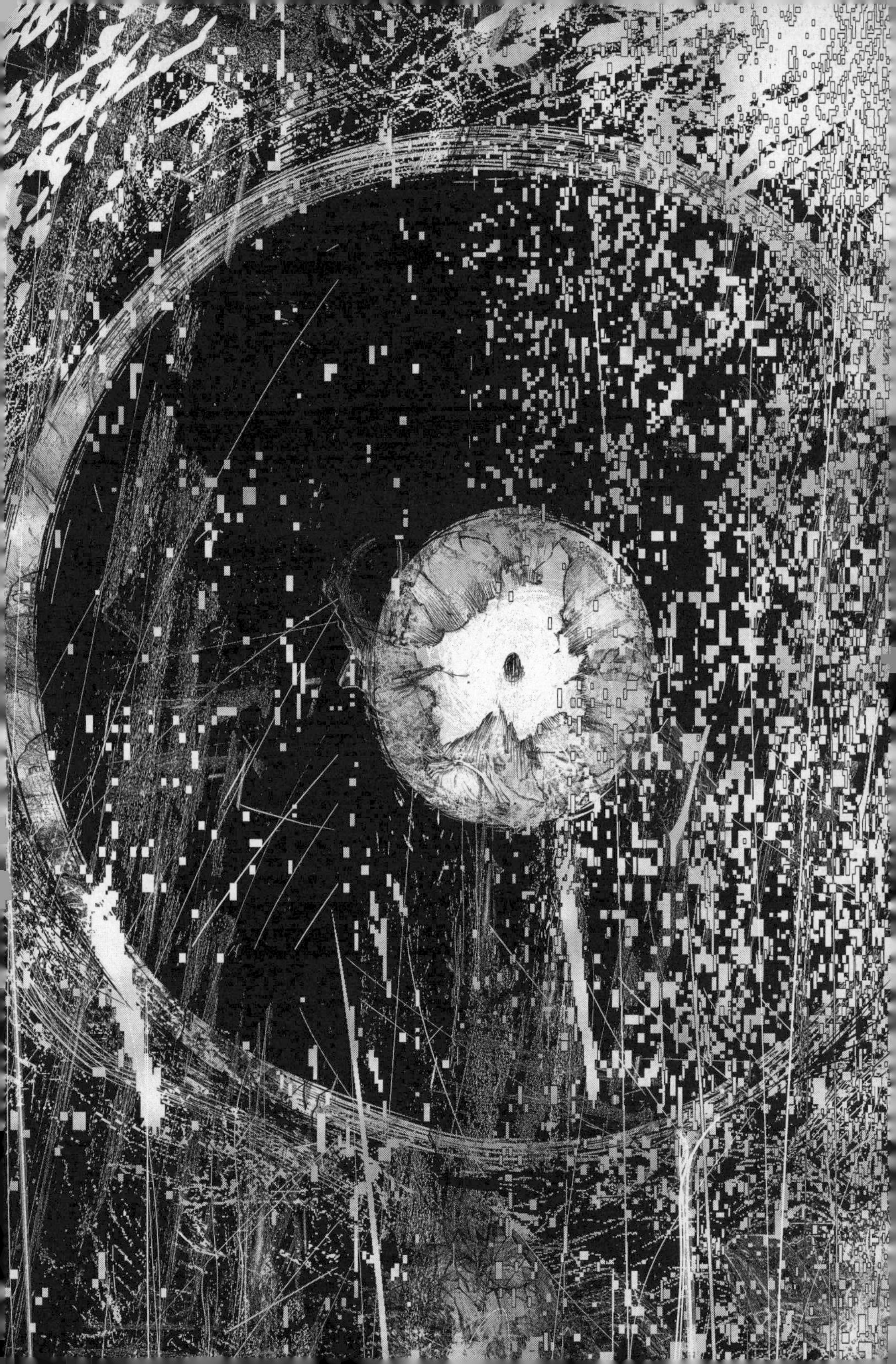

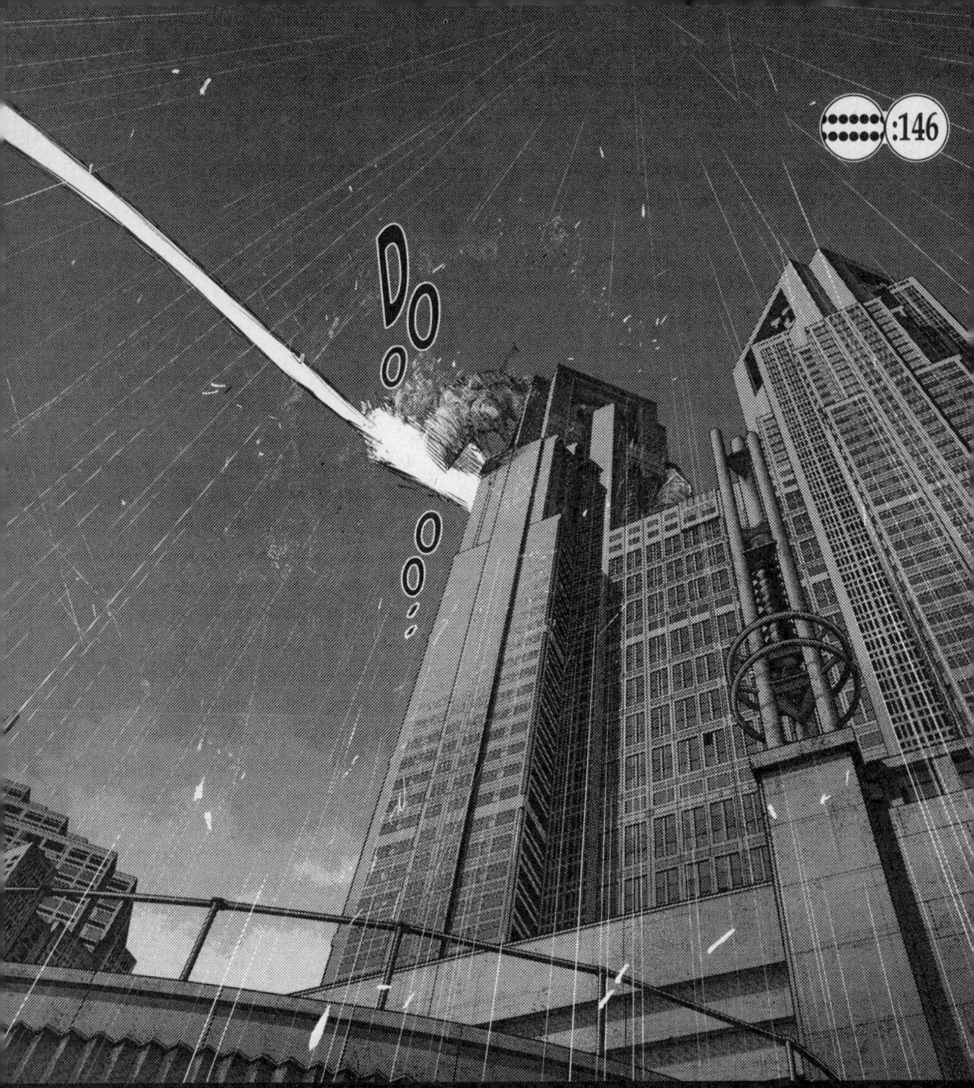
:146
DOOO
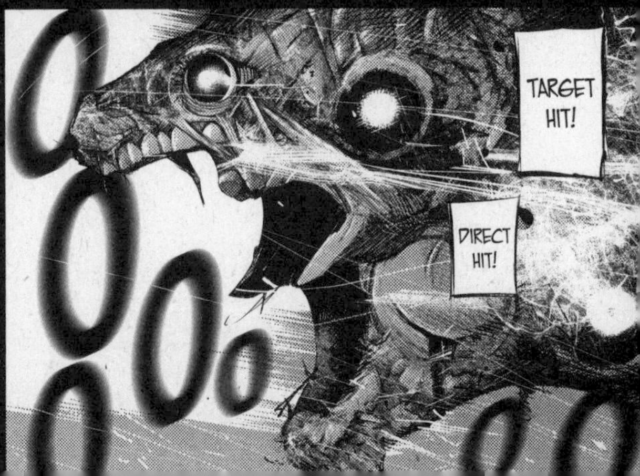
TARGET HIT!
DIRECT HIT!
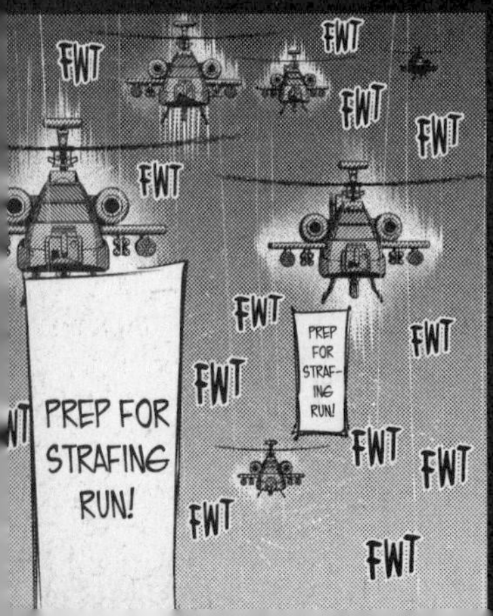
FWT
PREP FOR STRAF-ING RUN!
PREP FOR STRAFING RUN!

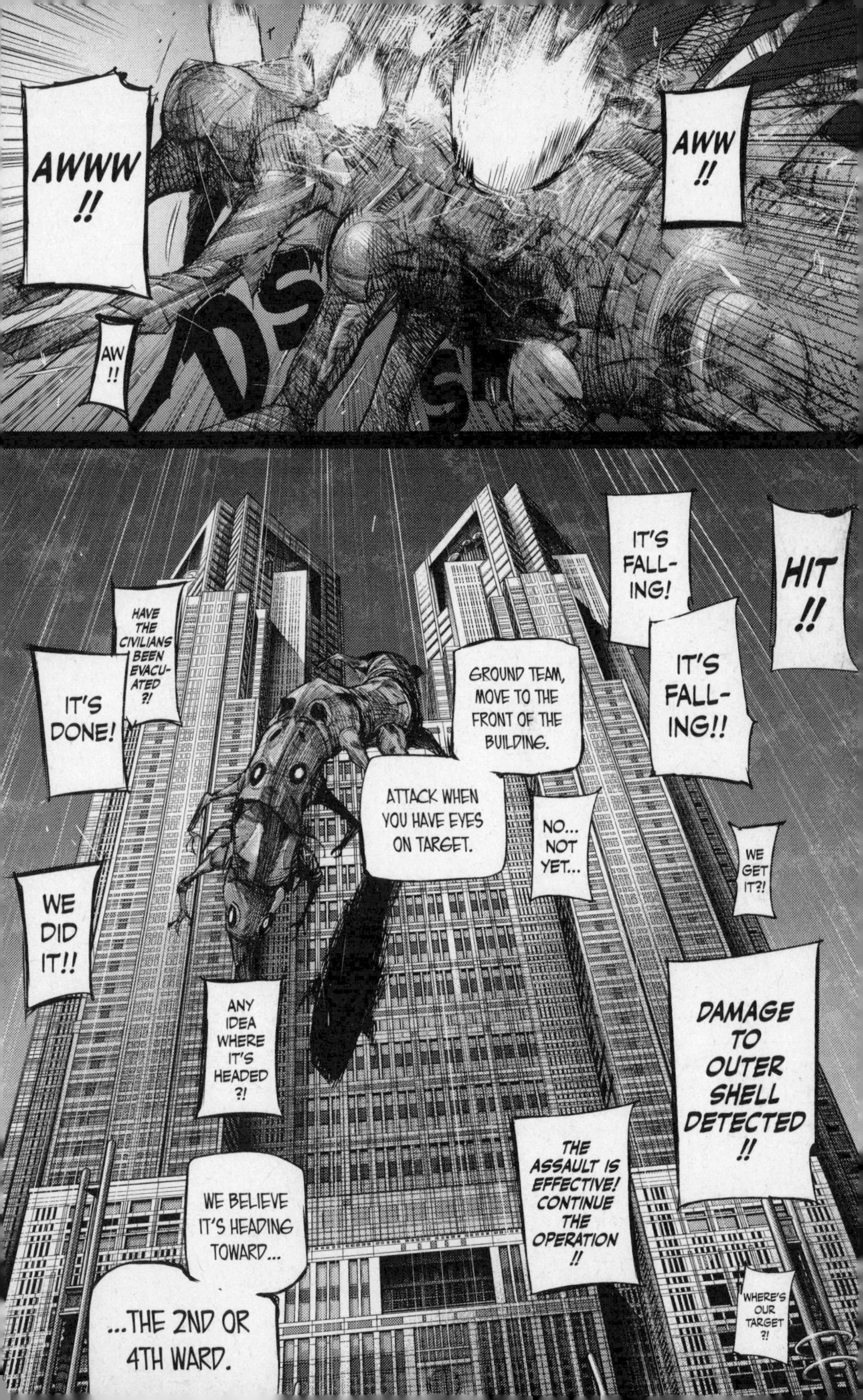
AWW !!
AWWW !!
AW !!
HIT !!
IT'S FALLING!
IT'S FALLING!!
GROUND TEAM, MOVE TO THE FRONT OF THE BUILDING.
ATTACK WHEN YOU HAVE EYES ON TARGET.
HAVE THE CIVILIANS BEEN EVACUATED ?!
IT'S DONE!
WE GET IT?!
NO... NOT YET...
WE DID IT!!
DAMAGE TO OUTER SHELL DETECTED !!
THE ASSAULT IS EFFECTIVE! CONTINUE THE OPERATION !!
ANY IDEA WHERE IT'S HEADED ?!
WE BELIEVE IT'S HEADING TOWARD...
...THE 2ND OR 4TH WARD.
WHERE'S OUR TARGET ?!

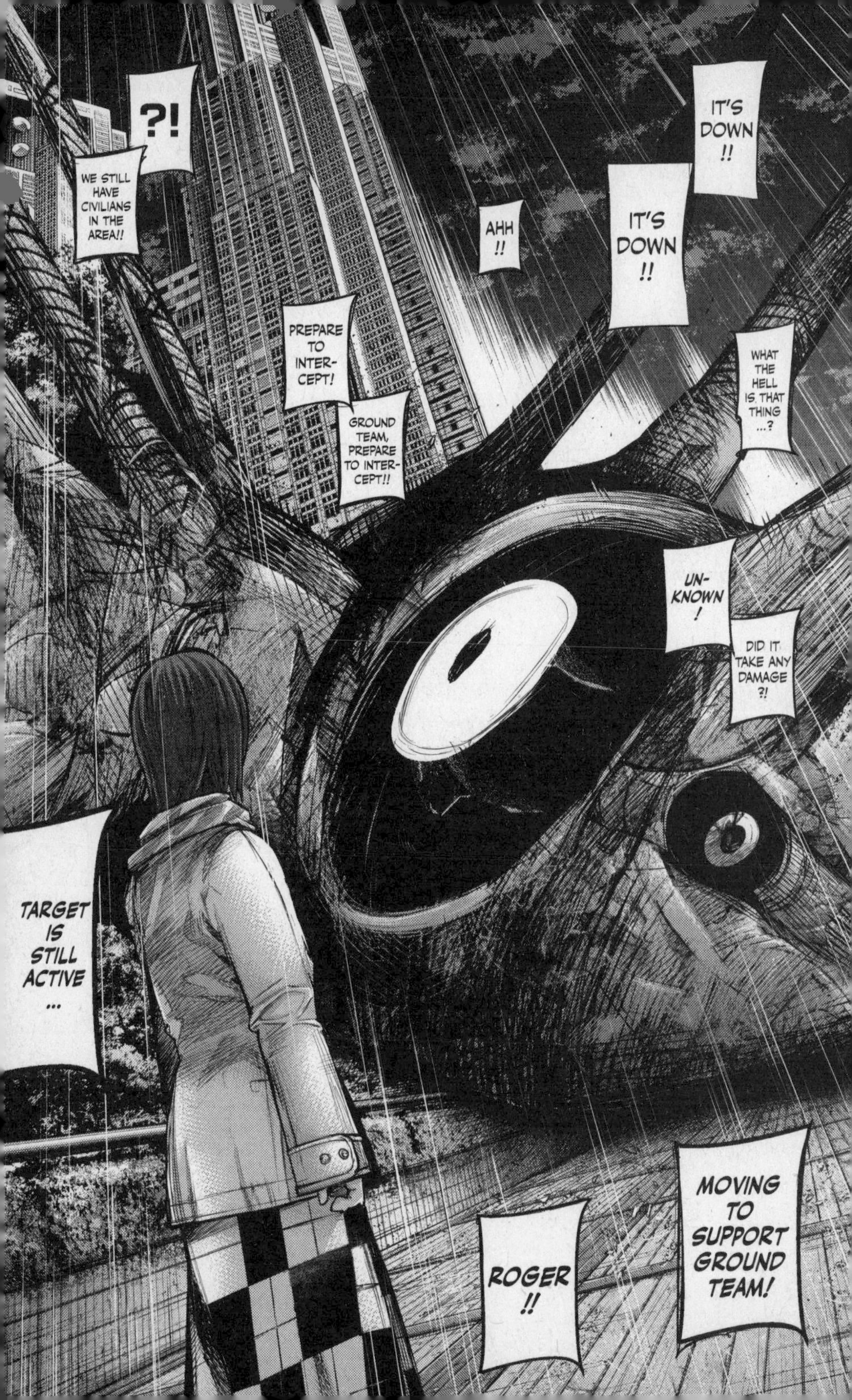
IT'S DOWN!!
IT'S DOWN!!
AHH!!
?!
WE STILL HAVE CIVILIANS IN THE AREA!!
WHAT THE HELL IS THAT THING...?
PREPARE TO INTER-CEPT!
GROUND TEAM, PREPARE TO INTER-CEPT!!
UN-KNOWN!
DID IT TAKE ANY DAMAGE?!
TARGET IS STILL ACTIVE...
MOVING TO SUPPORT GROUND TEAM!
ROGER!!

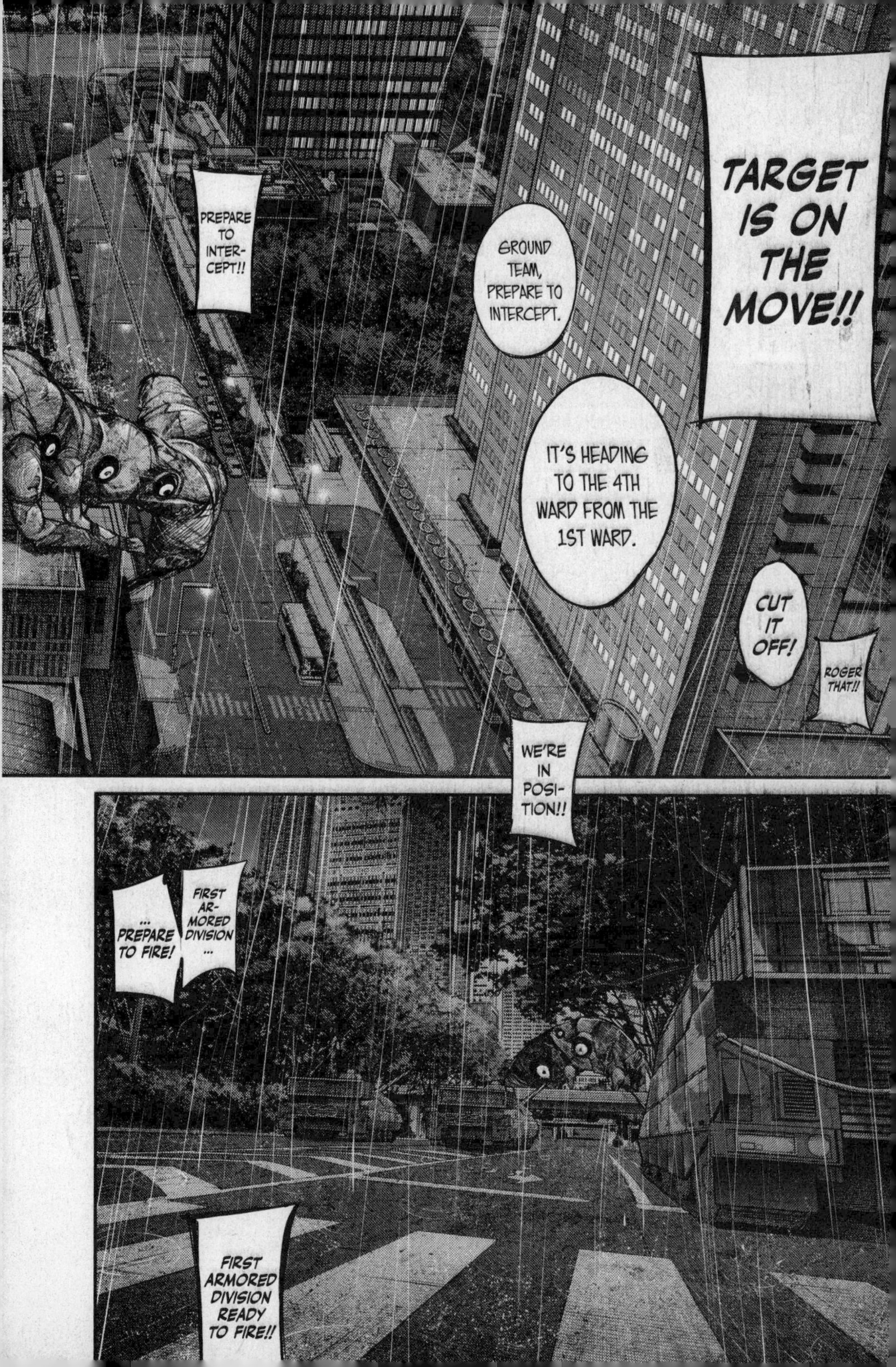
TARGET IS ON THE MOVE!!
GROUND TEAM, PREPARE TO INTERCEPT.
PREPARE TO INTER-CEPT!!
IT'S HEADING TO THE 4TH WARD FROM THE 1ST WARD.
CUT IT OFF!
ROGER THAT!!
WE'RE IN POSI-TION!!
FIRST AR-MORED DIVISION ...
... PREPARE TO FIRE!
FIRST ARMORED DIVISION READY TO FIRE!!

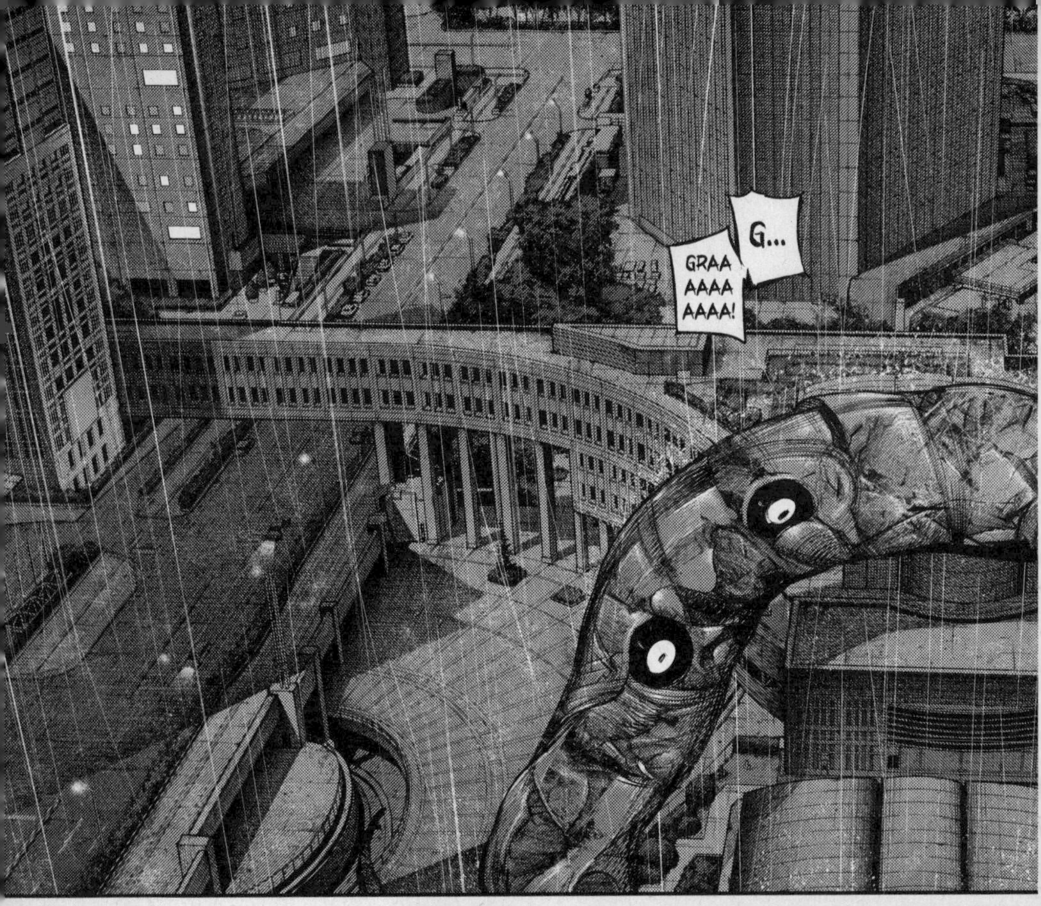
G...
GRAA AAAA AAAA!

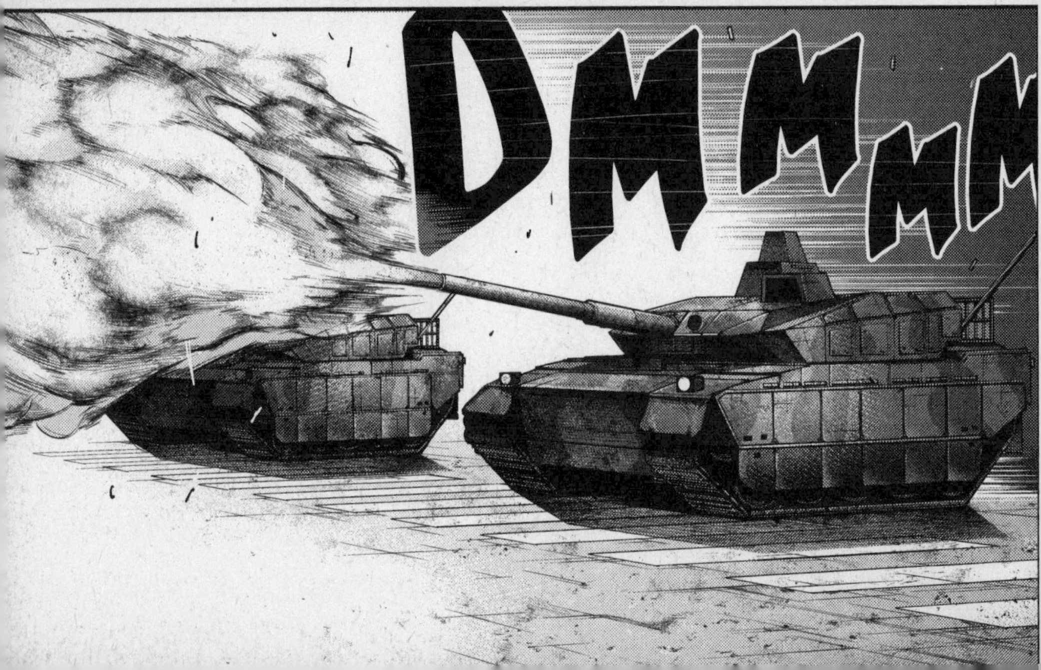
DMMMMM

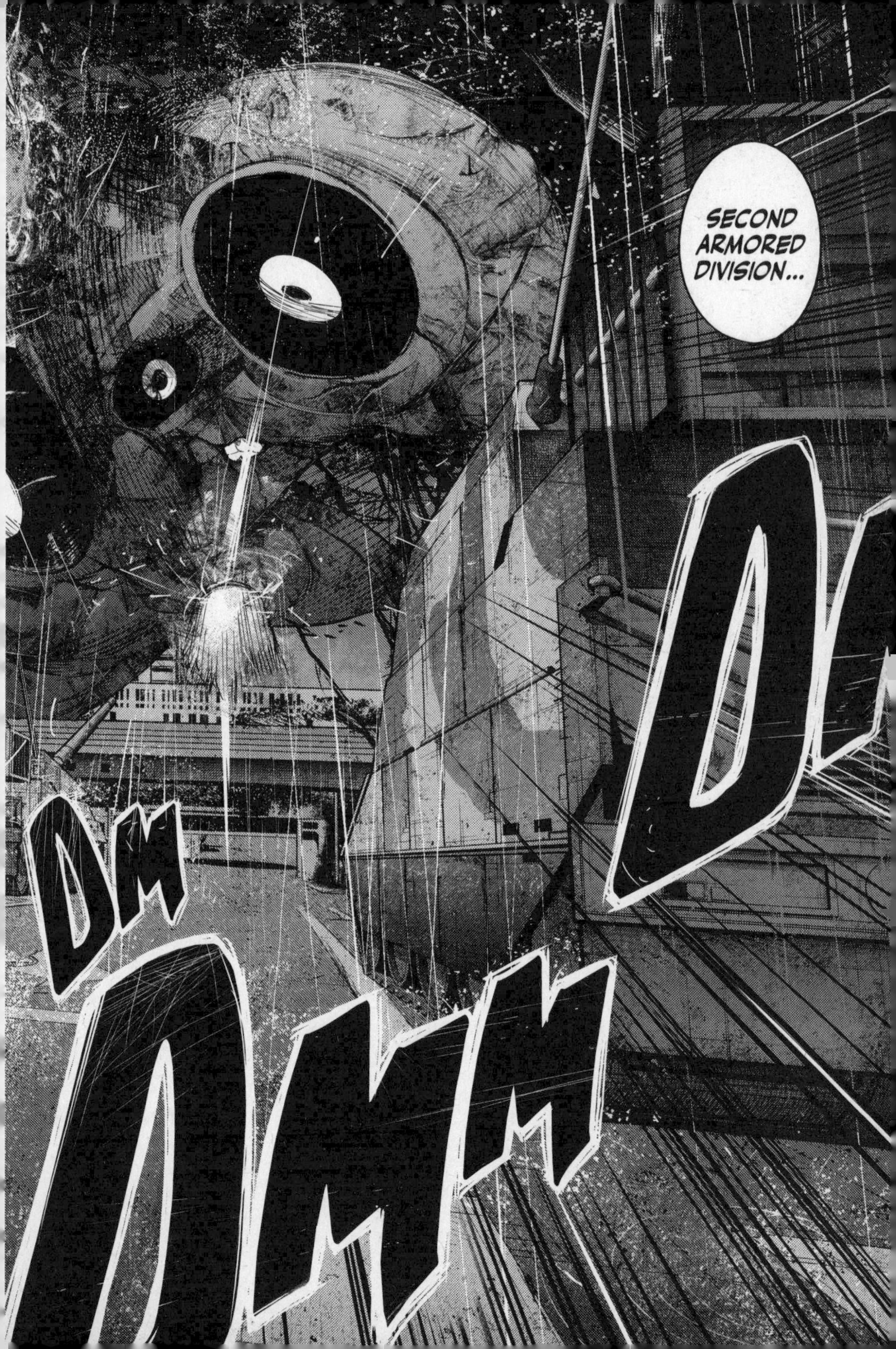
SECOND ARMORED DIVISION...

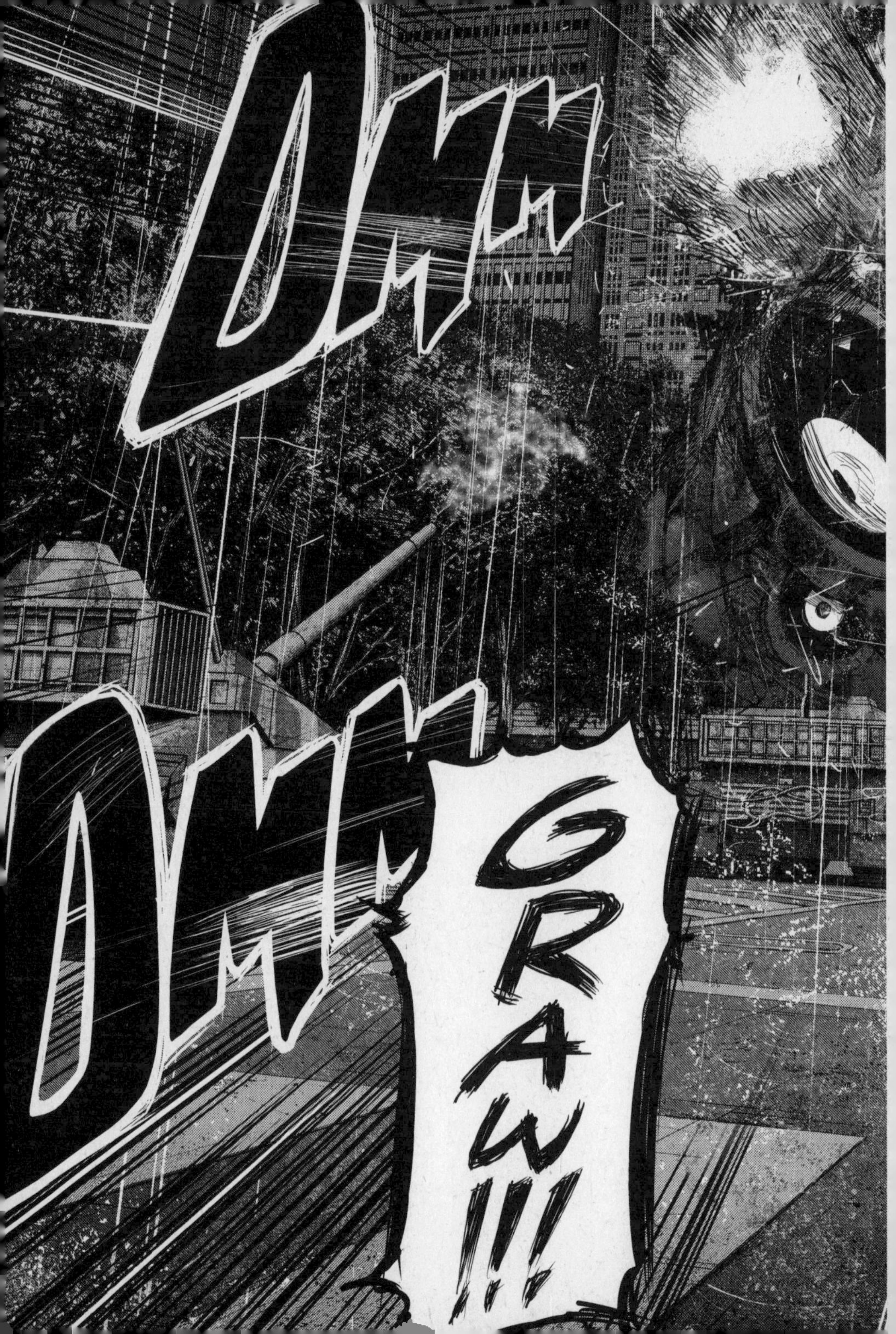
GRAW!!!

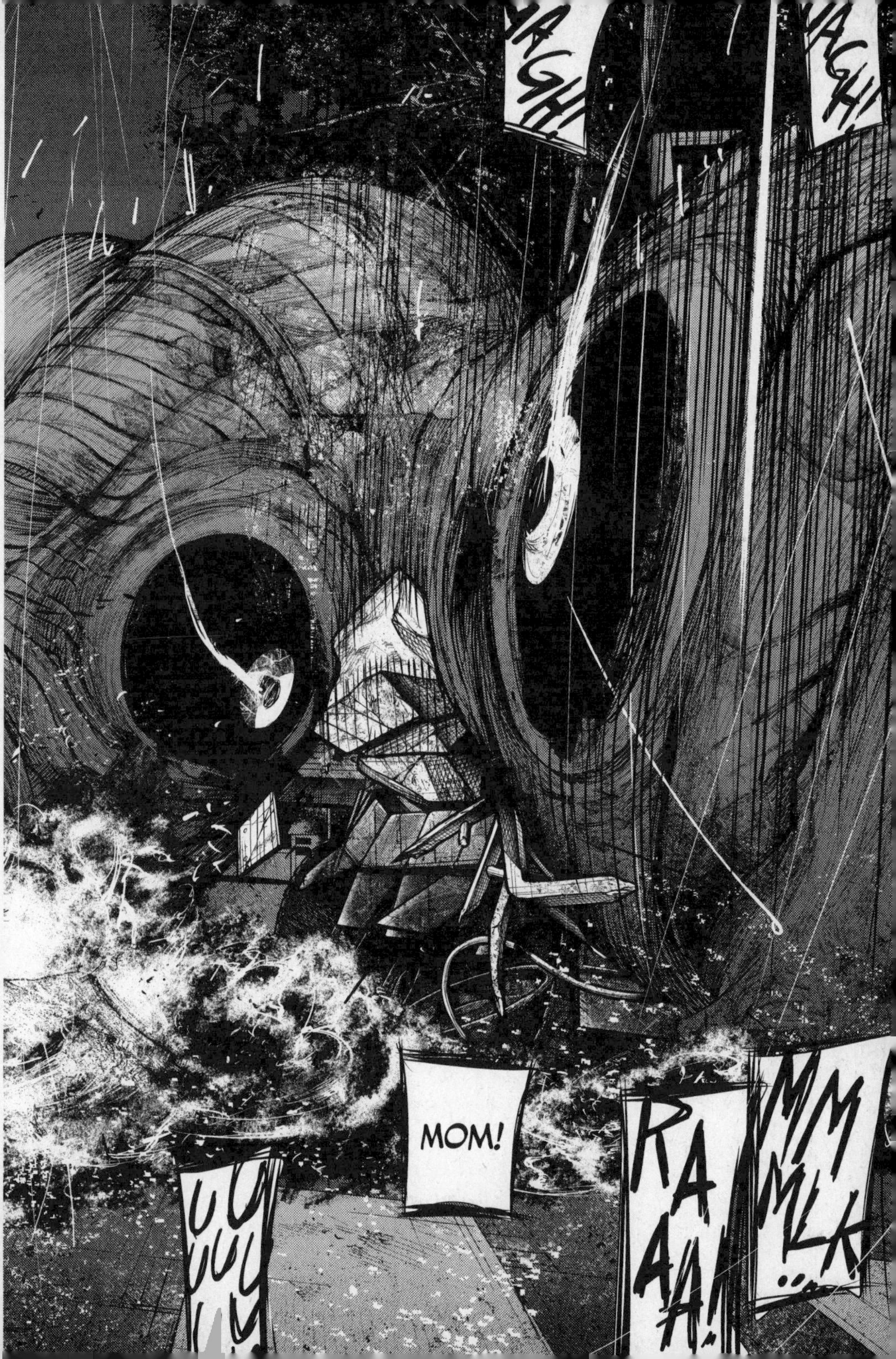
YAGH!
YAGH!
RAAAA!
MOM!

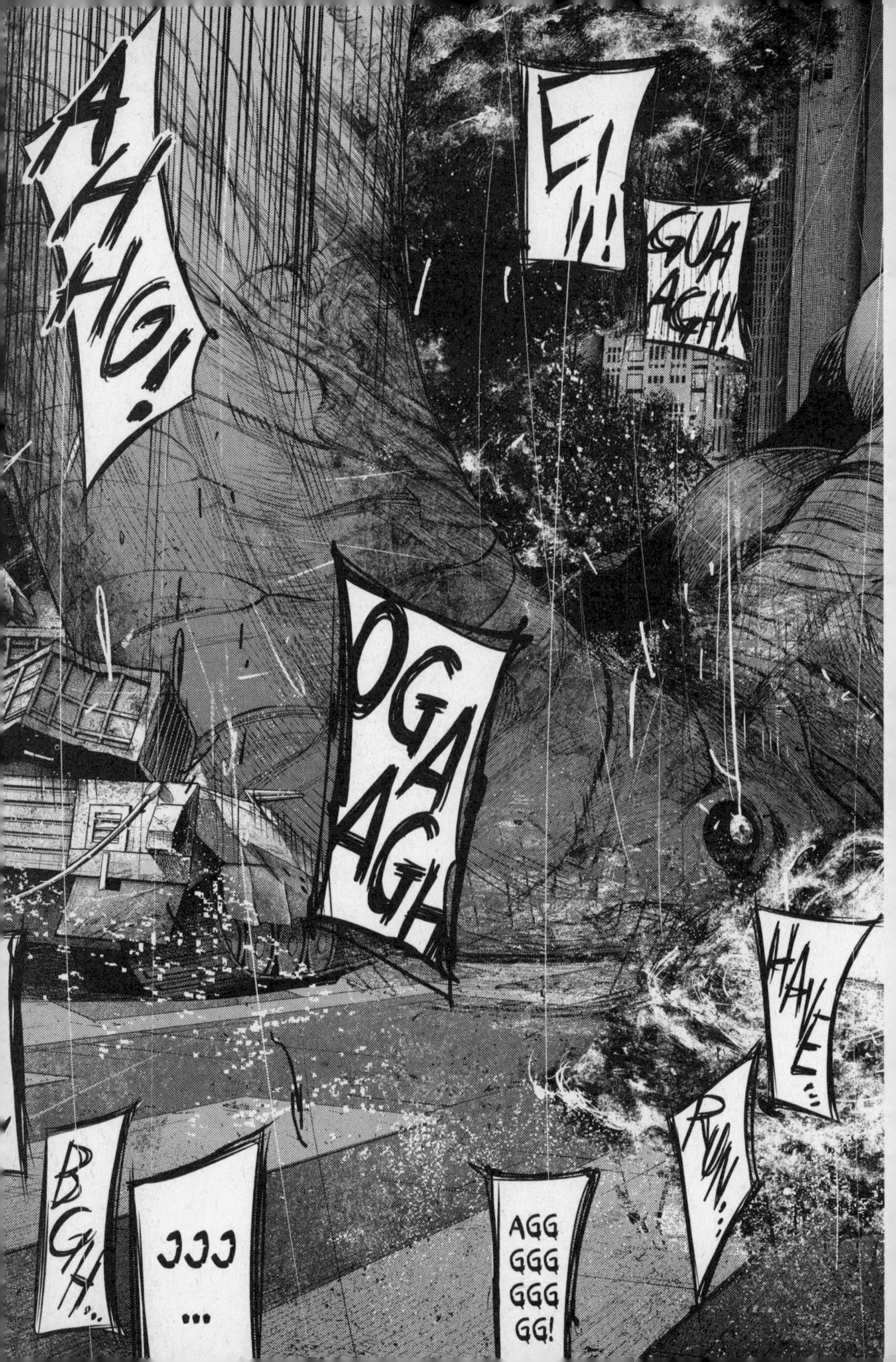
E!!!
GUAAGH!!
AHHO!
OGAAGH
HAVE...
RUN...
AGGGGGGGGGG!
JJJ...
BGH..

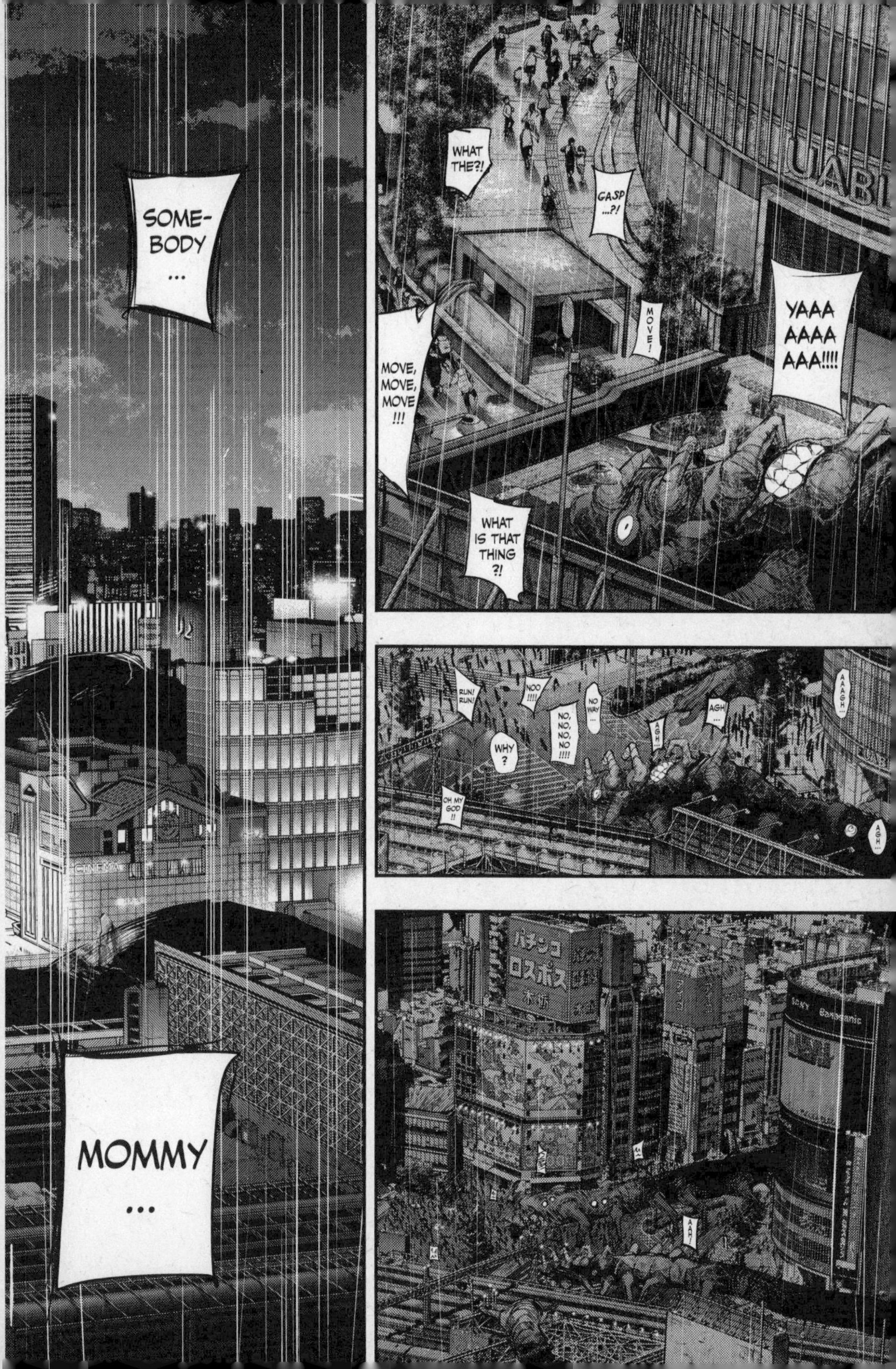
YAAA AAAA AAA!!!!
MOVE!
GASP ...?!
WHAT THE?!
MOVE, MOVE, MOVE !!!
WHAT IS THAT THING ?!
AAAGH...
AGH ...
AGH...
NO WAY ...
NO, NO, NO, NO !!!!
NOO !!!!
RUN! RUN!
WHY ?
OH MY GOD !!
AGH...
AAH!
SOME-BODY ...
MOMMY ...

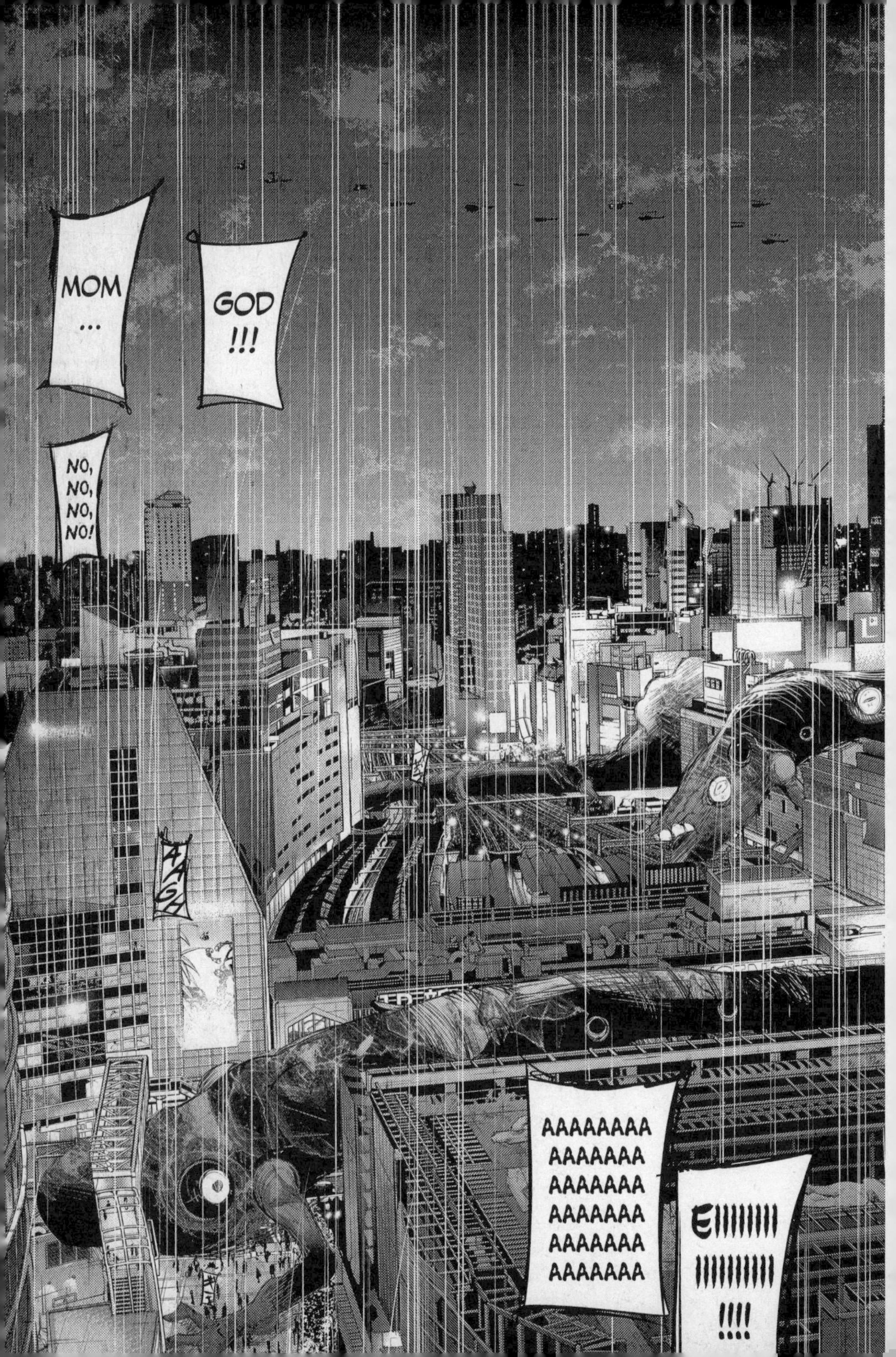
GOD !!!
MOM ...
NO, NO, NO, NO!
AAGH
AAAAAAAA AAAAAAA AAAAAAA AAAAAAA AAAAAAA AAAAAAA
EIIIIIIII IIIIIIIIII !!!!

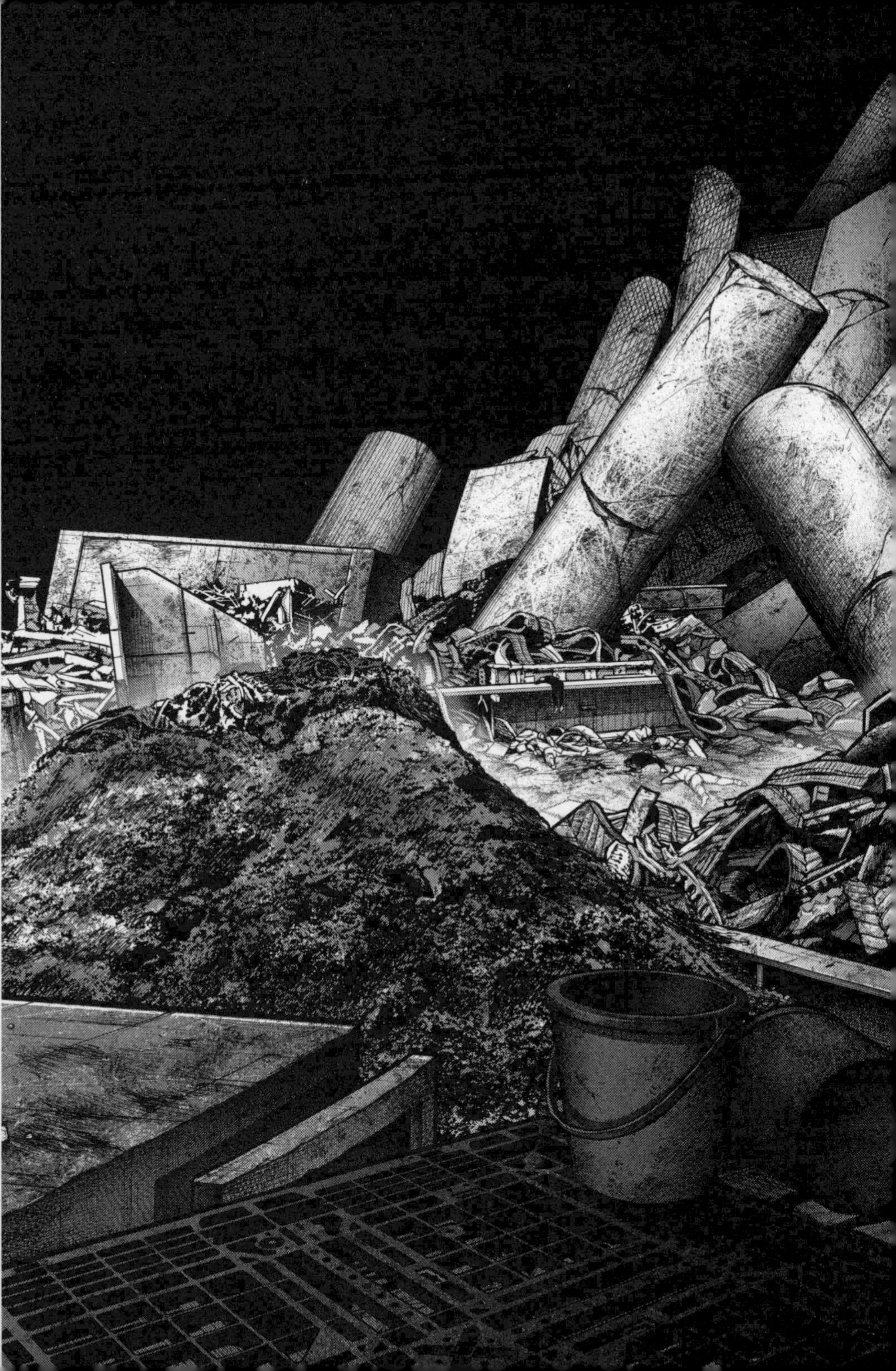

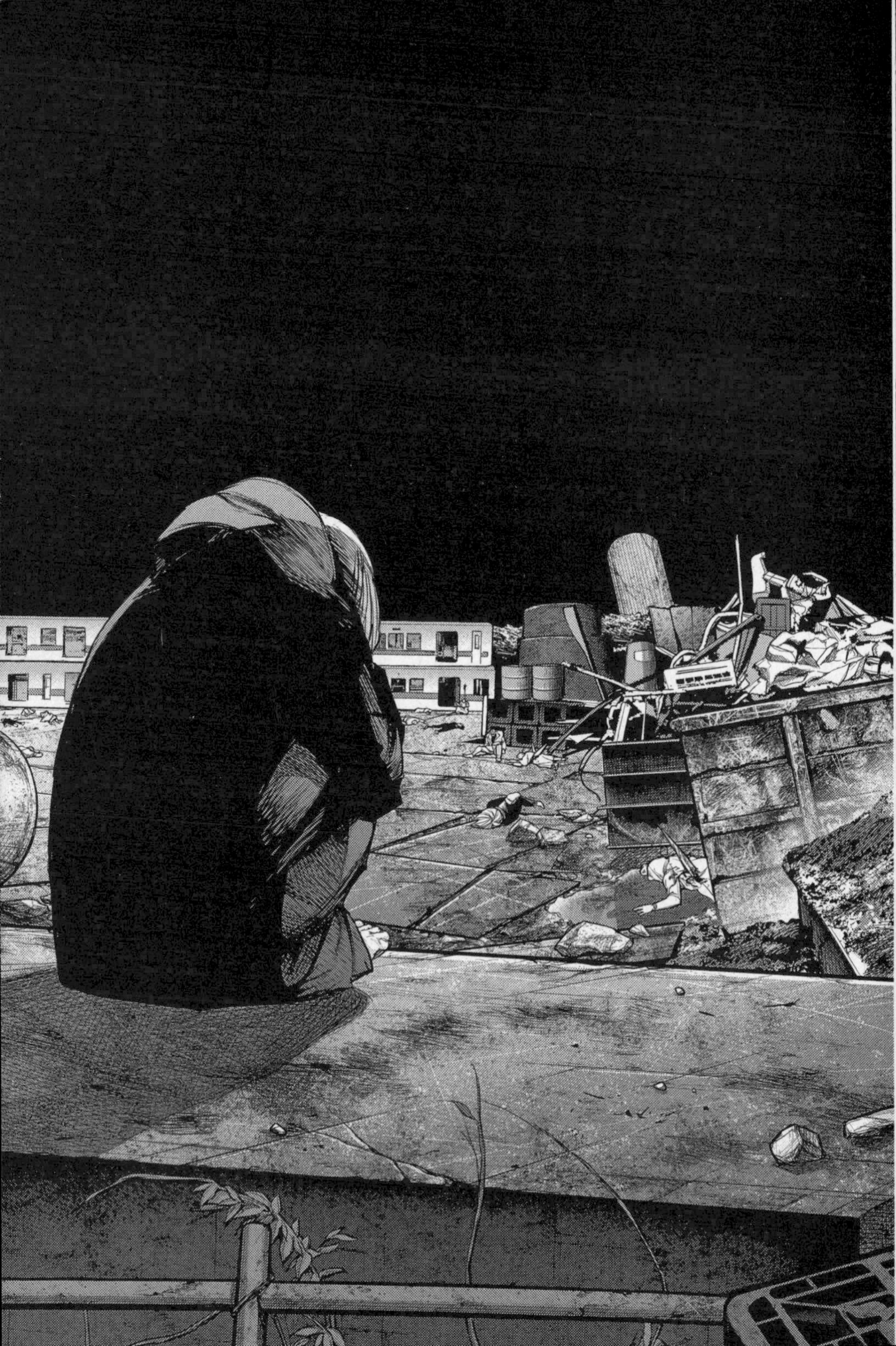

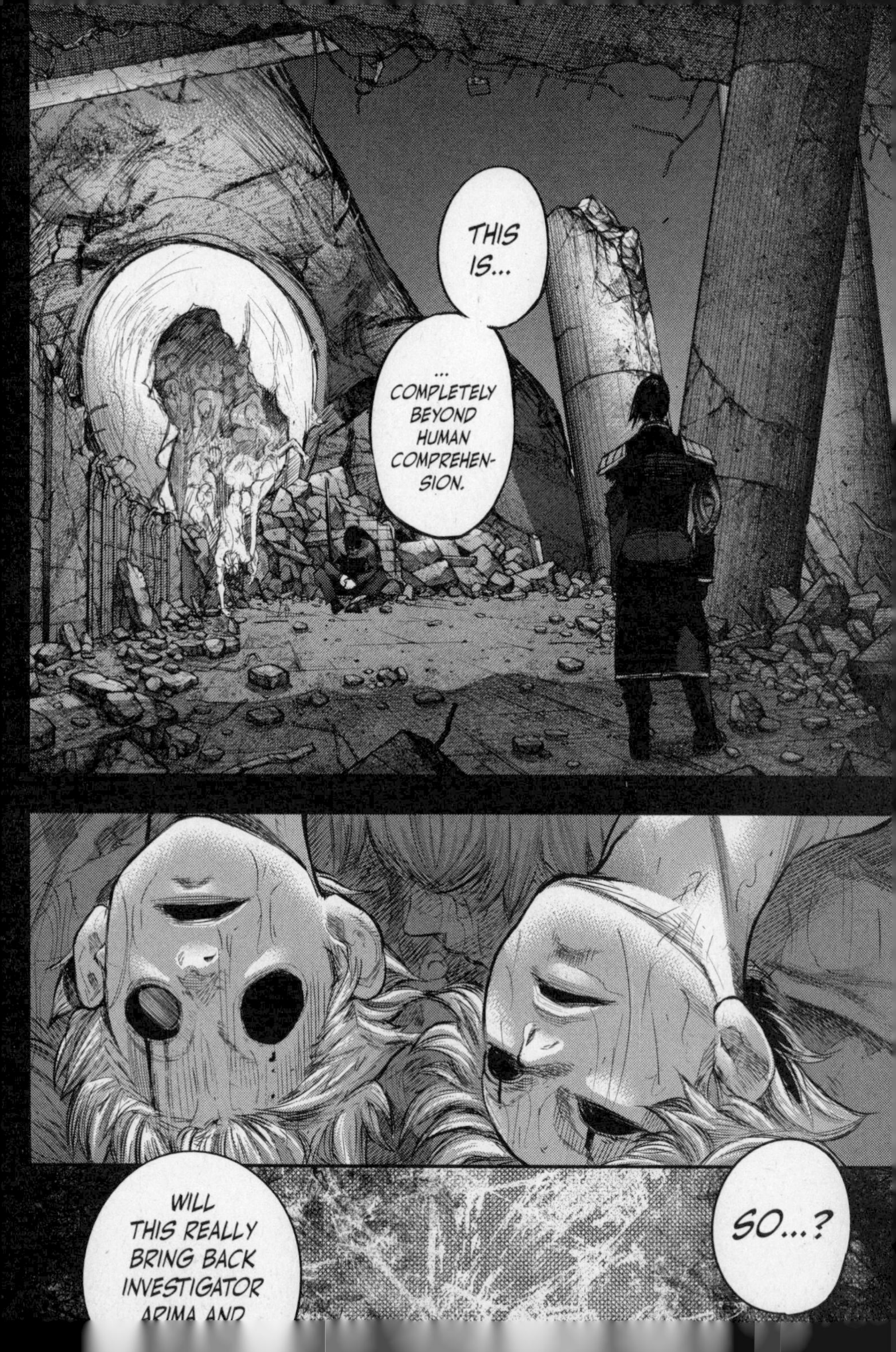
THIS IS...
...COMPLETELY BEYOND HUMAN COMPREHENSION.
SO...?
WILL THIS REALLY BRING BACK INVESTIGATOR ARIMA AND

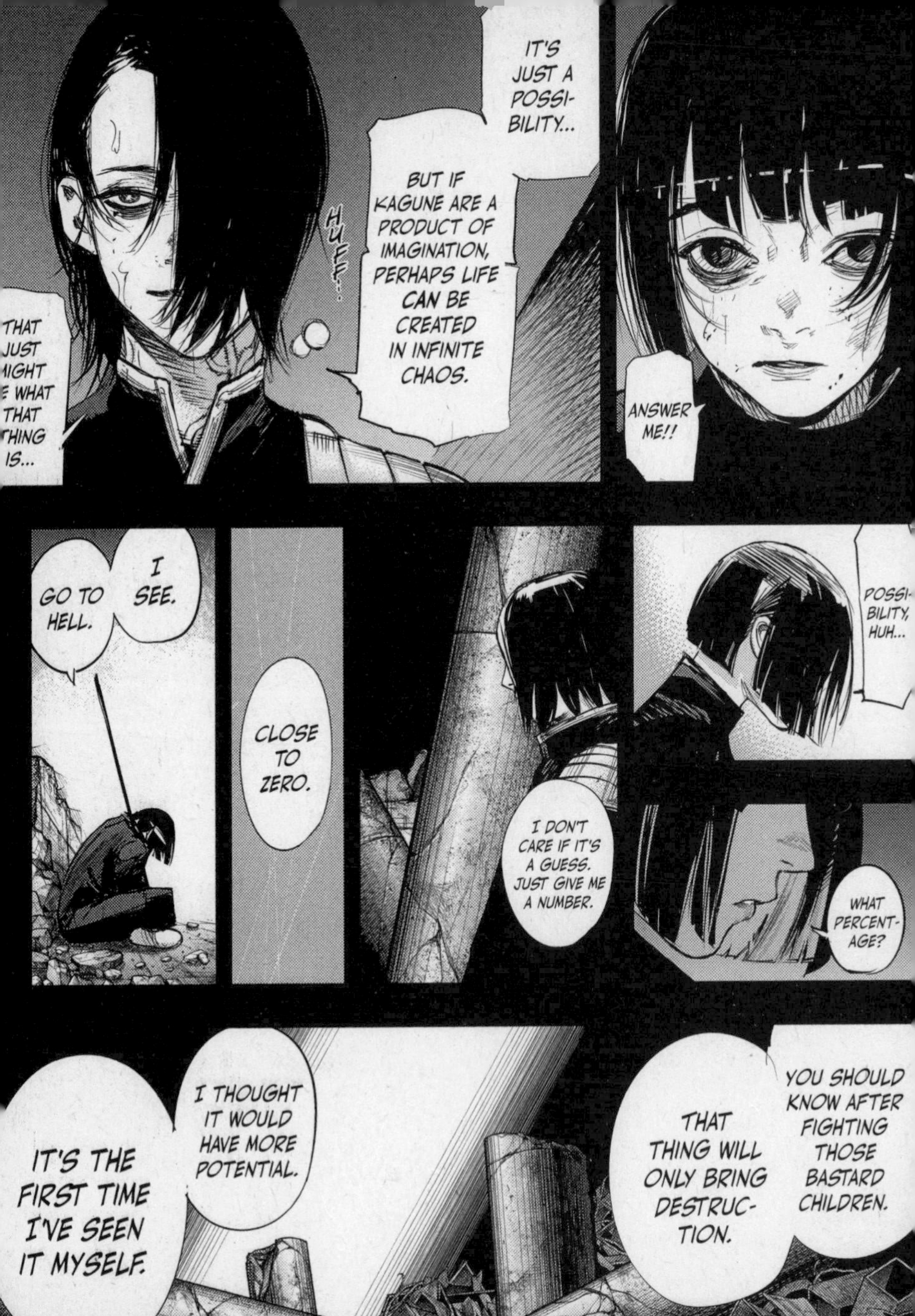
ANSWER ME!!
IT'S JUST A POSSIBILITY...
BUT IF KAGUNE ARE A PRODUCT OF IMAGINATION, PERHAPS LIFE CAN BE CREATED IN INFINITE CHAOS.
HUFF...
THAT JUST MIGHT E WHAT THAT THING IS...
POSSIBILITY, HUH...
WHAT PERCENTAGE?
I DON'T CARE IF IT'S A GUESS. JUST GIVE ME A NUMBER.
CLOSE TO ZERO.
I SEE.
GO TO HELL.
YOU SHOULD KNOW AFTER FIGHTING THOSE BASTARD CHILDREN.
THAT THING WILL ONLY BRING DESTRUCTION.
I THOUGHT IT WOULD HAVE MORE POTENTIAL.
IT'S THE FIRST TIME I'VE SEEN IT MYSELF.

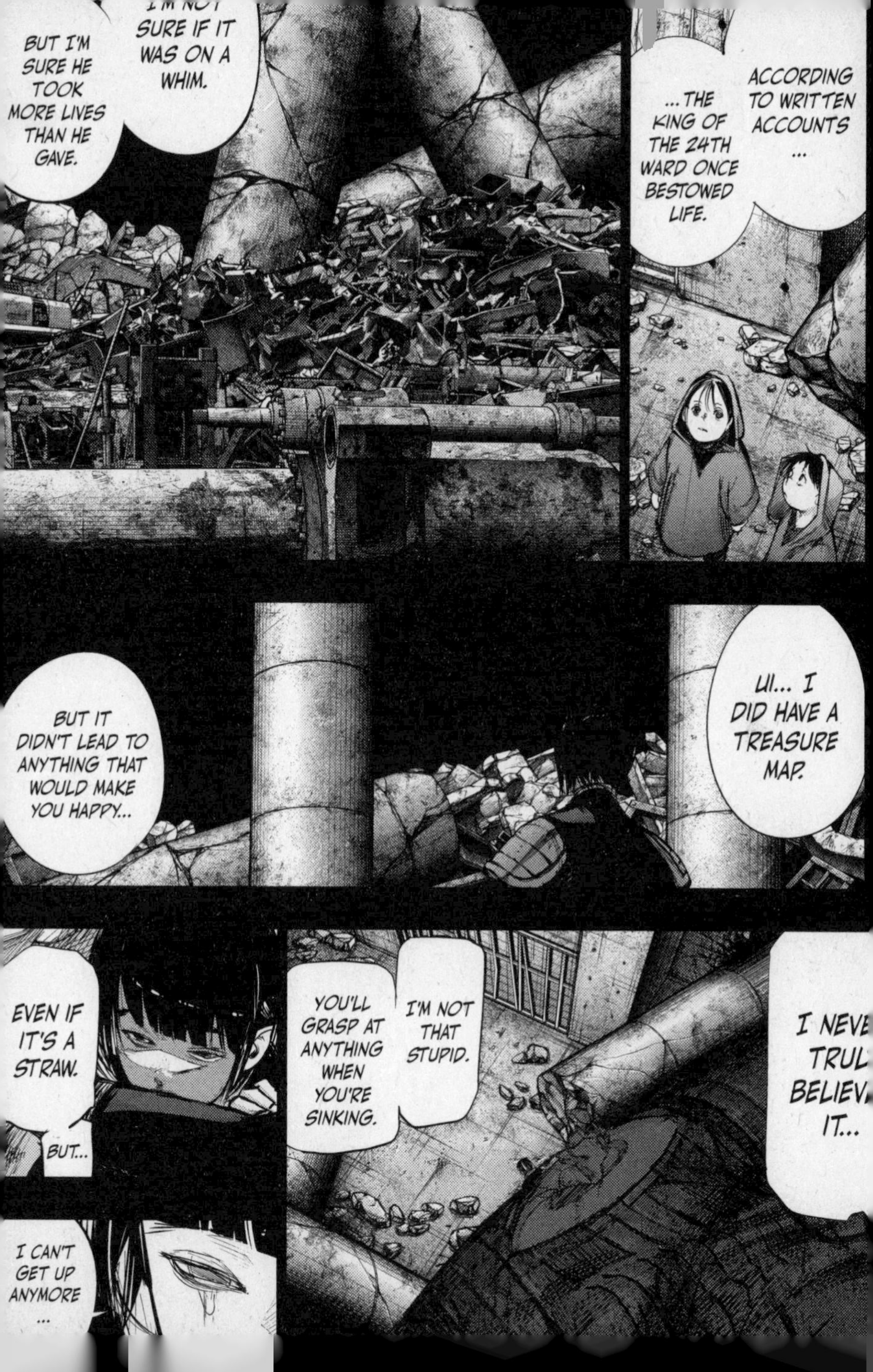
ACCORDING TO WRITTEN ACCOUNTS ...
...THE KING OF THE 24TH WARD ONCE BESTOWED LIFE.
I'M NOT SURE IF IT WAS ON A WHIM.
BUT I'M SURE HE TOOK MORE LIVES THAN HE GAVE.
UI... I DID HAVE A TREASURE MAP.
BUT IT DIDN'T LEAD TO ANYTHING THAT WOULD MAKE YOU HAPPY...
I NEVE TRUL BELIEV IT...
I'M NOT THAT STUPID.
YOU'LL GRASP AT ANYTHING WHEN YOU'RE SINKING.
EVEN IF IT'S A STRAW.
BUT...
I CAN'T GET UP ANYMORE ...

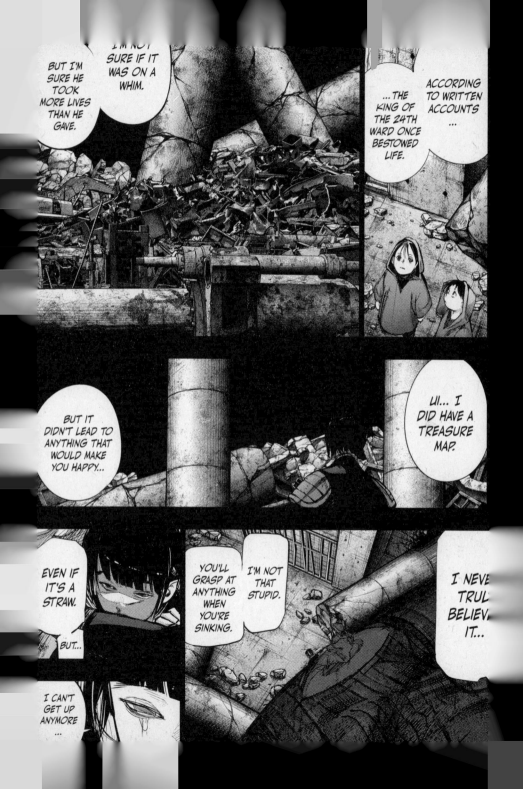

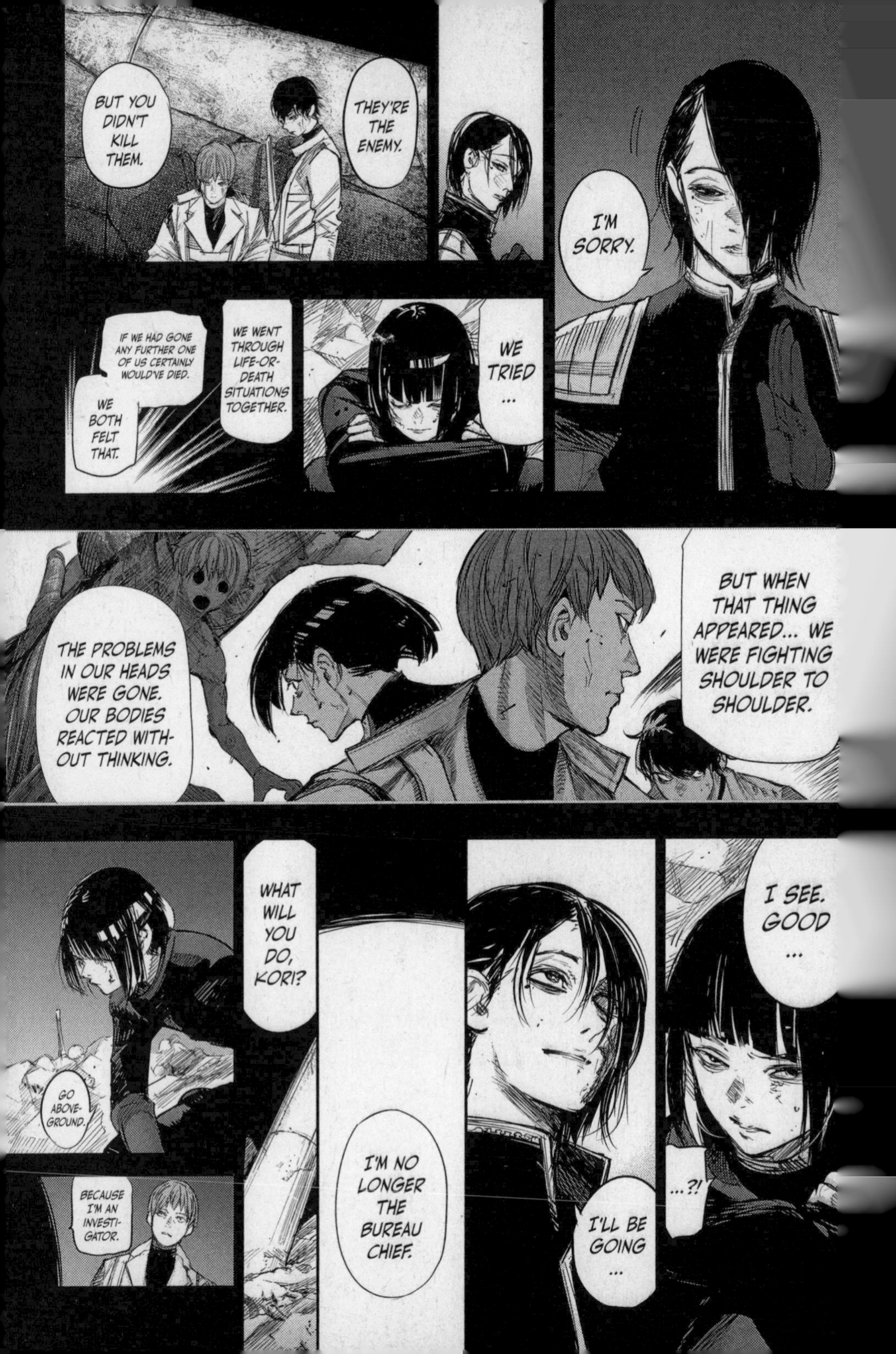
I'M SORRY.
THEY'RE THE ENEMY.
BUT YOU DIDN'T KILL THEM.
WE TRIED ...
WE WENT THROUGH LIFE-OR-DEATH SITUATIONS TOGETHER.
IF WE HAD GONE ANY FURTHER ONE OF US CERTAINLY WOULD'VE DIED.
WE BOTH FELT THAT.
BUT WHEN THAT THING APPEARED... WE WERE FIGHTING SHOULDER TO SHOULDER.
THE PROBLEMS IN OUR HEADS WERE GONE. OUR BODIES REACTED WITH-OUT THINKING.
I SEE. GOOD ...
...?!
I'LL BE GOING ...
I'M NO LONGER THE BUREAU CHIEF.
WHAT WILL YOU DO, KORI?
GO ABOVE-GROUND.
BECAUSE I'M AN INVESTI-GATOR.

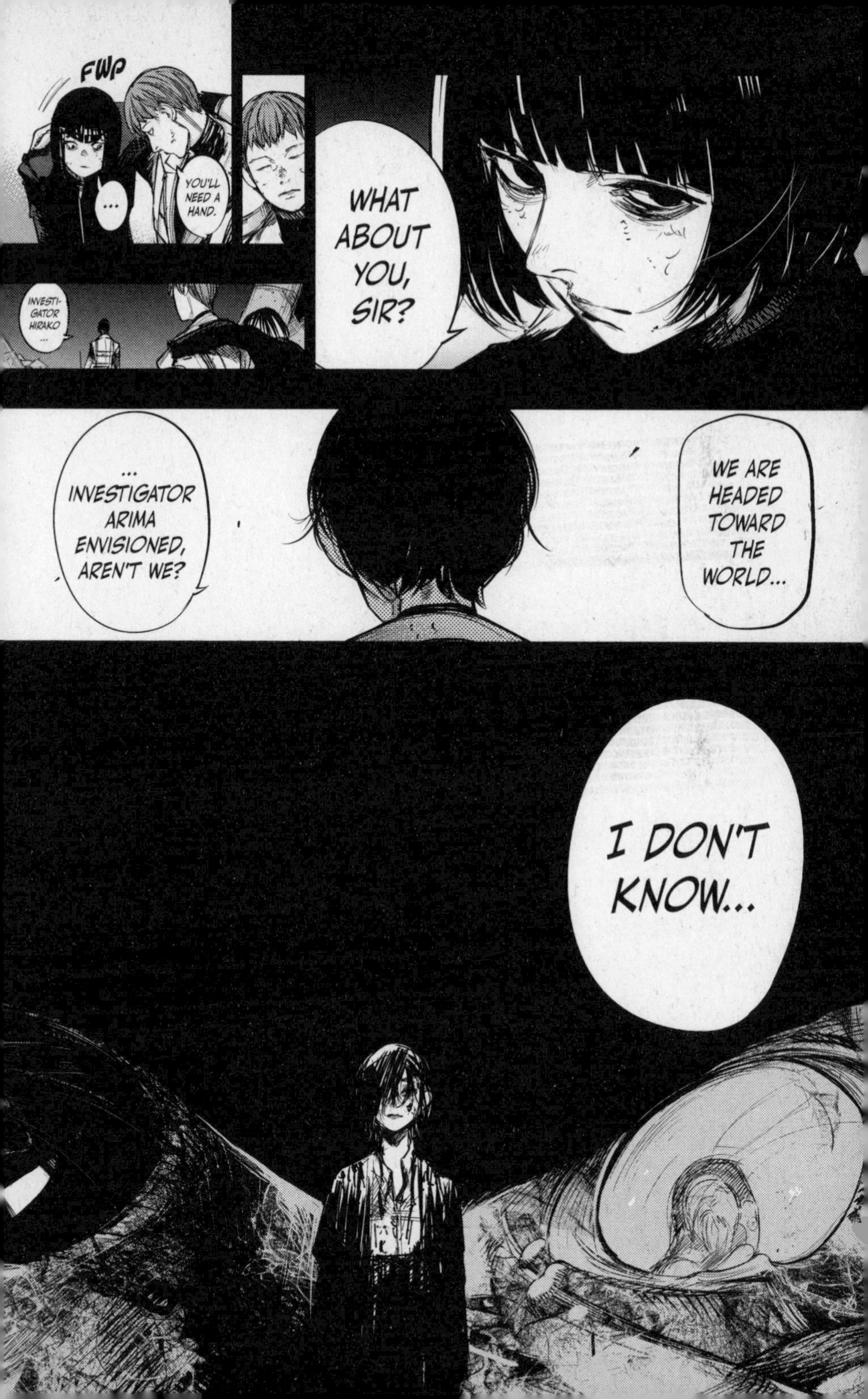
WHAT ABOUT YOU, SIR?
FWP
YOU'LL NEED A HAND.
...
INVESTIGATOR HIRAKO ...
WE ARE HEADED TOWARD THE WORLD...
... INVESTIGATOR ARIMA ENVISIONED, AREN'T WE?
I DON'T KNOW...

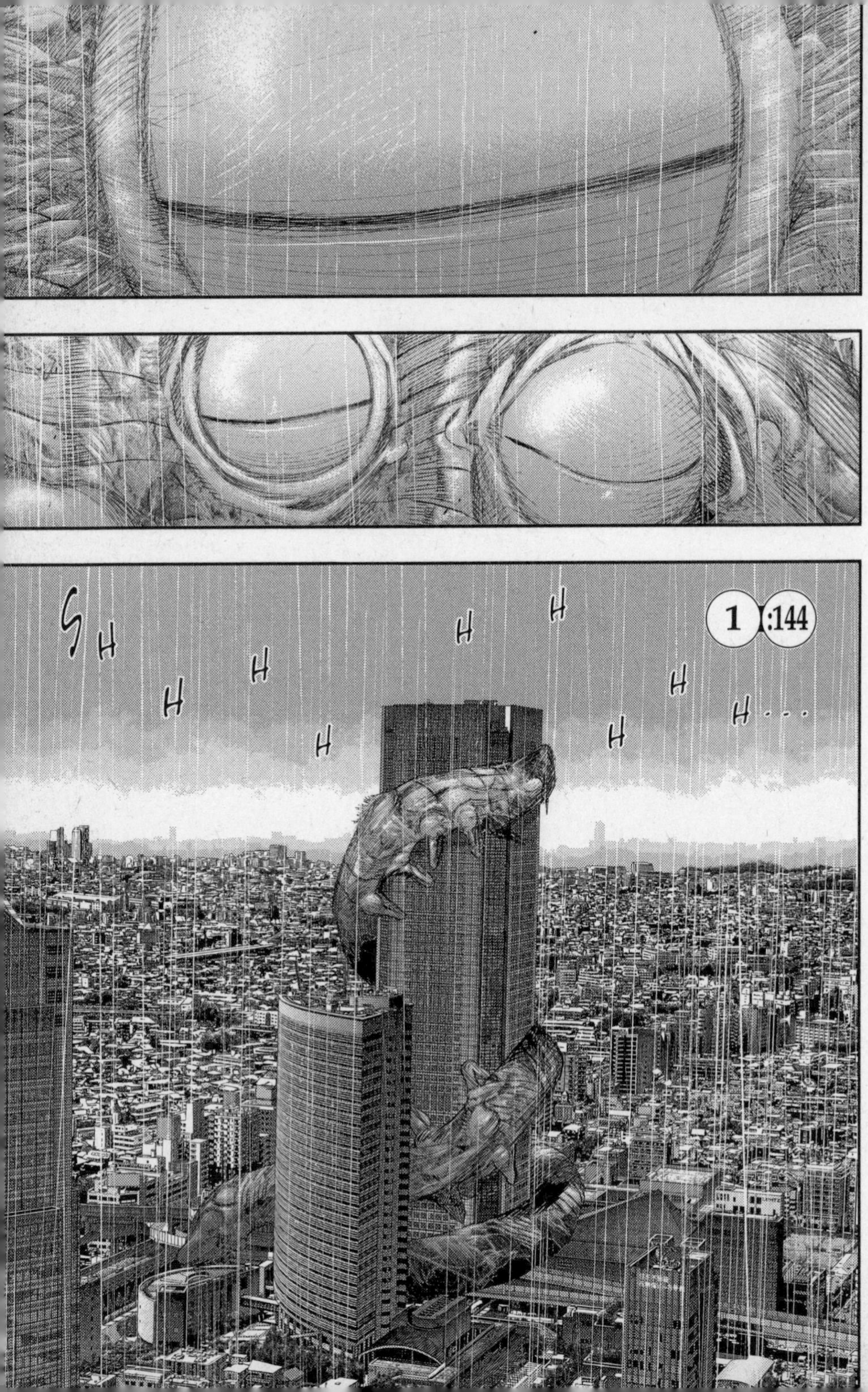

1:144
SHHHHHHHHH...

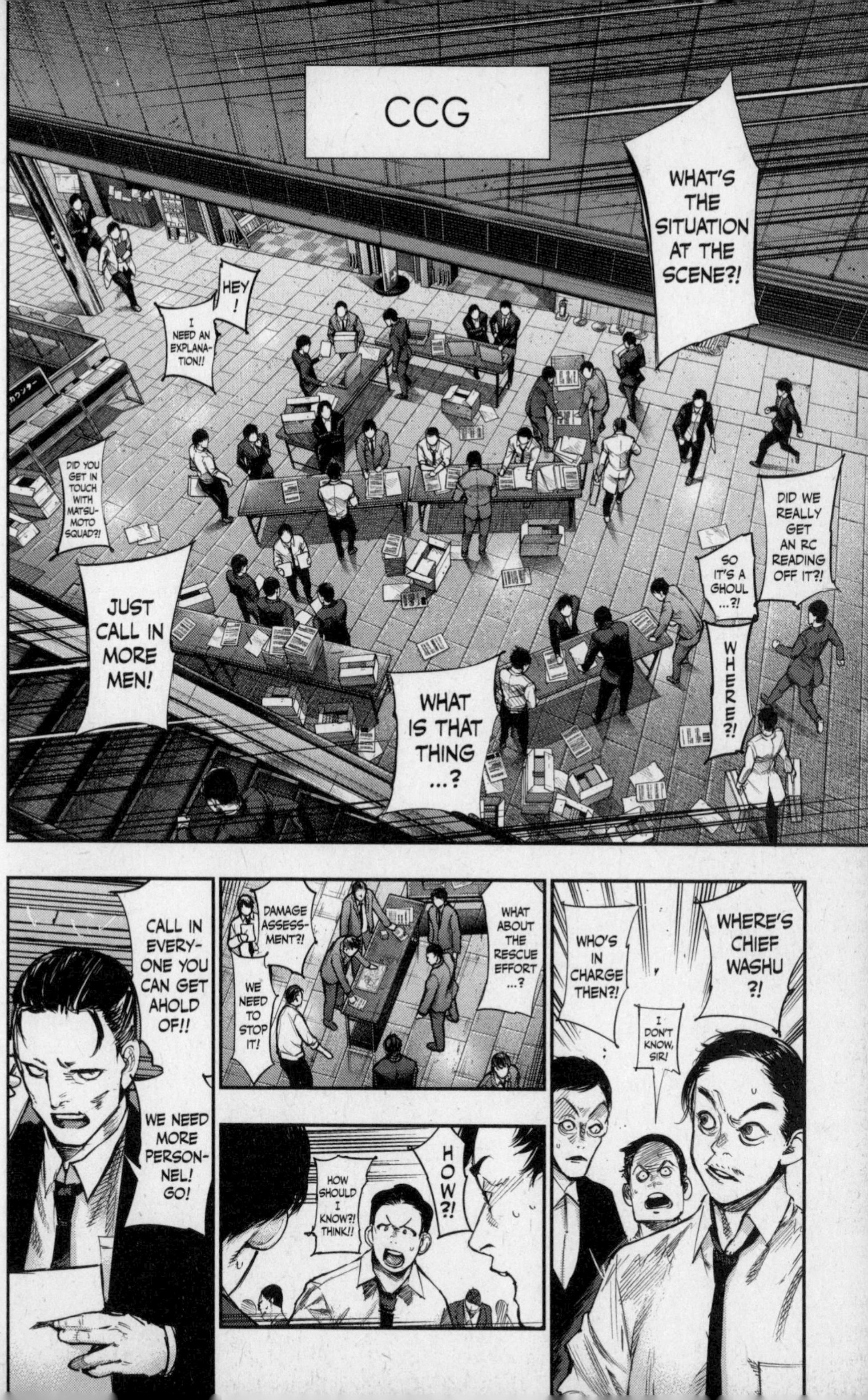
CCG
WHAT'S THE SITUATION AT THE SCENE?!
HEY!
I NEED AN EXPLANATION!!
DID WE REALLY GET AN RC READING OFF IT?!
SO IT'S A GHOUL...?!
DID YOU GET IN TOUCH WITH MATSUMOTO SQUAD?!
WHERE?!
WHAT IS THAT THING...?
JUST CALL IN MORE MEN!
WHERE'S CHIEF WASHU?!
WHO'S IN CHARGE THEN?!
I DON'T KNOW, SIR!
WHAT ABOUT THE RESCUE EFFORT...?
DAMAGE ASSESSMENT?!
WE NEED TO STOP IT!
HOW?!
HOW SHOULD I KNOW?! THINK!!
CALL IN EVERYONE YOU CAN GET AHOLD OF!!
WE NEED MORE PERSONNEL! GO!

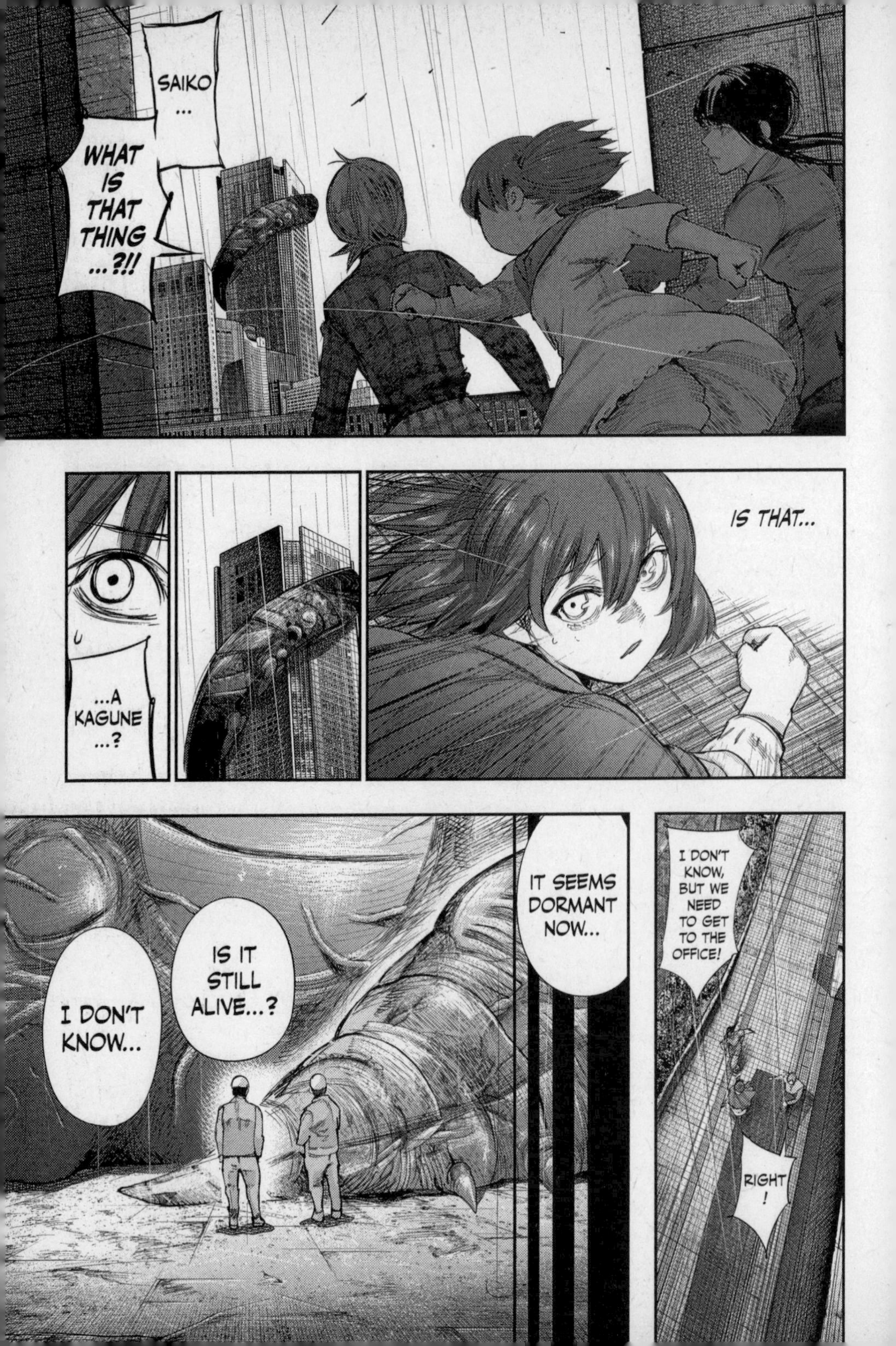
SAIKO...
WHAT IS THAT THING...?!!
IS THAT...
...A KAGUNE...?
I DON'T KNOW, BUT WE NEED TO GET TO THE OFFICE!
RIGHT!
IT SEEMS DORMANT NOW...
IS IT STILL ALIVE...?
I DON'T KNOW...

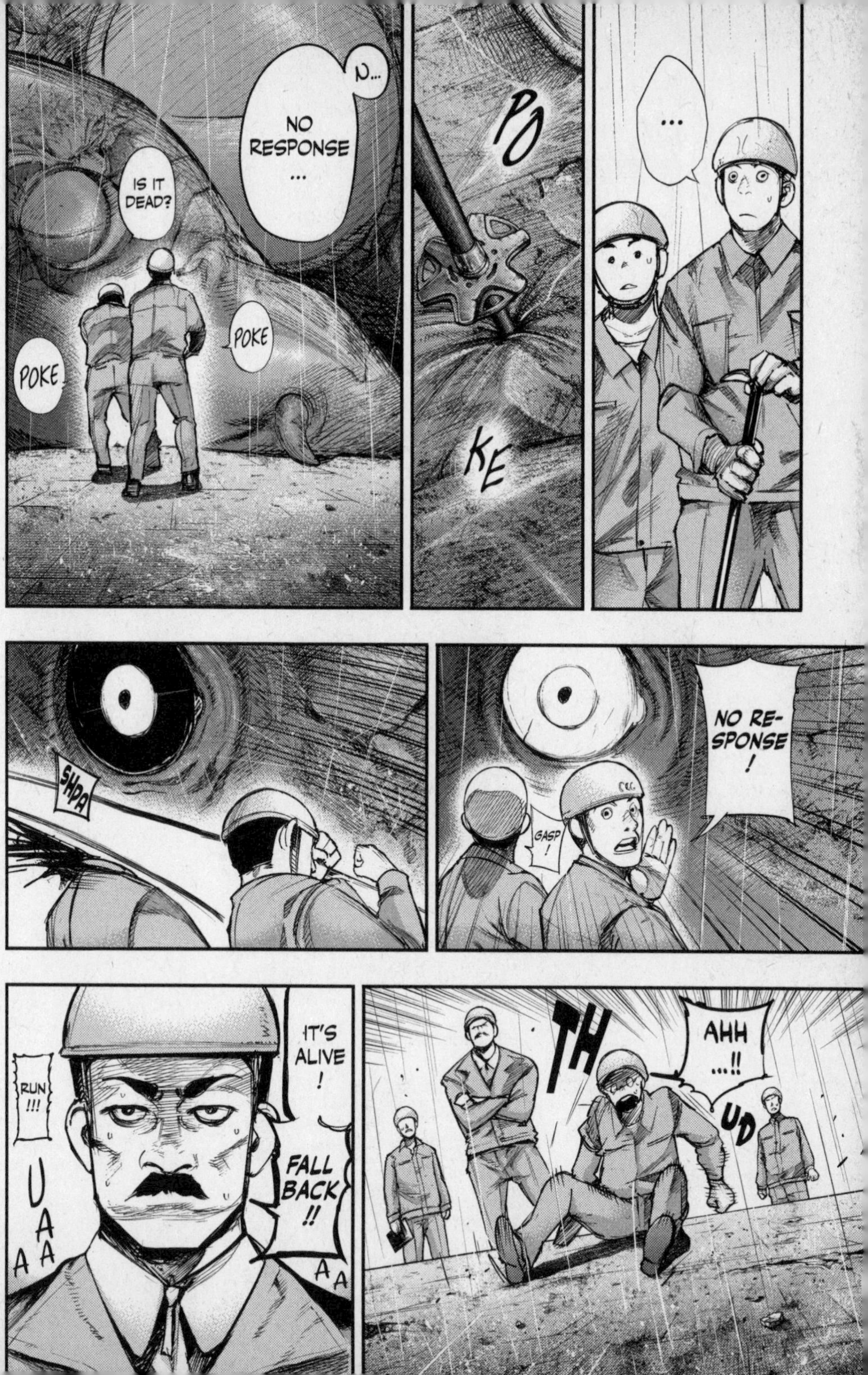
...
PO
KE
N... NO RESPONSE ...
IS IT DEAD?
POKE
POKE
NO RE-SPONSE !
GASP !
SHPA
AHH ...!!
TH
UD
IT'S ALIVE !
FALL BACK !!
RUN !!!
UAAAAA

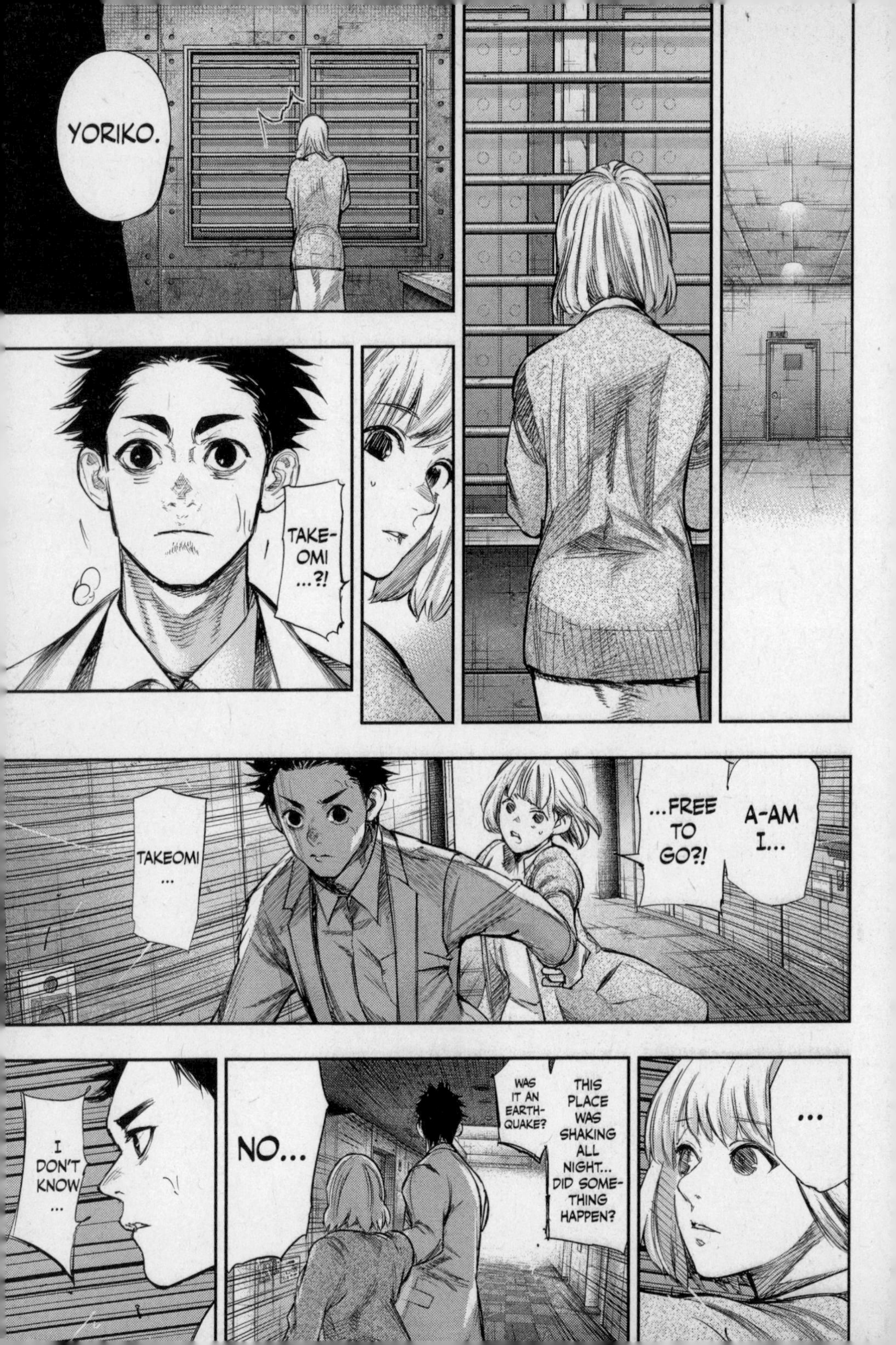
YORIKO.
TAKEOMI...?!
A-AM I...
...FREE TO GO?!
TAKEOMI...
...
THIS PLACE WAS SHAKING ALL NIGHT... DID SOMETHING HAPPEN?
WAS IT AN EARTHQUAKE?
NO...
I DON'T KNOW...

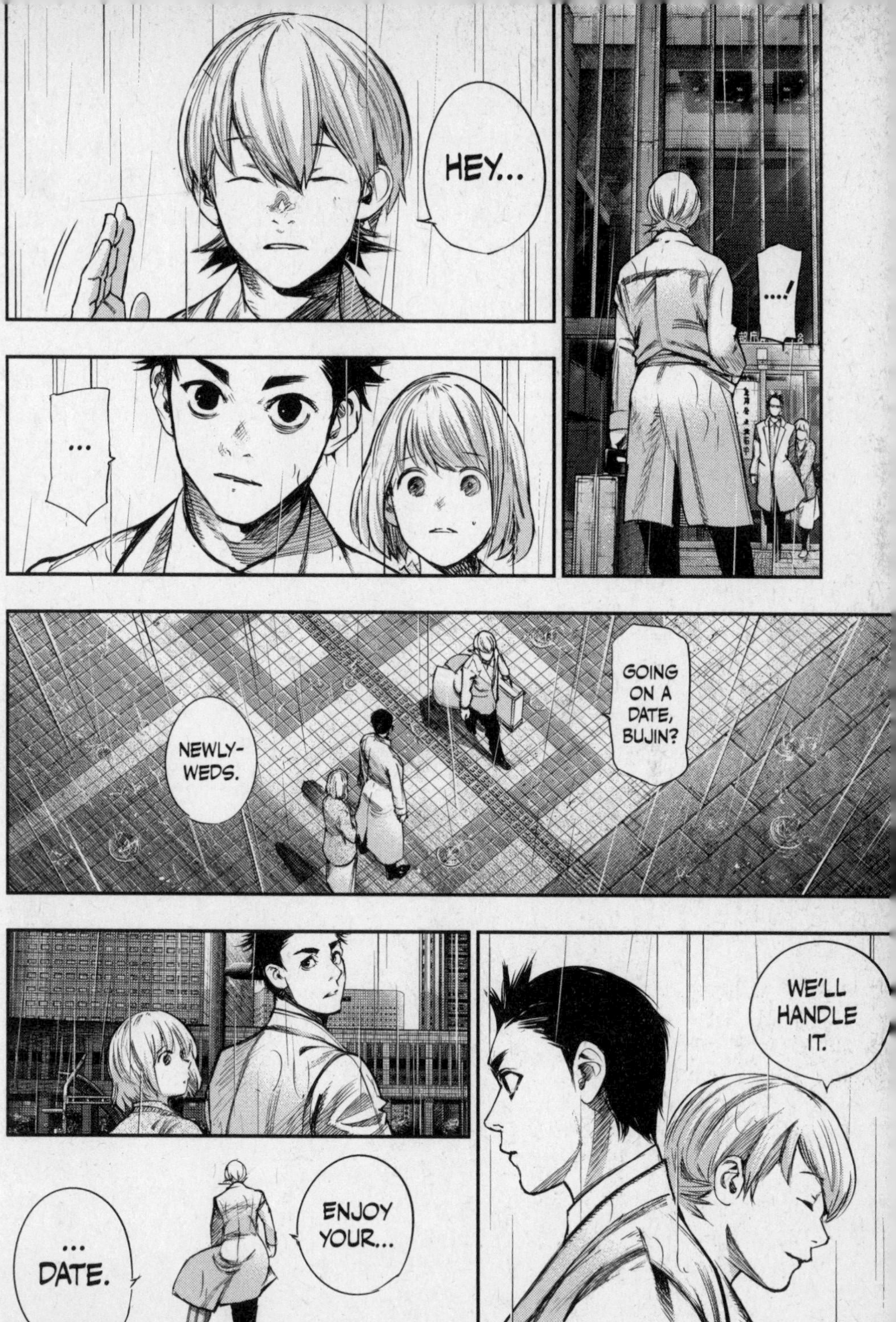
....!
HEY...
...
GOING ON A DATE, BUJIN?
NEWLY-WEDS.
WE'LL HANDLE IT.
ENJOY YOUR...
... DATE.

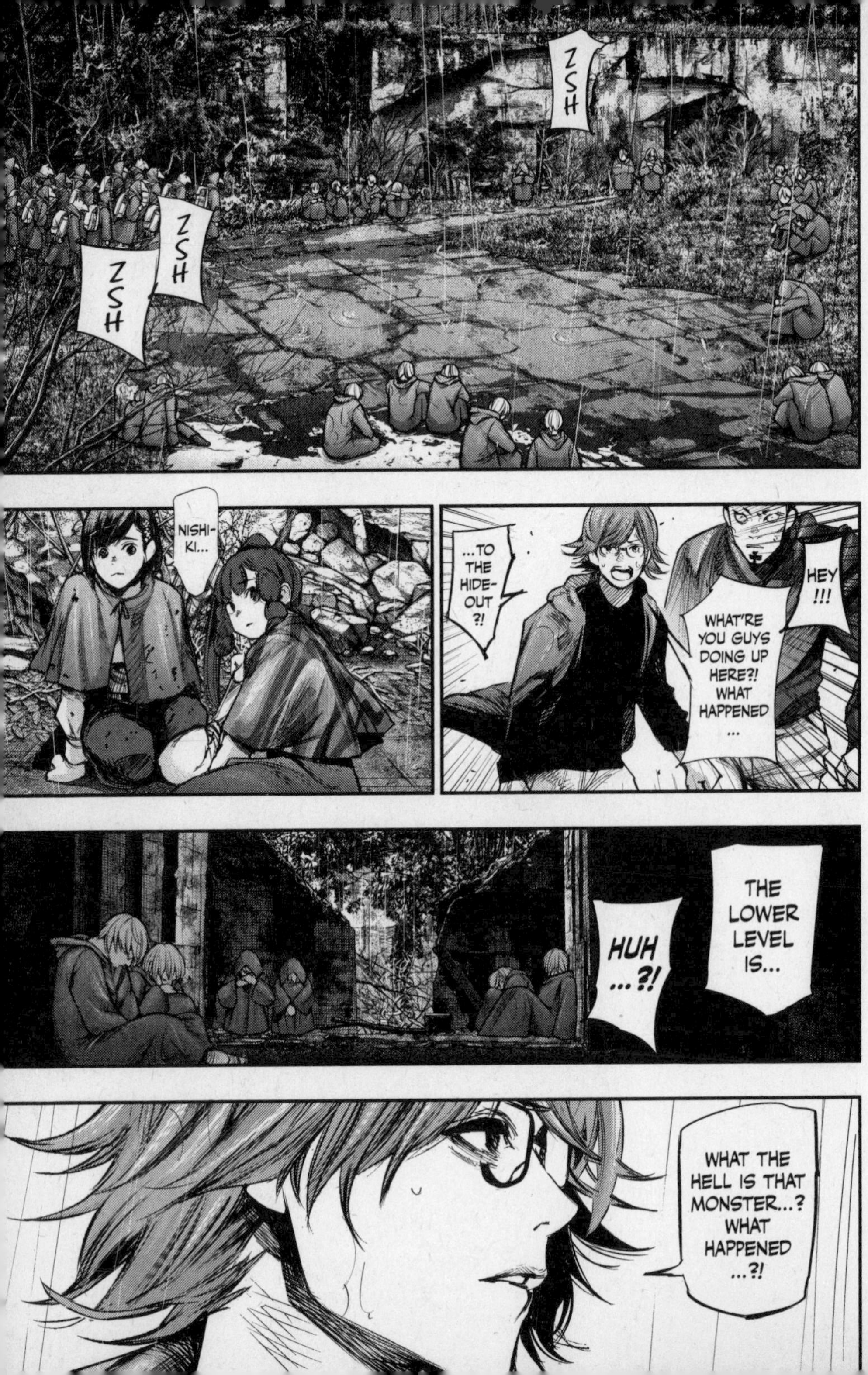
ZSH
ZSH
ZSH
HEY!!!
WHAT'RE YOU GUYS DOING UP HERE?! WHAT HAPPENED...
...TO THE HIDE-OUT?!
NISHIKI...
THE LOWER LEVEL IS...
HUH...?!
WHAT THE HELL IS THAT MONSTER...? WHAT HAPPENED...?!

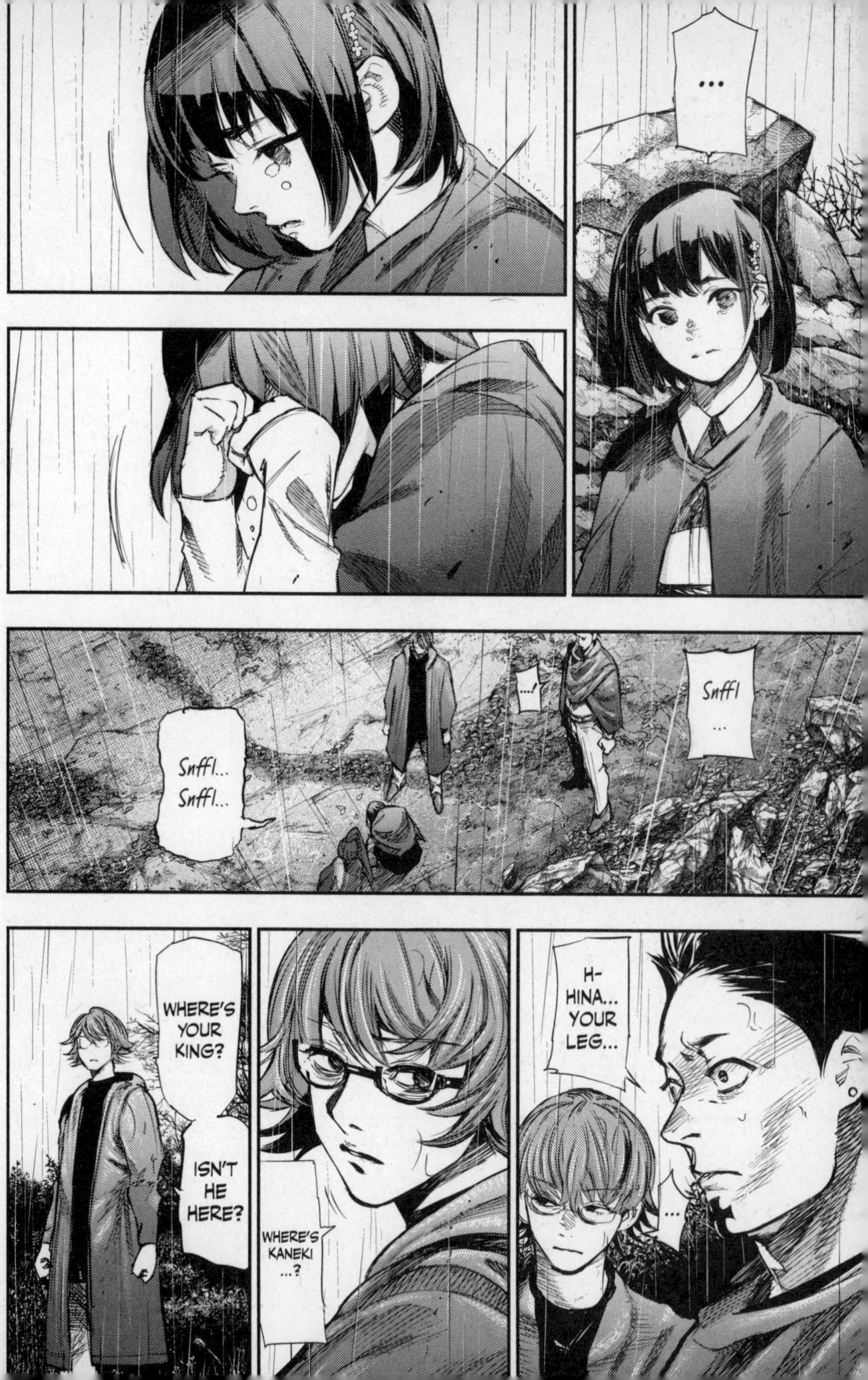
...
Snffl ...
...!
Snffl... Snffl...
H- HINA... YOUR LEG...
...
WHERE'S KANEKI ...?
WHERE'S YOUR KING?
ISN'T HE HERE?

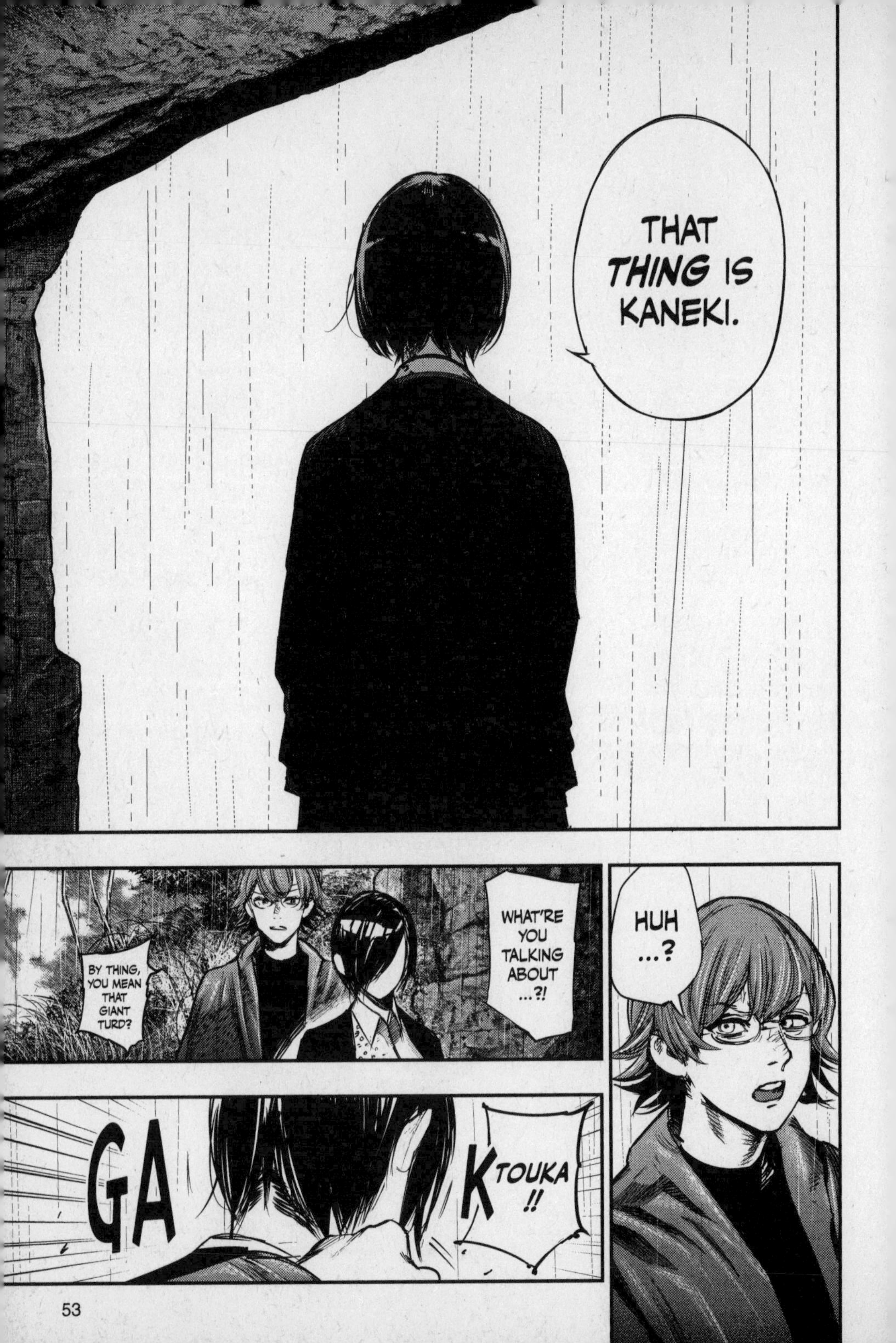
THAT THING IS KANEKI.
HUH ...?
WHAT'RE YOU TALKING ABOUT ...?!
BY THING, YOU MEAN THAT GIANT TURD?
GAK
TOUKA !!

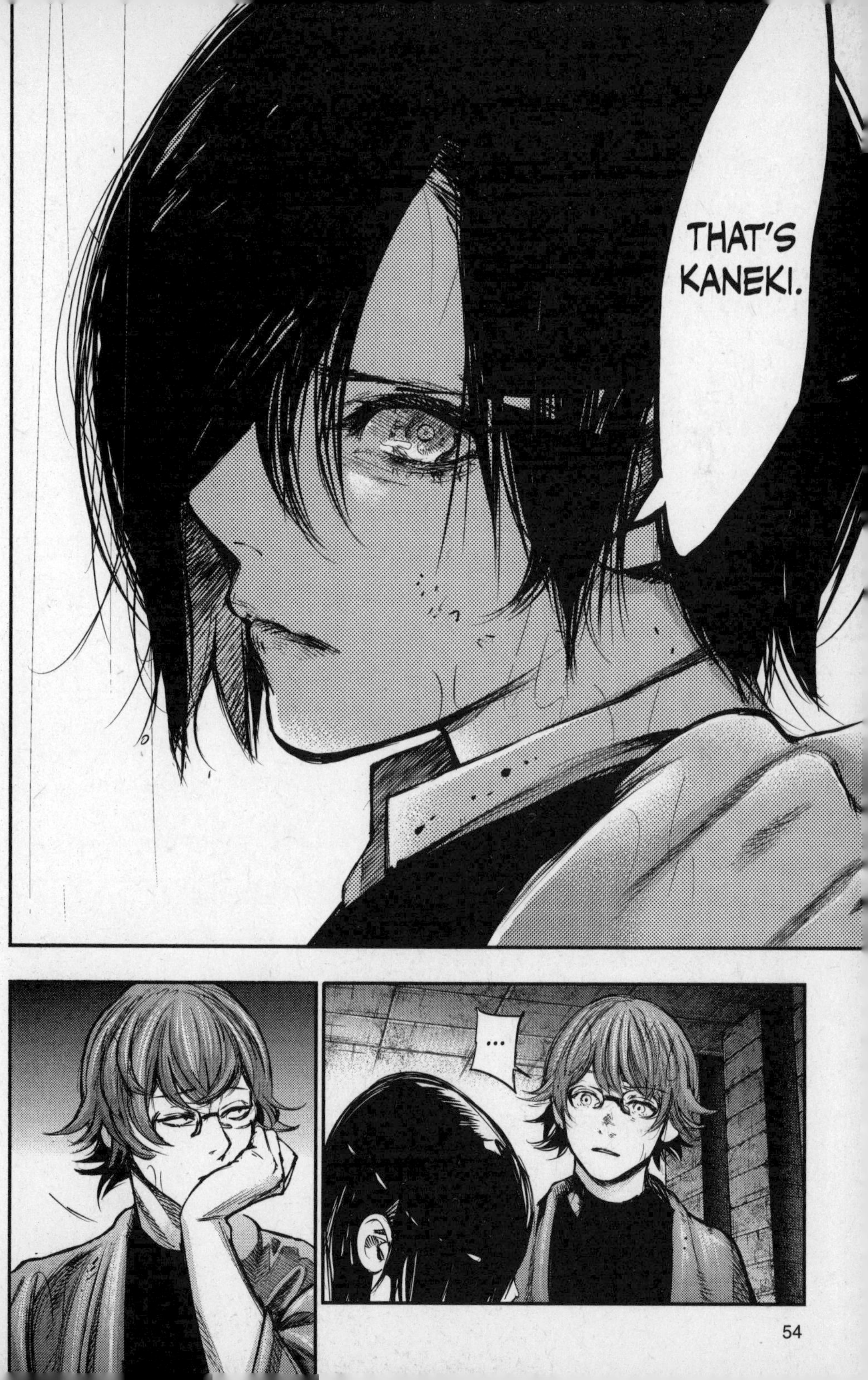
THAT'S KANEKI.
...

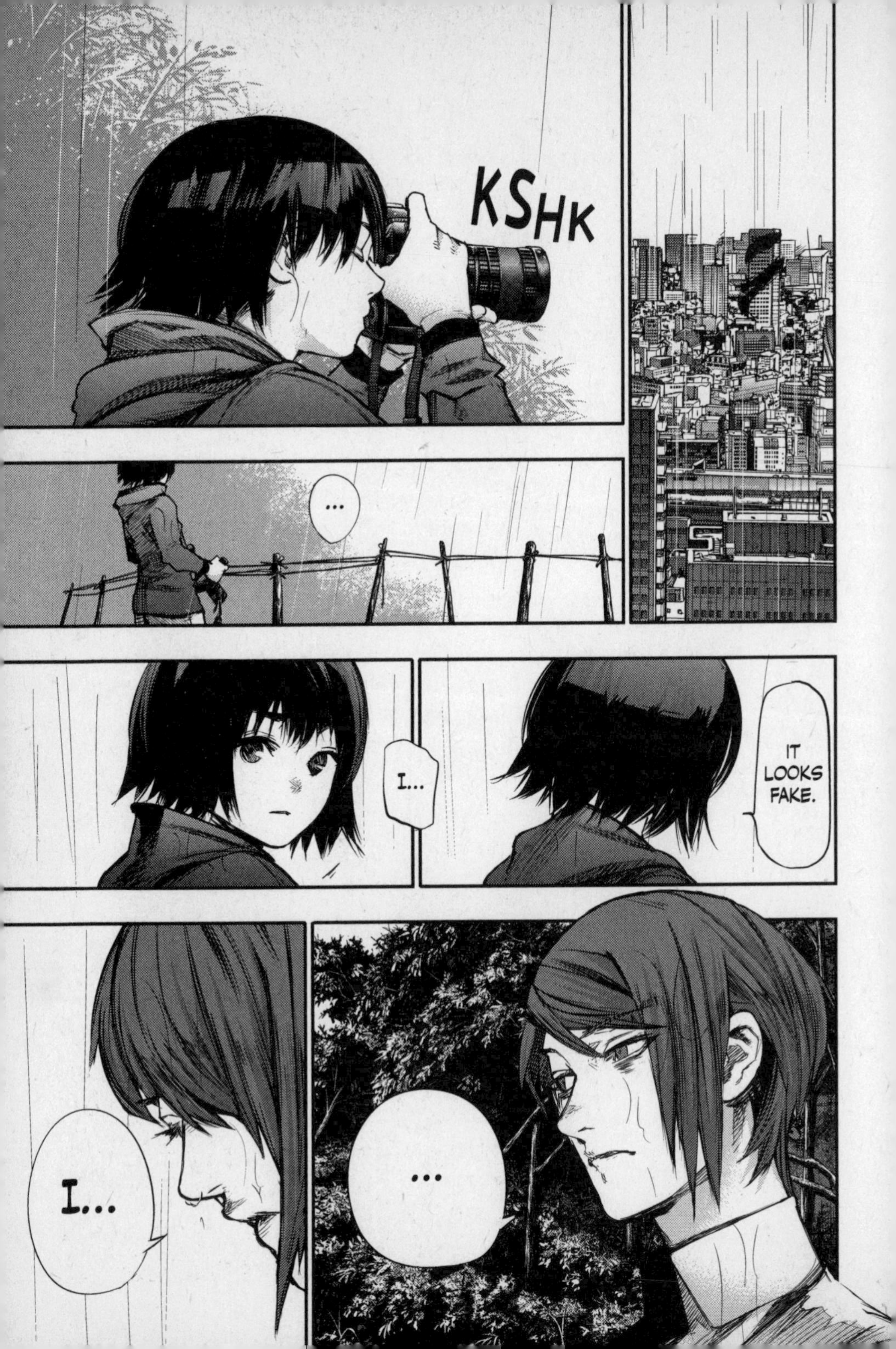
KSHK
...
IT LOOKS FAKE.
I...
...
I...

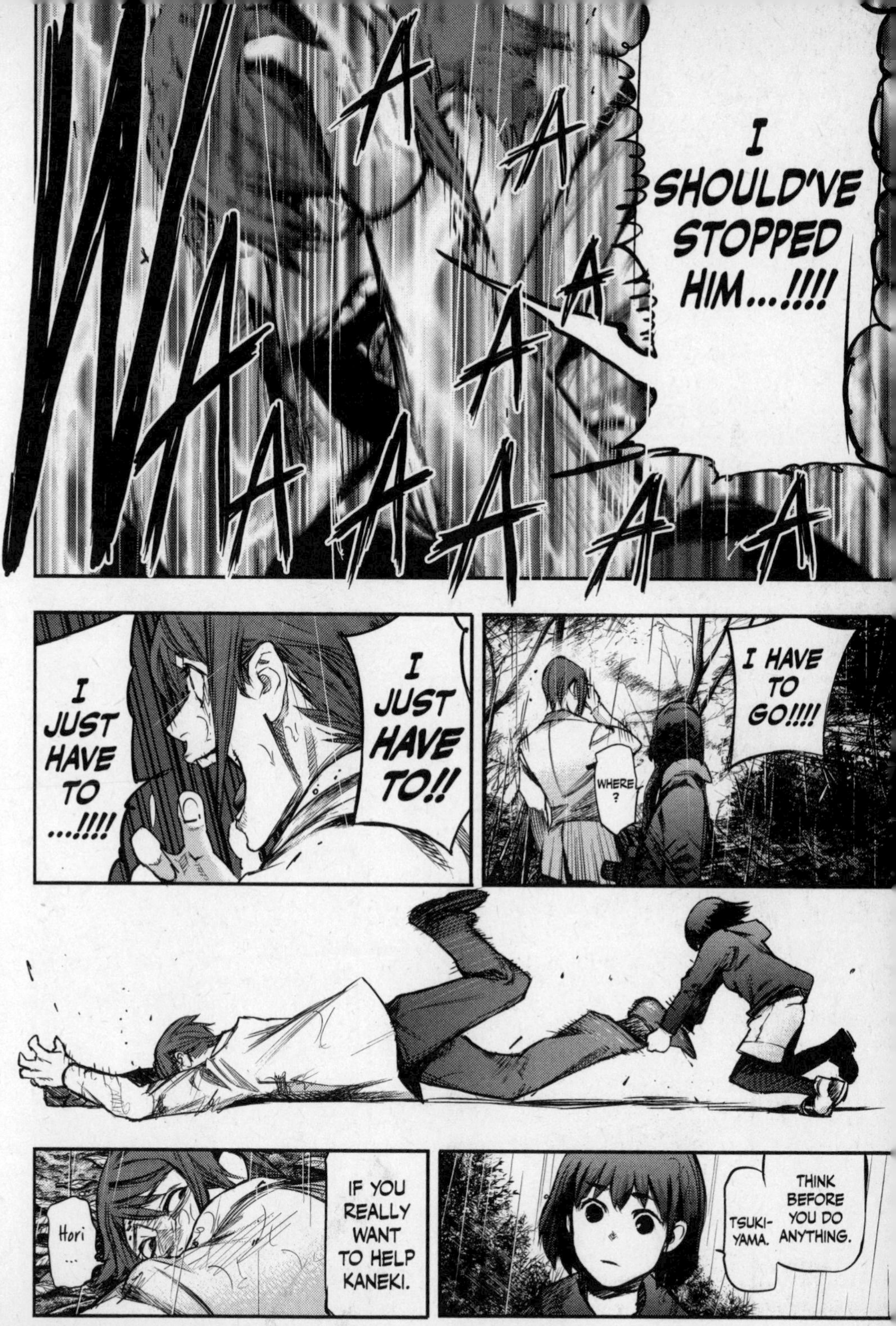
I SHOULD'VE STOPPED HIM...!!!!
WAAAAAAAAAAA
I HAVE TO GO!!!!
WHERE?
I JUST HAVE TO!!
I JUST HAVE TO ...!!!!
THINK BEFORE YOU DO ANYTHING.
TSUKI-YAMA.
IF YOU REALLY WANT TO HELP KANEKI.
Hori ...

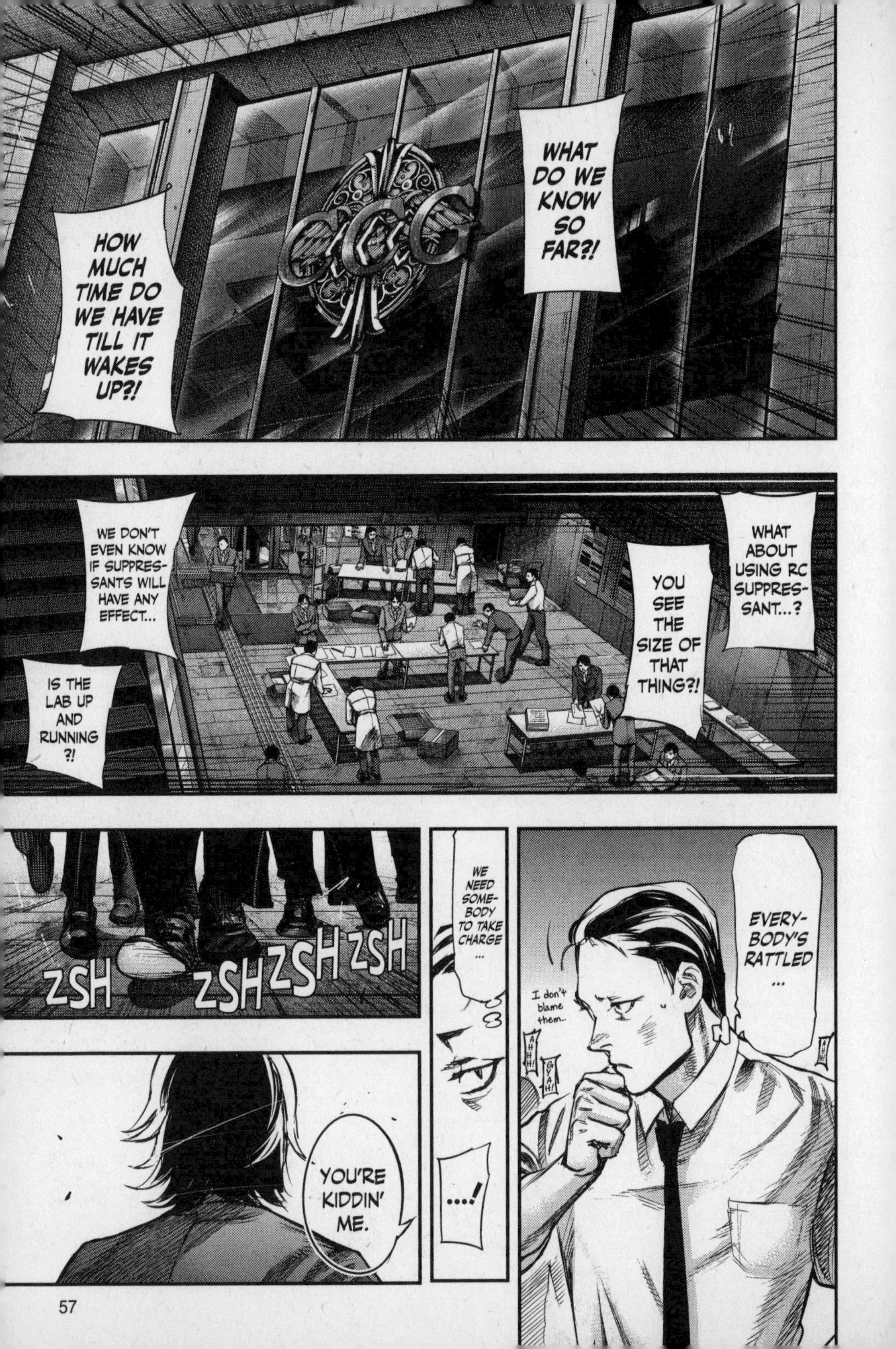
WHAT DO WE KNOW SO FAR?!
HOW MUCH TIME DO WE HAVE TILL IT WAKES UP?!
WHAT ABOUT USING RC SUPPRES-SANT...?
YOU SEE THE SIZE OF THAT THING?!
WE DON'T EVEN KNOW IF SUPPRES-SANTS WILL HAVE ANY EFFECT...
IS THE LAB UP AND RUNNING?!
EVERY-BODY'S RATTLED...
I don't blame them...
AHH!!
GYAH!
WE NEED SOME-BODY TO TAKE CHARGE...
...!
ZSH ZSH ZSH ZSH ZSH
YOU'RE KIDDIN' ME.

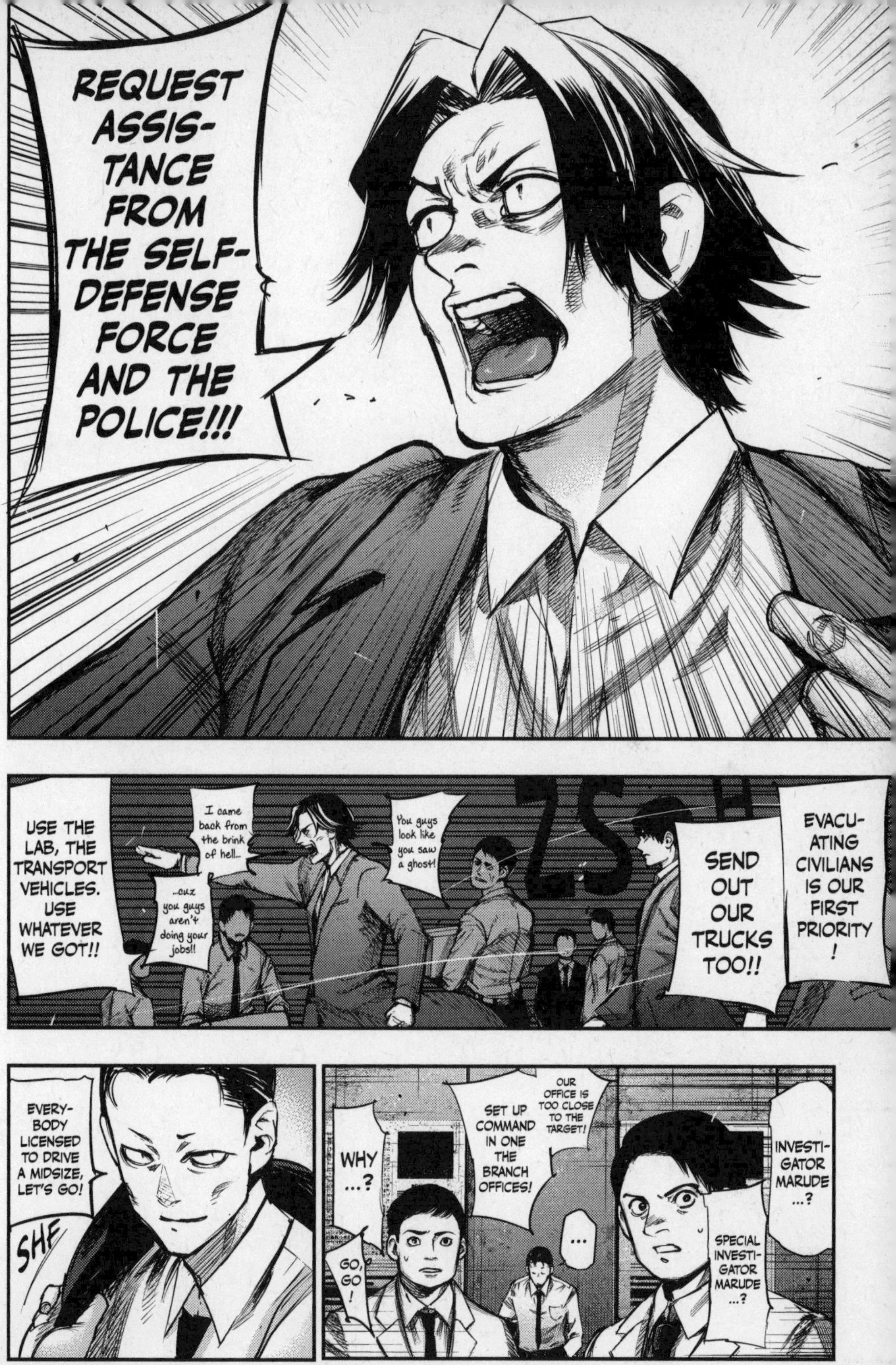
REQUEST ASSISTANCE FROM THE SELF-DEFENSE FORCE AND THE POLICE!!!
EVACUATING CIVILIANS IS OUR FIRST PRIORITY!
SEND OUT OUR TRUCKS TOO!!
You guys look like you saw a ghost!
I came back from the brink of hell...
...cuz you guys aren't doing your jobs!!
USE THE LAB, THE TRANSPORT VEHICLES. USE WHATEVER WE GOT!!
INVESTIGATOR MARUDE ...?
SPECIAL INVESTIGATOR MARUDE ...?
OUR OFFICE IS TOO CLOSE TO THE TARGET!
SET UP COMMAND IN ONE THE BRANCH OFFICES!
WHY ...?
...
GO, GO!
EVERYBODY LICENSED TO DRIVE A MIDSIZE, LET'S GO!
SHF

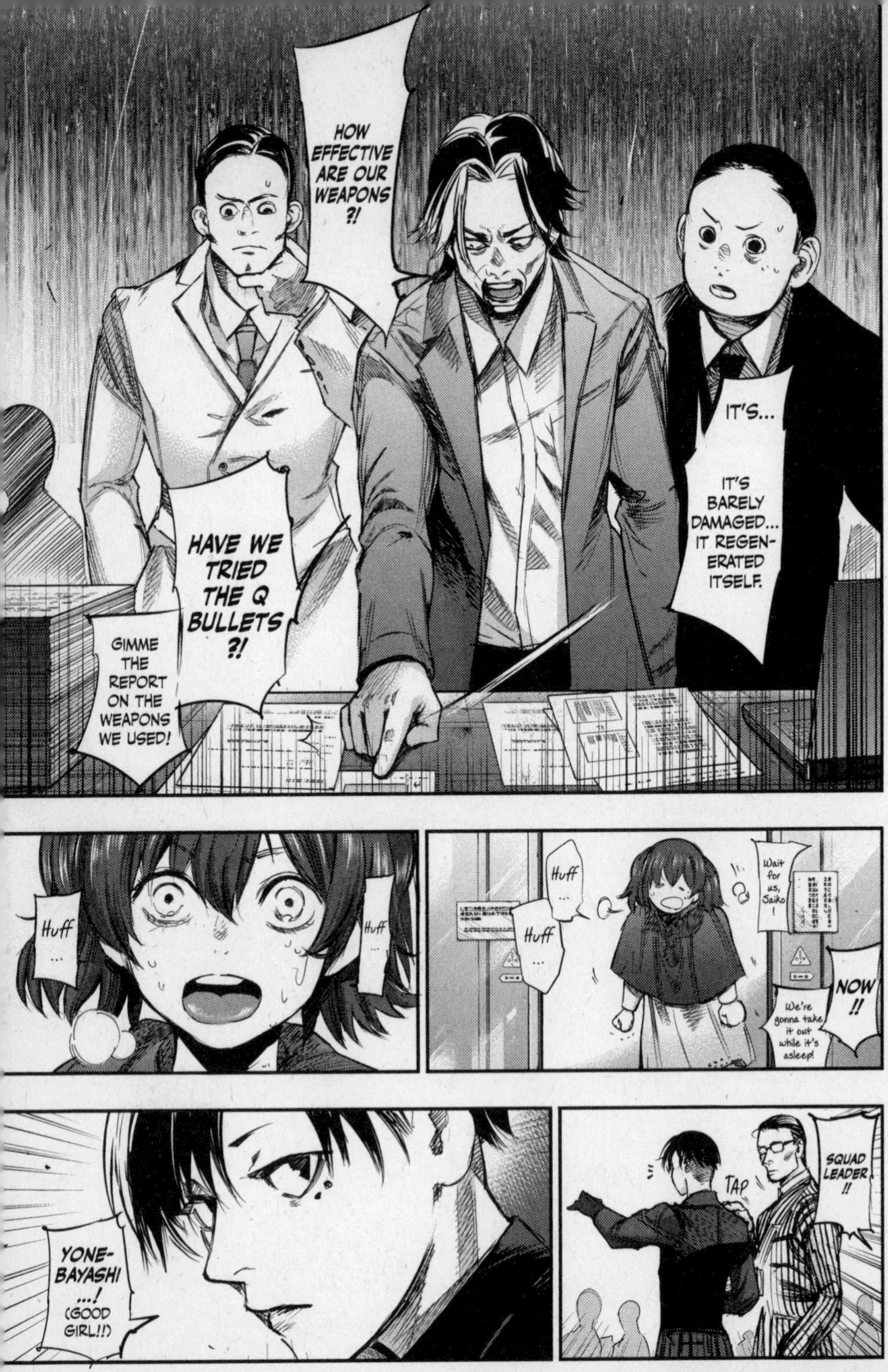
HOW EFFECTIVE ARE OUR WEAPONS ?!
IT'S...
IT'S BARELY DAMAGED... IT REGENERATED ITSELF.
HAVE WE TRIED THE Q BULLETS ?!
GIMME THE REPORT ON THE WEAPONS WE USED!
Wait for us, Saiko!
NOW!!
We're gonna take it out while it's asleep!
Huff...
Huff...
Huff...
Huff...
SQUAD LEADER!!
TAP
YONE-BAYASHI...!
(GOOD GIRL!!)

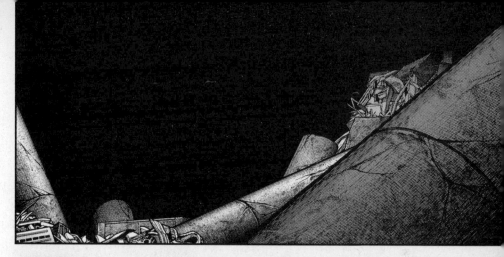

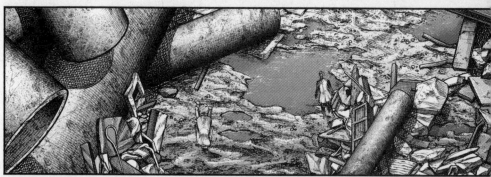

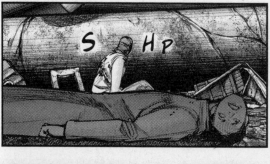

S Hp

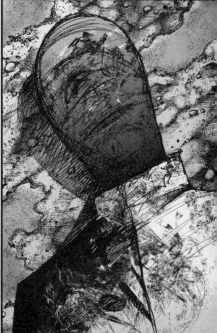

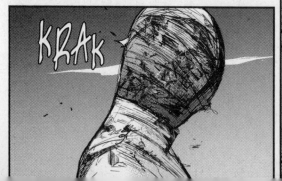

KRAK

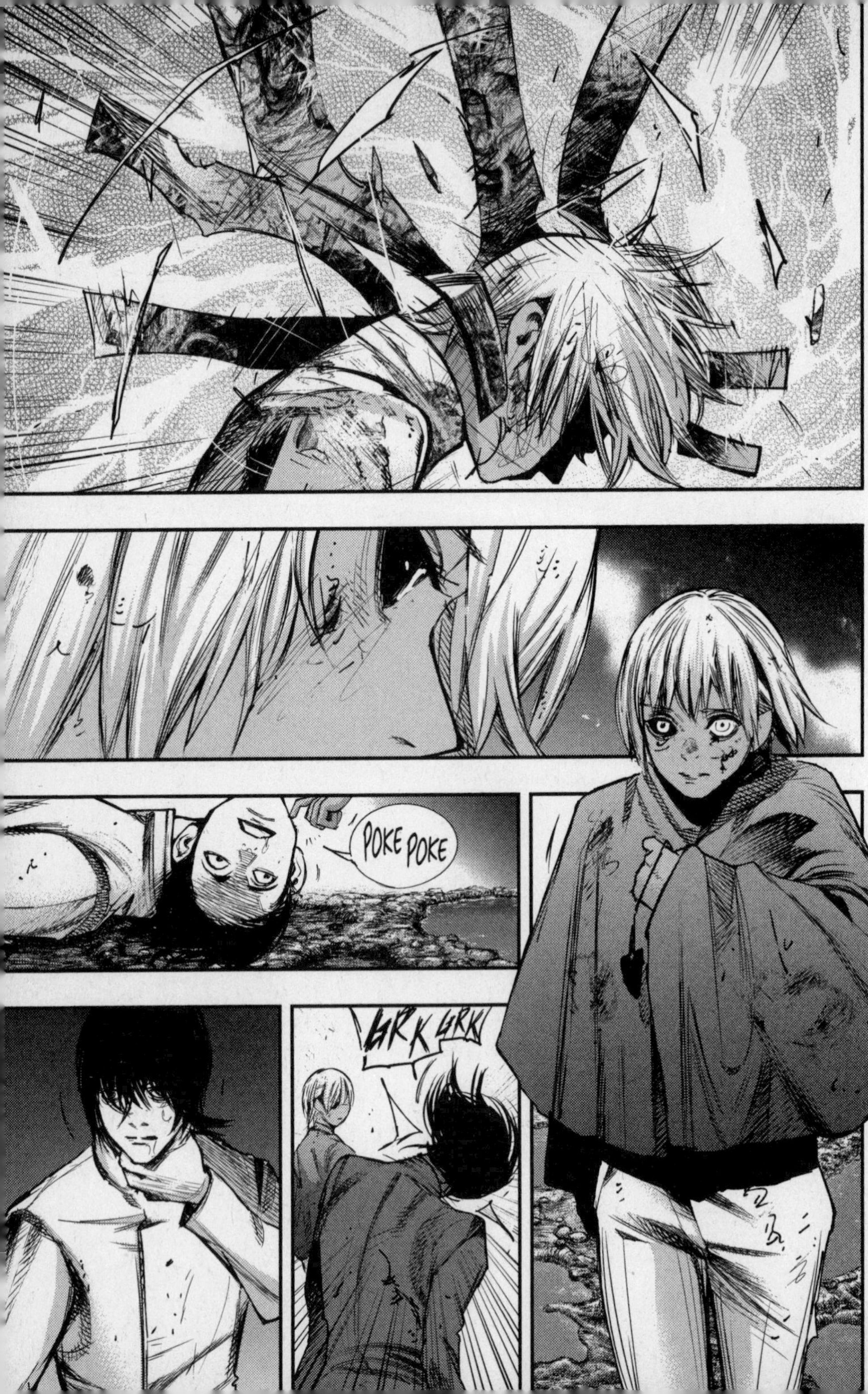
POKE POKE
GRK GRK

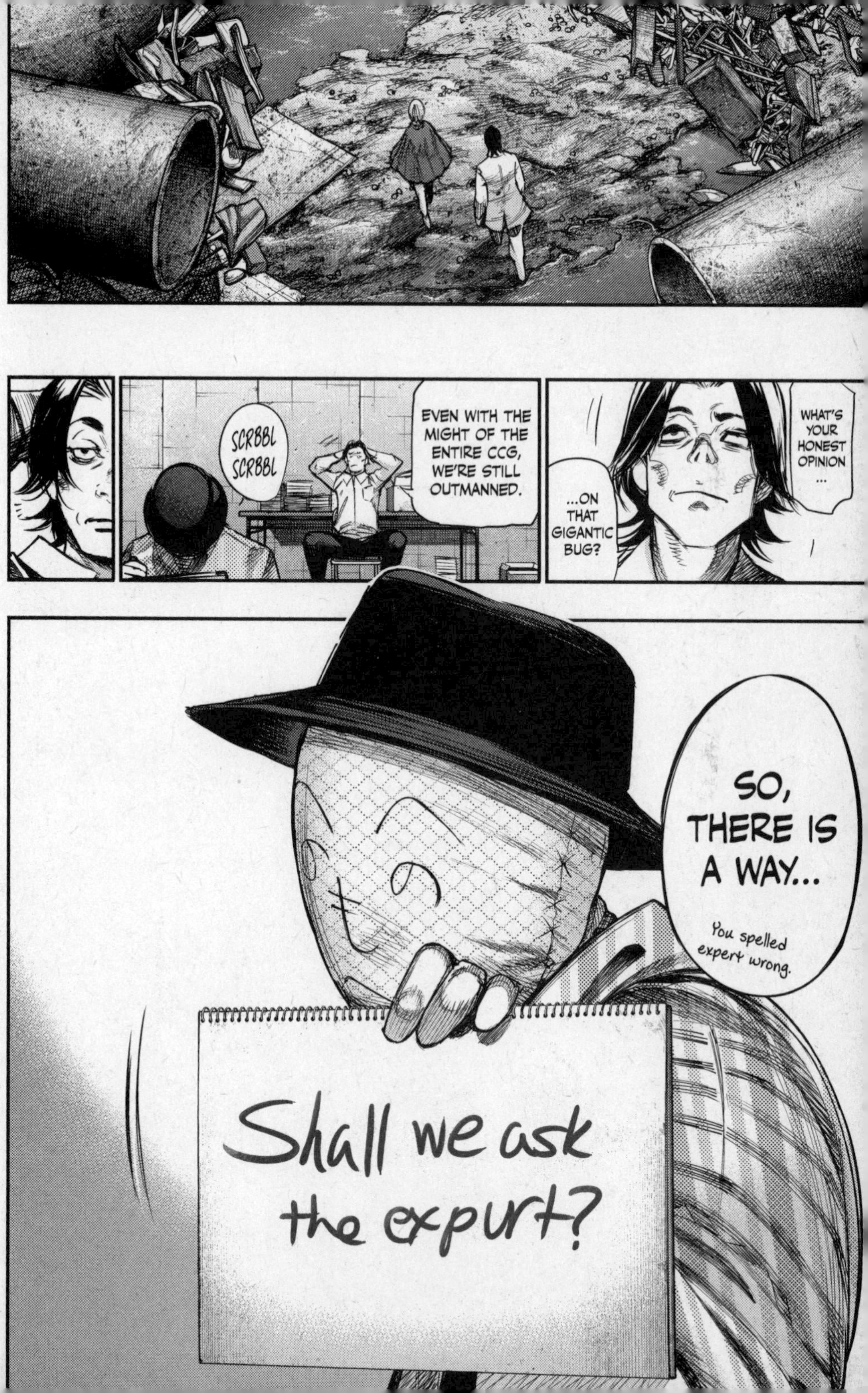
WHAT'S YOUR HONEST OPINION ...
...ON THAT GIGANTIC BUG?
EVEN WITH THE MIGHT OF THE ENTIRE CCG, WE'RE STILL OUTMANNED.
SCRBBL SCRBBL
SO, THERE IS A WAY...
You spelled expert wrong.
Shall we ask the expurt?

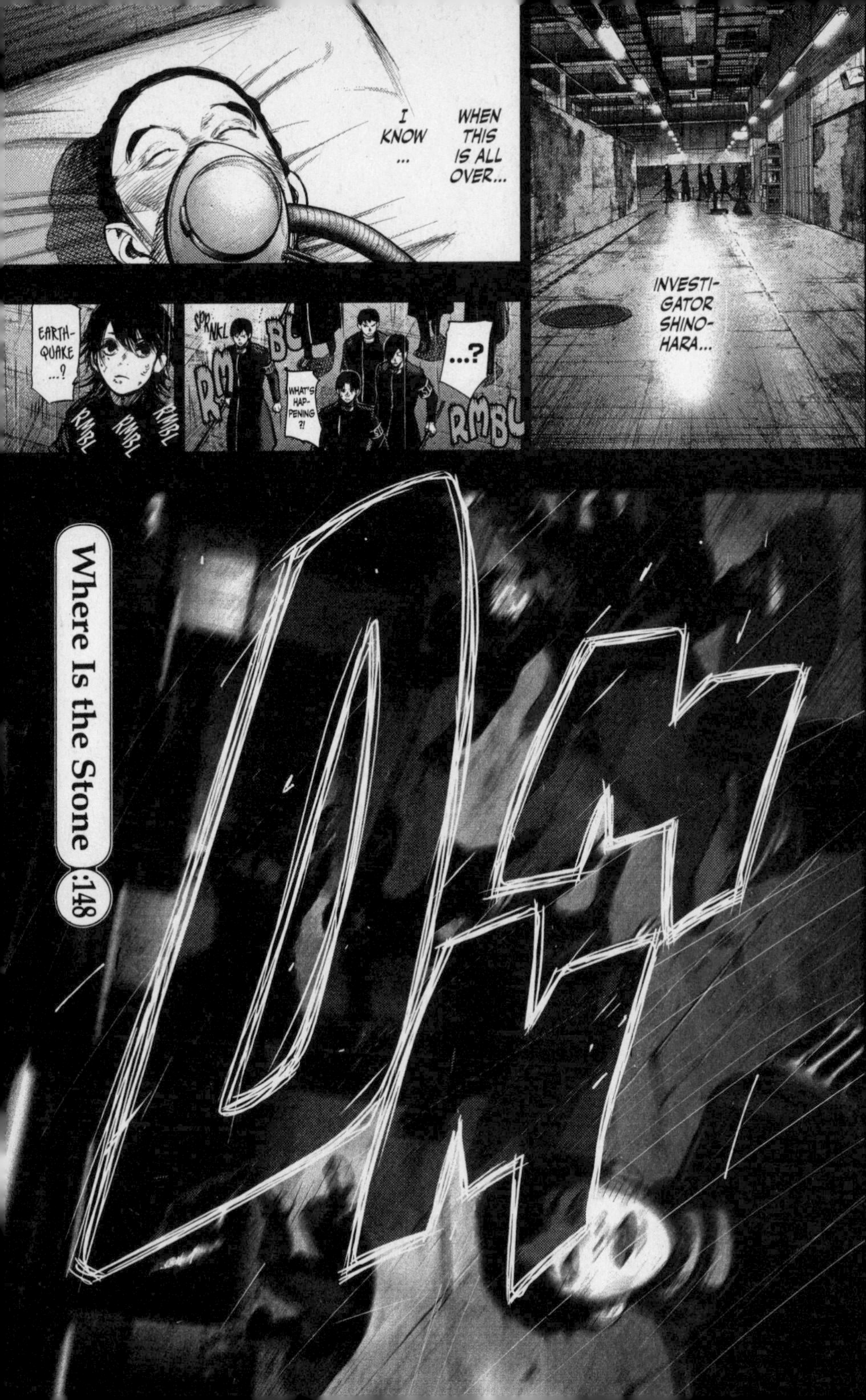
INVESTI-GATOR SHINO-HARA...
WHEN THIS IS ALL OVER...
I KNOW...
...?
RMBL
WHAT'S HAP-PENING?!
EARTH-QUAKE...?
RMBL
RMBL
RMBL
Where Is the Stone :148

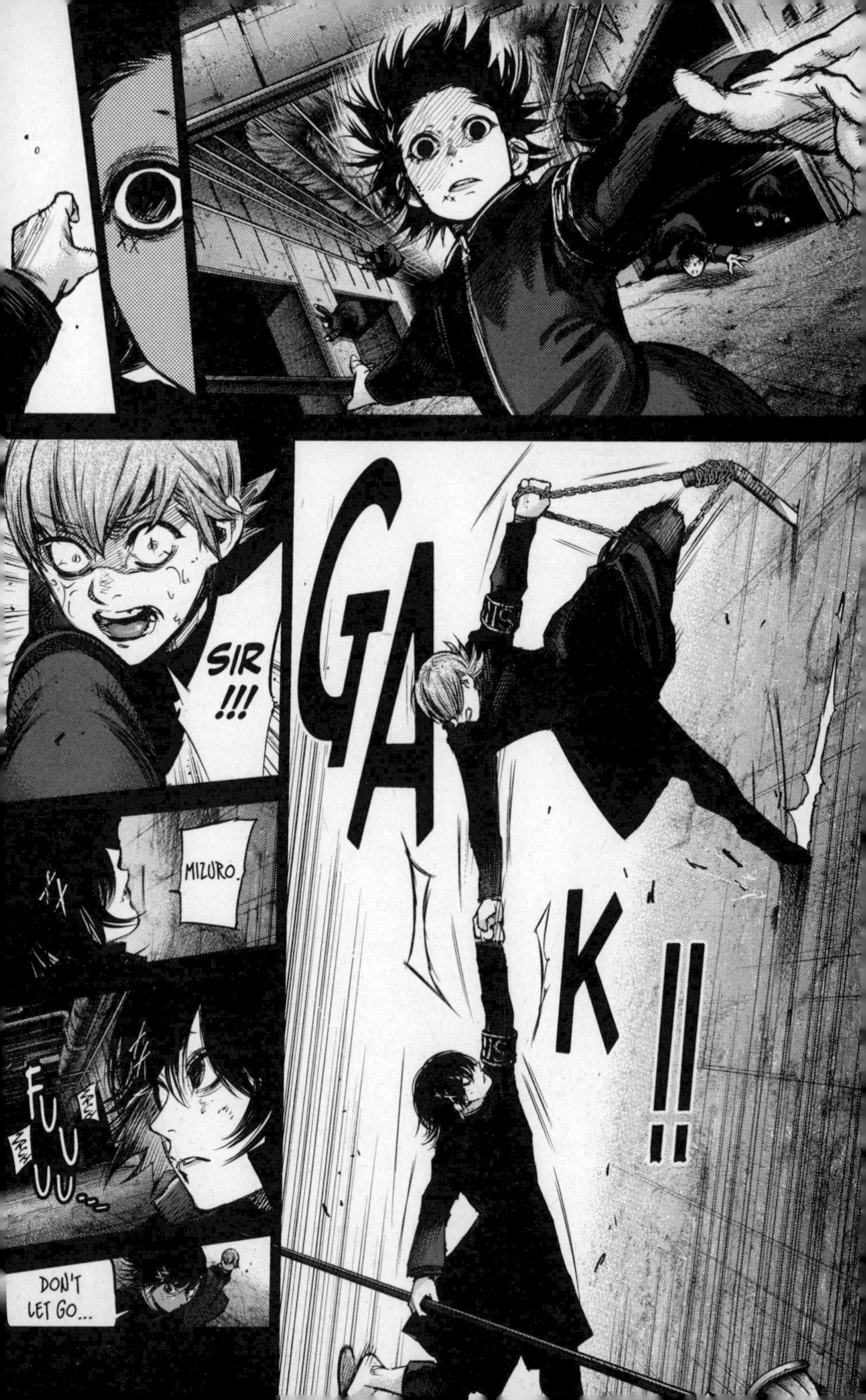
GAK!!
SIR!!!
MIZURO.
FUUUU...
DON'T LET GO...

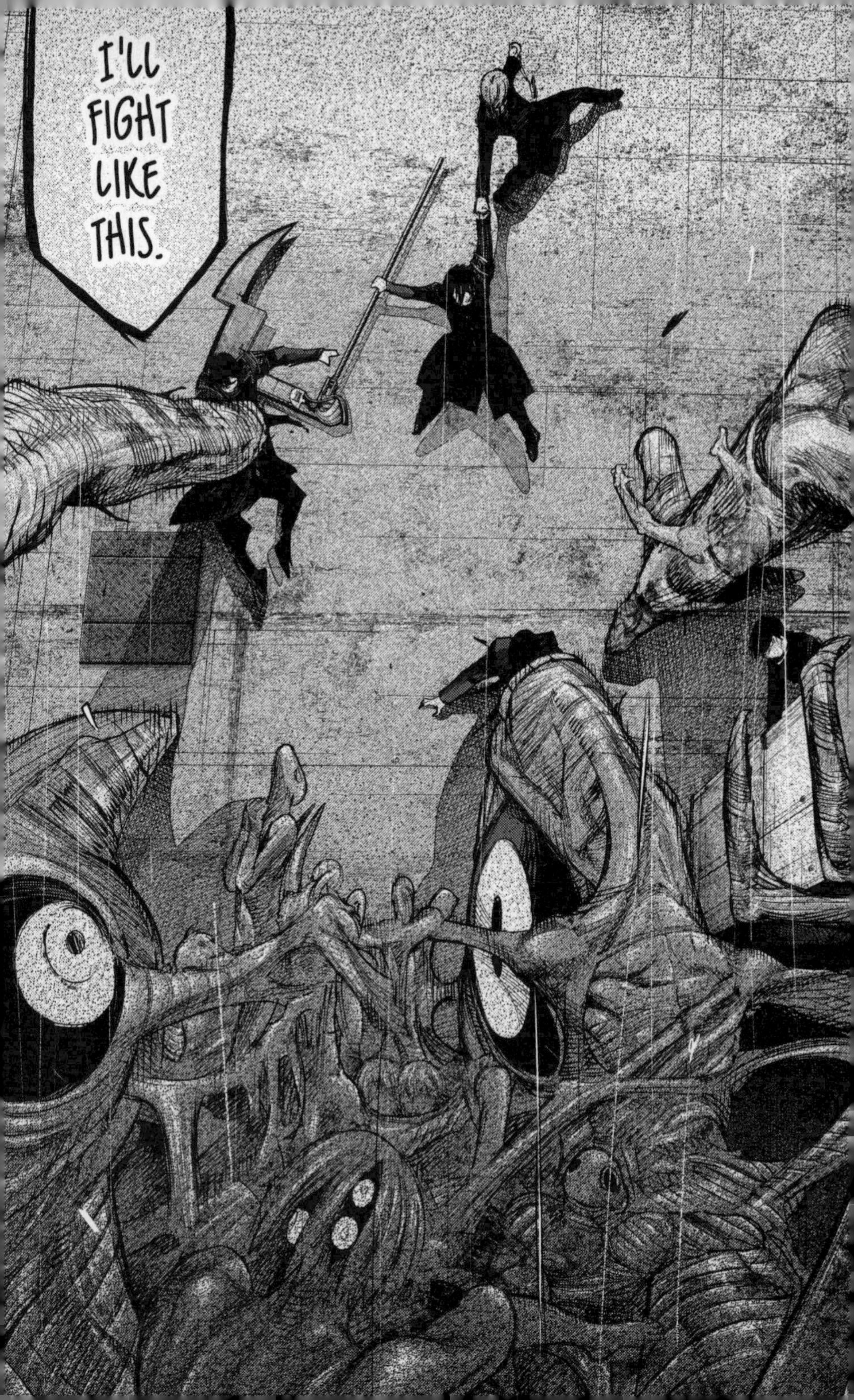
I'LL FIGHT LIKE THIS.

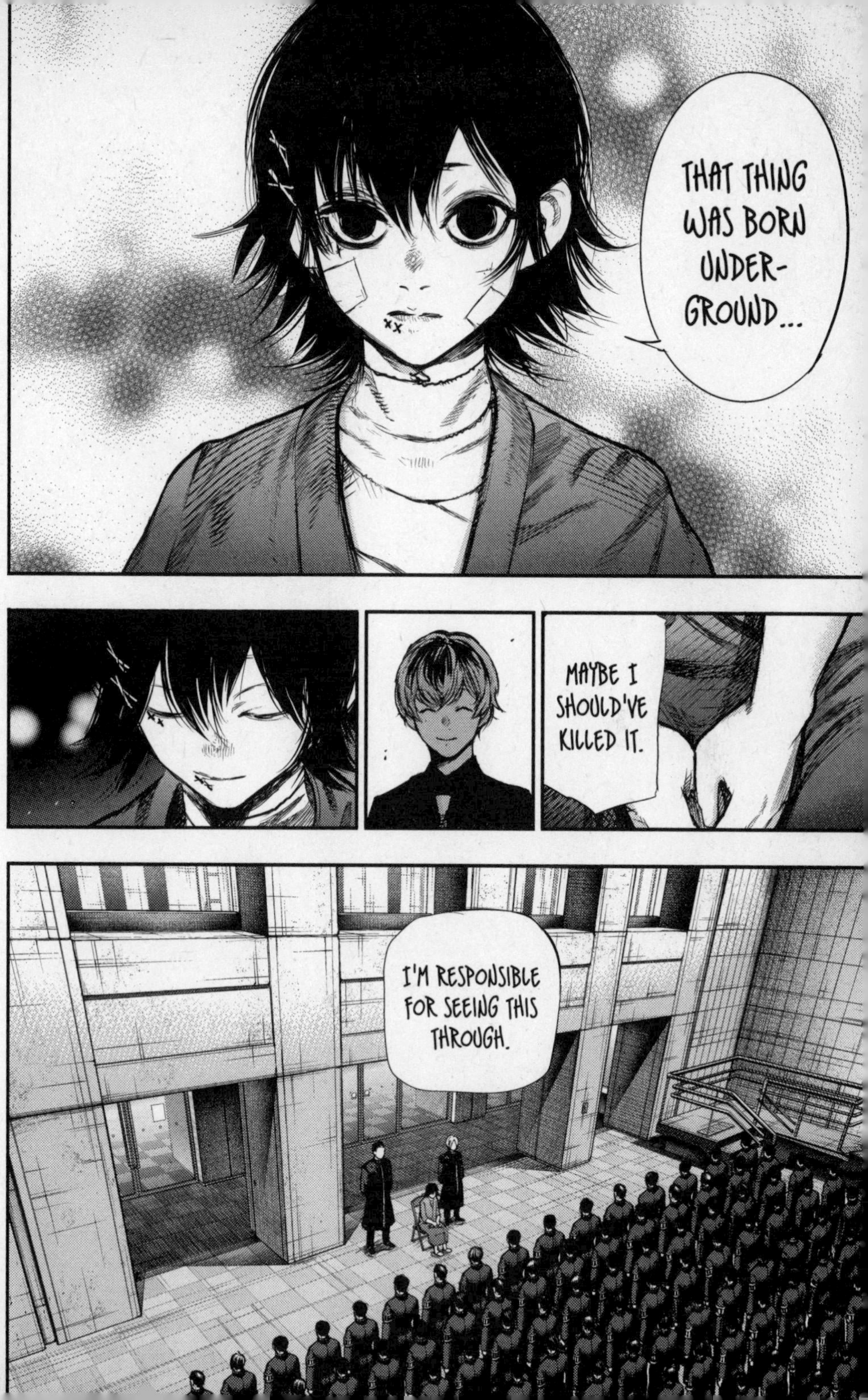
THAT THING WAS BORN UNDER-GROUND...
MAYBE I SHOULD'VE KILLED IT.
I'M RESPONSIBLE FOR SEEING THIS THROUGH.

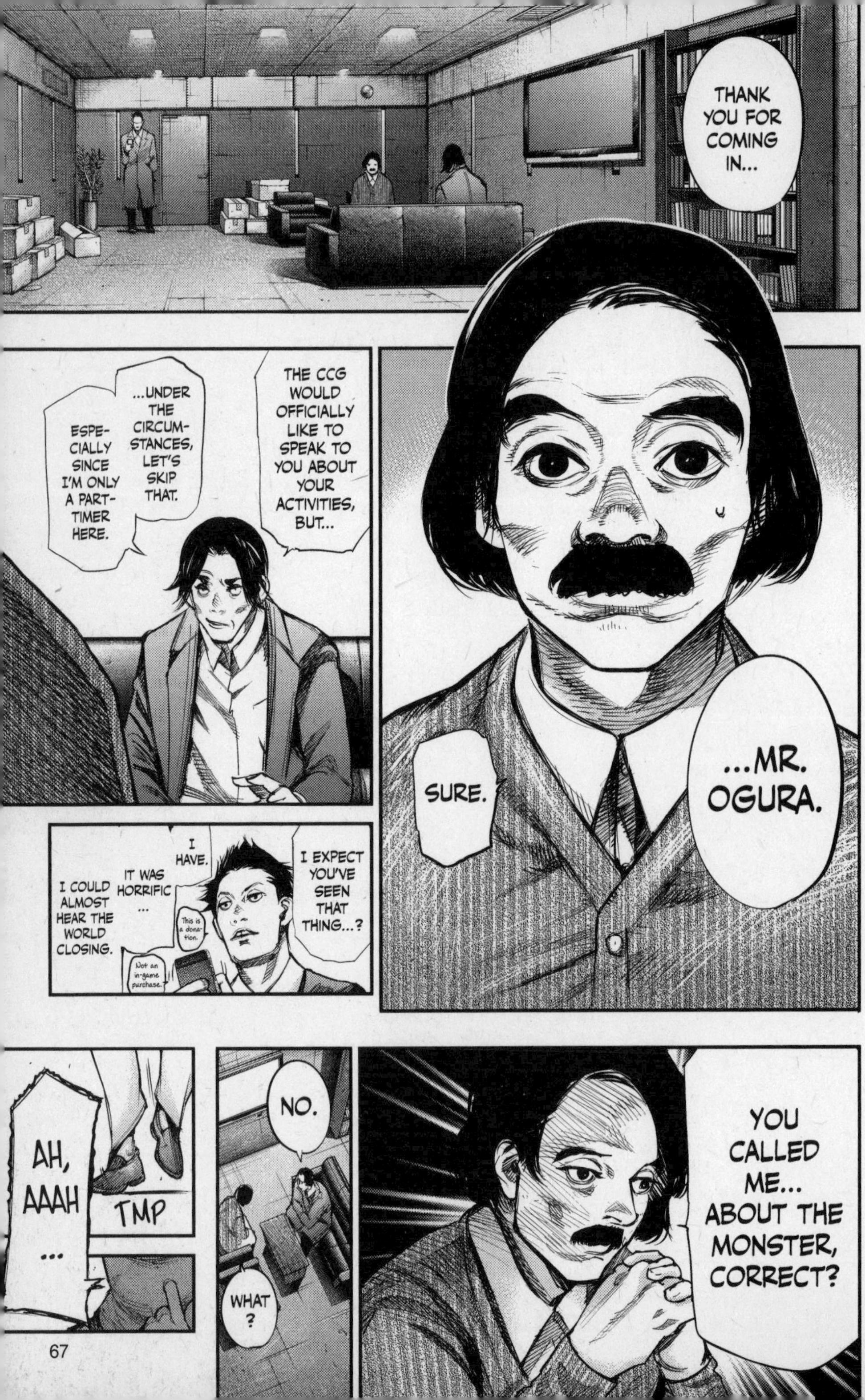
THANK YOU FOR COMING IN...
...MR. OGURA.
SURE.
THE CCG WOULD OFFICIALLY LIKE TO SPEAK TO YOU ABOUT YOUR ACTIVITIES, BUT...
...UNDER THE CIRCUM-STANCES, LET'S SKIP THAT.
ESPE-CIALLY SINCE I'M ONLY A PART-TIMER HERE.
I EXPECT YOU'VE SEEN THAT THING...?
I HAVE.
IT WAS HORRIFIC...
I COULD ALMOST HEAR THE WORLD CLOSING.
This is a dona-tion.
Not an in-game purchase.
YOU CALLED ME... ABOUT THE MONSTER, CORRECT?
NO.
WHAT?
TMP
AH, AAAH...

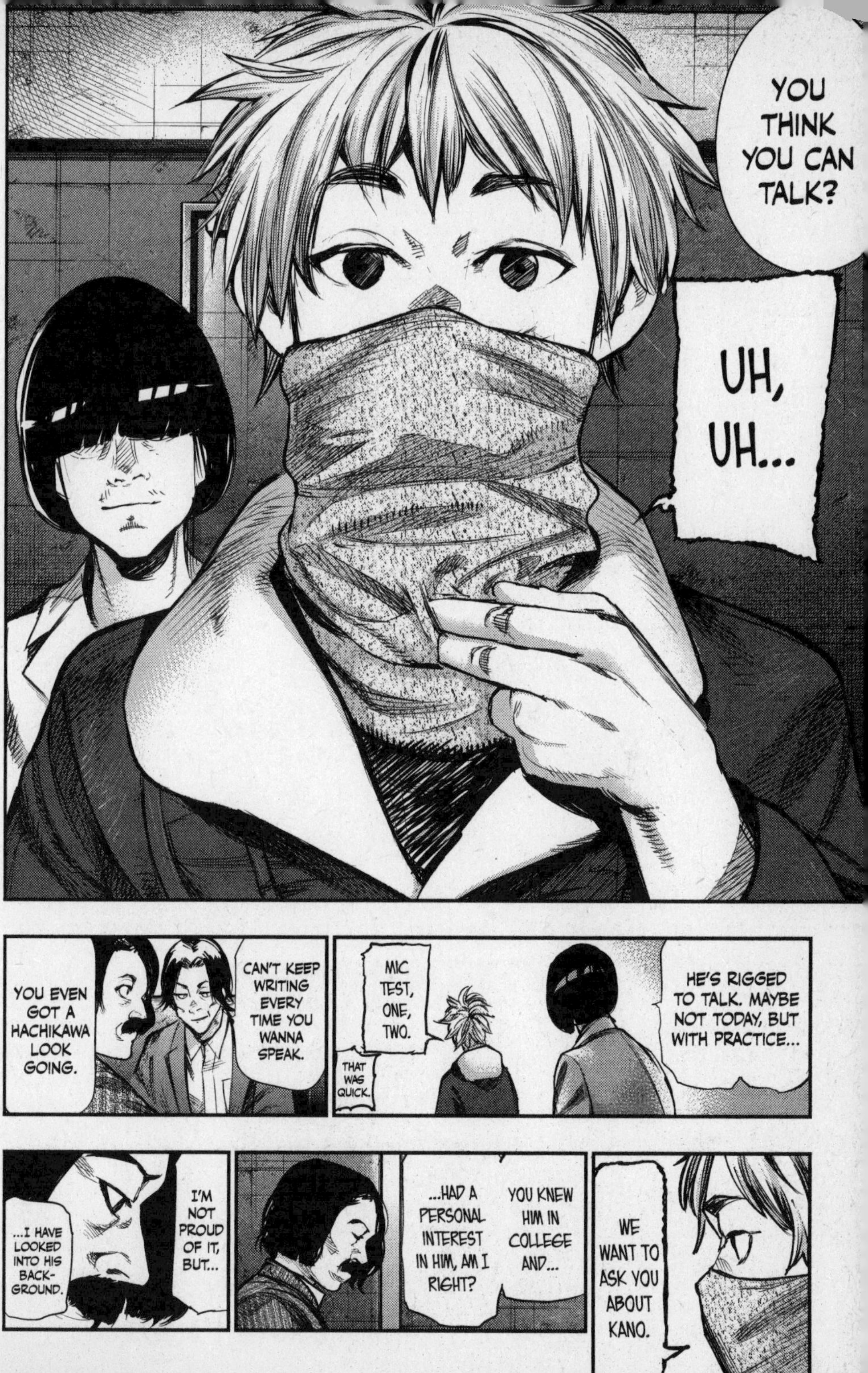
YOU THINK YOU CAN TALK?
UH, UH...
HE'S RIGGED TO TALK. MAYBE NOT TODAY, BUT WITH PRACTICE...
MIC TEST, ONE, TWO.
THAT WAS QUICK.
CAN'T KEEP WRITING EVERY TIME YOU WANNA SPEAK.
YOU EVEN GOT A HACHIKAWA LOOK GOING.
WE WANT TO ASK YOU ABOUT KANO.
YOU KNEW HIM IN COLLEGE AND...
...HAD A PERSONAL INTEREST IN HIM, AM I RIGHT?
I'M NOT PROUD OF IT, BUT...
...I HAVE LOOKED INTO HIS BACK-GROUND.

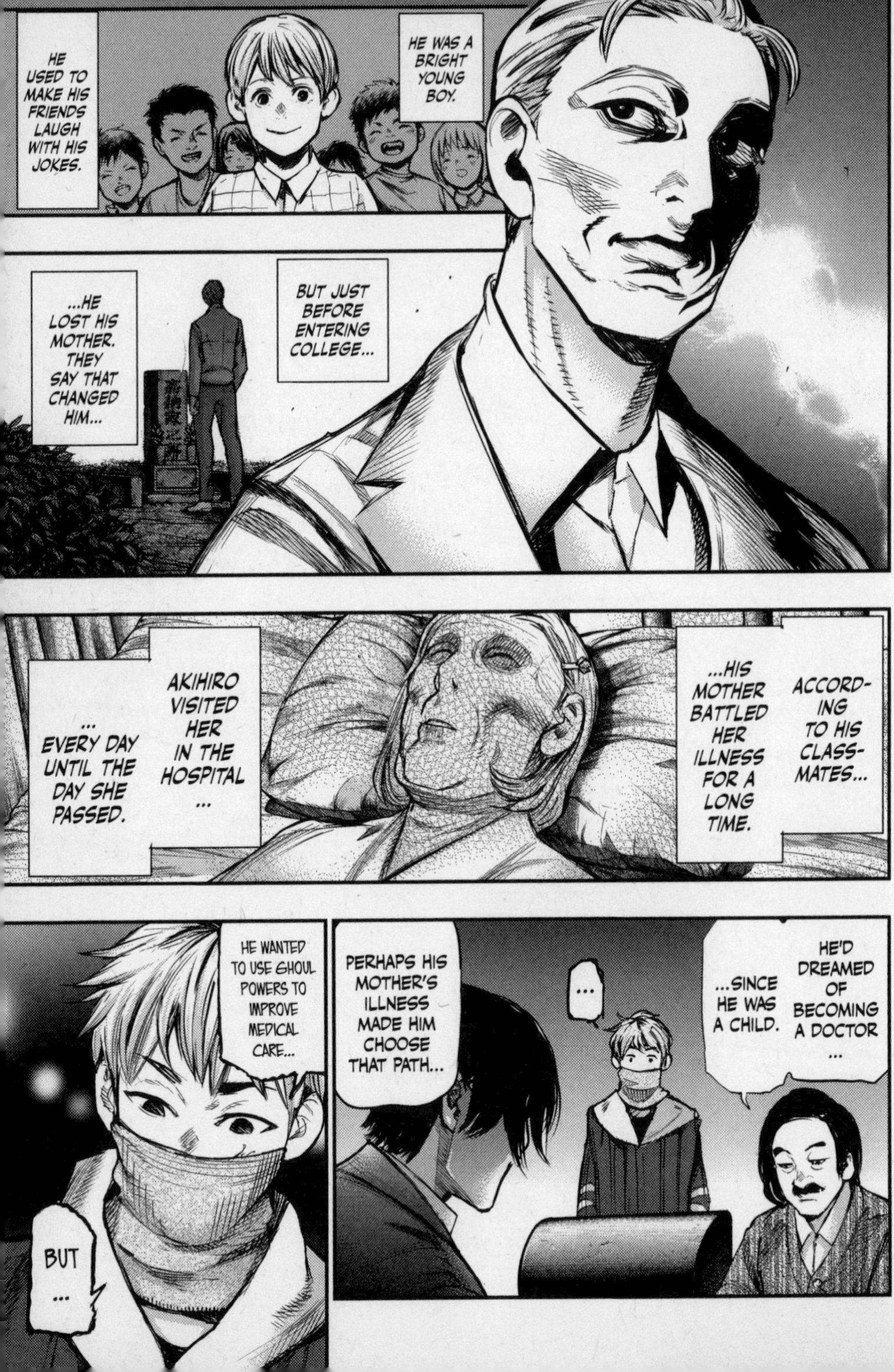
HE WAS A BRIGHT YOUNG BOY.
HE USED TO MAKE HIS FRIENDS LAUGH WITH HIS JOKES.
BUT JUST BEFORE ENTERING COLLEGE...
...HE LOST HIS MOTHER. THEY SAY THAT CHANGED HIM...
ACCORD-ING TO HIS CLASS-MATES...
...HIS MOTHER BATTLED HER ILLNESS FOR A LONG TIME.
AKIHIRO VISITED HER IN THE HOSPITAL...
... EVERY DAY UNTIL THE DAY SHE PASSED.
HE'D DREAMED OF BECOMING A DOCTOR...
...SINCE HE WAS A CHILD.
...
PERHAPS HIS MOTHER'S ILLNESS MADE HIM CHOOSE THAT PATH...
HE WANTED TO USE GHOUL POWERS TO IMPROVE MEDICAL CARE...
BUT...

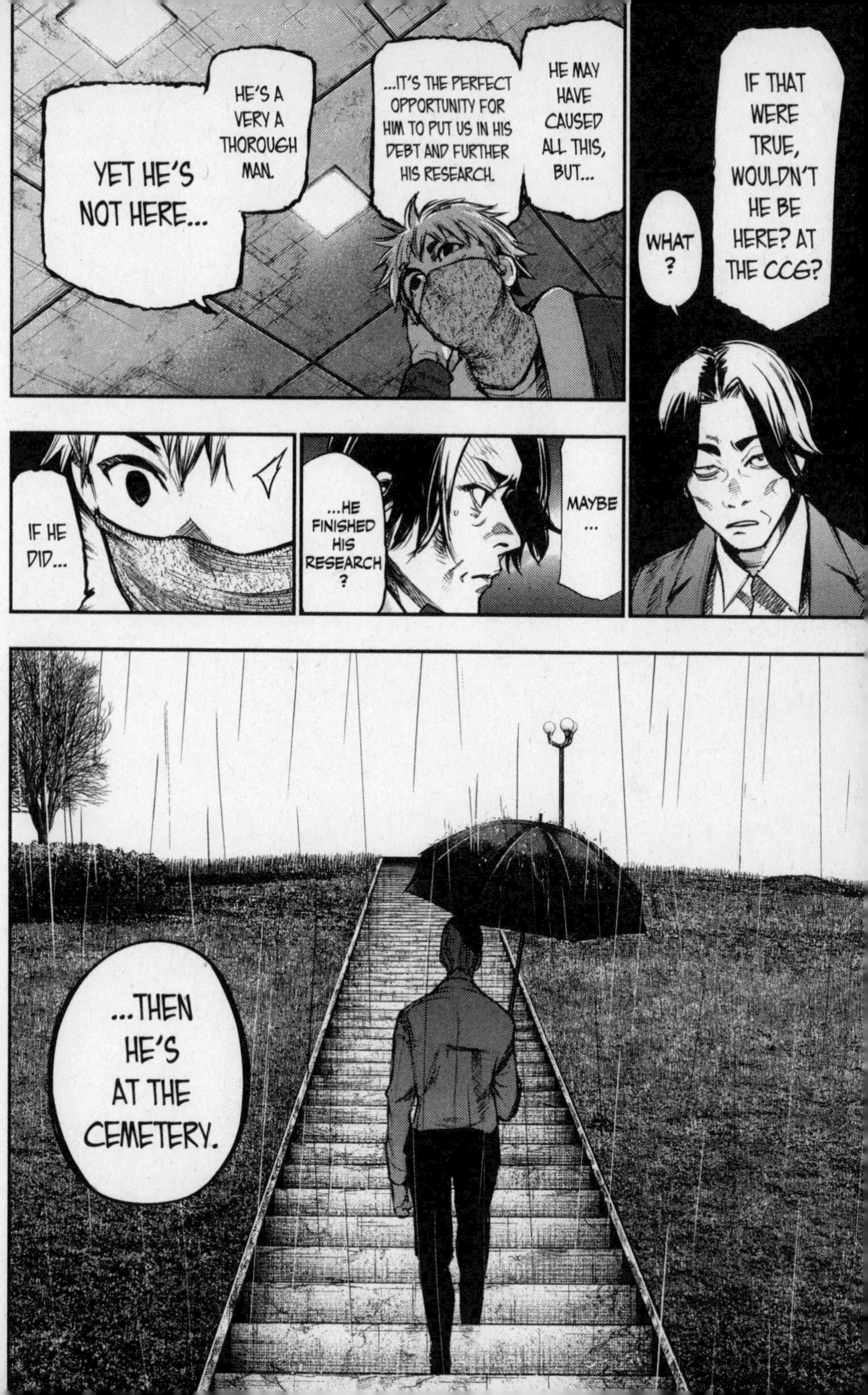
IF THAT WERE TRUE, WOULDN'T HE BE HERE? AT THE CCG?
WHAT?
HE MAY HAVE CAUSED ALL THIS, BUT...
...IT'S THE PERFECT OPPORTUNITY FOR HIM TO PUT US IN HIS DEBT AND FURTHER HIS RESEARCH.
HE'S A VERY A THOROUGH MAN.
YET HE'S NOT HERE...
MAYBE...
...HE FINISHED HIS RESEARCH?
IF HE DID...
...THEN HE'S AT THE CEMETERY.

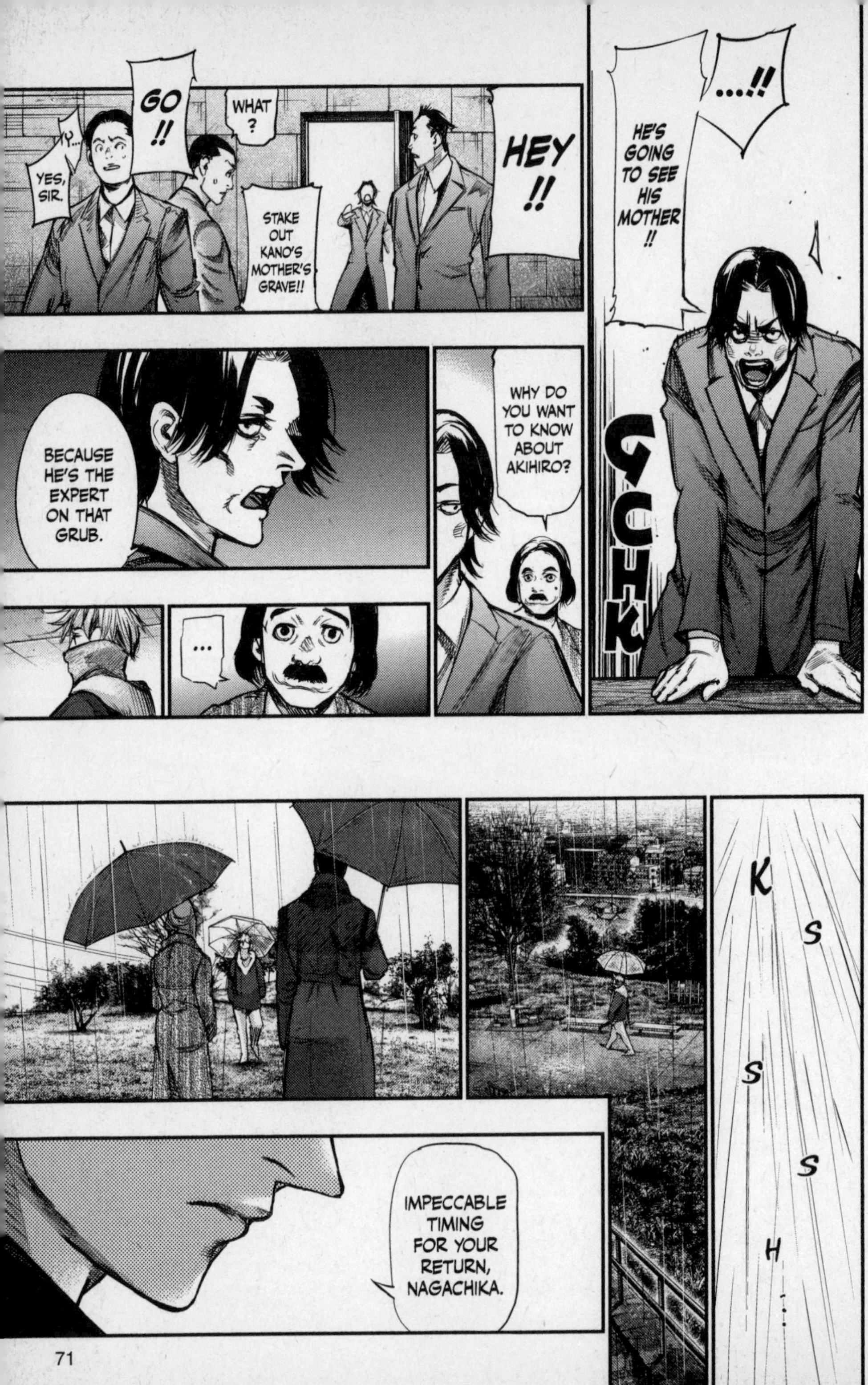
...!!
HE'S GOING TO SEE HIS MOTHER!!
GCHK
HEY!!
WHAT?
STAKE OUT KANO'S MOTHER'S GRAVE!!
GO!!
Y...
YES, SIR.
WHY DO YOU WANT TO KNOW ABOUT AKIHIRO?
BECAUSE HE'S THE EXPERT ON THAT GRUB.
...
KSSSH...
IMPECCABLE TIMING FOR YOUR RETURN, NAGACHIKA.

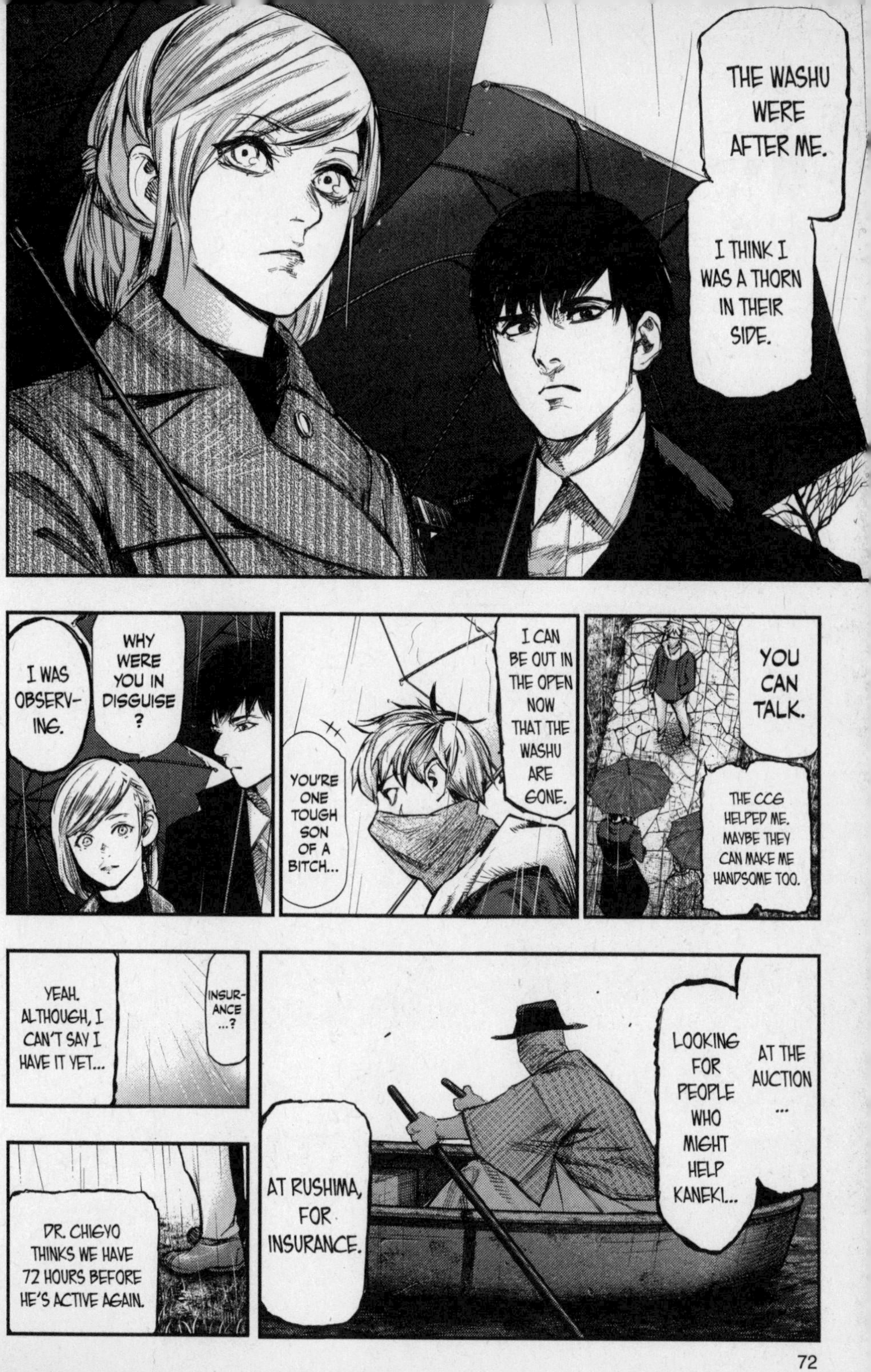
THE WASHU WERE AFTER ME.
I THINK I WAS A THORN IN THEIR SIDE.
YOU CAN TALK.
THE CCG HELPED ME. MAYBE THEY CAN MAKE ME HANDSOME TOO.
I CAN BE OUT IN THE OPEN NOW THAT THE WASHU ARE GONE.
YOU'RE ONE TOUGH SON OF A BITCH...
WHY WERE YOU IN DISGUISE?
I WAS OBSERV-ING.
AT THE AUCTION...
LOOKING FOR PEOPLE WHO MIGHT HELP KANEKI...
AT RUSHIMA, FOR INSURANCE.
INSUR-ANCE...?
YEAH. ALTHOUGH, I CAN'T SAY I HAVE IT YET...
DR. CHIGYO THINKS WE HAVE 72 HOURS BEFORE HE'S ACTIVE AGAIN.

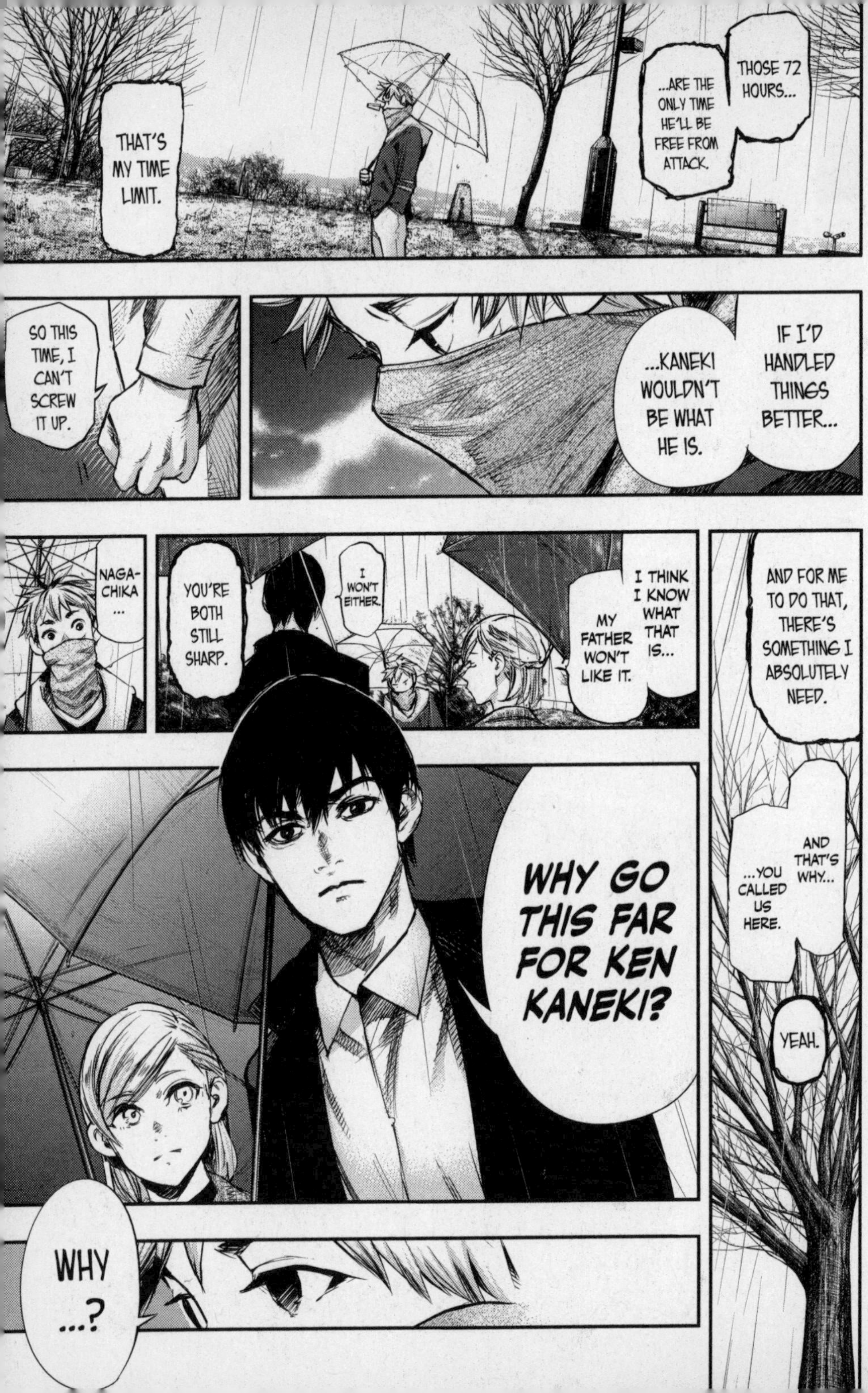
THOSE 72 HOURS...
...ARE THE ONLY TIME HE'LL BE FREE FROM ATTACK.
THAT'S MY TIME LIMIT.
IF I'D HANDLED THINGS BETTER...
...KANEKI WOULDN'T BE WHAT HE IS.
SO THIS TIME, I CAN'T SCREW IT UP.
AND FOR ME TO DO THAT, THERE'S SOMETHING I ABSOLUTELY NEED.
AND THAT'S WHY...
...YOU CALLED US HERE.
YEAH.
I THINK I KNOW WHAT THAT IS...
MY FATHER WON'T LIKE IT.
I WON'T EITHER.
YOU'RE BOTH STILL SHARP.
NAGA-CHIKA ...
WHY GO THIS FAR FOR KEN KANEKI?
WHY ...?

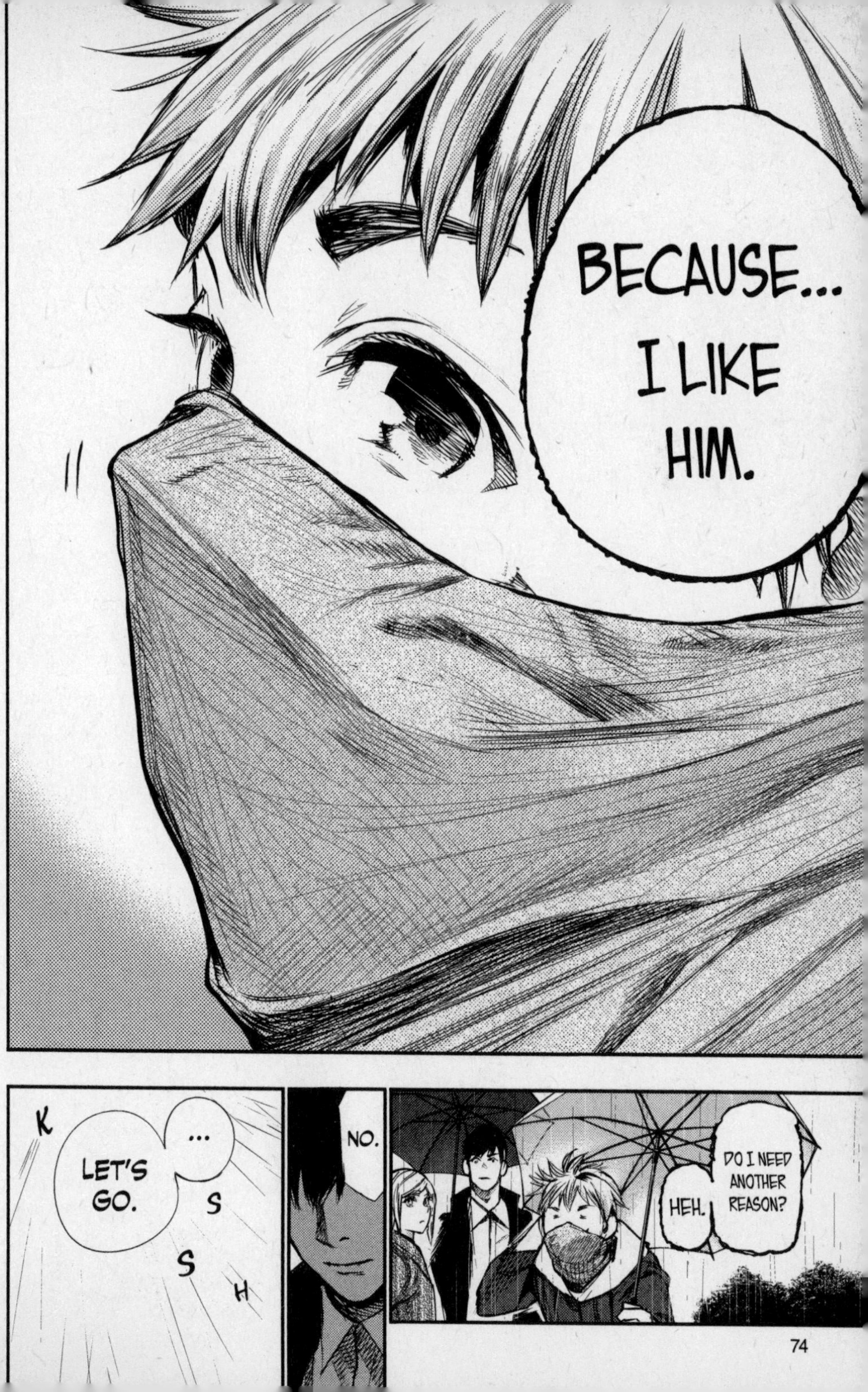
BECAUSE... I LIKE HIM.
DO I NEED ANOTHER REASON?
HEH.
NO.
...
LET'S GO.
K S S H

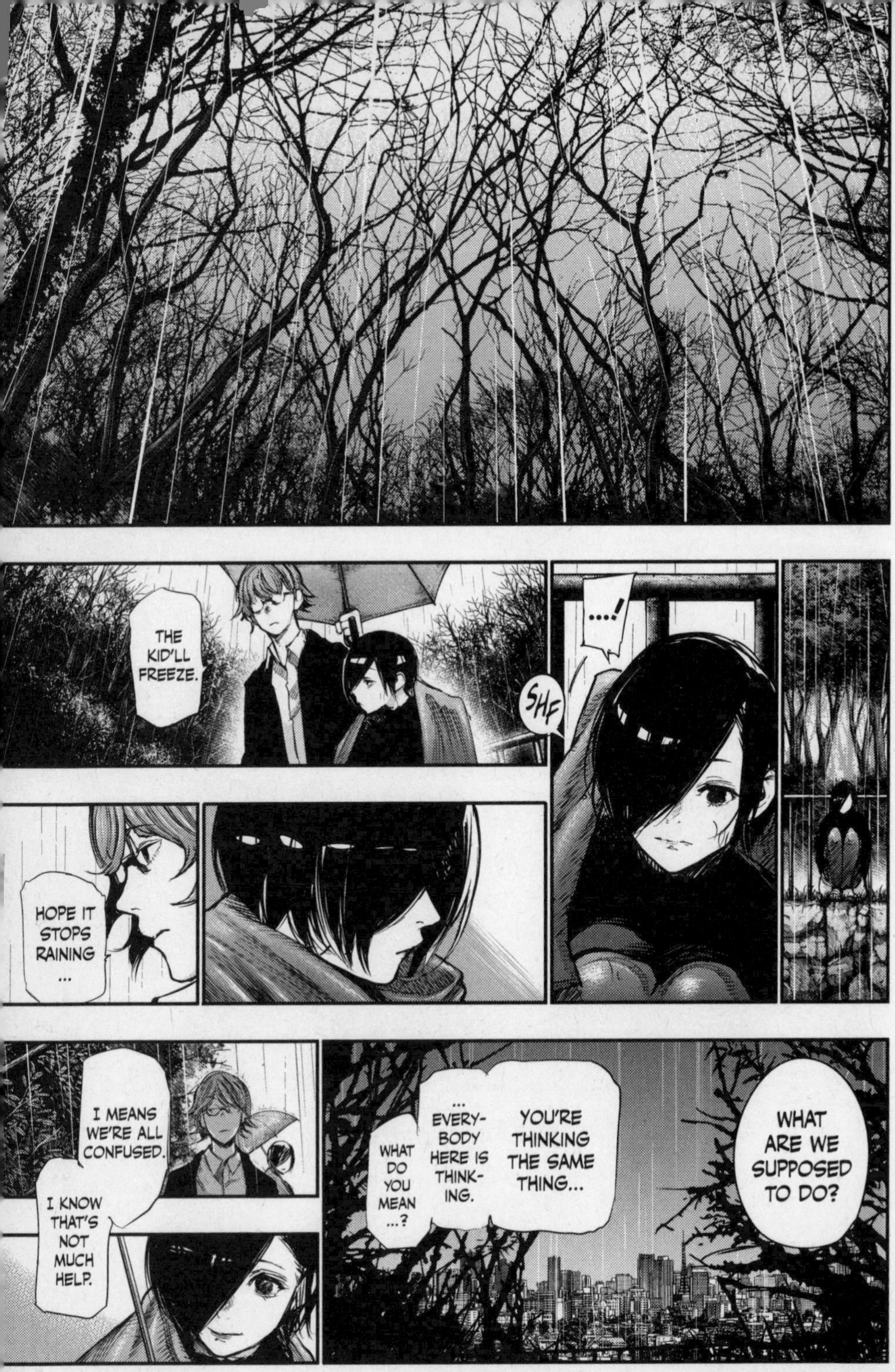
...!
SHF
THE KID'LL FREEZE.
HOPE IT STOPS RAINING ...
WHAT ARE WE SUPPOSED TO DO?
YOU'RE THINKING THE SAME THING...
... EVERY-BODY HERE IS THINK-ING.
WHAT DO YOU MEAN ...?
I MEANS WE'RE ALL CONFUSED.
I KNOW THAT'S NOT MUCH HELP.

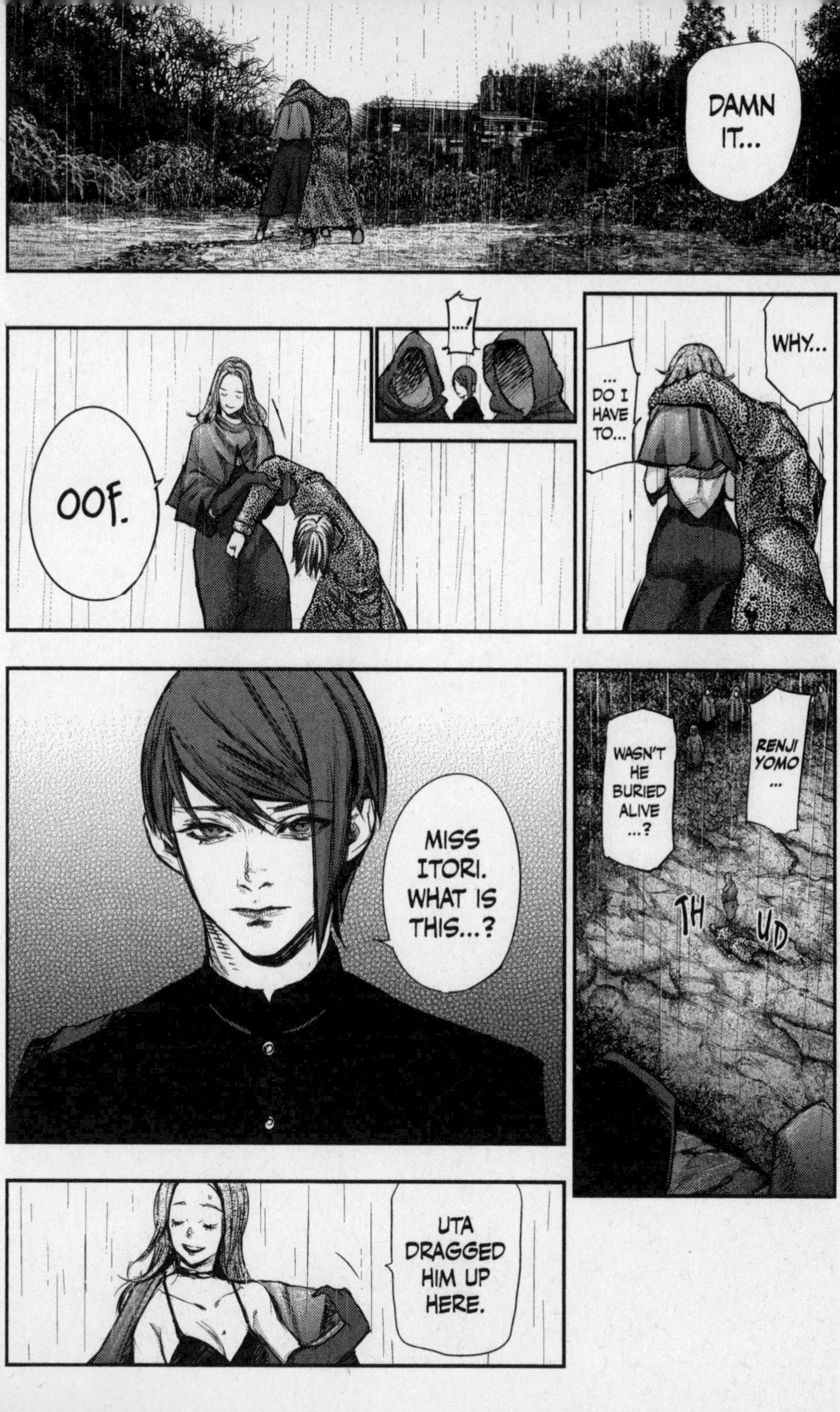
DAMN IT...
WHY...
...DO I HAVE TO...
...!
OOF.
RENJI YOMO...
WASN'T HE BURIED ALIVE...?
TH UD
MISS ITORI. WHAT IS THIS...?
UTA DRAGGED HIM UP HERE.

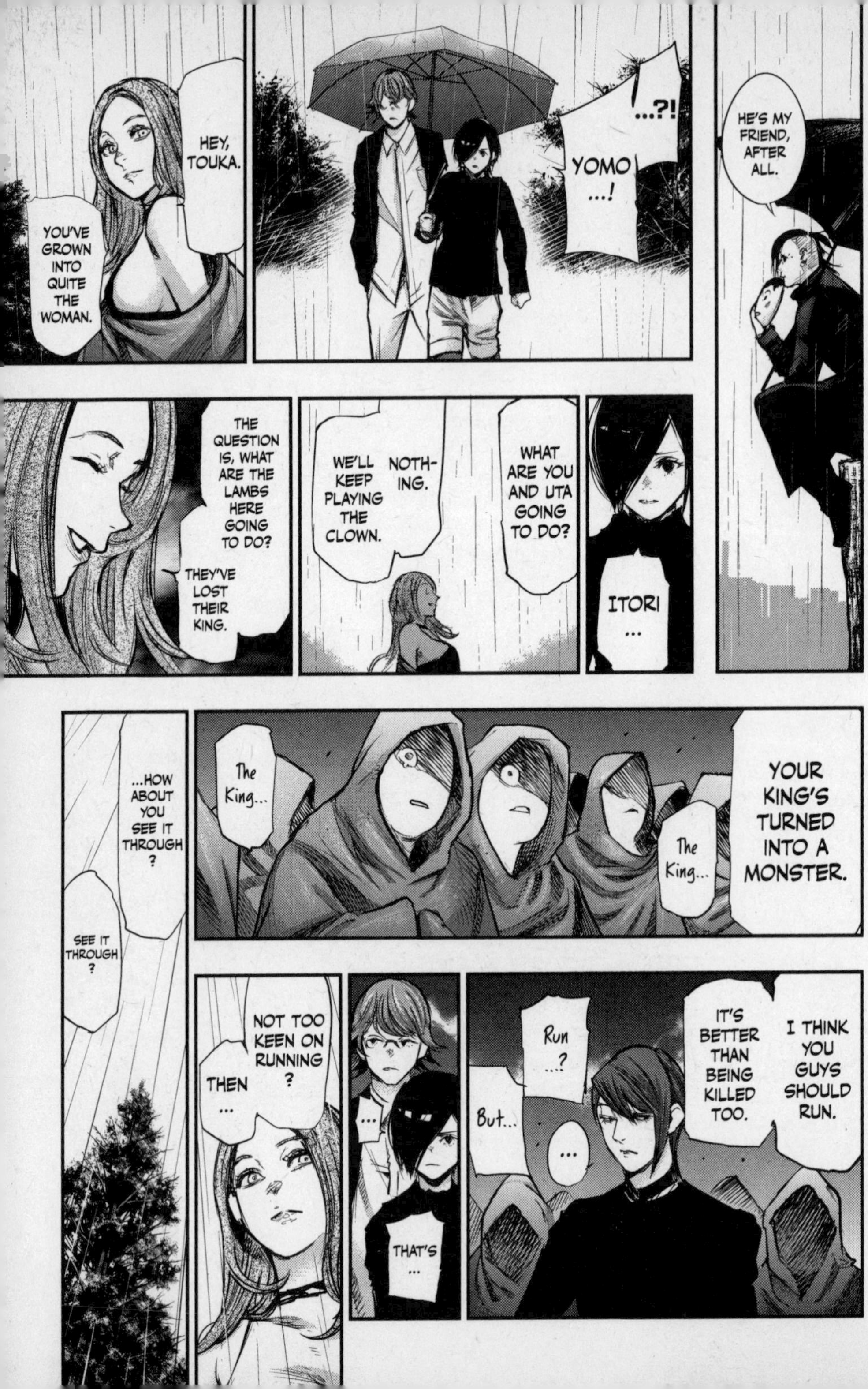

HE'S MY FRIEND, AFTER ALL.
...?!
YOMO ...!
HEY, TOUKA.
YOU'VE GROWN INTO QUITE THE WOMAN.
ITORI ...
WHAT ARE YOU AND UTA GOING TO DO?
NOTH-ING.
WE'LL KEEP PLAYING THE CLOWN.
THE QUESTION IS, WHAT ARE THE LAMBS HERE GOING TO DO?
THEY'VE LOST THEIR KING.
YOUR KING'S TURNED INTO A MONSTER.
The King...
The King...
I THINK YOU GUYS SHOULD RUN.
IT'S BETTER THAN BEING KILLED TOO.
Run ...?
But...
...
...
THAT'S ...
NOT TOO KEEN ON RUNNING ?
THEN ...
...HOW ABOUT YOU SEE IT THROUGH ?
SEE IT THROUGH ?

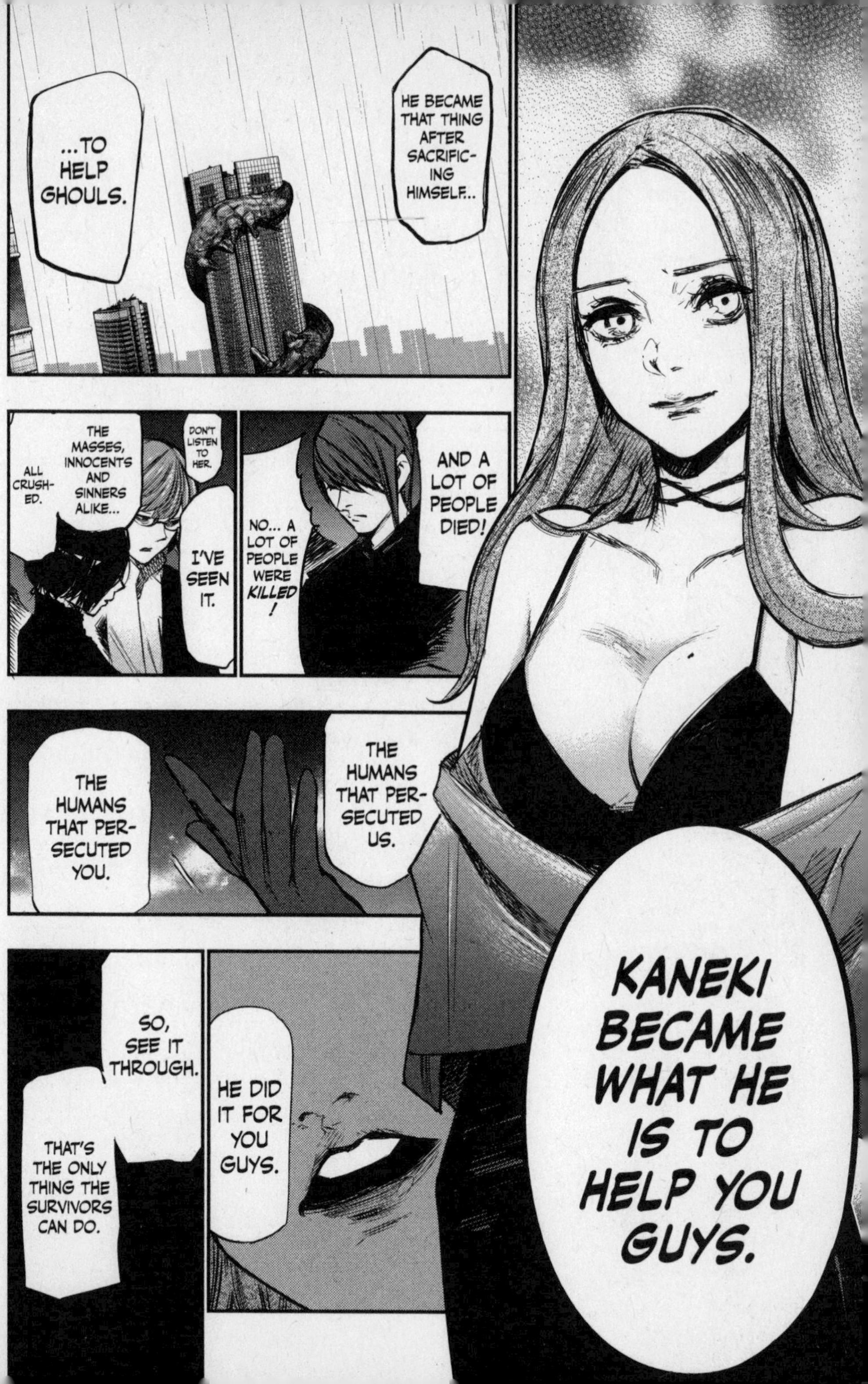
KANEKI BECAME WHAT HE IS TO HELP YOU GUYS.
HE BECAME THAT THING AFTER SACRIFIC-ING HIMSELF...
...TO HELP GHOULS.
AND A LOT OF PEOPLE DIED!
NO... A LOT OF PEOPLE WERE *KILLED*!
DON'T LISTEN TO HER.
I'VE SEEN IT.
THE MASSES, INNOCENTS AND SINNERS ALIKE...
ALL CRUSH-ED.
THE HUMANS THAT PER-SECUTED US.
THE HUMANS THAT PER-SECUTED YOU.
HE DID IT FOR YOU GUYS.
SO, SEE IT THROUGH.
THAT'S THE ONLY THING THE SURVIVORS CAN DO.

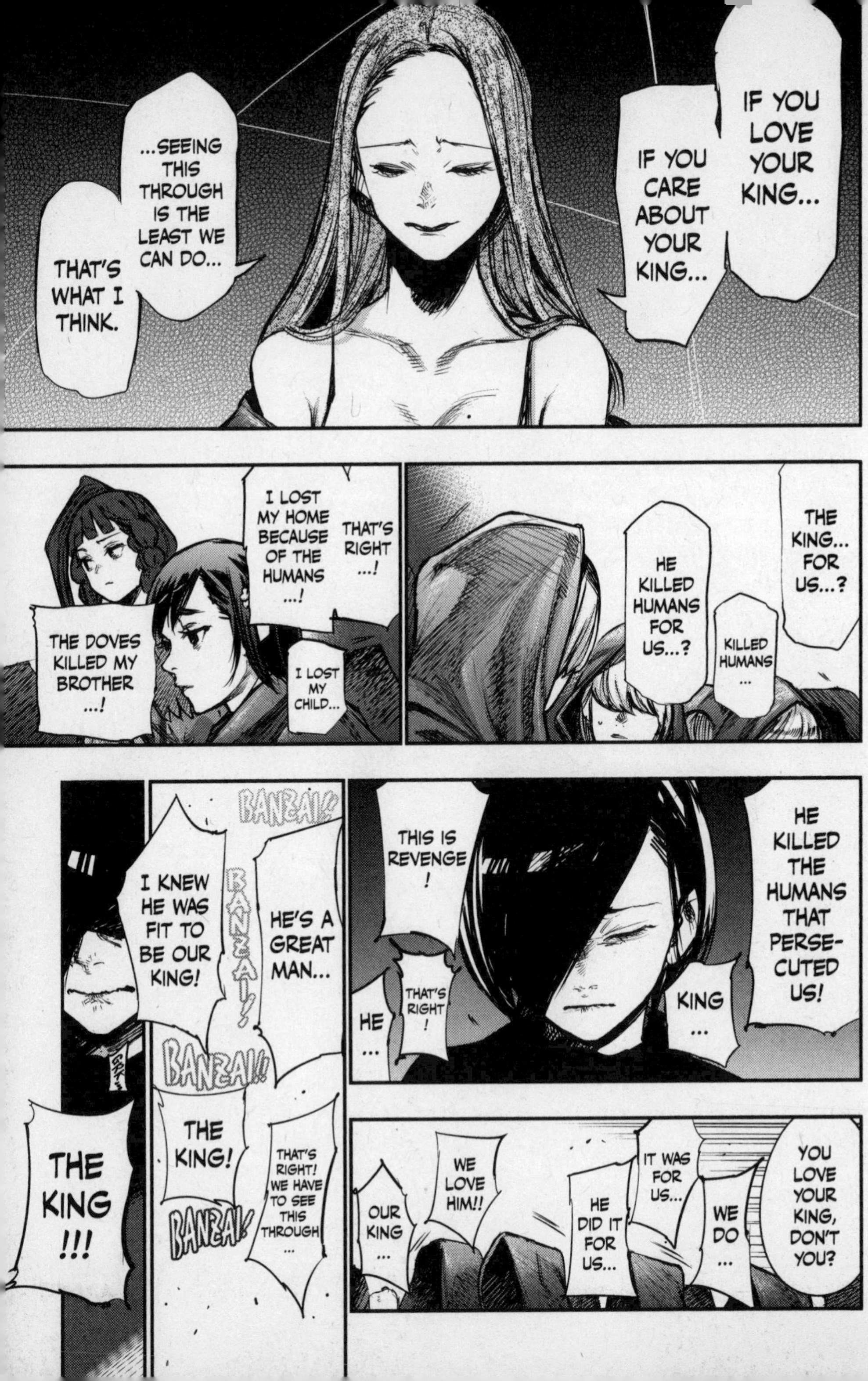
IF YOU LOVE YOUR KING...
IF YOU CARE ABOUT YOUR KING...
...SEEING THIS THROUGH IS THE LEAST WE CAN DO...
THAT'S WHAT I THINK.
THE KING... FOR US...?
HE KILLED HUMANS FOR US...?
KILLED HUMANS ...
THAT'S RIGHT ...!
I LOST MY HOME BECAUSE OF THE HUMANS ...!
I LOST MY CHILD...
THE DOVES KILLED MY BROTHER ...!
HE KILLED THE HUMANS THAT PERSE-CUTED US!
THIS IS REVENGE !
KING ...
THAT'S RIGHT !
HE ...
YOU LOVE YOUR KING, DON'T YOU?
IT WAS FOR US...
WE DO ...
HE DID IT FOR US...
WE LOVE HIM!!
OUR KING ...
BANZAI!!
HE'S A GREAT MAN...
I KNEW HE WAS FIT TO BE OUR KING!
BANZAI!
BANZAI!!
THE KING!
THAT'S RIGHT! WE HAVE TO SEE THIS THROUGH ...
BANZAI!
THE KING !!!

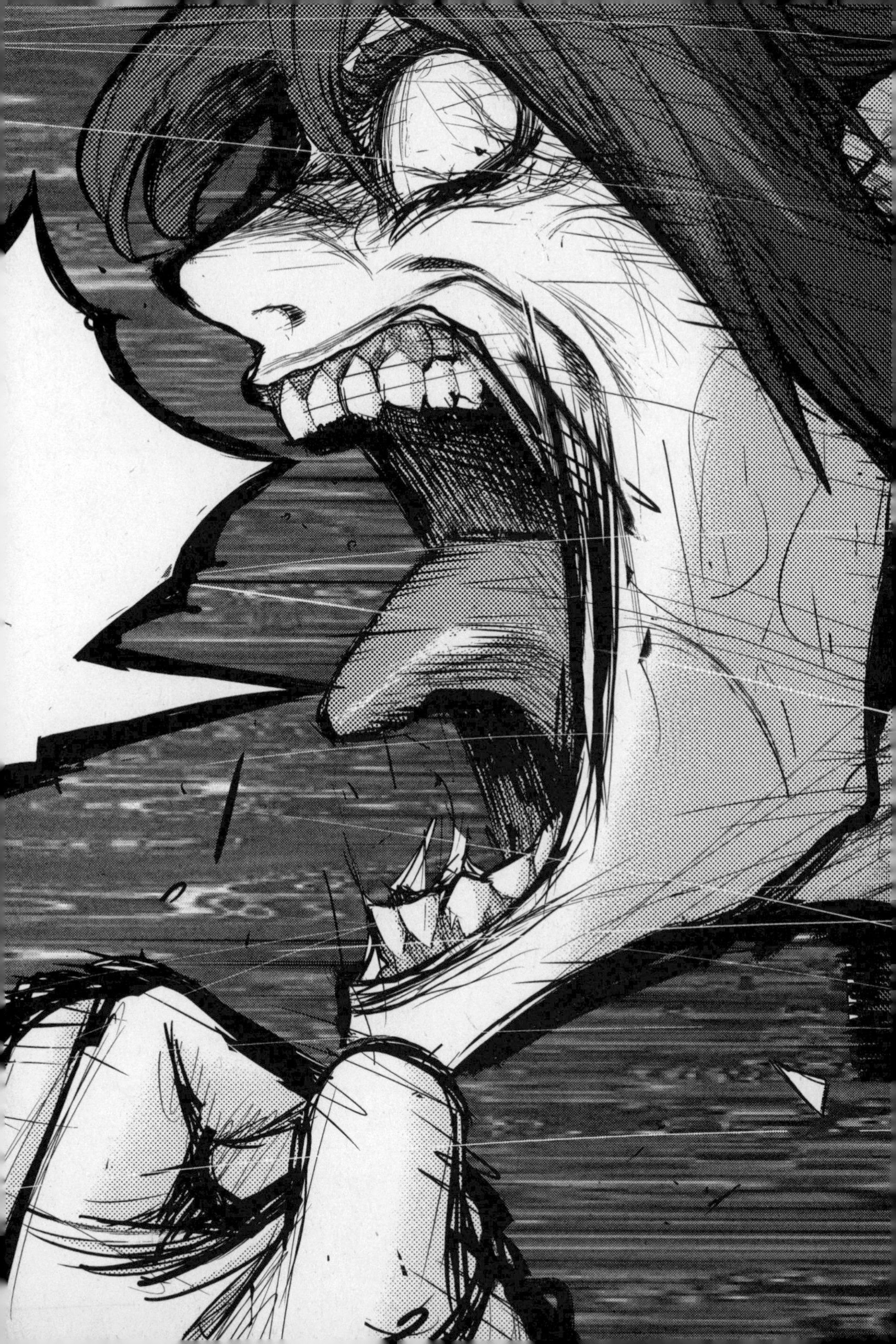

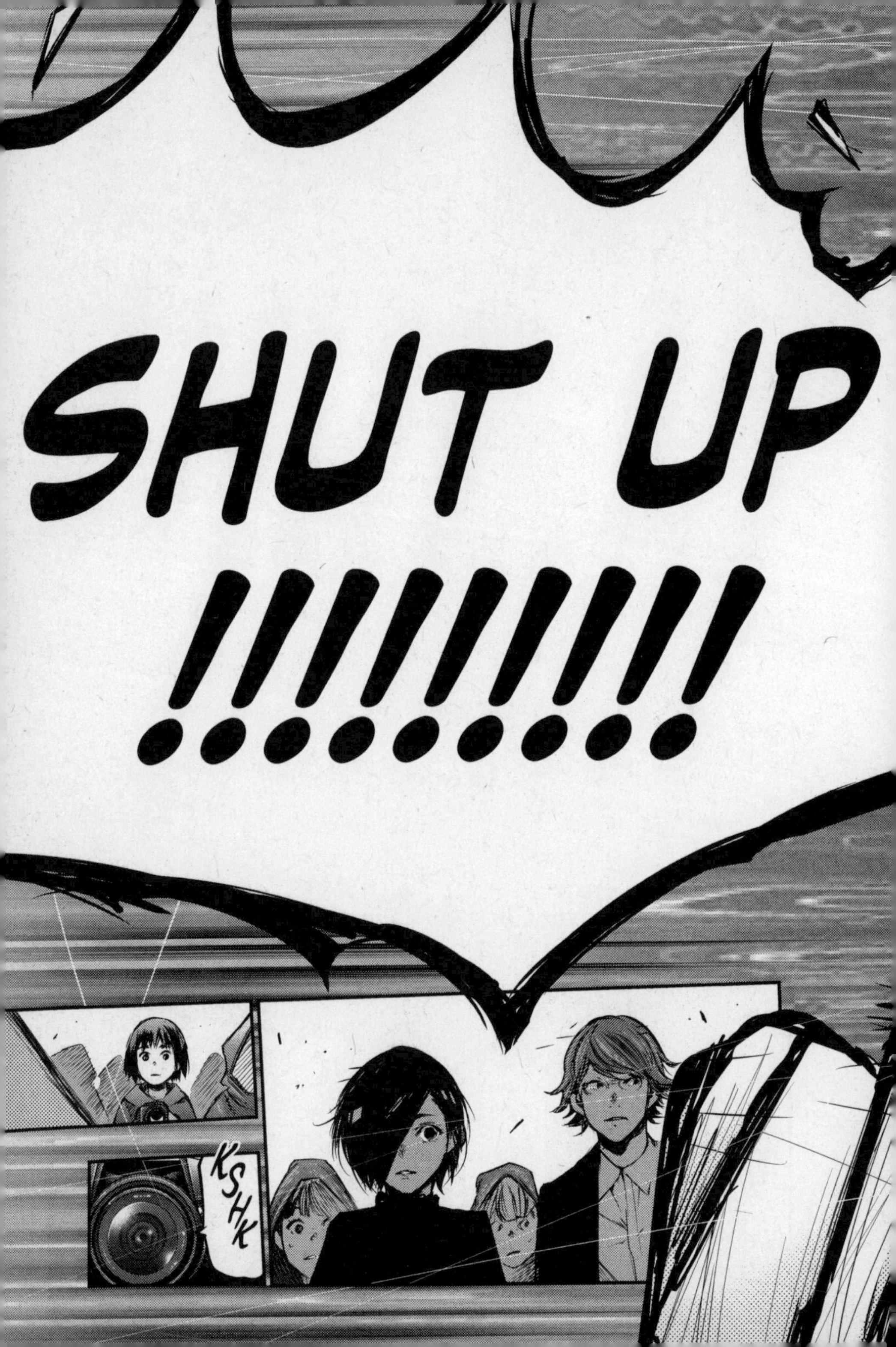
SHUT UP !!!!!!!!!
KSHK

TOKYO GHOUL:re

Irresistible Force :149

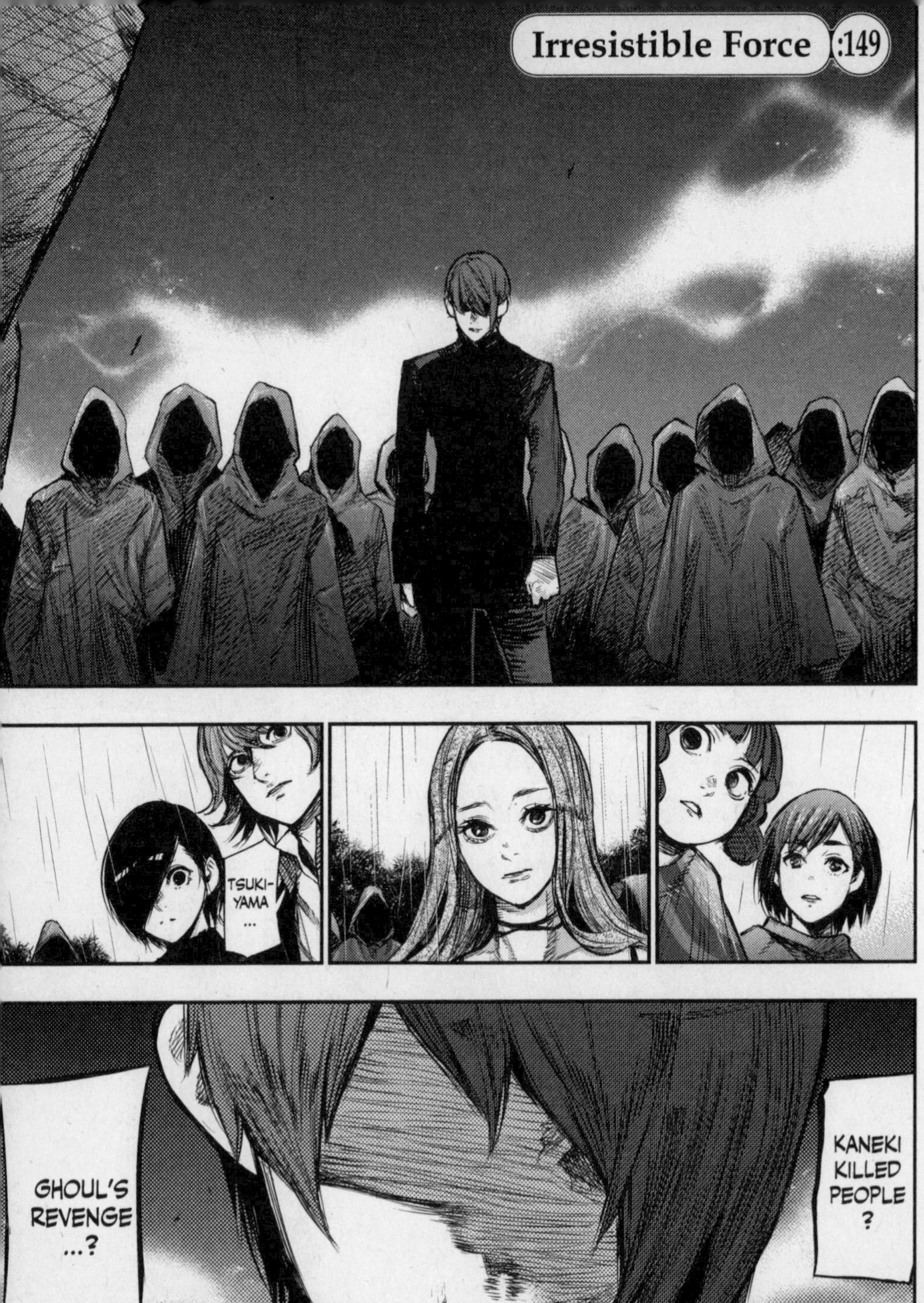
TSUKI-YAMA ...
KANEKI KILLED PEOPLE ?
GHOUL'S REVENGE ...?

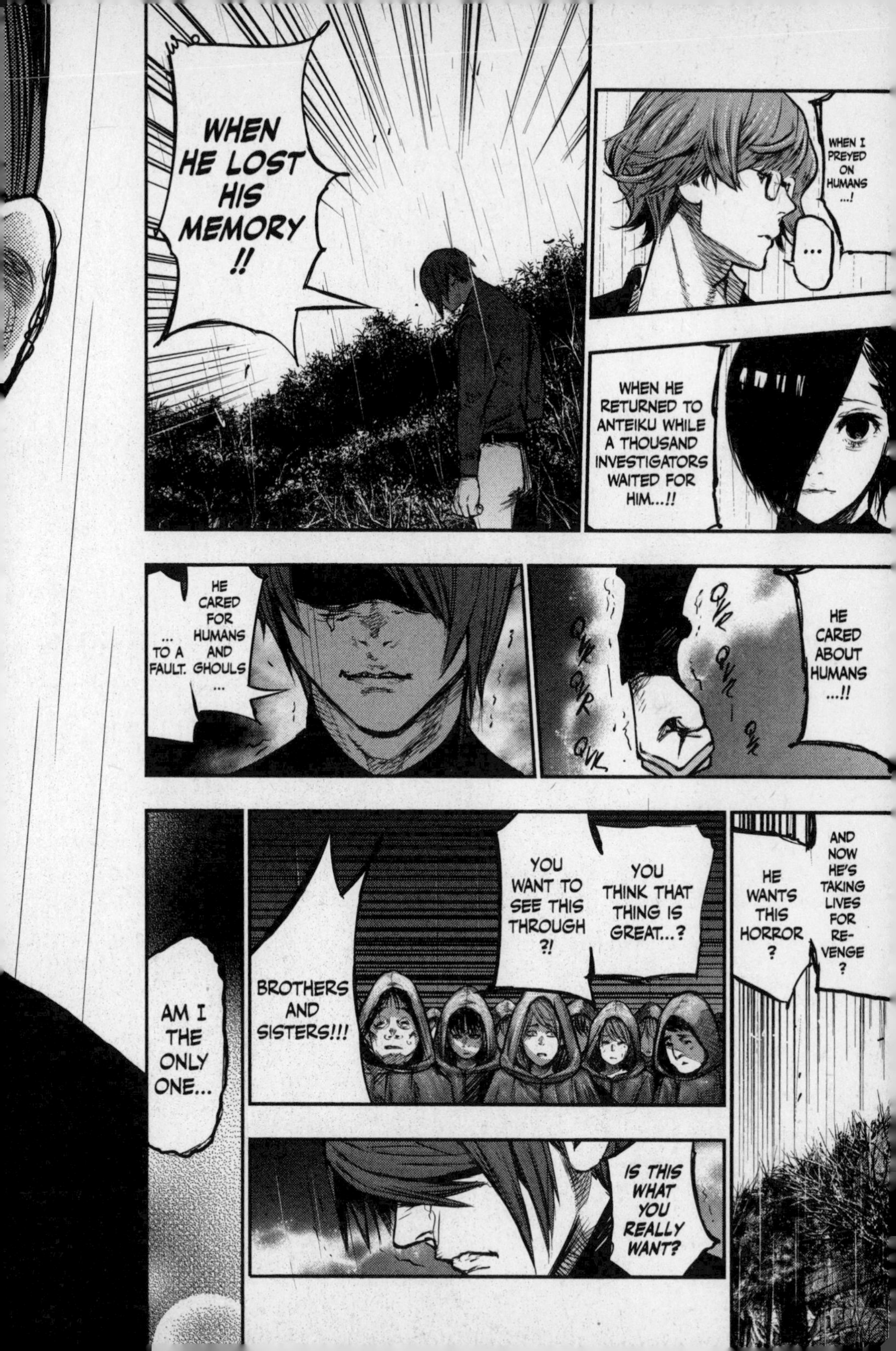
WHEN I PREYED ON HUMANS ...!
...
WHEN HE RETURNED TO ANTEIKU WHILE A THOUSAND INVESTIGATORS WAITED FOR HIM...!!
WHEN HE LOST HIS MEMORY !!
HE CARED ABOUT HUMANS ...!!
QVR QVR QVR
QVR QVR QVR QVK
HE CARED FOR HUMANS AND GHOULS ...
... TO A FAULT.
AND NOW HE'S TAKING LIVES FOR RE-VENGE?
HE WANTS THIS HORROR?
YOU THINK THAT THING IS GREAT...?
YOU WANT TO SEE THIS THROUGH ?!
BROTHERS AND SISTERS!!!
IS THIS WHAT YOU REALLY WANT?
AM I THE ONLY ONE...

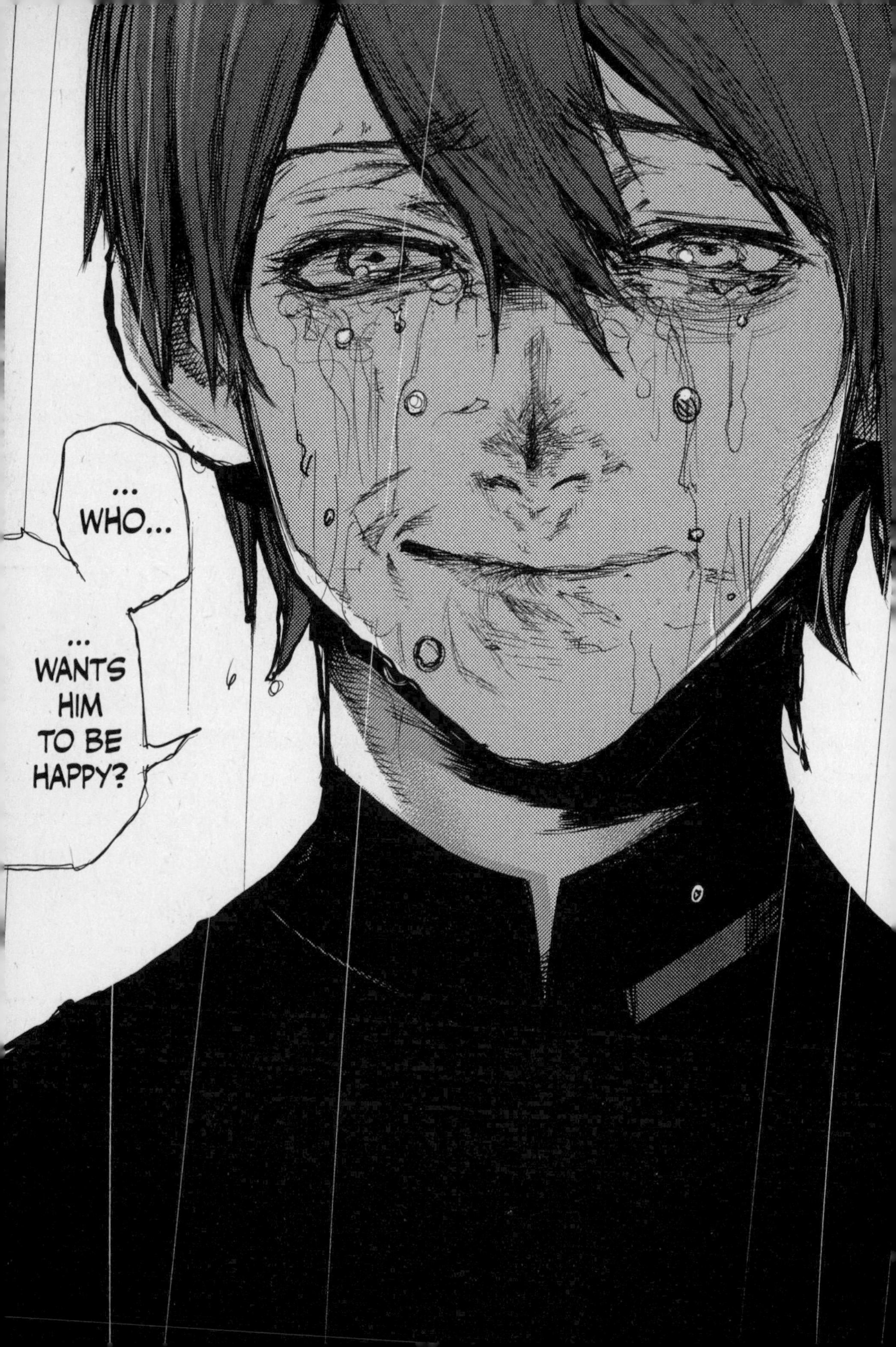
... WHO...
... WANTS HIM TO BE HAPPY?

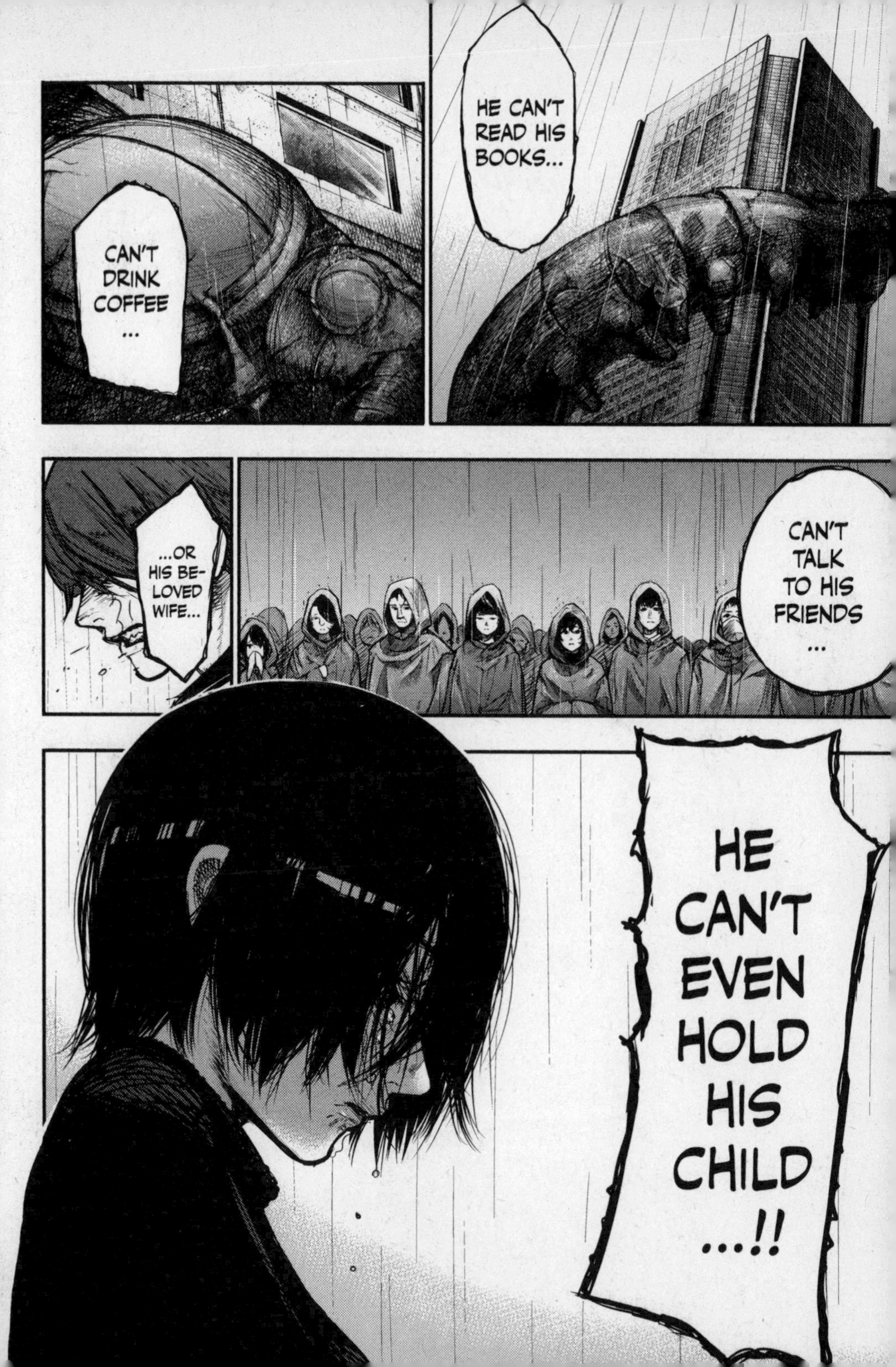
HE CAN'T READ HIS BOOKS...
CAN'T DRINK COFFEE ...
CAN'T TALK TO HIS FRIENDS ...
...OR HIS BE-LOVED WIFE...
HE CAN'T EVEN HOLD HIS CHILD ...!!

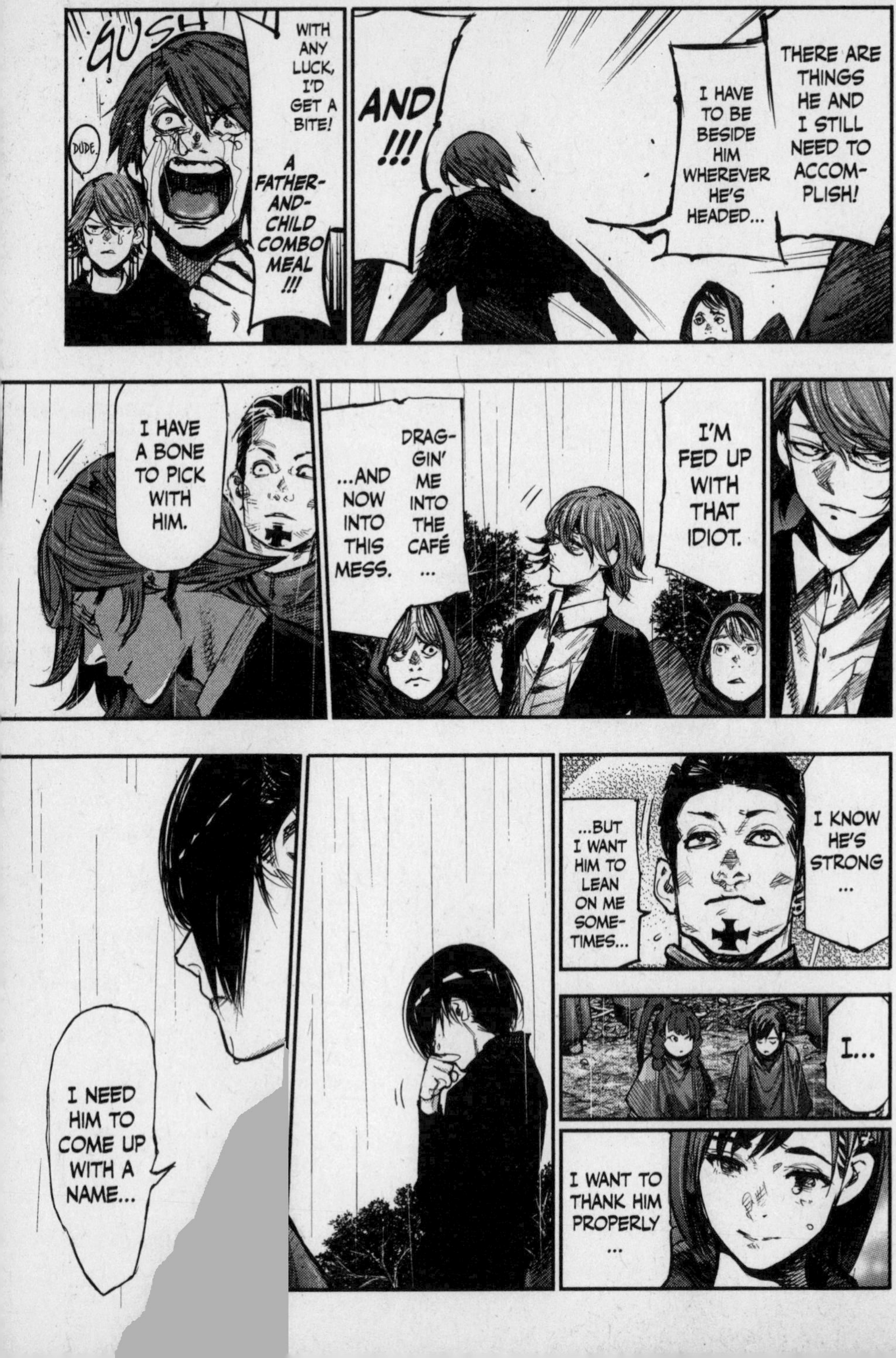
THERE ARE THINGS HE AND I STILL NEED TO ACCOMPLISH!
I HAVE TO BE BESIDE HIM WHEREVER HE'S HEADED...
AND !!!
WITH ANY LUCK, I'D GET A BITE!
A FATHER-AND-CHILD COMBO MEAL !!!
GUSH
DUDE.
I'M FED UP WITH THAT IDIOT.
DRAGGIN' ME INTO THE CAFÉ ...
...AND NOW INTO THIS MESS.
I HAVE A BONE TO PICK WITH HIM.
I KNOW HE'S STRONG ...
...BUT I WANT HIM TO LEAN ON ME SOMETIMES...
I...
I WANT TO THANK HIM PROPERLY ...
I NEED HIM TO COME UP WITH A NAME...

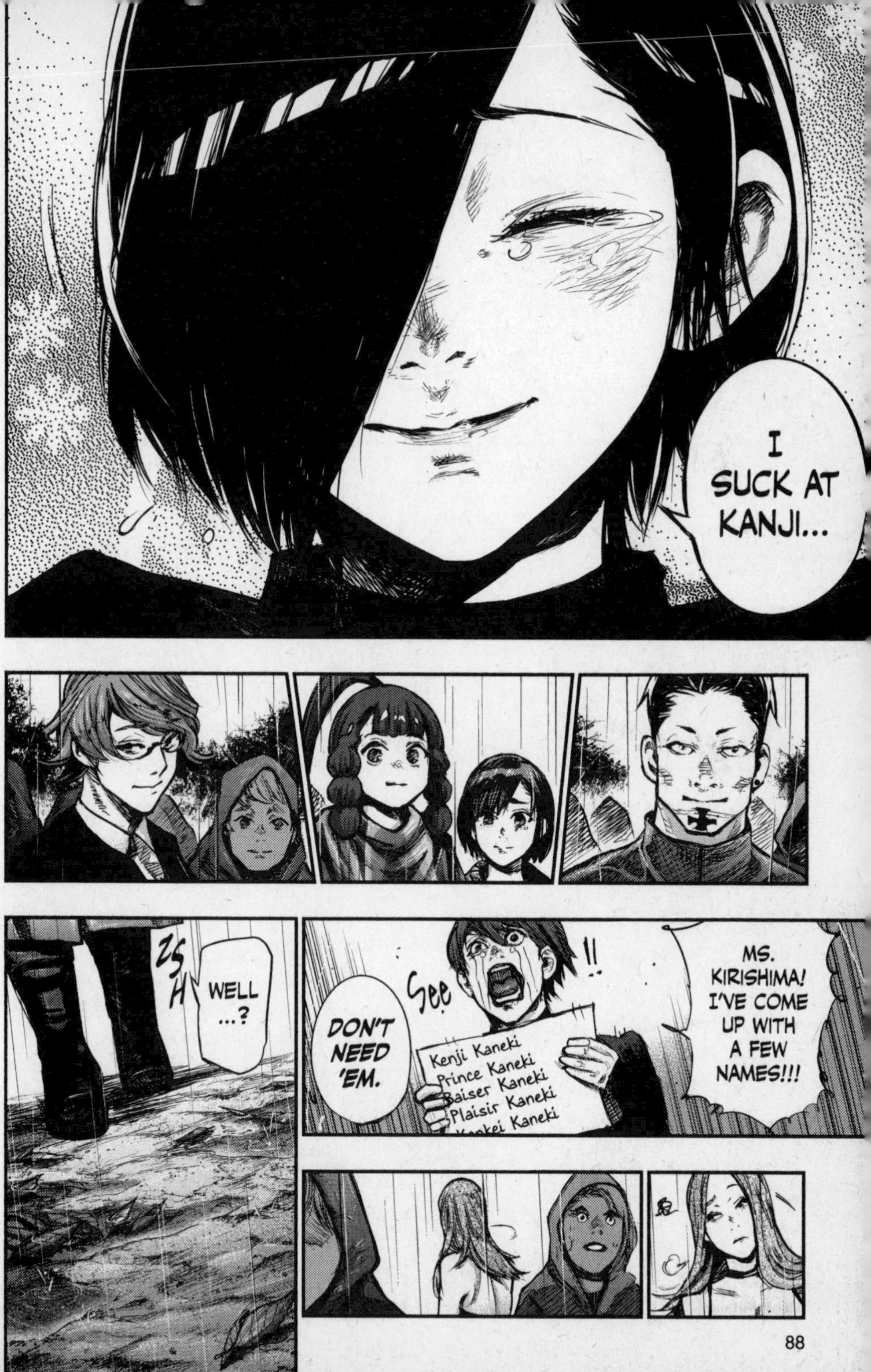
I SUCK AT KANJI...
MS. KIRISHIMA! I'VE COME UP WITH A FEW NAMES!!!
!!
See
Kenji Kaneki
Prince Kaneki
Baiser Kaneki
Plaisir Kaneki
Kankei Kaneki
DON'T NEED 'EM.
ZSH
WELL ...?

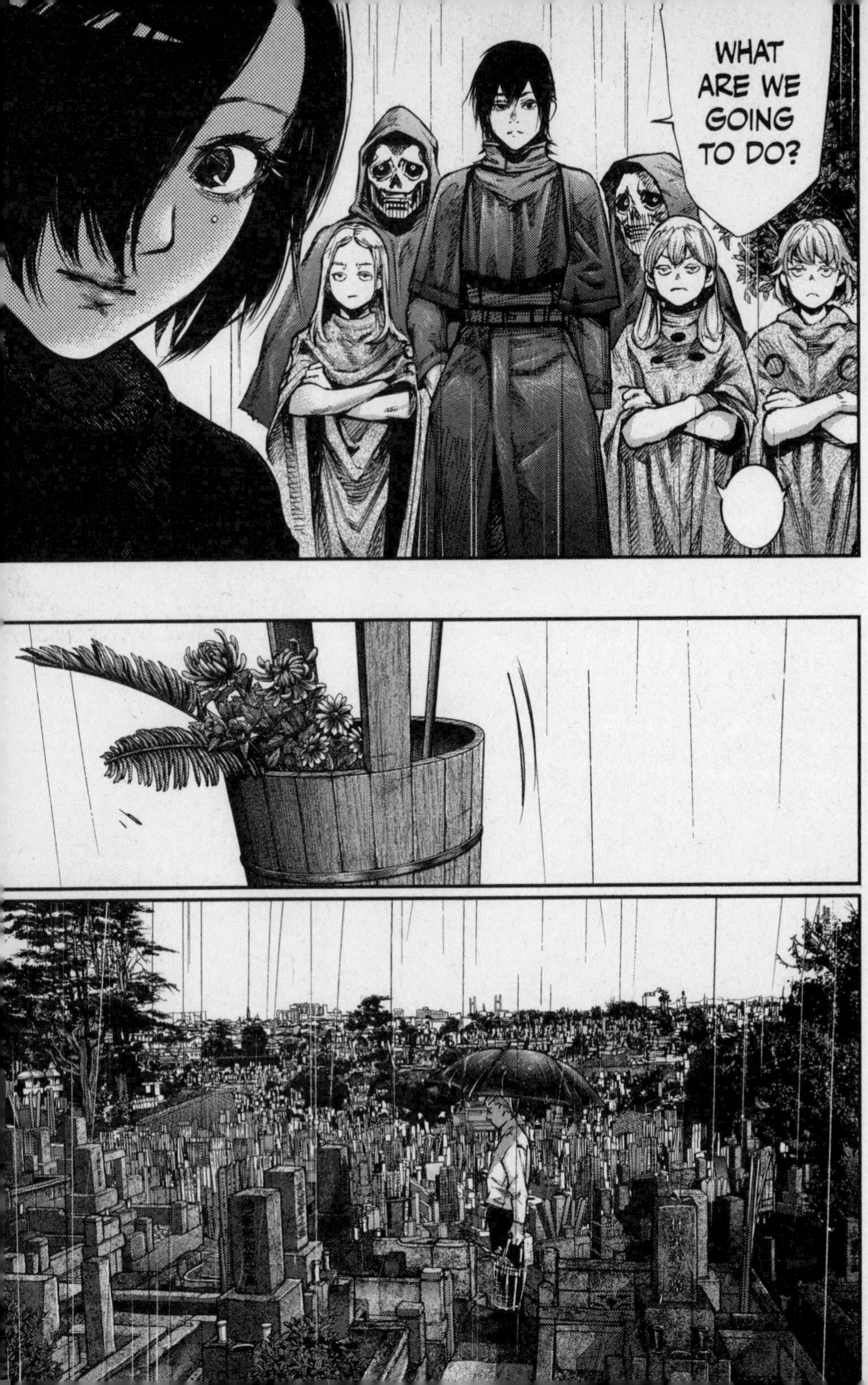
WHAT ARE WE GOING TO DO?

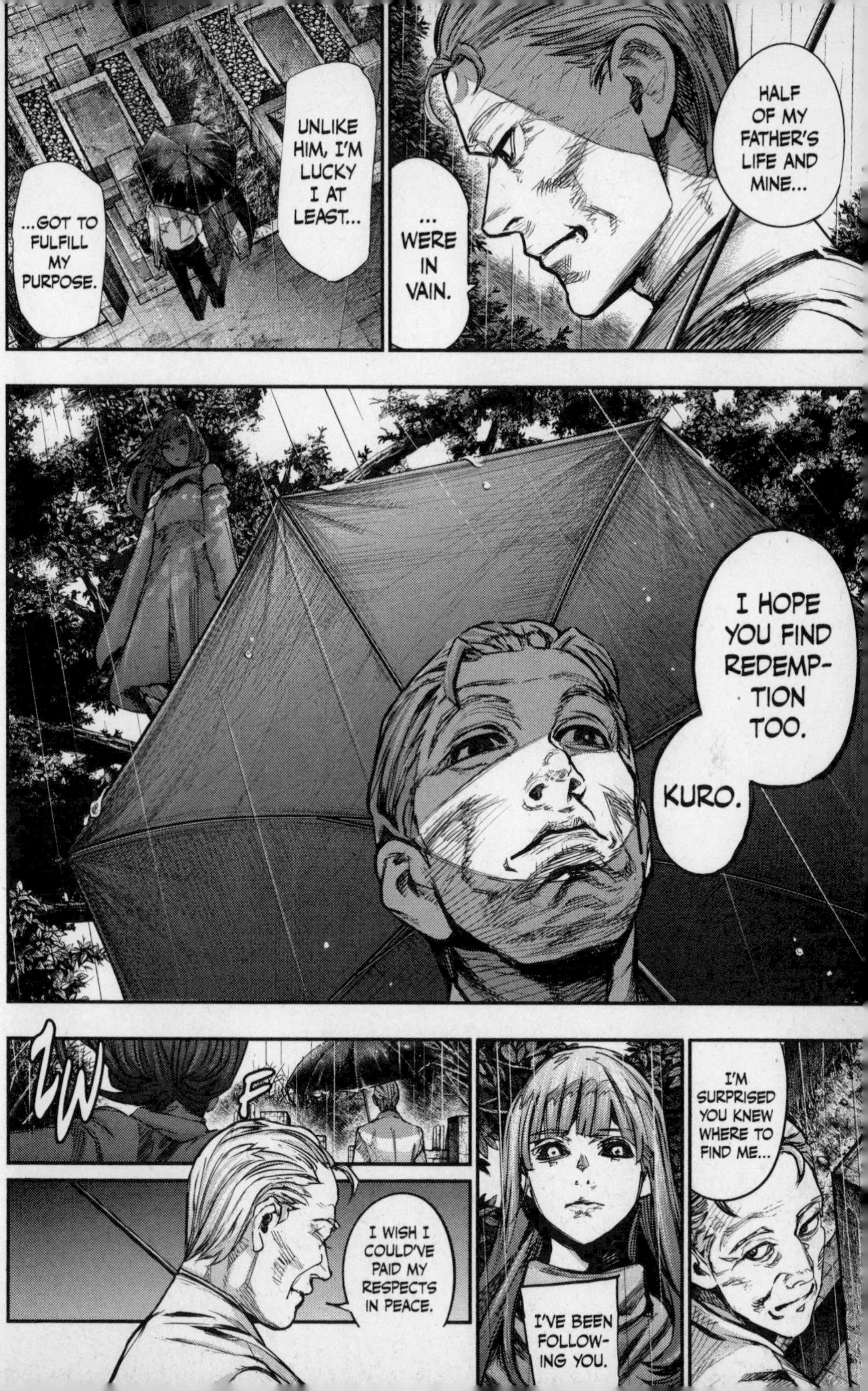

HALF OF MY FATHER'S LIFE AND MINE...
...WERE IN VAIN.
UNLIKE HIM, I'M LUCKY I AT LEAST...
...GOT TO FULFILL MY PURPOSE.
I HOPE YOU FIND REDEMPTION TOO.
KURO.
I'M SURPRISED YOU KNEW WHERE TO FIND ME...
I'VE BEEN FOLLOWING YOU.
ZW F
I WISH I COULD'VE PAID MY RESPECTS IN PEACE.

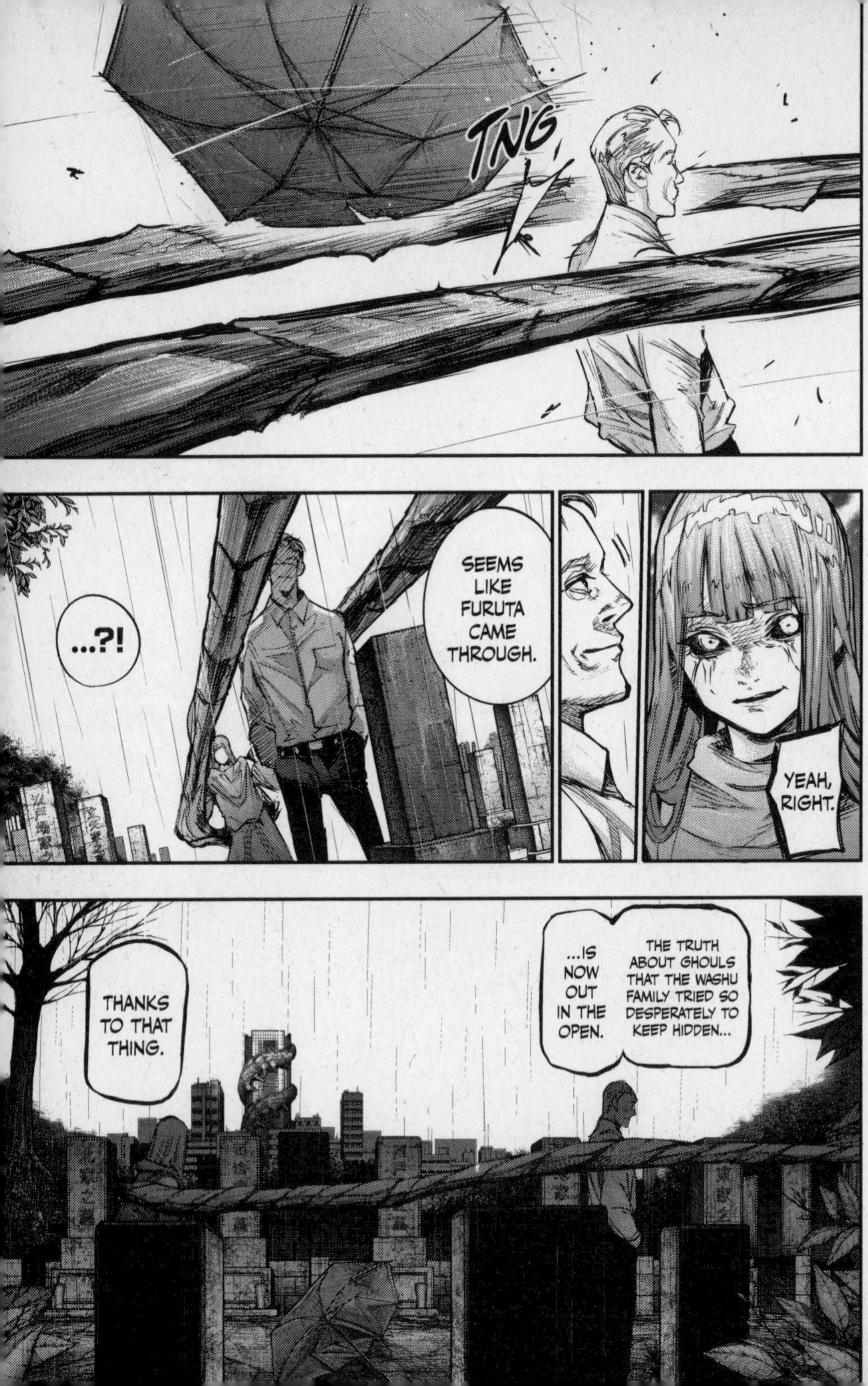
TNG
YEAH, RIGHT.
SEEMS LIKE FURUTA CAME THROUGH.
...?!
THE TRUTH ABOUT GHOULS THAT THE WASHU FAMILY TRIED SO DESPERATELY TO KEEP HIDDEN...
...IS NOW OUT IN THE OPEN.
THANKS TO THAT THING.

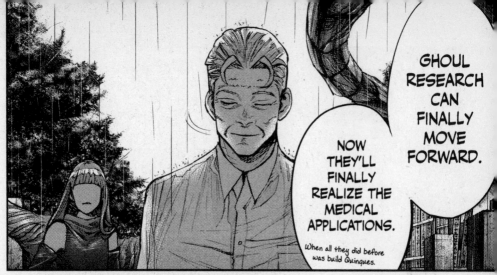

GHOUL RESEARCH CAN FINALLY MOVE FORWARD.

NOW THEY'LL FINALLY REALIZE THE MEDICAL APPLICATIONS.

When all they did before was build Quinques.

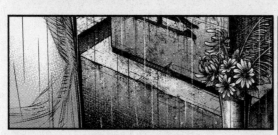

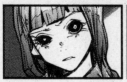

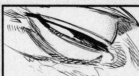

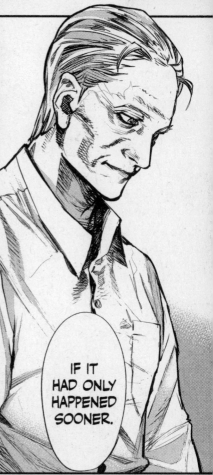

IF IT HAD ONLY HAPPENED SOONER.

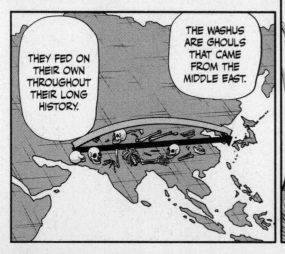

THE WASHUS ARE GHOULS THAT CAME FROM THE MIDDLE EAST.

THEY FED ON THEIR OWN THROUGHOUT THEIR LONG HISTORY.

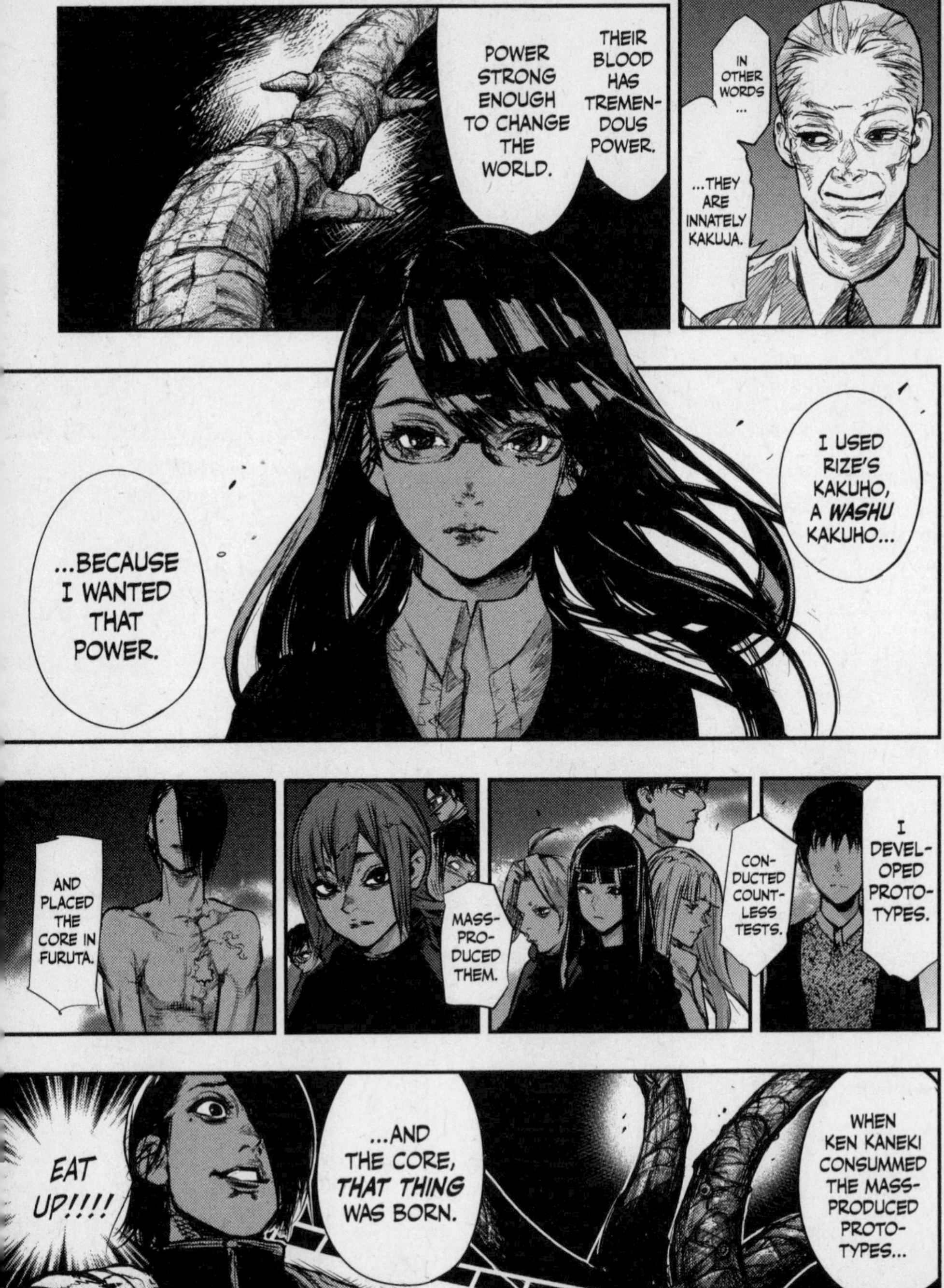
IN OTHER WORDS...
...THEY ARE INNATELY KAKUJA.
THEIR BLOOD HAS TREMENDOUS POWER.
POWER STRONG ENOUGH TO CHANGE THE WORLD.
I USED RIZE'S KAKUHO, A *WASHU* KAKUHO...
...BECAUSE I WANTED THAT POWER.
I DEVELOPED PROTOTYPES.
CONDUCTED COUNTLESS TESTS.
MASS-PRODUCED THEM.
AND PLACED THE CORE IN FURUTA.
WHEN KEN KANEKI CONSUMMED THE MASS-PRODUCED PROTOTYPES...
...AND THE CORE, *THAT THING* WAS BORN.
EAT UP!!!!

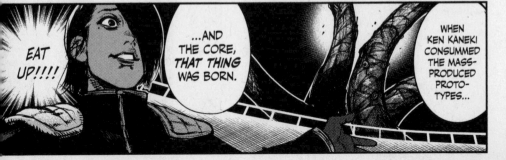

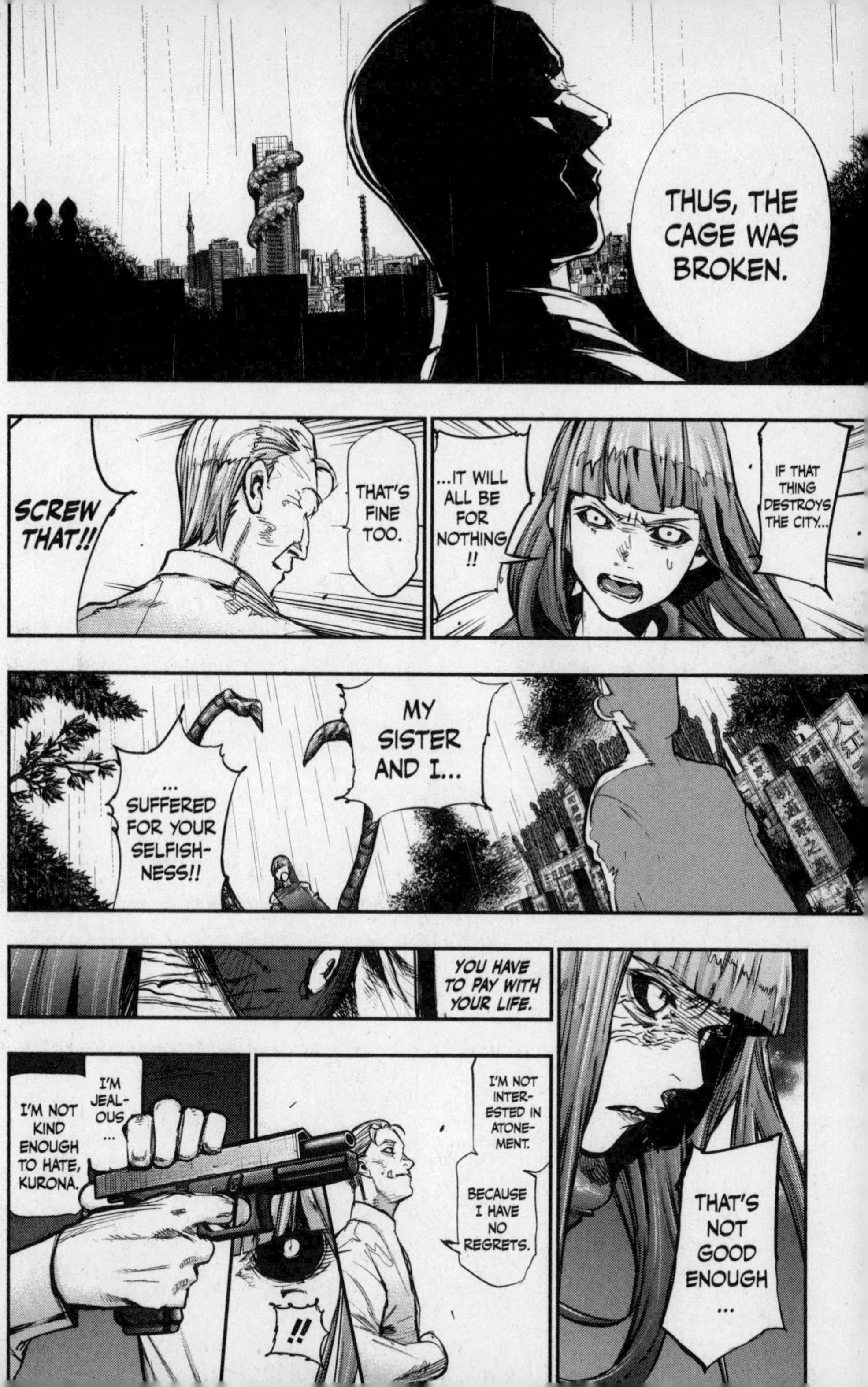
THUS, THE CAGE WAS BROKEN.
IF THAT THING DESTROYS THE CITY...
...IT WILL ALL BE FOR NOTHING!!
THAT'S FINE TOO.
SCREW THAT!!!
MY SISTER AND I...
...SUFFERED FOR YOUR SELFISHNESS!!
THAT'S NOT GOOD ENOUGH...
YOU HAVE TO PAY WITH YOUR LIFE.
I'M NOT INTERESTED IN ATONEMENT.
BECAUSE I HAVE NO REGRETS.
!!
I'M JEALOUS...
I'M NOT KIND ENOUGH TO HATE, KURONA.

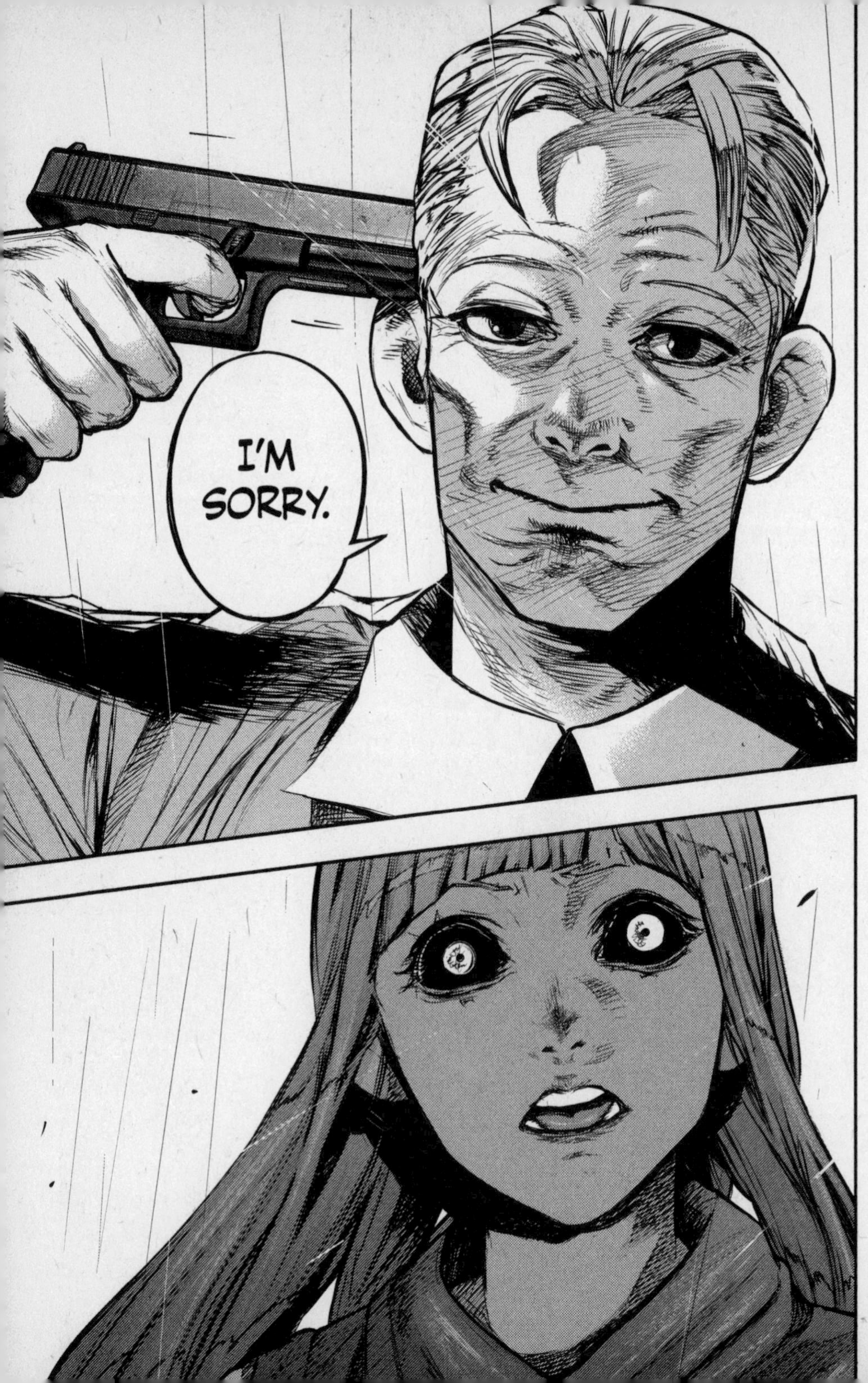
I'M SORRY.

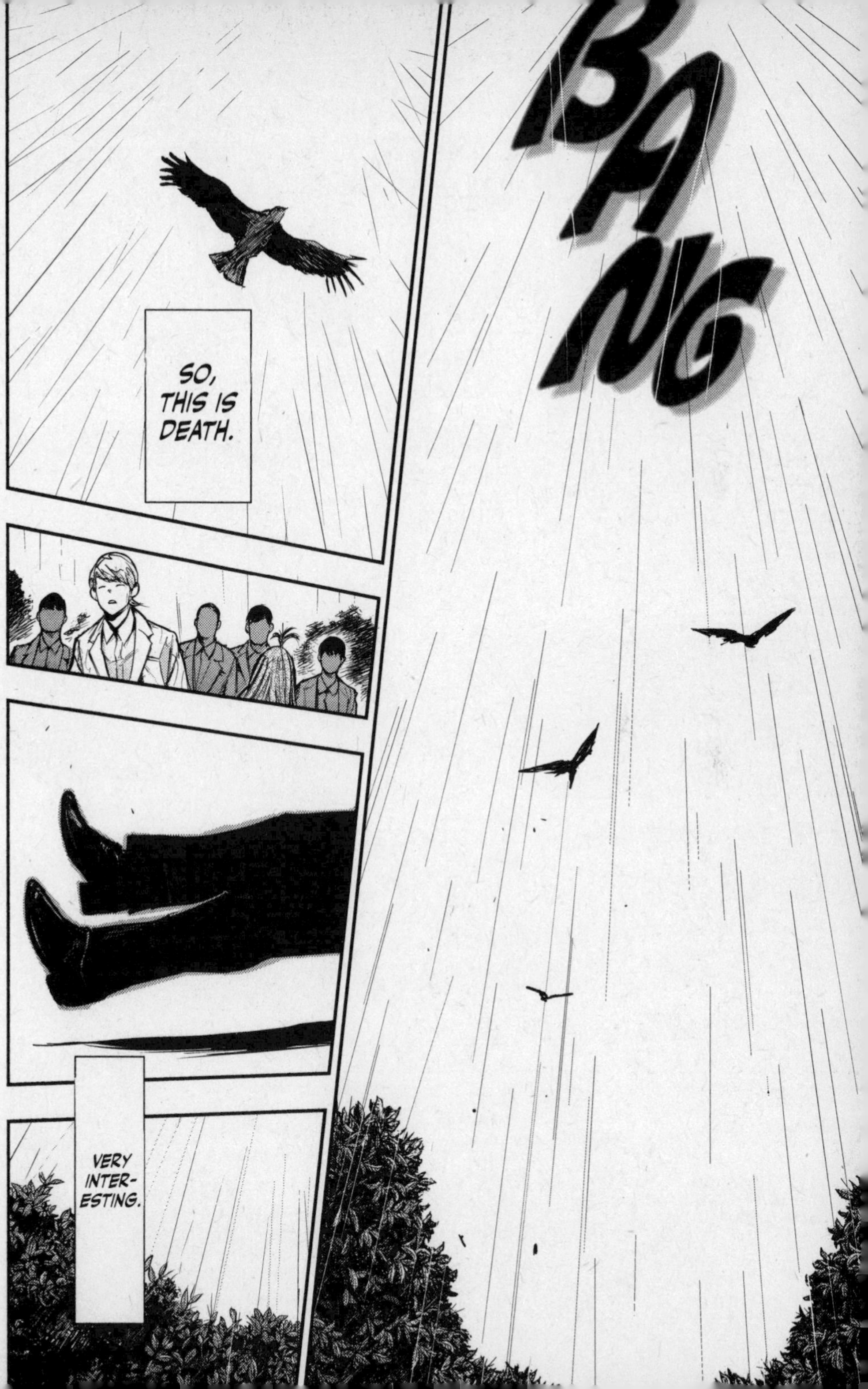
BANG
SO, THIS IS DEATH.
VERY INTER-ESTING.

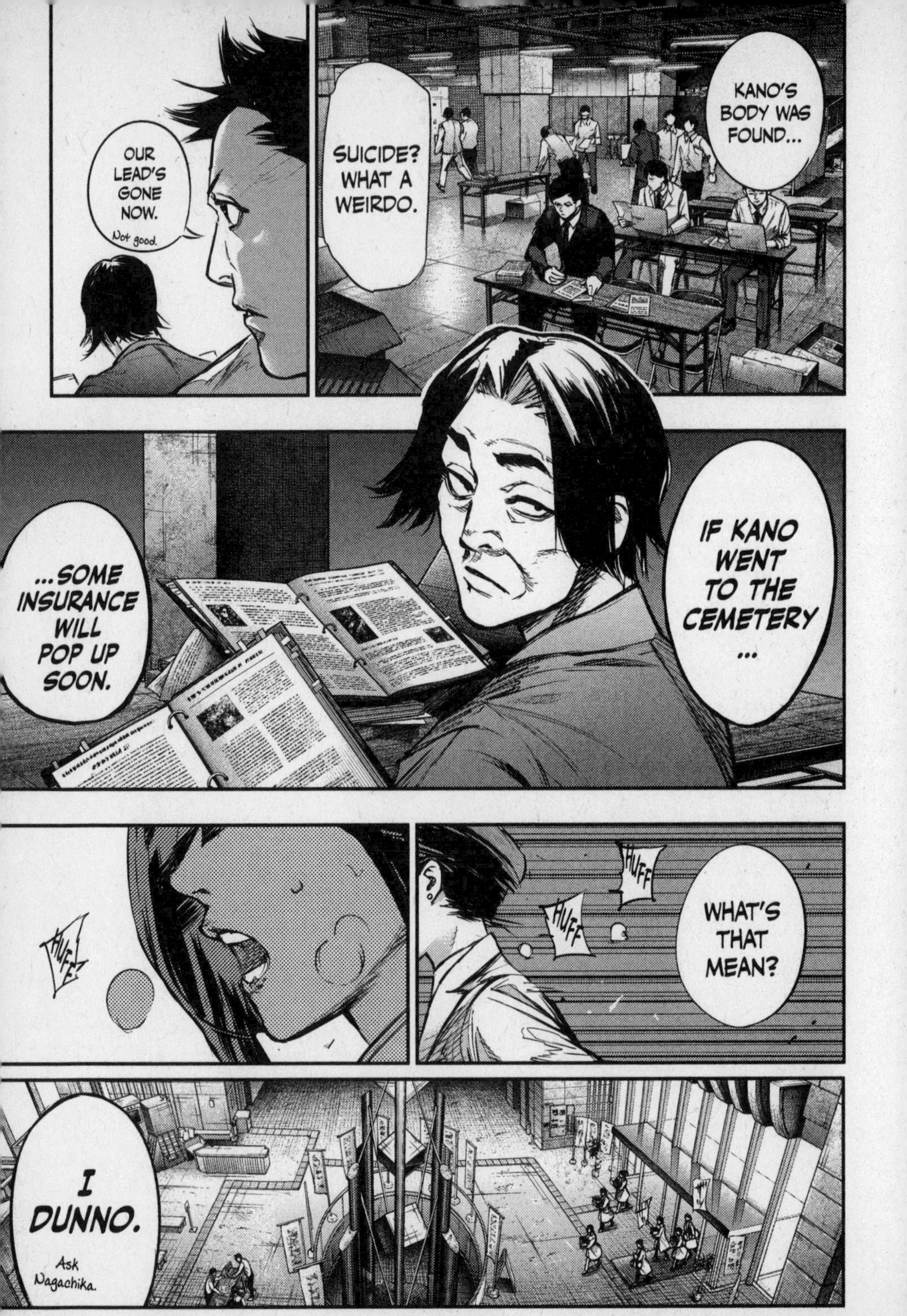
KANO'S BODY WAS FOUND...
SUICIDE? WHAT A WEIRDO.
OUR LEAD'S GONE NOW.
Not good.
IF KANO WENT TO THE CEMETERY ...
...SOME INSURANCE WILL POP UP SOON.
HUFF
HUFF
WHAT'S THAT MEAN?
HUFF
I DUNNO.
Ask Nagachika.

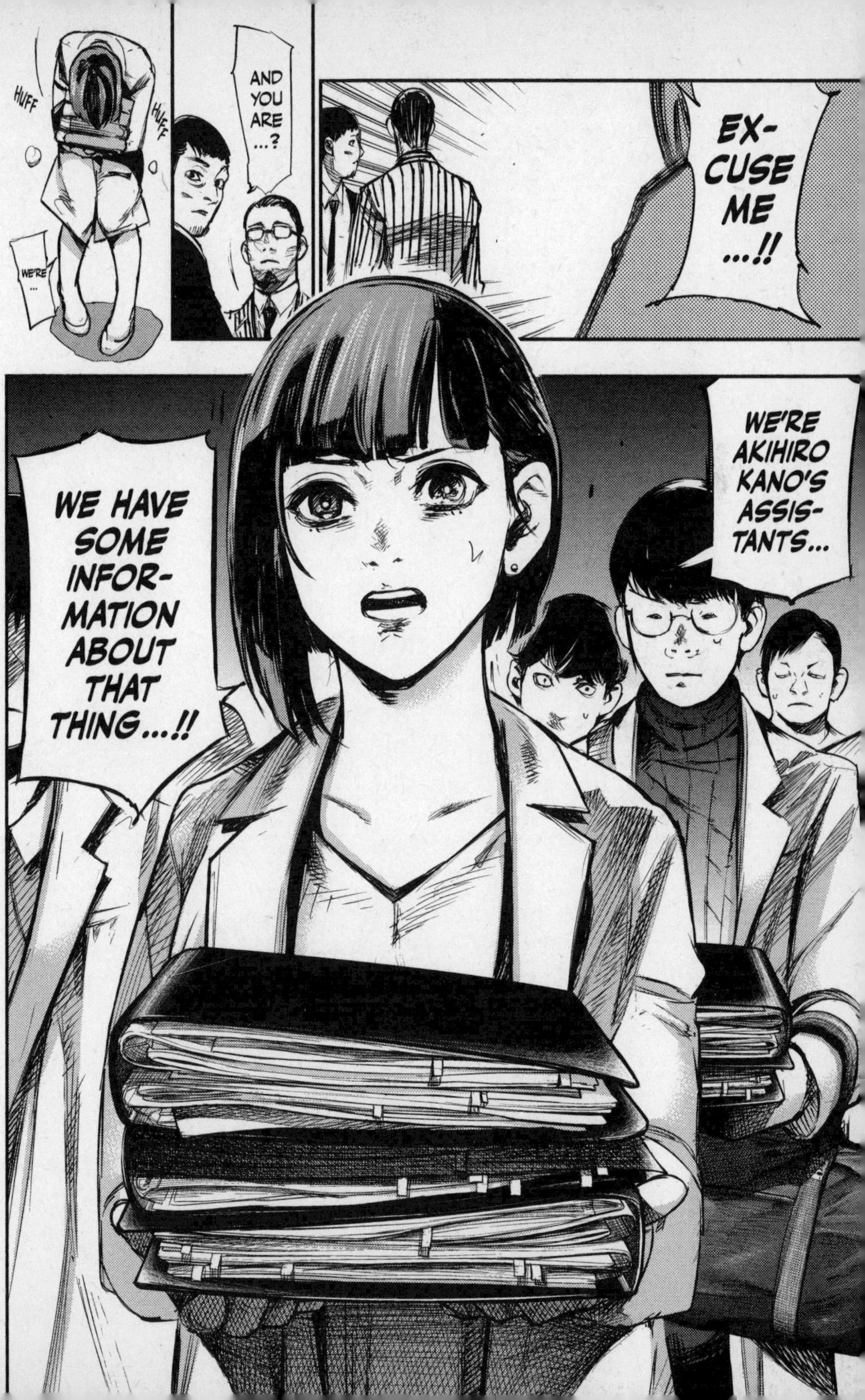
EX-CUSE ME ...!!
AND YOU ARE ...?
HUFF
HUFF
WE'RE ...
WE'RE AKIHIRO KANO'S ASSIS-TANTS...
WE HAVE SOME INFOR-MATION ABOUT THAT THING...!!

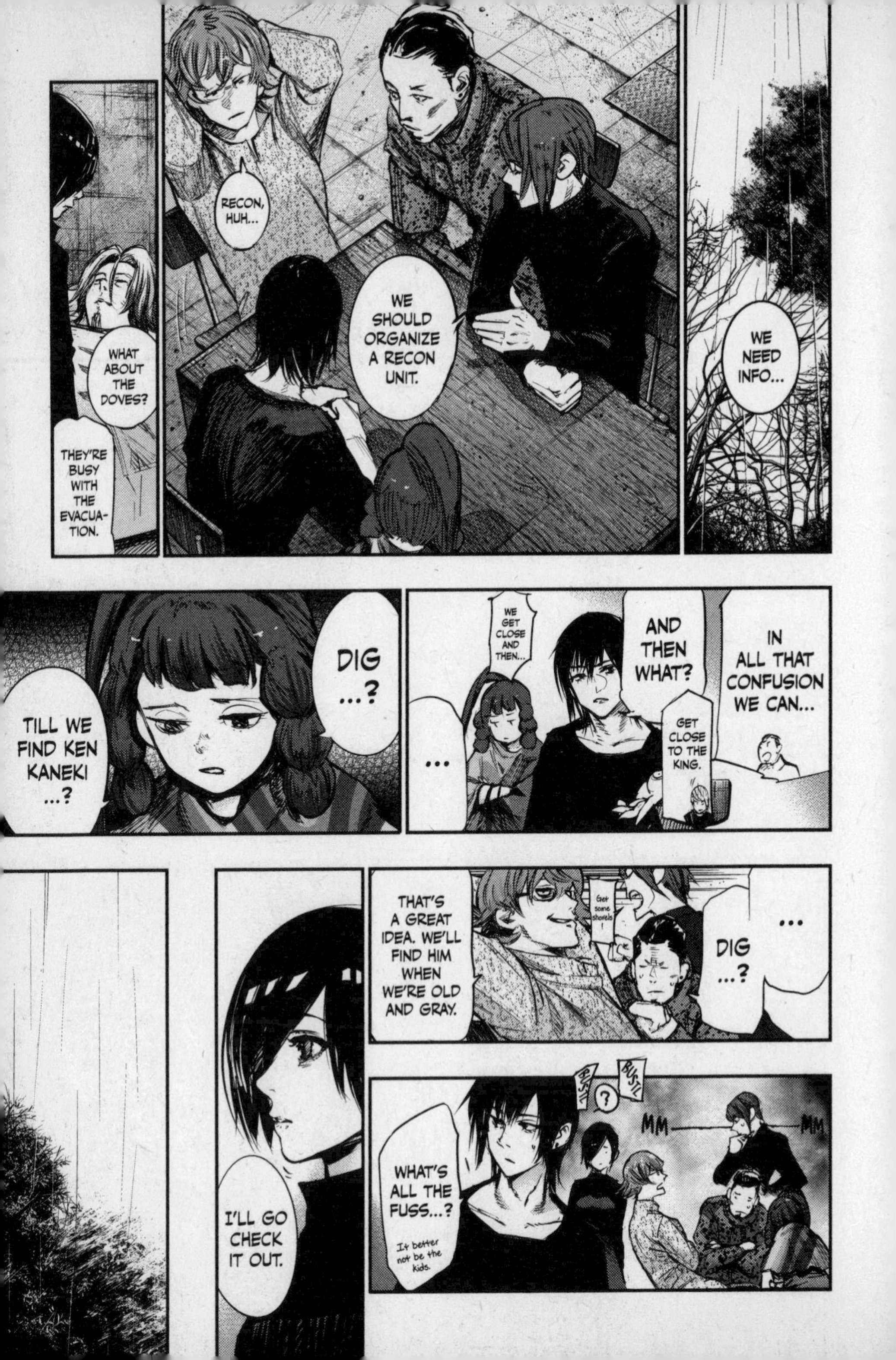
WE NEED INFO...
WE SHOULD ORGANIZE A RECON UNIT.
RECON, HUH...
WHAT ABOUT THE DOVES?
THEY'RE BUSY WITH THE EVACUA-TION.
IN ALL THAT CONFUSION WE CAN...
AND THEN WHAT?
GET CLOSE TO THE KING.
WE GET CLOSE AND THEN...
...
DIG ...?
TILL WE FIND KEN KANEKI ...?
...
DIG ...?
Get some shovels!
THAT'S A GREAT IDEA. WE'LL FIND HIM WHEN WE'RE OLD AND GRAY.
BUSTL
BUSTL
?
MM
MM
WHAT'S ALL THE FUSS...?
It better not be the kids.
I'LL GO CHECK IT OUT.

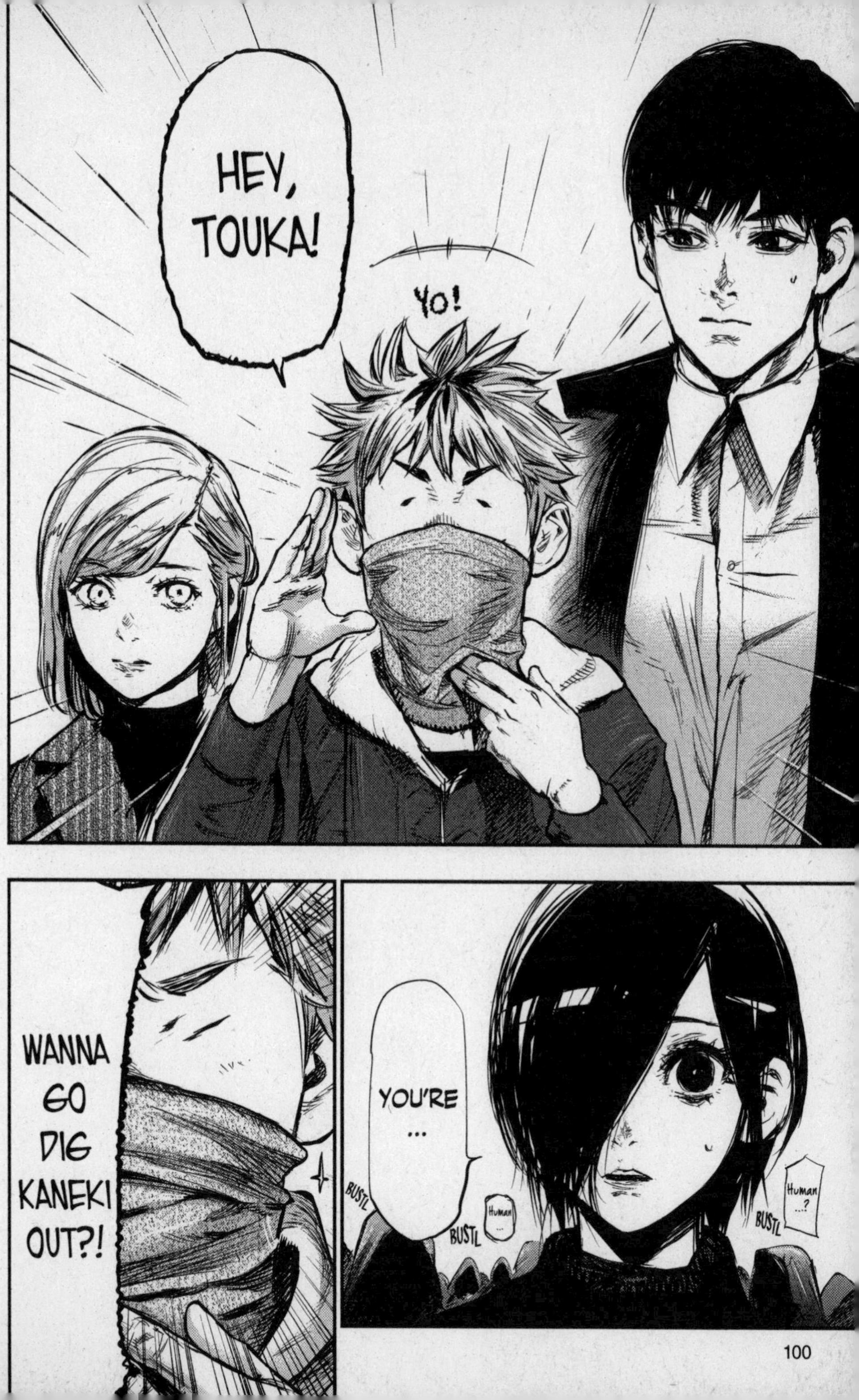
HEY, TOUKA!
YO!
YOU'RE ...
Human ...?
BUSTL
BUSTL
Human ...
BUSTL
BUSTL
WANNA GO DIG KANEKI OUT?!

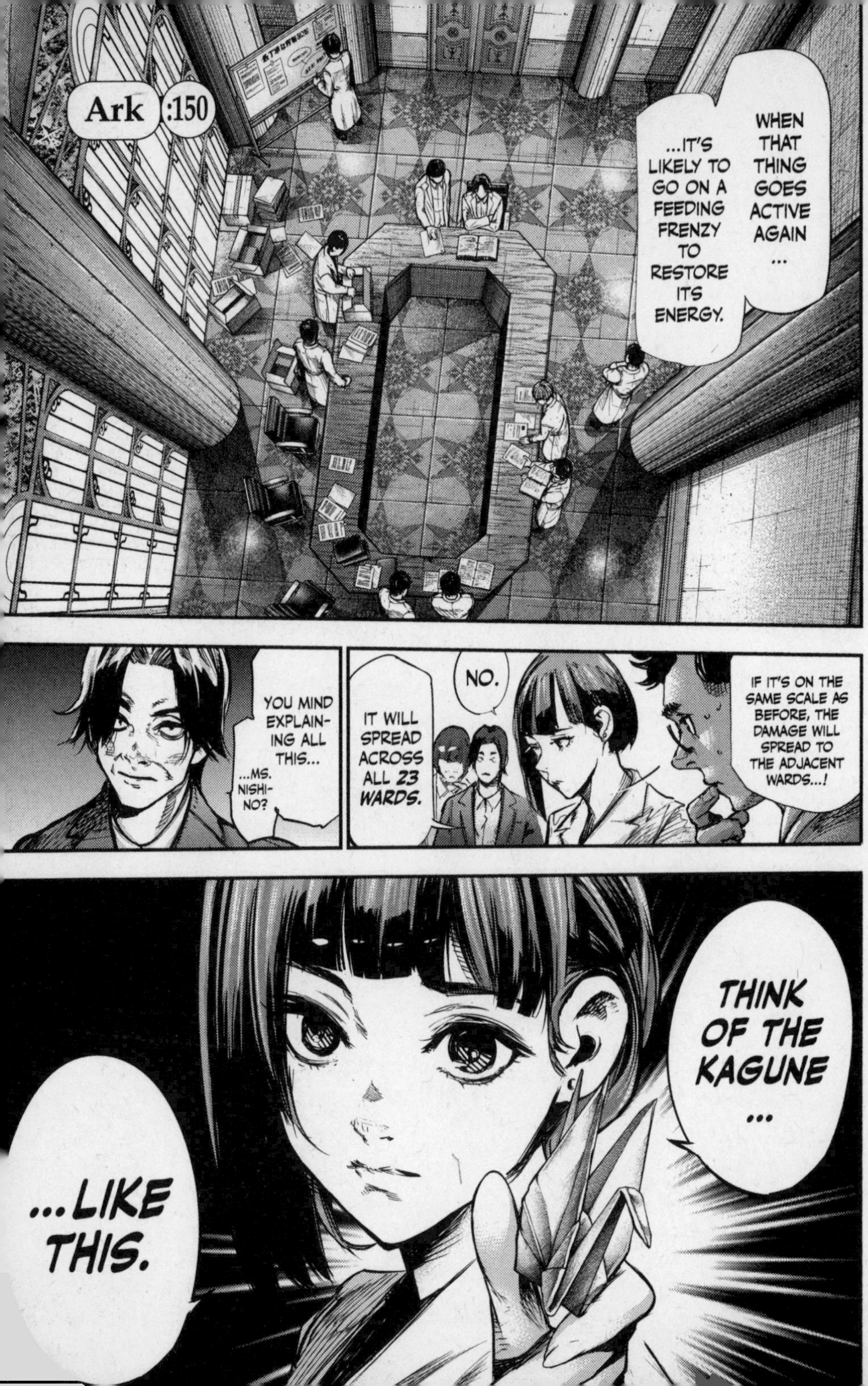
WHEN THAT THING GOES ACTIVE AGAIN ...
...IT'S LIKELY TO GO ON A FEEDING FRENZY TO RESTORE ITS ENERGY.
Ark :150
IF IT'S ON THE SAME SCALE AS BEFORE, THE DAMAGE WILL SPREAD TO THE ADJACENT WARDS...!
NO.
IT WILL SPREAD ACROSS ALL 23 WARDS.
YOU MIND EXPLAINING ALL THIS...
...MS. NISHINO?
THINK OF THE KAGUNE ...
...LIKE THIS.

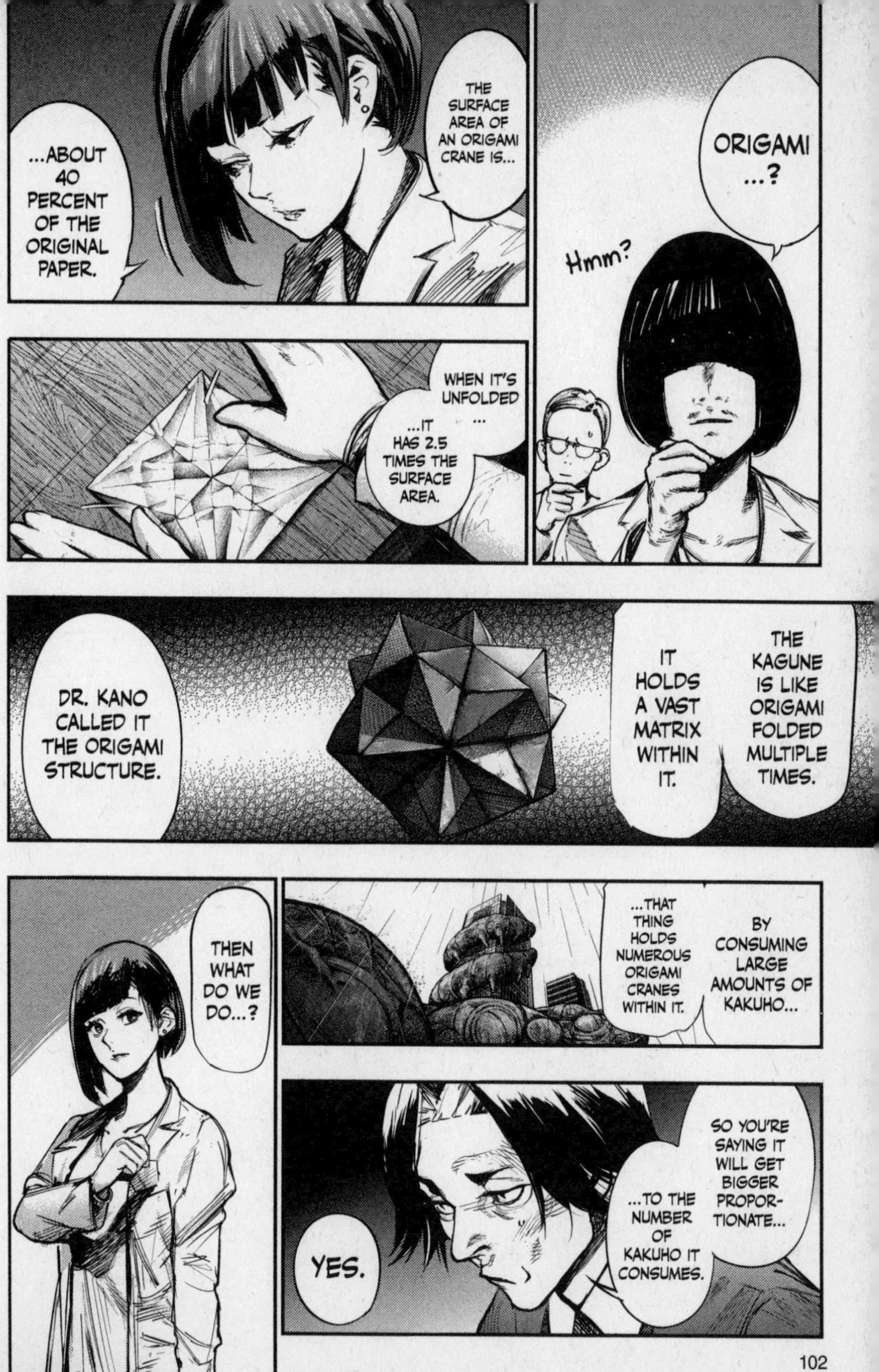
ORIGAMI ...?
Hmm?
THE SURFACE AREA OF AN ORIGAMI CRANE IS...
...ABOUT 40 PERCENT OF THE ORIGINAL PAPER.
WHEN IT'S UNFOLDED ...
...IT HAS 2.5 TIMES THE SURFACE AREA.
THE KAGUNE IS LIKE ORIGAMI FOLDED MULTIPLE TIMES.
IT HOLDS A VAST MATRIX WITHIN IT.
DR. KANO CALLED IT THE ORIGAMI STRUCTURE.
BY CONSUMING LARGE AMOUNTS OF KAKUHO...
...THAT THING HOLDS NUMEROUS ORIGAMI CRANES WITHIN IT.
SO YOU'RE SAYING IT WILL GET BIGGER PROPORTIONATE...
...TO THE NUMBER OF KAKUHO IT CONSUMES.
YES.
THEN WHAT DO WE DO...?

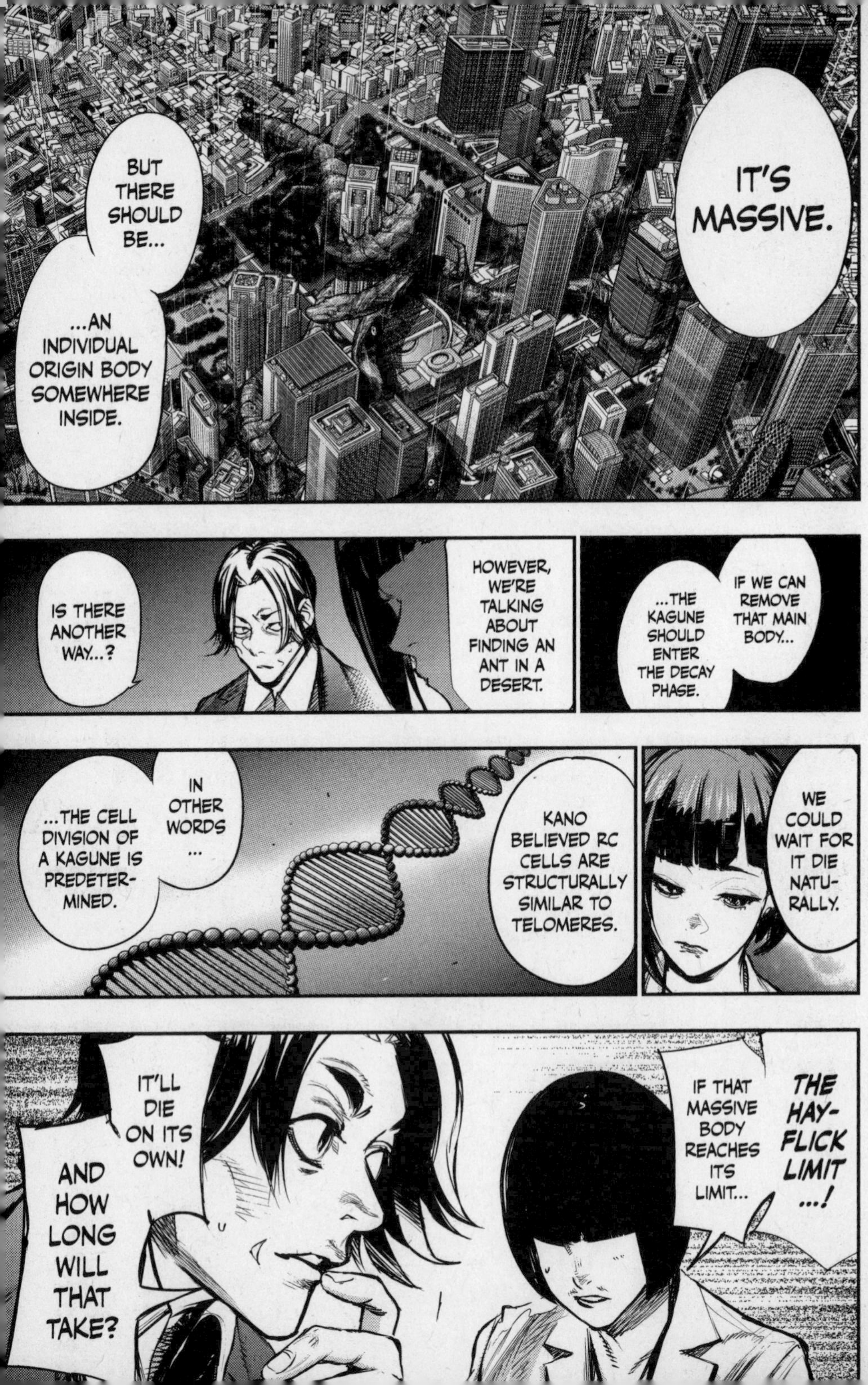
IT'S MASSIVE.
BUT THERE SHOULD BE...
...AN INDIVIDUAL ORIGIN BODY SOMEWHERE INSIDE.
IF WE CAN REMOVE THAT MAIN BODY...
...THE KAGUNE SHOULD ENTER THE DECAY PHASE.
HOWEVER, WE'RE TALKING ABOUT FINDING AN ANT IN A DESERT.
IS THERE ANOTHER WAY...?
WE COULD WAIT FOR IT DIE NATURALLY.
KANO BELIEVED RC CELLS ARE STRUCTURALLY SIMILAR TO TELOMERES.
IN OTHER WORDS...
...THE CELL DIVISION OF A KAGUNE IS PREDETERMINED.
THE HAYFLICK LIMIT...!
IF THAT MASSIVE BODY REACHES ITS LIMIT...
IT'LL DIE ON ITS OWN!
AND HOW LONG WILL THAT TAKE?

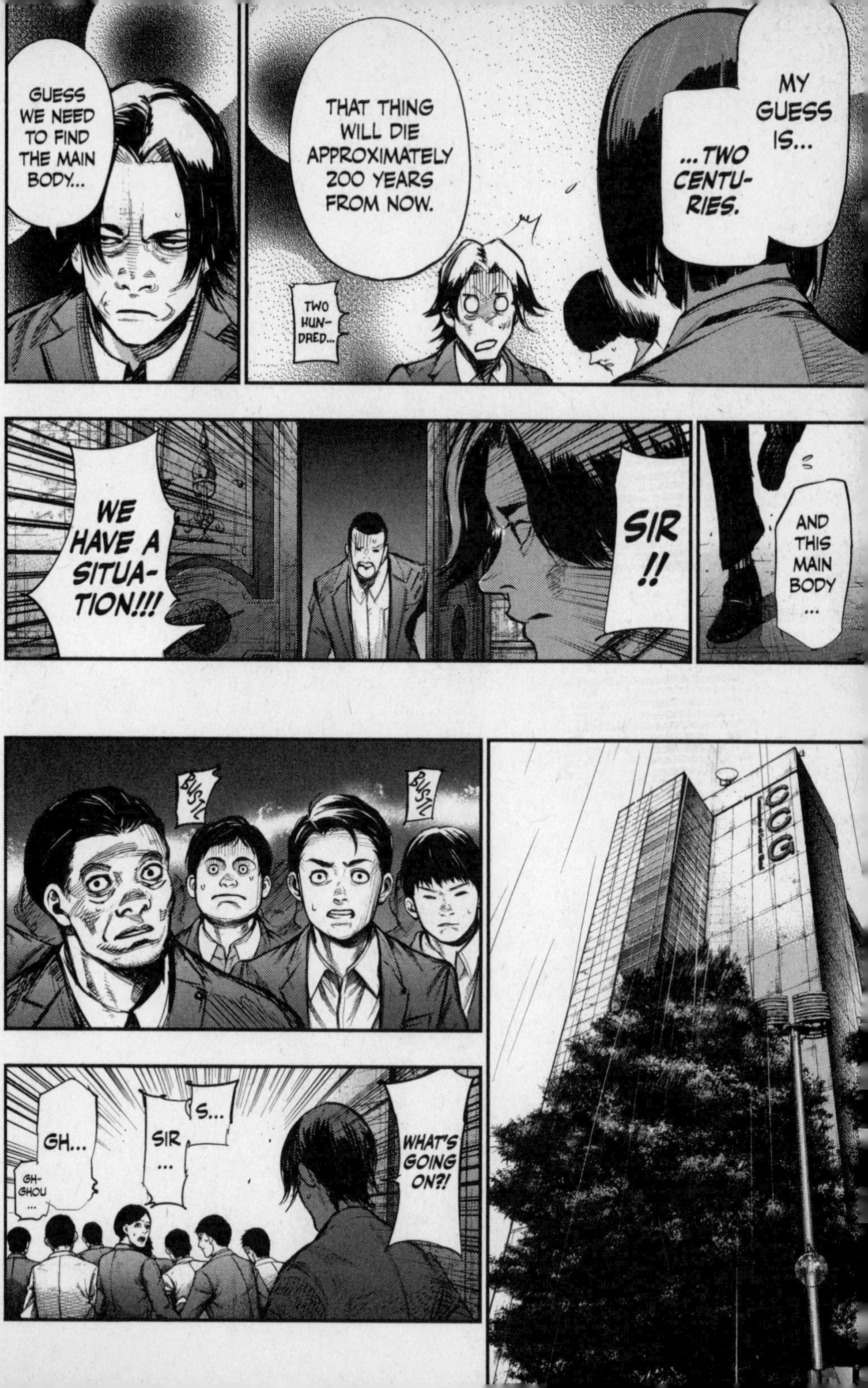
MY GUESS IS...
...TWO CENTURIES.
THAT THING WILL DIE APPROXIMATELY 200 YEARS FROM NOW.
TWO HUNDRED...
GUESS WE NEED TO FIND THE MAIN BODY...
AND THIS MAIN BODY ...
SIR !!
WE HAVE A SITUATION!!!
CCG
BUSTL
BUSTL
WHAT'S GOING ON?!
S...
SIR ...
GH...
GH-GHOU ...

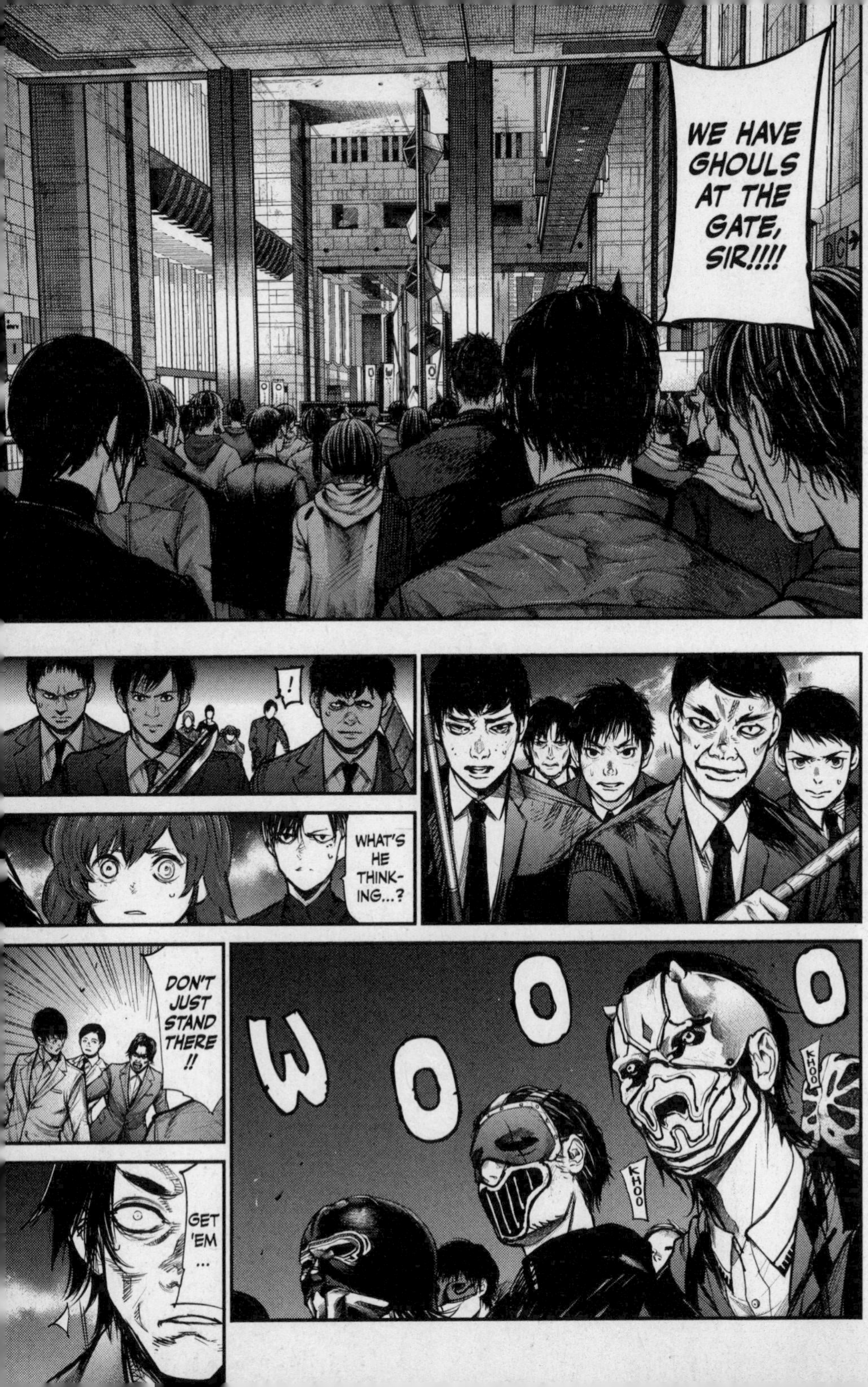
WE HAVE GHOULS AT THE GATE, SIR!!!!
!
WHAT'S HE THINKING...?
3OOO
KHOO
KHOO
DON'T JUST STAND THERE!!
GET 'EM ...

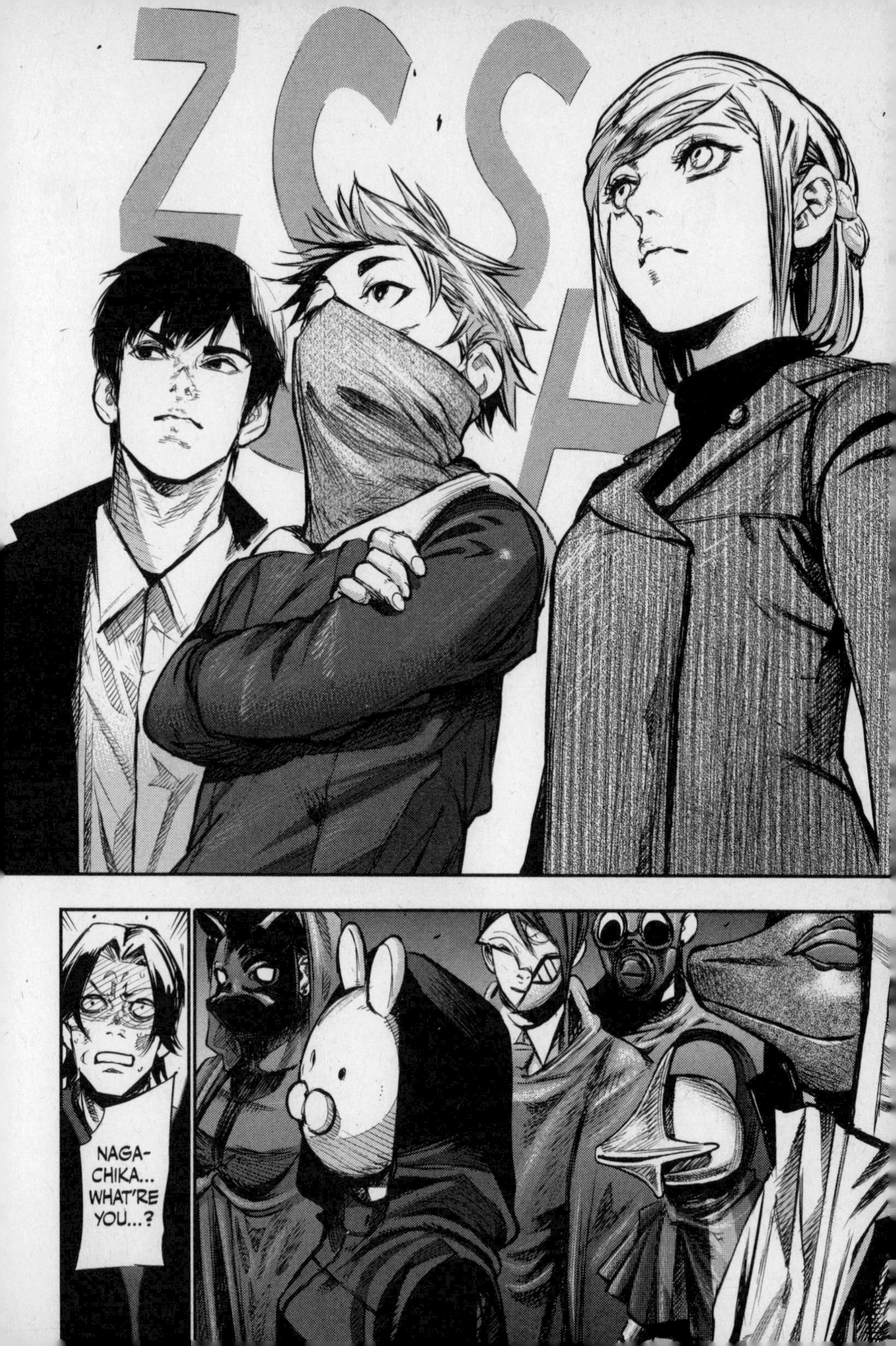
NAGA-CHIKA... WHAT'RE YOU...?

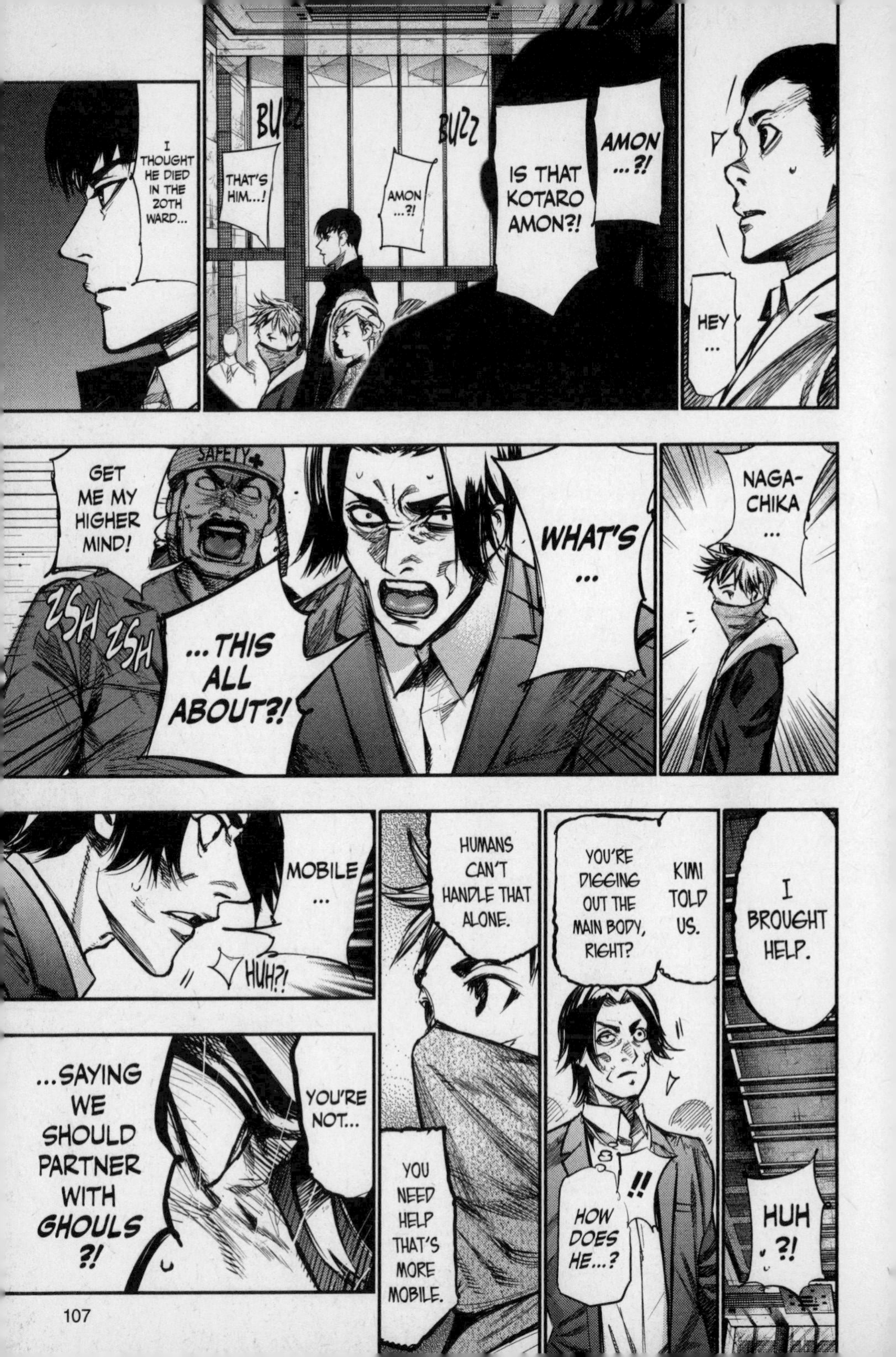
HEY ...
AMON ...?!
IS THAT KOTARO AMON?!
BUZZ
AMON ...?!
BUZZ
THAT'S HIM...!
I THOUGHT HE DIED IN THE 20TH WARD...
NAGA-CHIKA ...
WHAT'S ...
...THIS ALL ABOUT?!
GET ME MY HIGHER MIND!
ZSH ZSH
I BROUGHT HELP.
HUH ?!
KIMI TOLD US.
YOU'RE DIGGING OUT THE MAIN BODY, RIGHT?
!!
HOW DOES HE...?
HUMANS CAN'T HANDLE THAT ALONE.
YOU NEED HELP THAT'S MORE MOBILE.
MOBILE ...
HUH?!
YOU'RE NOT...
...SAYING WE SHOULD PARTNER WITH GHOULS ?!

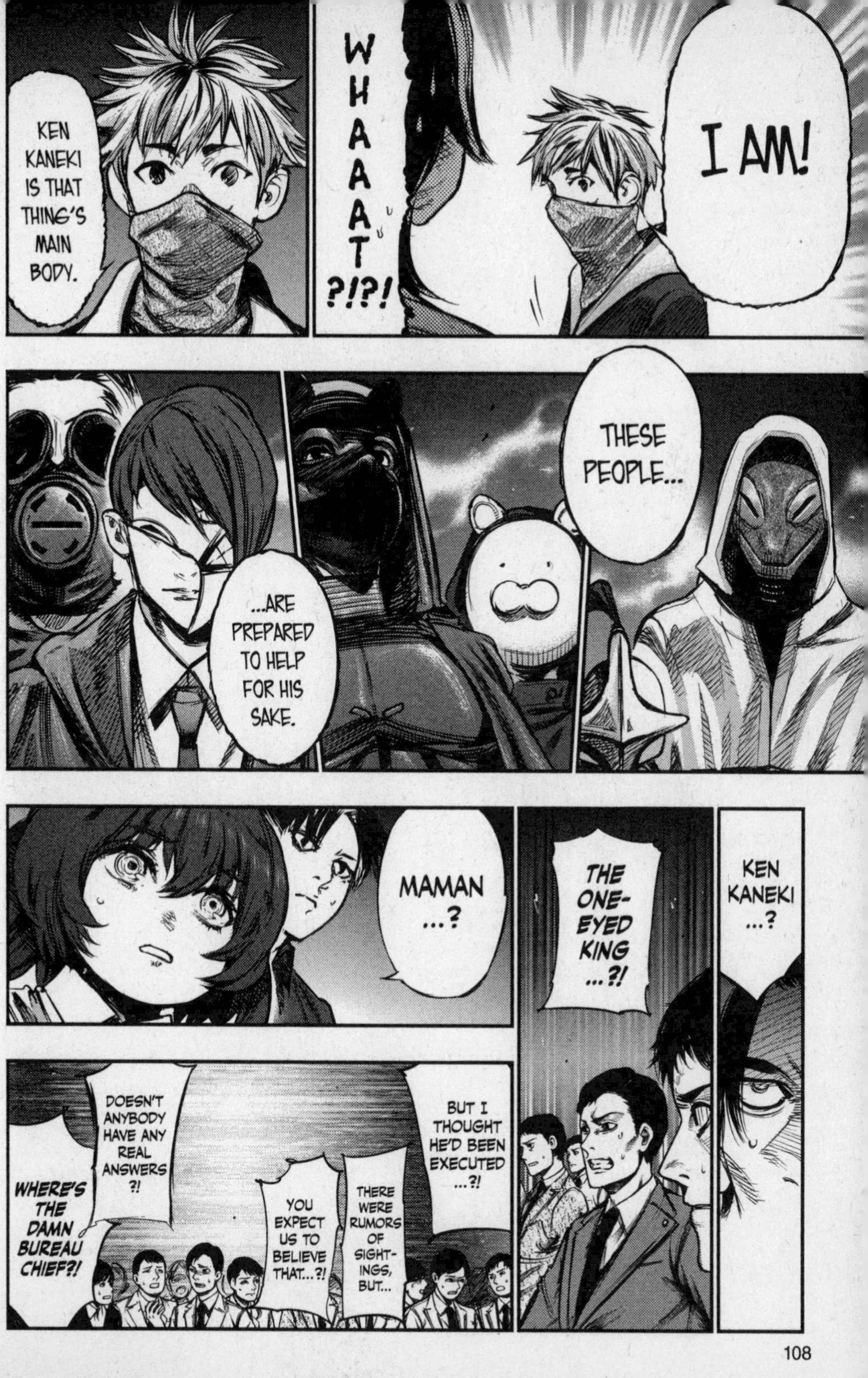
I AM!
WHAAAT ?!?!
KEN KANEKI IS THAT THING'S MAIN BODY.
THESE PEOPLE...
...ARE PREPARED TO HELP FOR HIS SAKE.
KEN KANEKI ...?
THE ONE-EYED KING ...?!
MAMAN ...?
BUT I THOUGHT HE'D BEEN EXECUTED ...?!
THERE WERE RUMORS OF SIGHT-INGS, BUT...
YOU EXPECT US TO BELIEVE THAT...?!
DOESN'T ANYBODY HAVE ANY REAL ANSWERS ?!
WHERE'S THE DAMN BUREAU CHIEF?!

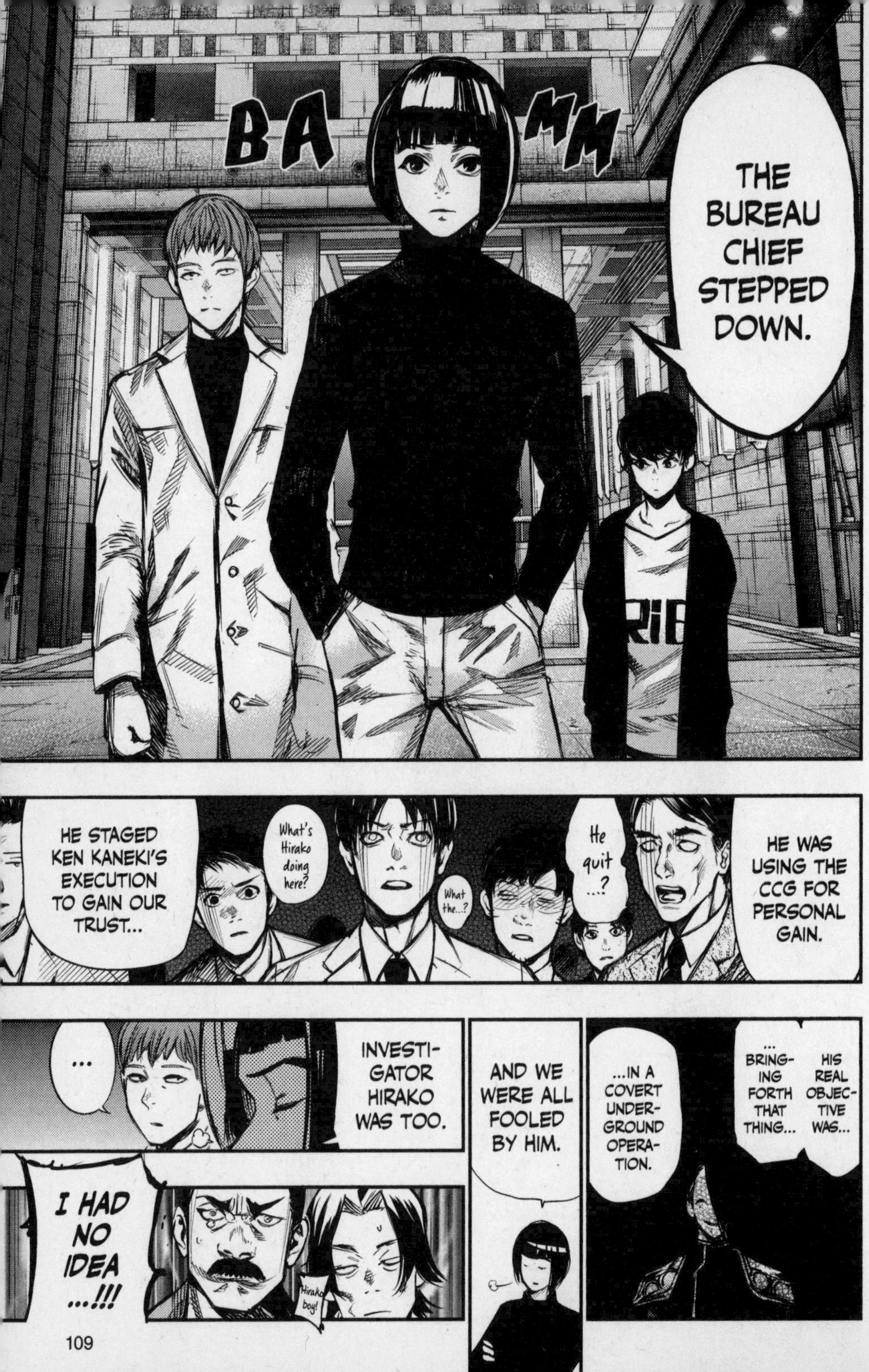
BAMM
THE BUREAU CHIEF STEPPED DOWN.
HE WAS USING THE CCG FOR PERSONAL GAIN.
He quit ...?
What the...?
What's Hirako doing here?
HE STAGED KEN KANEKI'S EXECUTION TO GAIN OUR TRUST...
HIS REAL OBJECTIVE WAS...
...BRING-ING FORTH THAT THING...
...IN A COVERT UNDER-GROUND OPERA-TION.
AND WE WERE ALL FOOLED BY HIM.
INVESTI-GATOR HIRAKO WAS TOO.
...
I HAD NO IDEA ...!!!
Hirako boy!

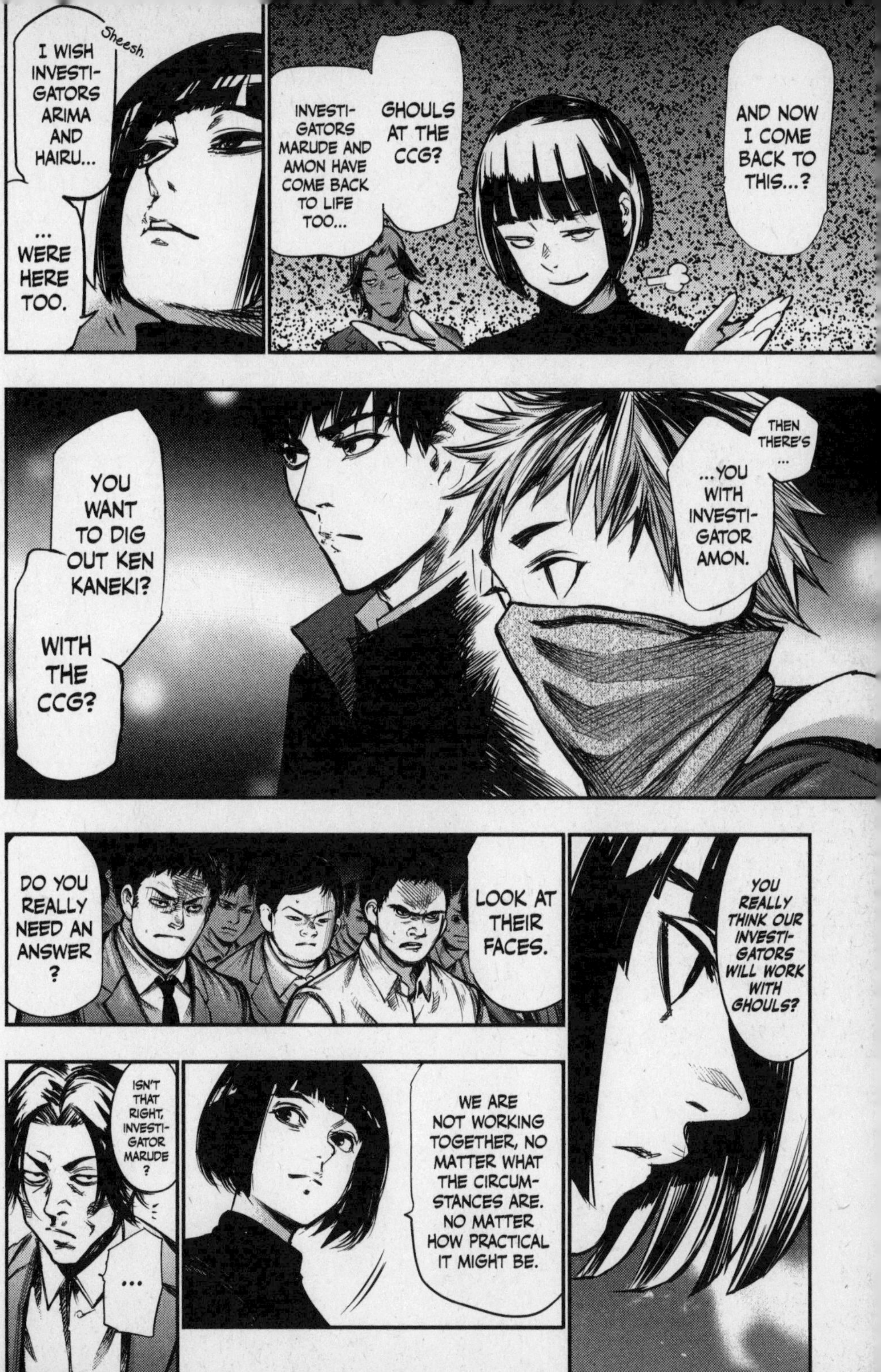
AND NOW I COME BACK TO THIS...?
GHOULS AT THE CCG?
INVESTIGATORS MARUDE AND AMON HAVE COME BACK TO LIFE TOO...
Sheesh.
I WISH INVESTIGATORS ARIMA AND HAIRU...
...WERE HERE TOO.
THEN THERE'S ...
...YOU WITH INVESTIGATOR AMON.
YOU WANT TO DIG OUT KEN KANEKI?
WITH THE CCG?
YOU REALLY THINK OUR INVESTIGATORS WILL WORK WITH GHOULS?
LOOK AT THEIR FACES.
DO YOU REALLY NEED AN ANSWER?
WE ARE NOT WORKING TOGETHER, NO MATTER WHAT THE CIRCUMSTANCES ARE. NO MATTER HOW PRACTICAL IT MIGHT BE.
ISN'T THAT RIGHT, INVESTIGATOR MARUDE?
...

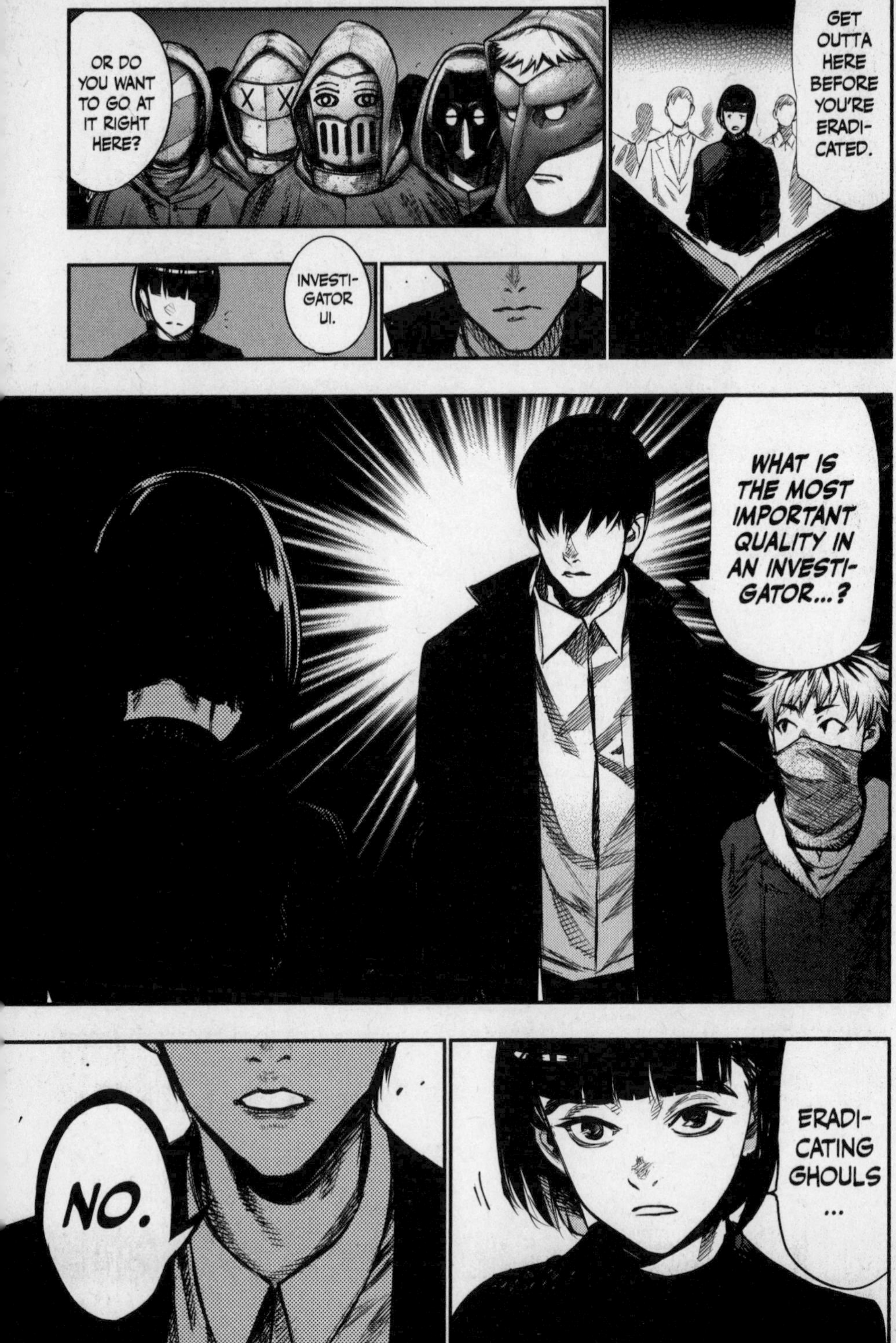
GET OUTTA HERE BEFORE YOU'RE ERADI-CATED.
OR DO YOU WANT TO GO AT IT RIGHT HERE?
INVESTI-GATOR UI.
WHAT IS THE MOST IMPORTANT QUALITY IN AN INVESTI-GATOR...?
ERADI-CATING GHOULS ...
NO.

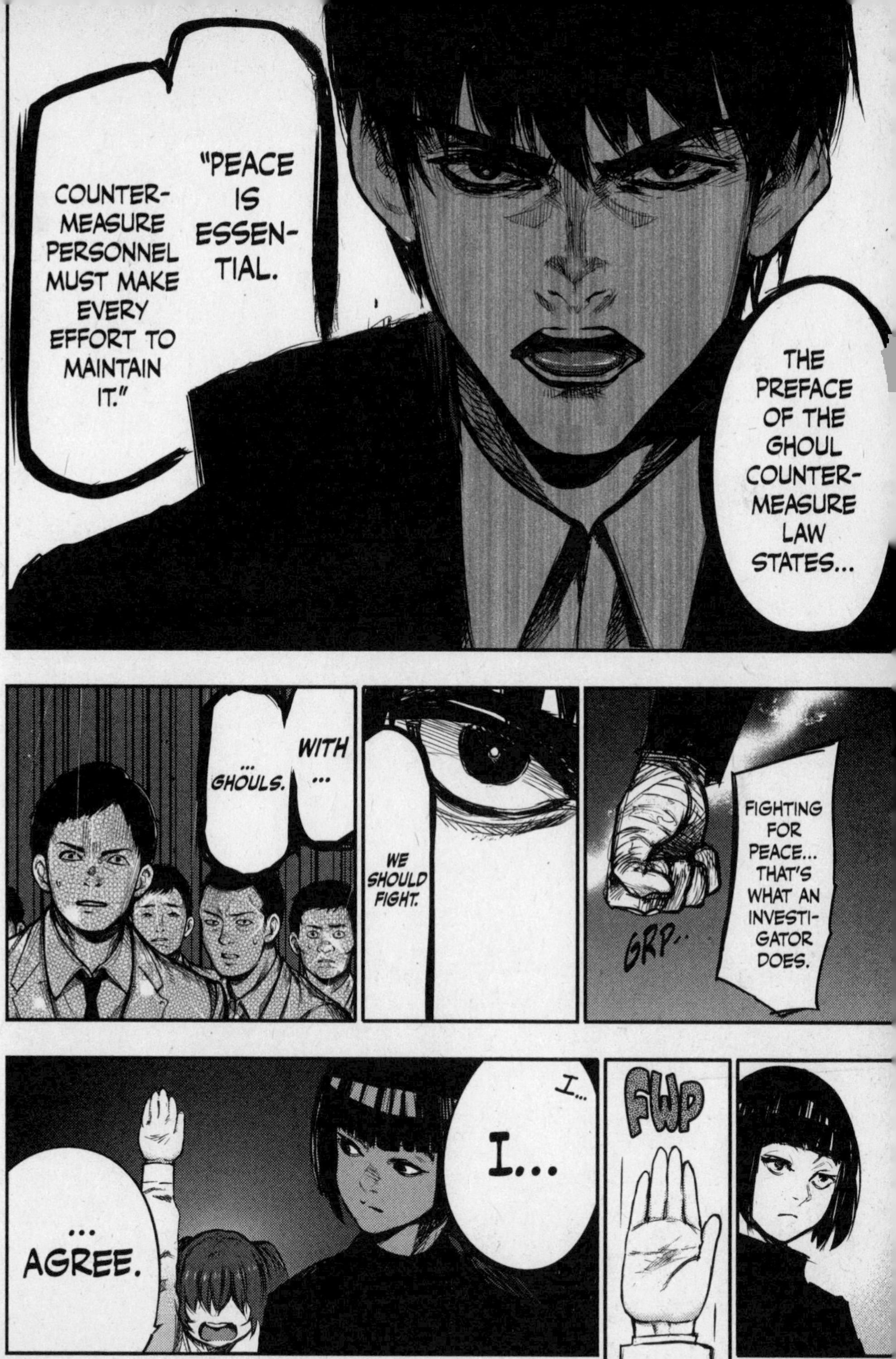
THE PREFACE OF THE GHOUL COUNTER-MEASURE LAW STATES...
"PEACE IS ESSEN-TIAL.
COUNTER-MEASURE PERSONNEL MUST MAKE EVERY EFFORT TO MAINTAIN IT."
FIGHTING FOR PEACE... THAT'S WHAT AN INVESTI-GATOR DOES.
GRP..
WE SHOULD FIGHT.
WITH ...
... GHOULS.
FWP
I...
I...
... AGREE.

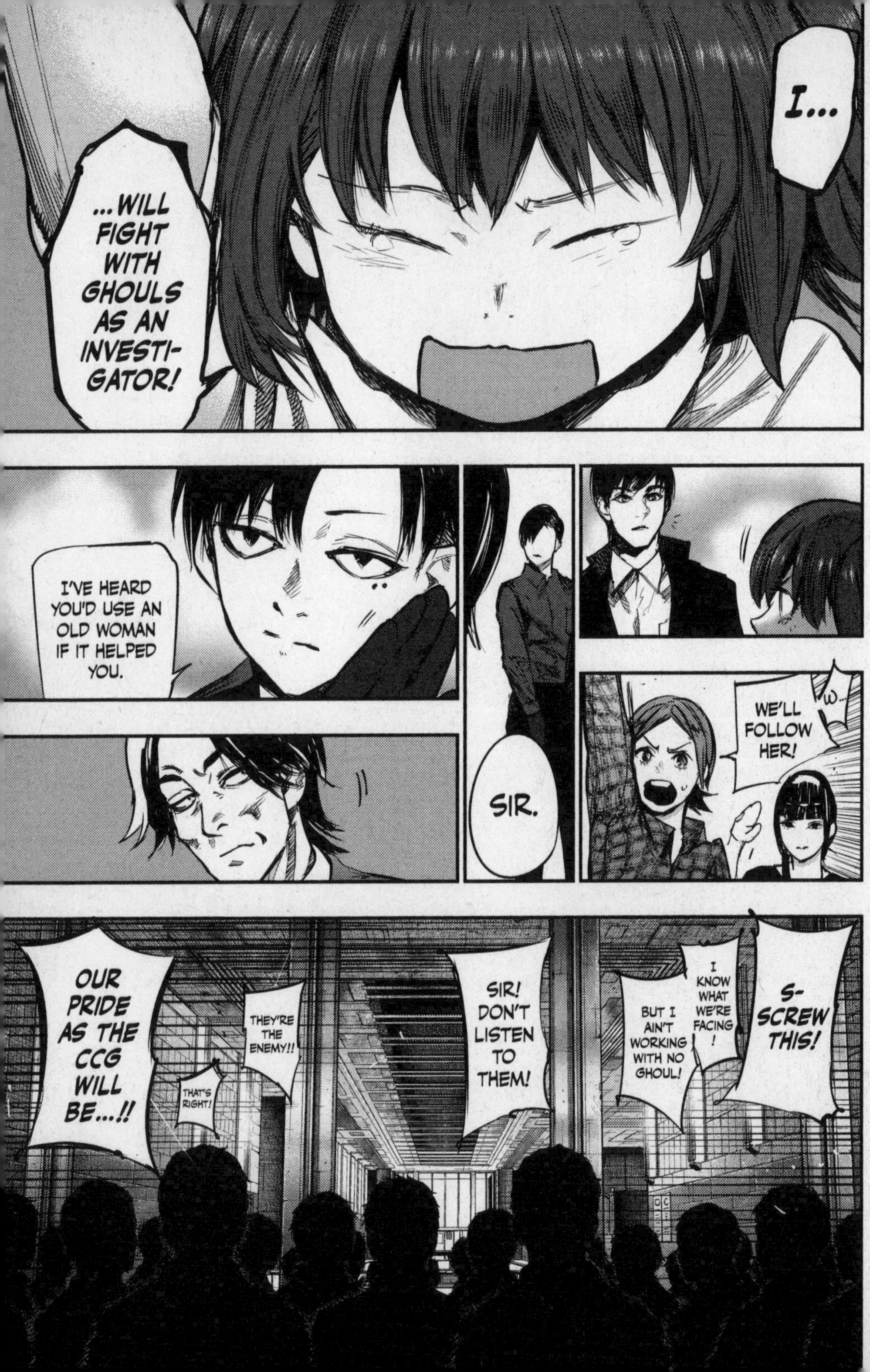
I...
...WILL FIGHT WITH GHOULS AS AN INVESTIGATOR!
W...
WE'LL FOLLOW HER!
SIR.
I'VE HEARD YOU'D USE AN OLD WOMAN IF IT HELPED YOU.
S-SCREW THIS!
I KNOW WHAT WE'RE FACING!
BUT I AIN'T WORKING WITH NO GHOUL!
SIR! DON'T LISTEN TO THEM!
THEY'RE THE ENEMY!!
THAT'S RIGHT!
OUR PRIDE AS THE CCG WILL BE...!!

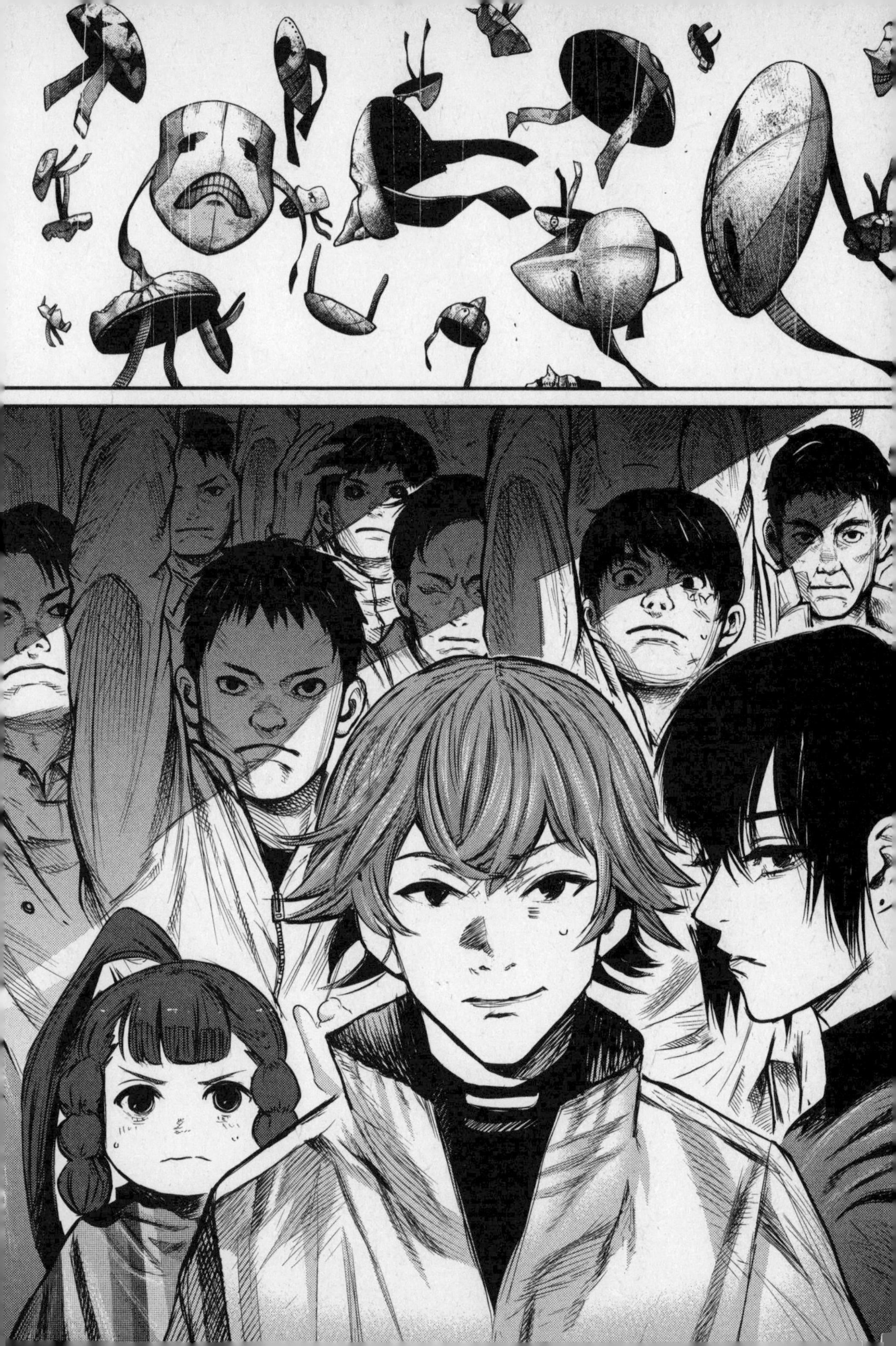

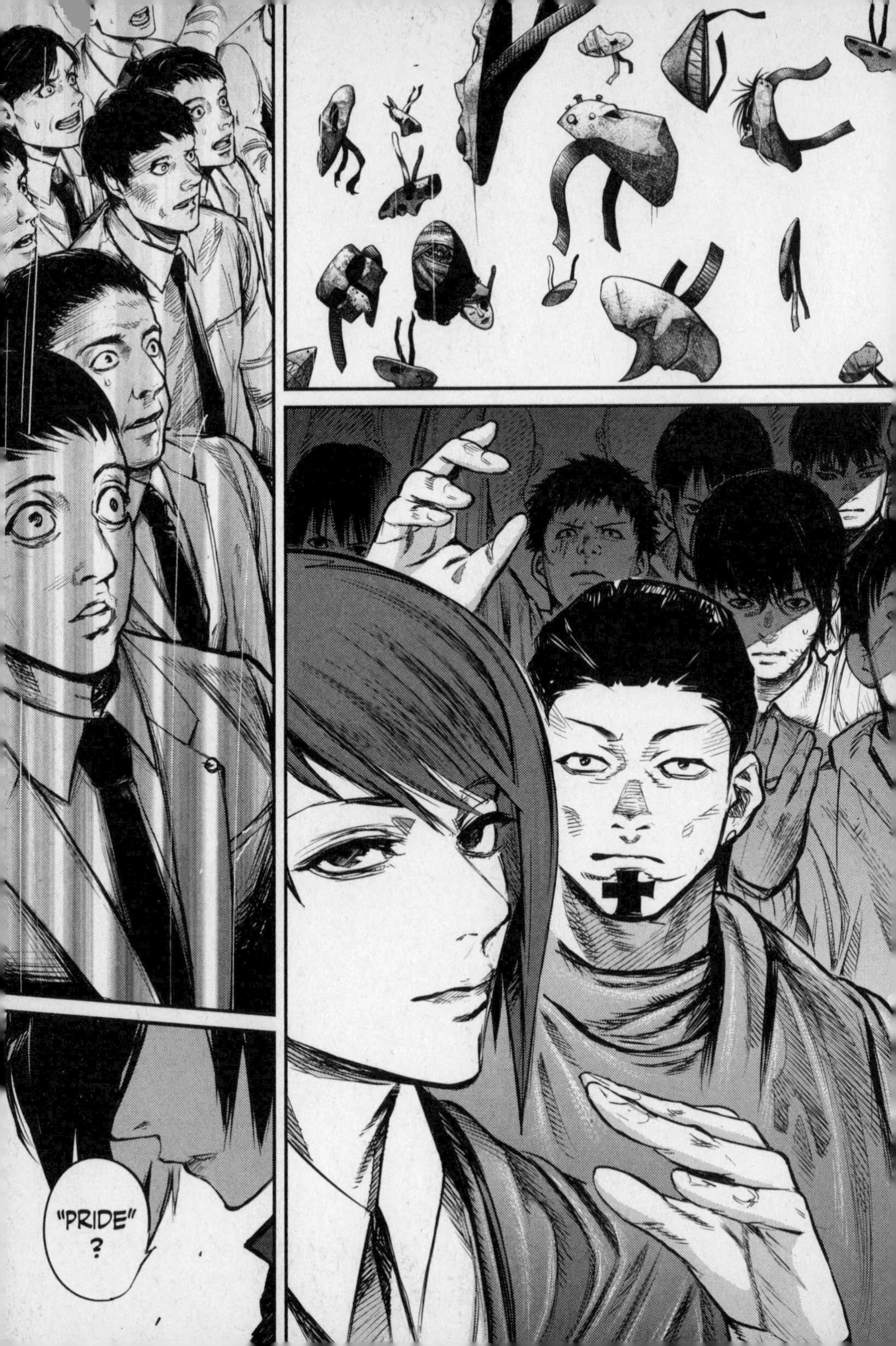
"PRIDE"?

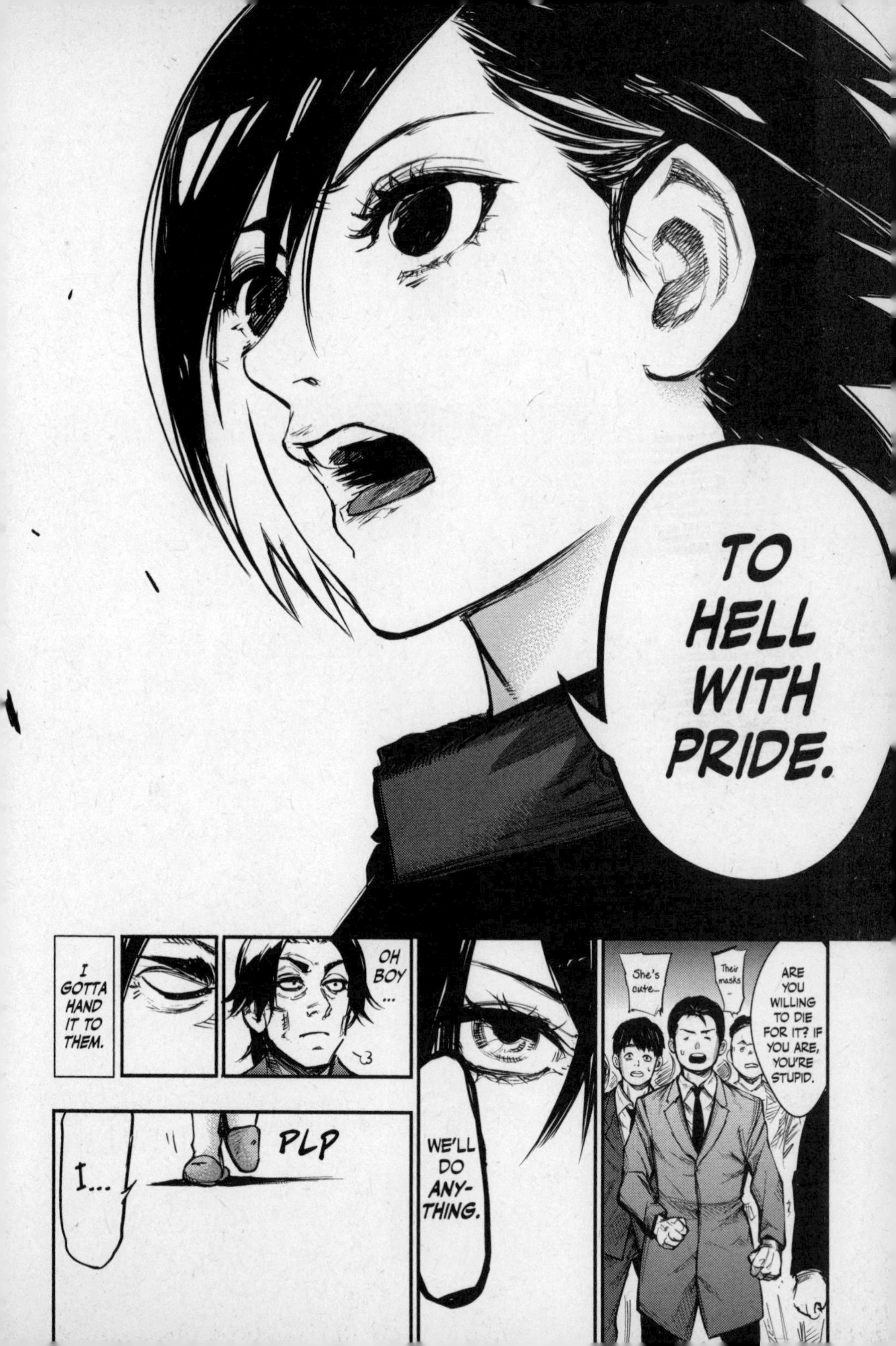
TO HELL WITH PRIDE.
ARE YOU WILLING TO DIE FOR IT? IF YOU ARE, YOU'RE STUPID.
Their masks...
She's cute...
WE'LL DO ANY-THING.
OH BOY...
I GOTTA HAND IT TO THEM.
PLP
I...

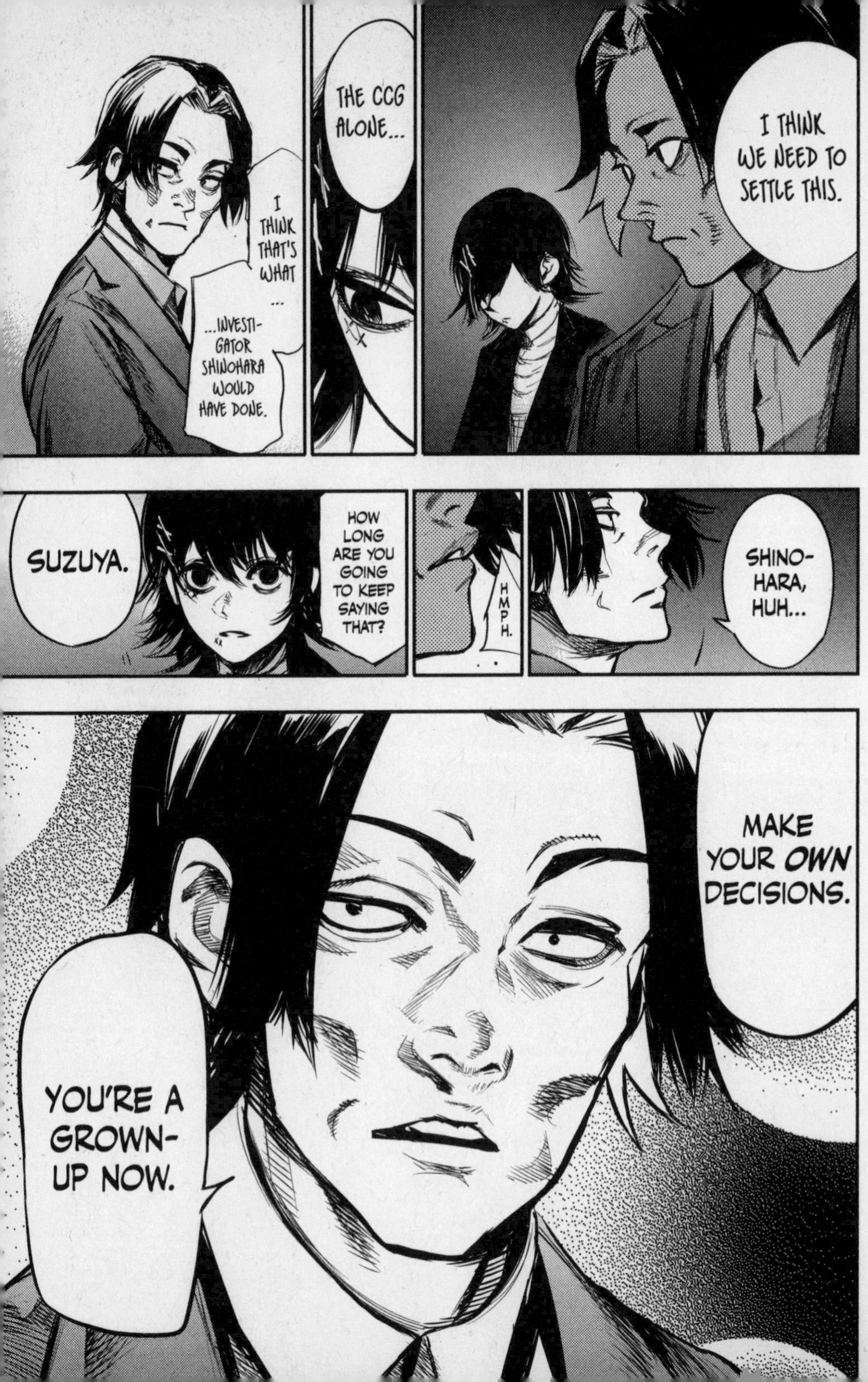
I THINK WE NEED TO SETTLE THIS.
THE CCG ALONE...
I THINK THAT'S WHAT ...
...INVESTIGATOR SHINOHARA WOULD HAVE DONE.
SHINO-HARA, HUH...
HMPH.
HOW LONG ARE YOU GOING TO KEEP SAYING THAT?
SUZUYA.
MAKE YOUR *OWN* DECISIONS.
YOU'RE A GROWN-UP NOW.

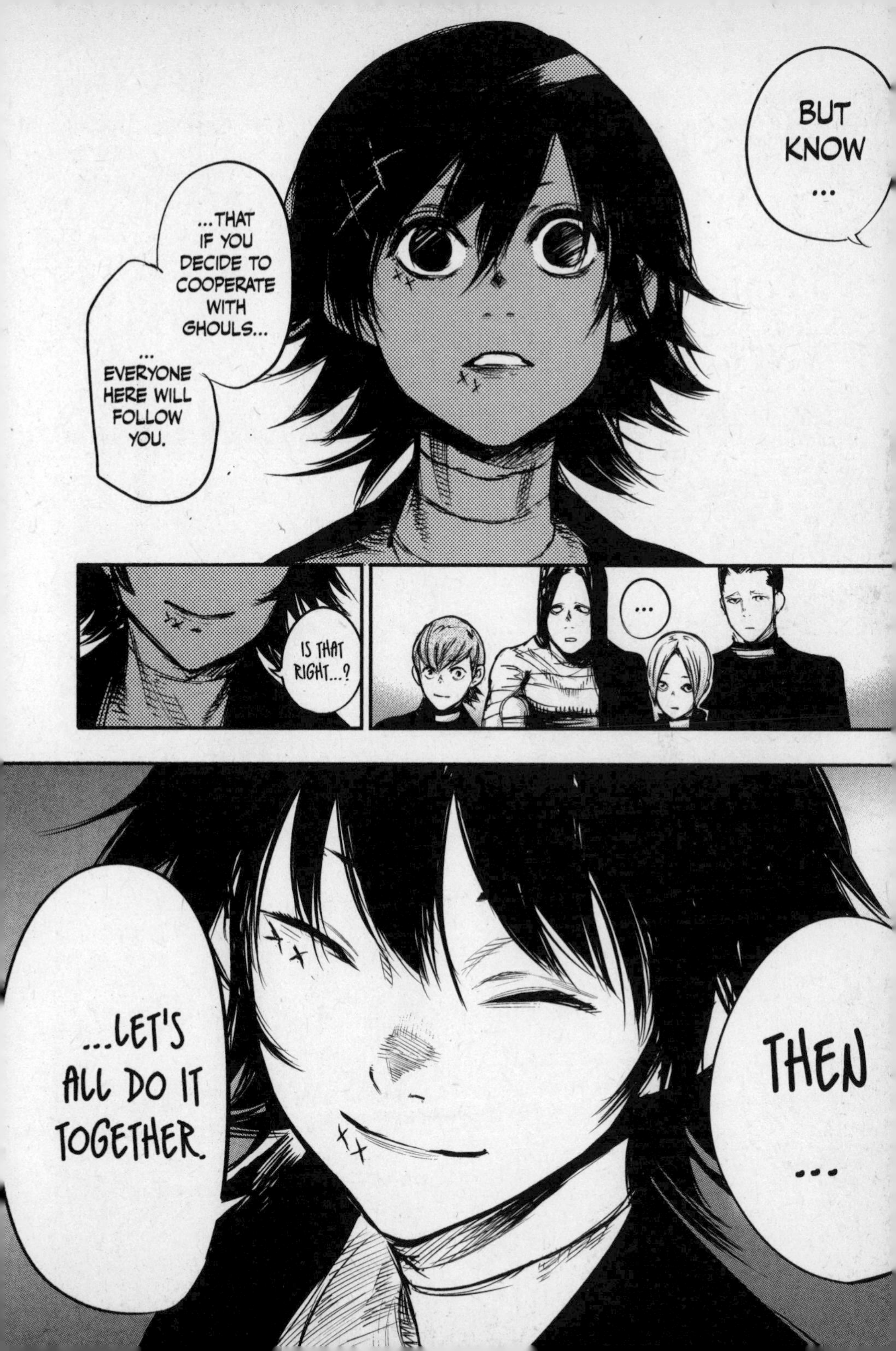
BUT KNOW ...
...THAT IF YOU DECIDE TO COOPERATE WITH GHOULS...
... EVERYONE HERE WILL FOLLOW YOU.
...
IS THAT RIGHT...?
THEN ...
...LET'S ALL DO IT TOGETHER.

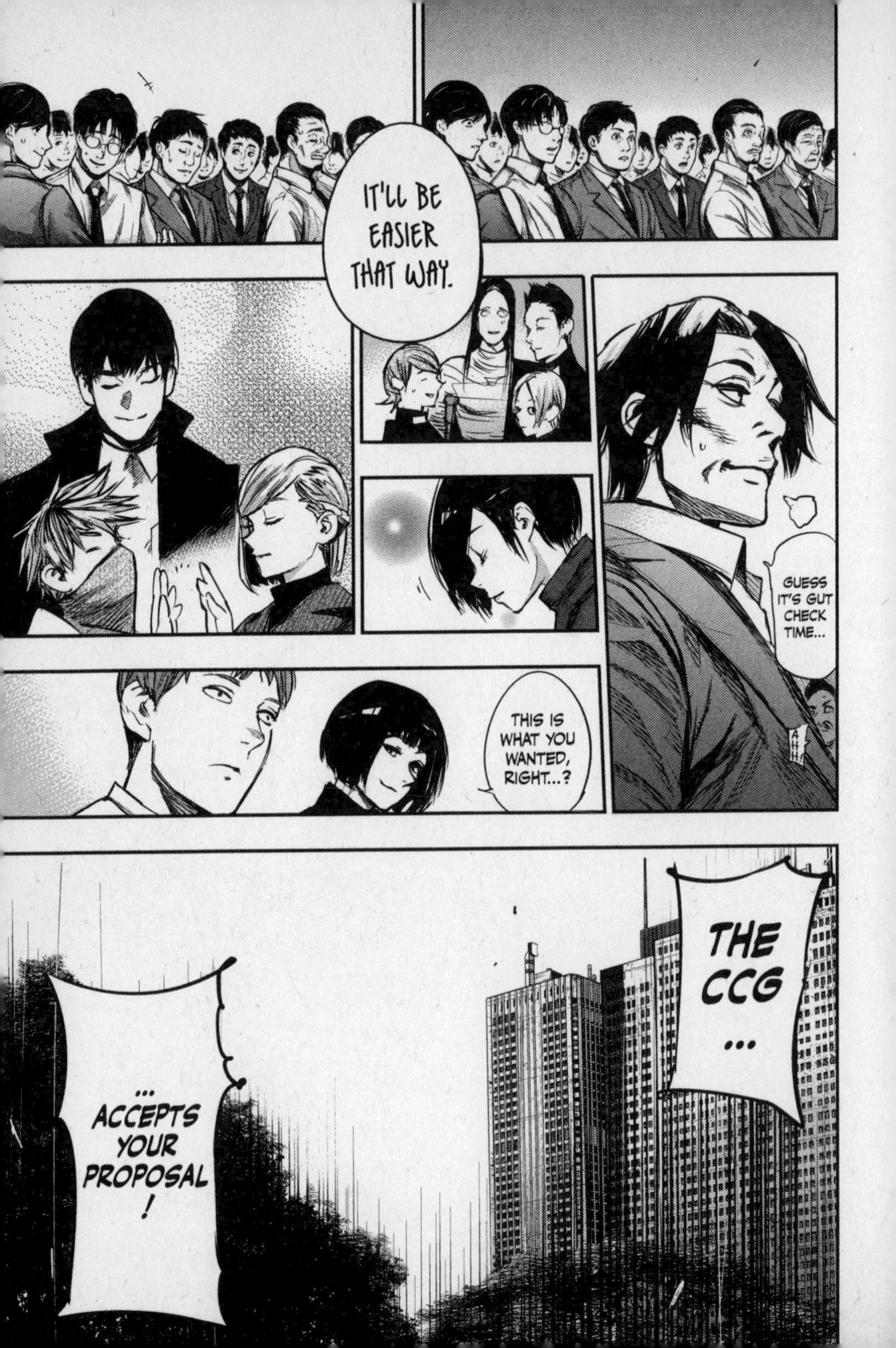
IT'LL BE EASIER THAT WAY.
GUESS IT'S GUT CHECK TIME...
AHH!
THIS IS WHAT YOU WANTED, RIGHT...?
THE CCG ...
... ACCEPTS YOUR PROPOSAL !

TOKYO GHOUL:re

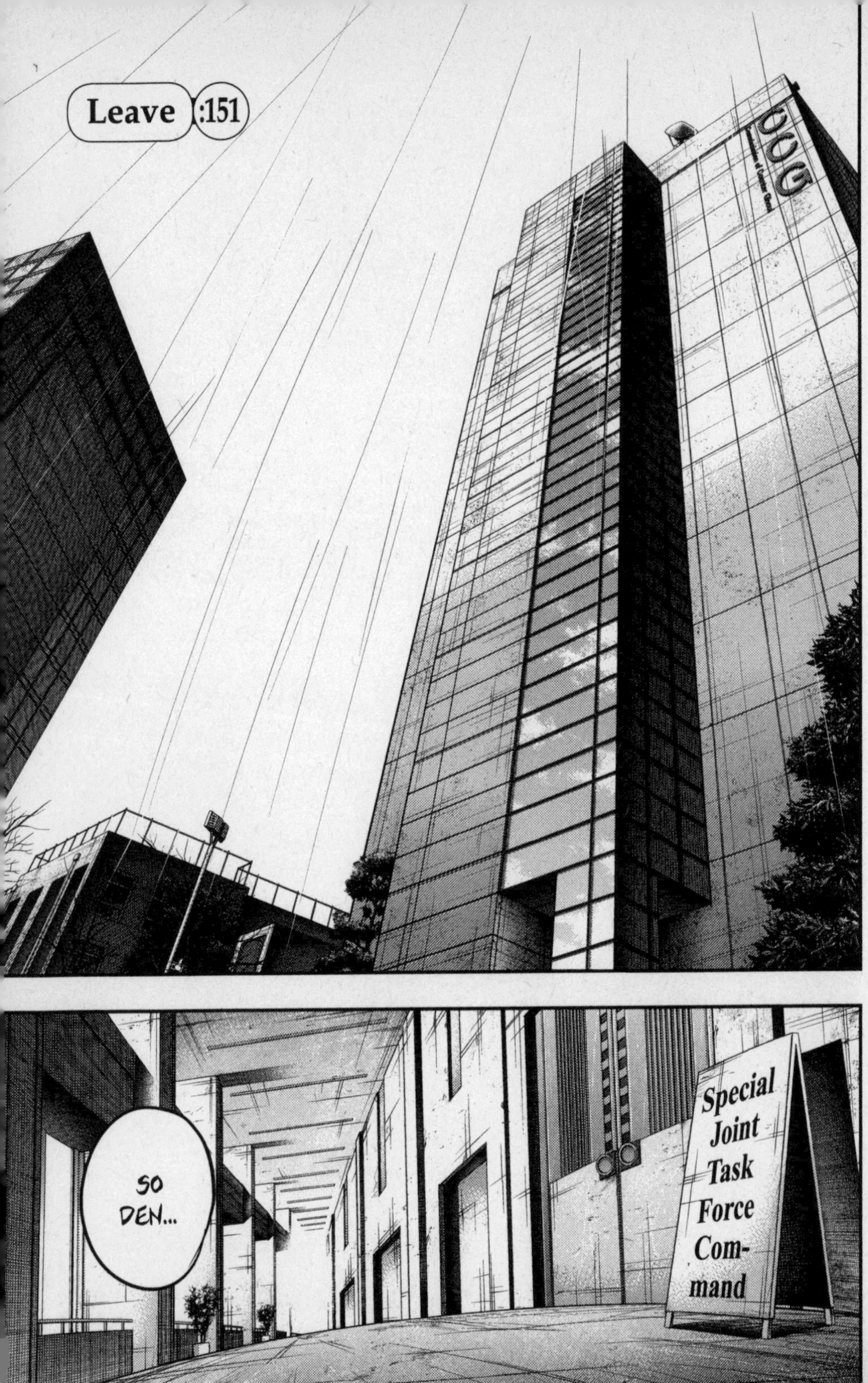
Leave :151
Special Joint Task Force Com-mand
SO DEN...

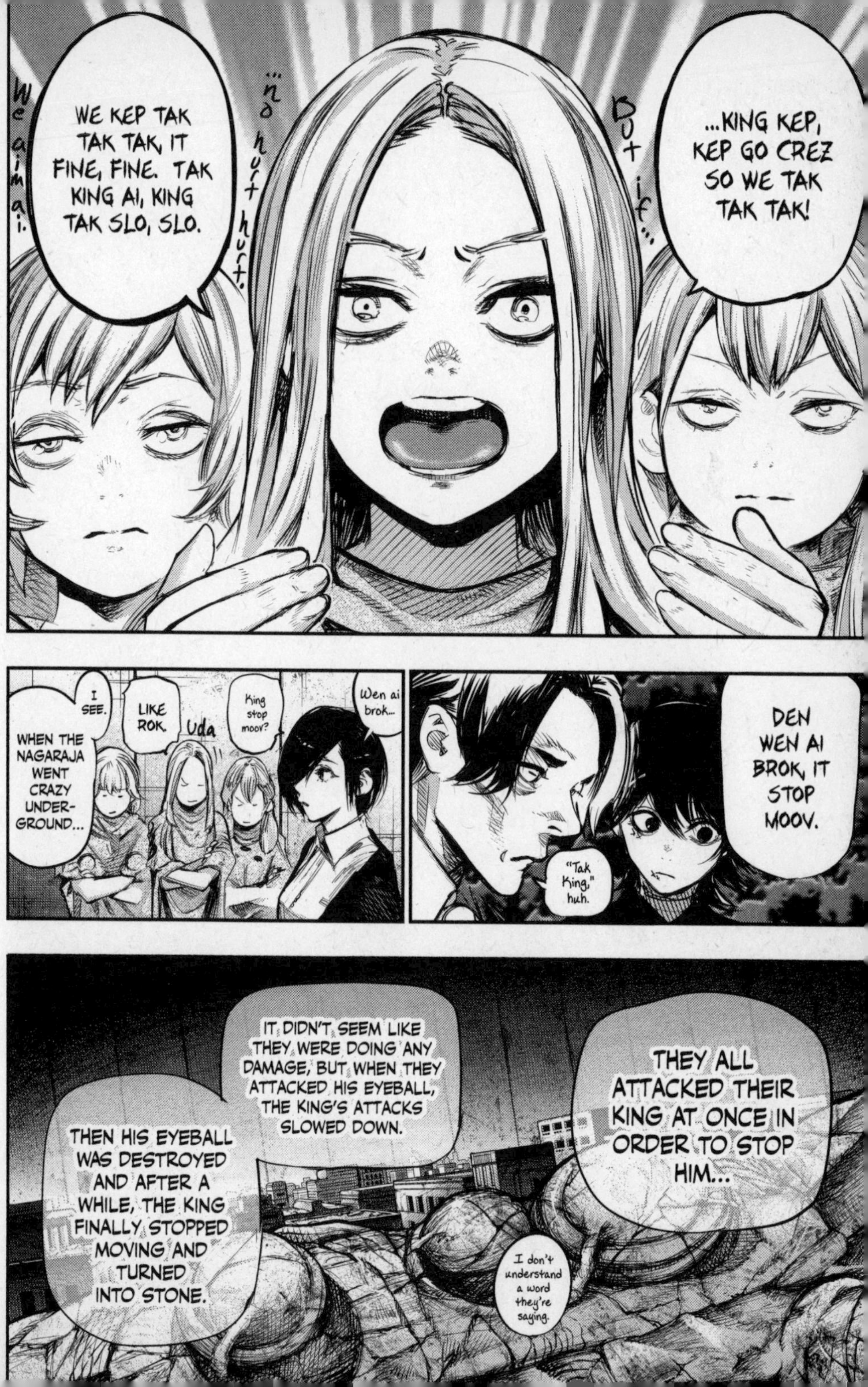
But if...
...KING KEP, KEP GO CREZ SO WE TAK TAK TAK!
...no hurt hurt.
We aimai.
WE KEP TAK TAK TAK, IT FINE, FINE. TAK KING AI, KING TAK SLO, SLO.
DEN WEN AI BROK, IT STOP MOOV.
"Tak King," huh.
Wen ai brok...
King stop moov?
Uda
LIKE ROK.
I SEE.
WHEN THE NAGARAJA WENT CRAZY UNDERGROUND...
THEY ALL ATTACKED THEIR KING AT ONCE IN ORDER TO STOP HIM...
IT DIDN'T SEEM LIKE THEY WERE DOING ANY DAMAGE, BUT WHEN THEY ATTACKED HIS EYEBALL, THE KING'S ATTACKS SLOWED DOWN.
THEN HIS EYEBALL WAS DESTROYED AND AFTER A WHILE, THE KING FINALLY STOPPED MOVING AND TURNED INTO STONE.
I don't understand a word they're saying.

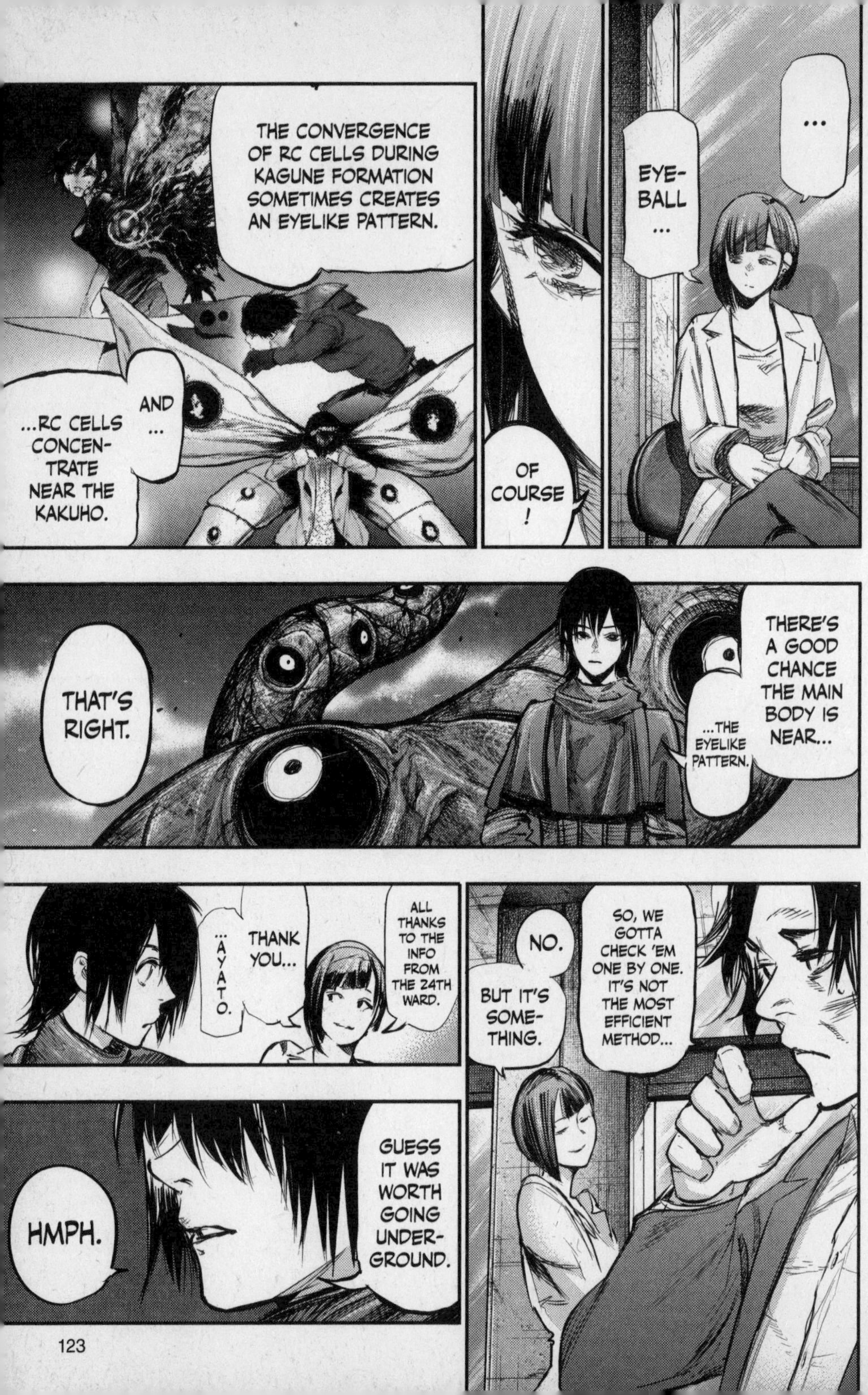
...
EYE-BALL...
OF COURSE!
THE CONVERGENCE OF RC CELLS DURING KAGUNE FORMATION SOMETIMES CREATES AN EYELIKE PATTERN.
AND...
...RC CELLS CONCENTRATE NEAR THE KAKUHO.
THERE'S A GOOD CHANCE THE MAIN BODY IS NEAR...
...THE EYELIKE PATTERN.
THAT'S RIGHT.
SO, WE GOTTA CHECK 'EM ONE BY ONE. IT'S NOT THE MOST EFFICIENT METHOD...
NO.
BUT IT'S SOMETHING.
ALL THANKS TO THE INFO FROM THE 24TH WARD.
THANK YOU...
...AYATO.
GUESS IT WAS WORTH GOING UNDERGROUND.
HMPH.

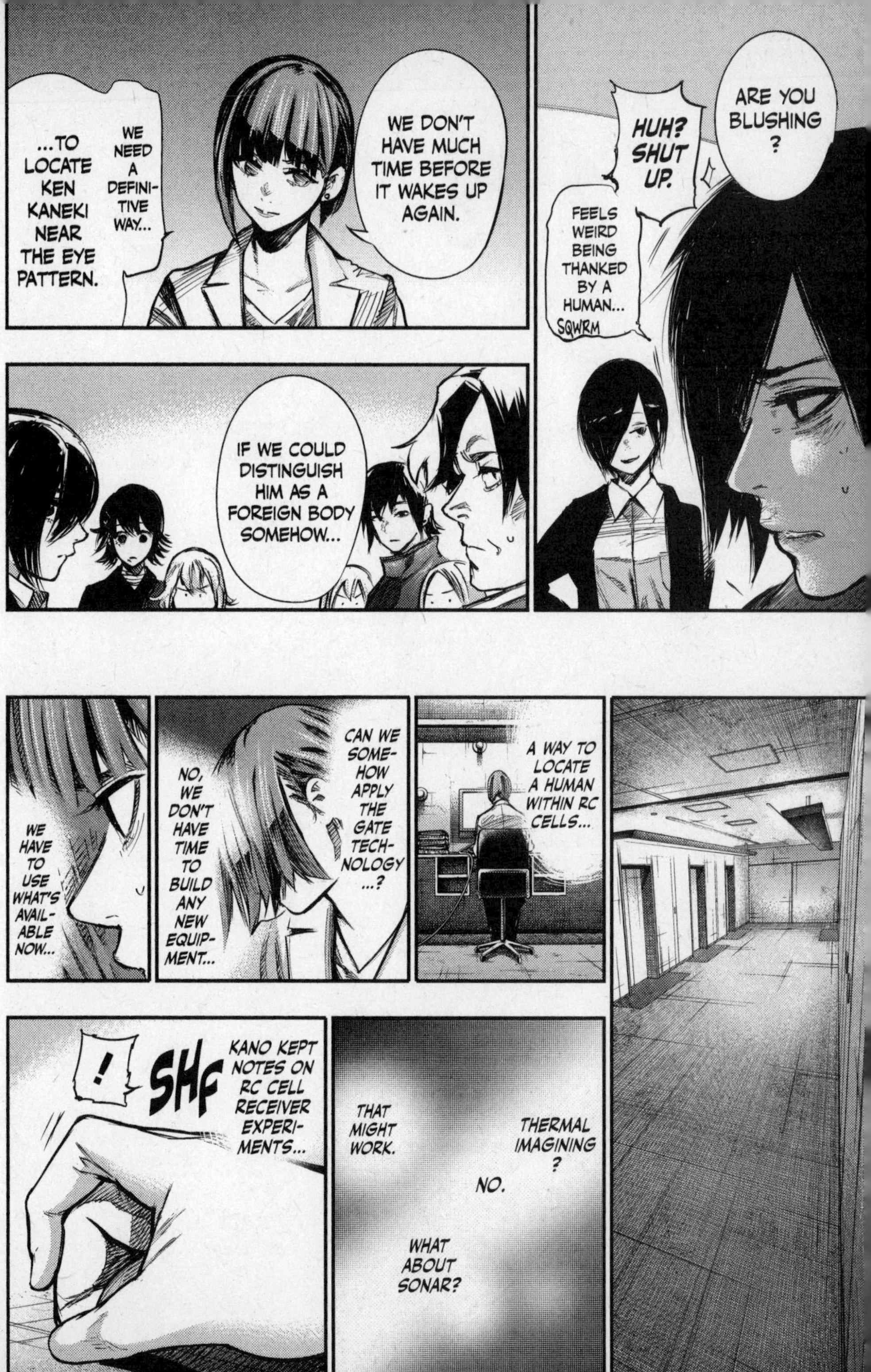
ARE YOU BLUSHING?
HUH? SHUT UP.
FEELS WEIRD BEING THANKED BY A HUMAN...
SQWRM
WE DON'T HAVE MUCH TIME BEFORE IT WAKES UP AGAIN.
WE NEED A DEFINITIVE WAY...
...TO LOCATE KEN KANEKI NEAR THE EYE PATTERN.
IF WE COULD DISTINGUISH HIM AS A FOREIGN BODY SOMEHOW...
A WAY TO LOCATE A HUMAN WITHIN RC CELLS...
CAN WE SOMEHOW APPLY THE GATE TECHNOLOGY...?
NO, WE DON'T HAVE TIME TO BUILD ANY NEW EQUIPMENT...
WE HAVE TO USE WHAT'S AVAILABLE NOW...
THERMAL IMAGINING?
NO.
WHAT ABOUT SONAR?
THAT MIGHT WORK.
!
SHF
KANO KEPT NOTES ON RC CELL RECEIVER EXPERIMENTS...

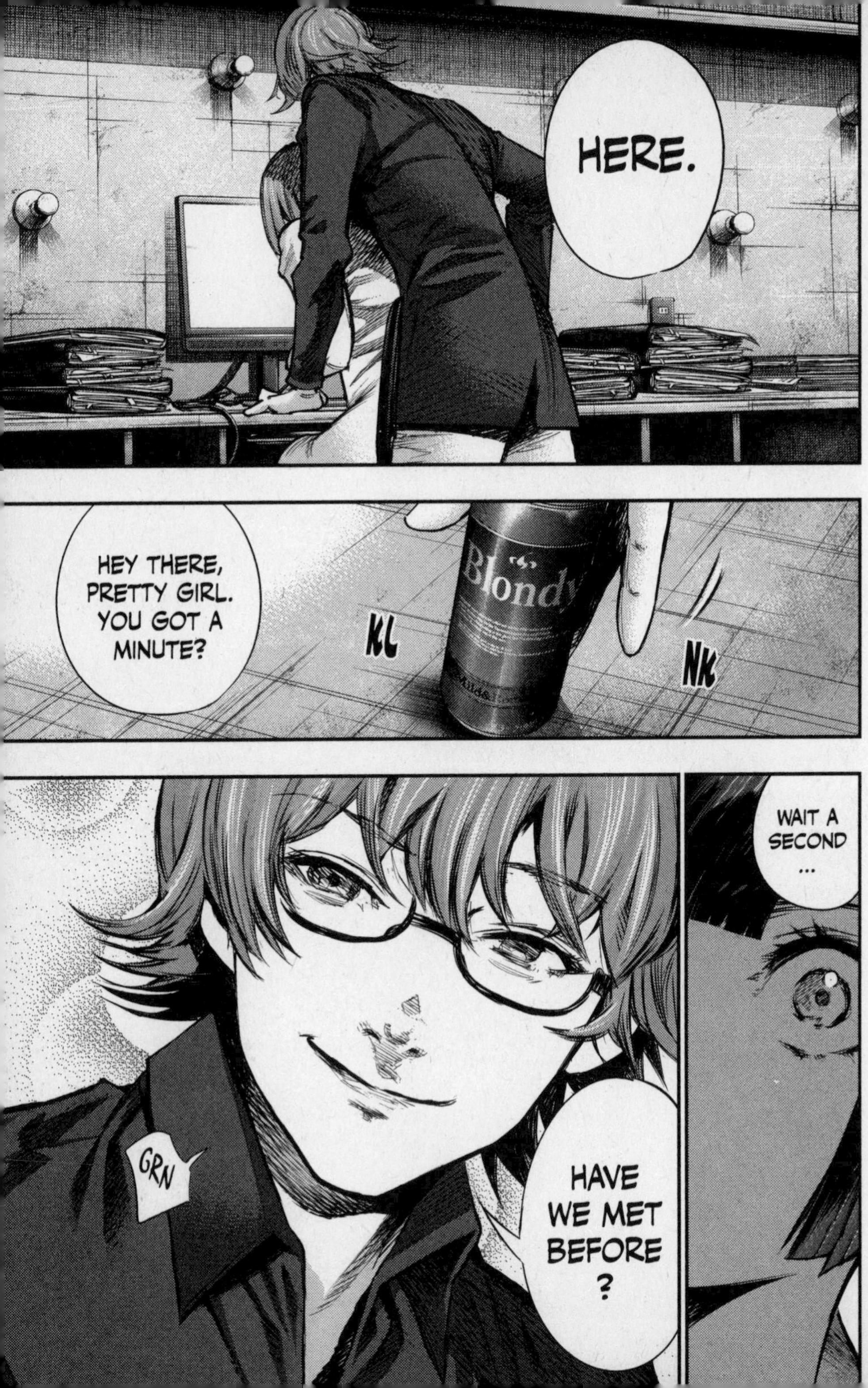
HERE.
HEY THERE, PRETTY GIRL. YOU GOT A MINUTE?
Blondy
KL
NK
WAIT A SECOND ...
GRN
HAVE WE MET BEFORE ?

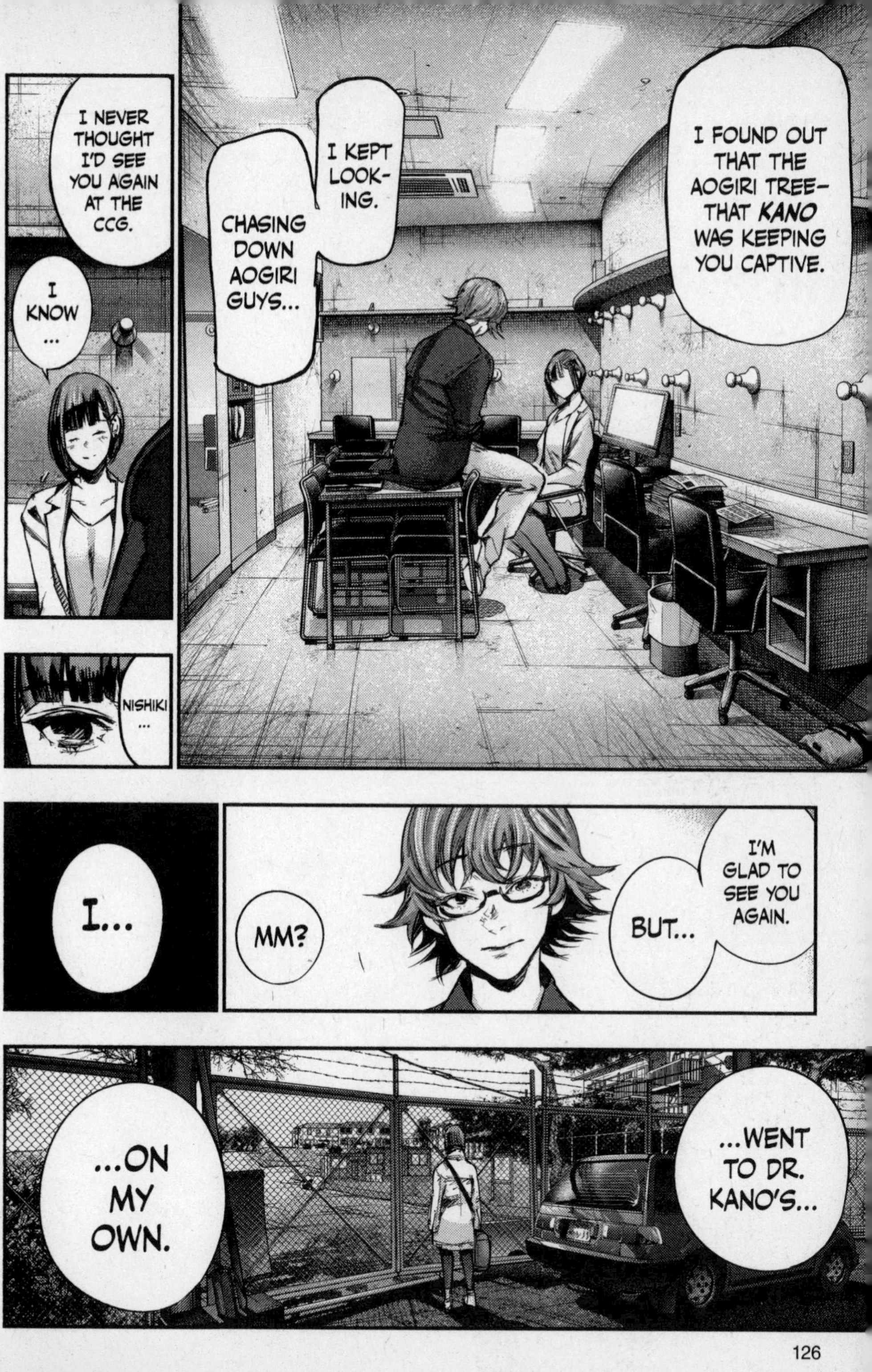
I FOUND OUT THAT THE AOGIRI TREE— THAT *KANO* WAS KEEPING YOU CAPTIVE.
I KEPT LOOKING.
CHASING DOWN AOGIRI GUYS...
I NEVER THOUGHT I'D SEE YOU AGAIN AT THE CCG.
I KNOW...
NISHIKI...
I'M GLAD TO SEE YOU AGAIN.
BUT...
MM?
I...
...WENT TO DR. KANO'S...
...ON MY OWN.

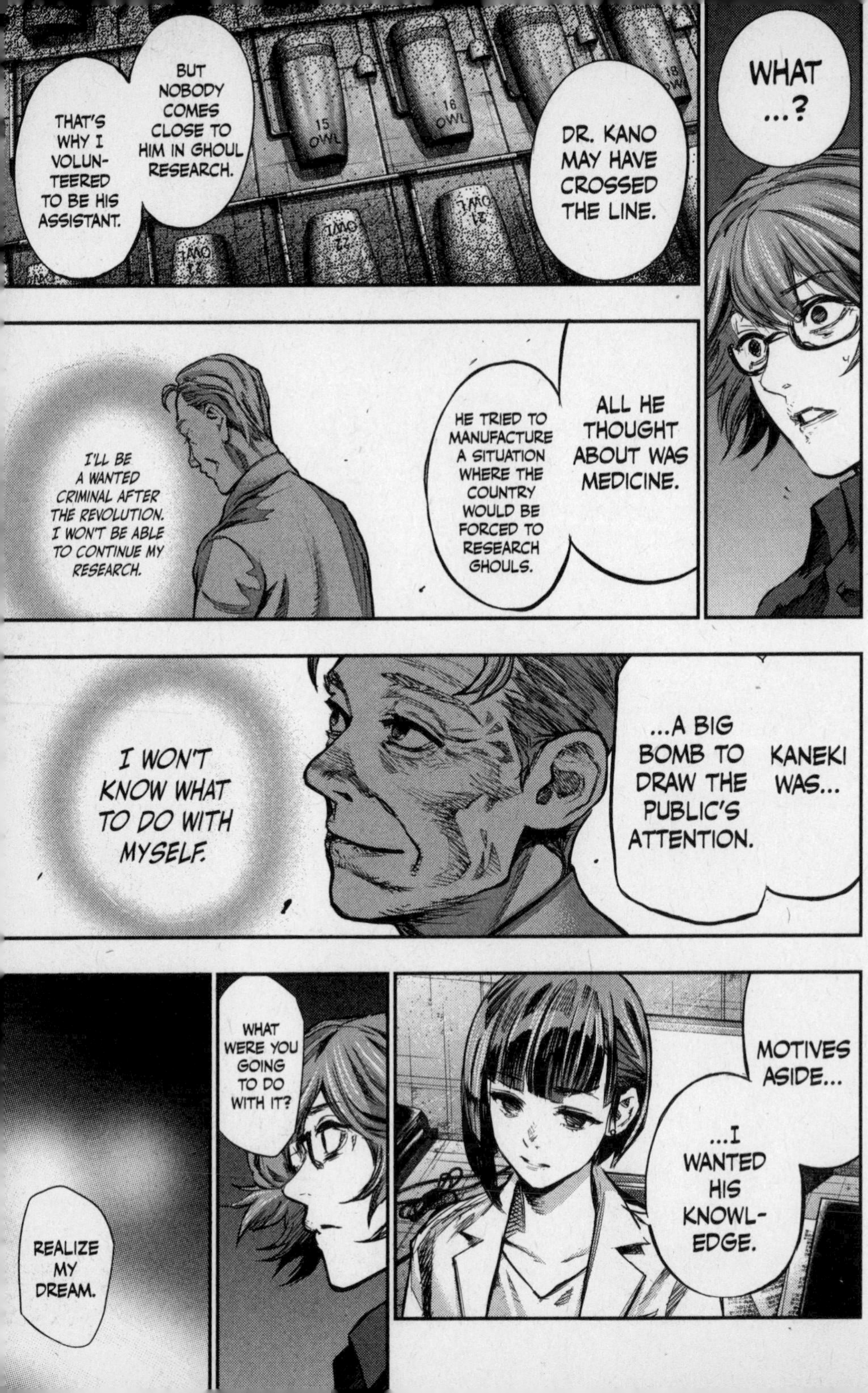
DR. KANO MAY HAVE CROSSED THE LINE.
BUT NOBODY COMES CLOSE TO HIM IN GHOUL RESEARCH.
THAT'S WHY I VOLUNTEERED TO BE HIS ASSISTANT.
WHAT ...?
ALL HE THOUGHT ABOUT WAS MEDICINE.
HE TRIED TO MANUFACTURE A SITUATION WHERE THE COUNTRY WOULD BE FORCED TO RESEARCH GHOULS.
I'LL BE A WANTED CRIMINAL AFTER THE REVOLUTION. I WON'T BE ABLE TO CONTINUE MY RESEARCH.
KANEKI WAS...
...A BIG BOMB TO DRAW THE PUBLIC'S ATTENTION.
I WON'T KNOW WHAT TO DO WITH MYSELF.
MOTIVES ASIDE...
...I WANTED HIS KNOWLEDGE.
WHAT WERE YOU GOING TO DO WITH IT?
REALIZE MY DREAM.

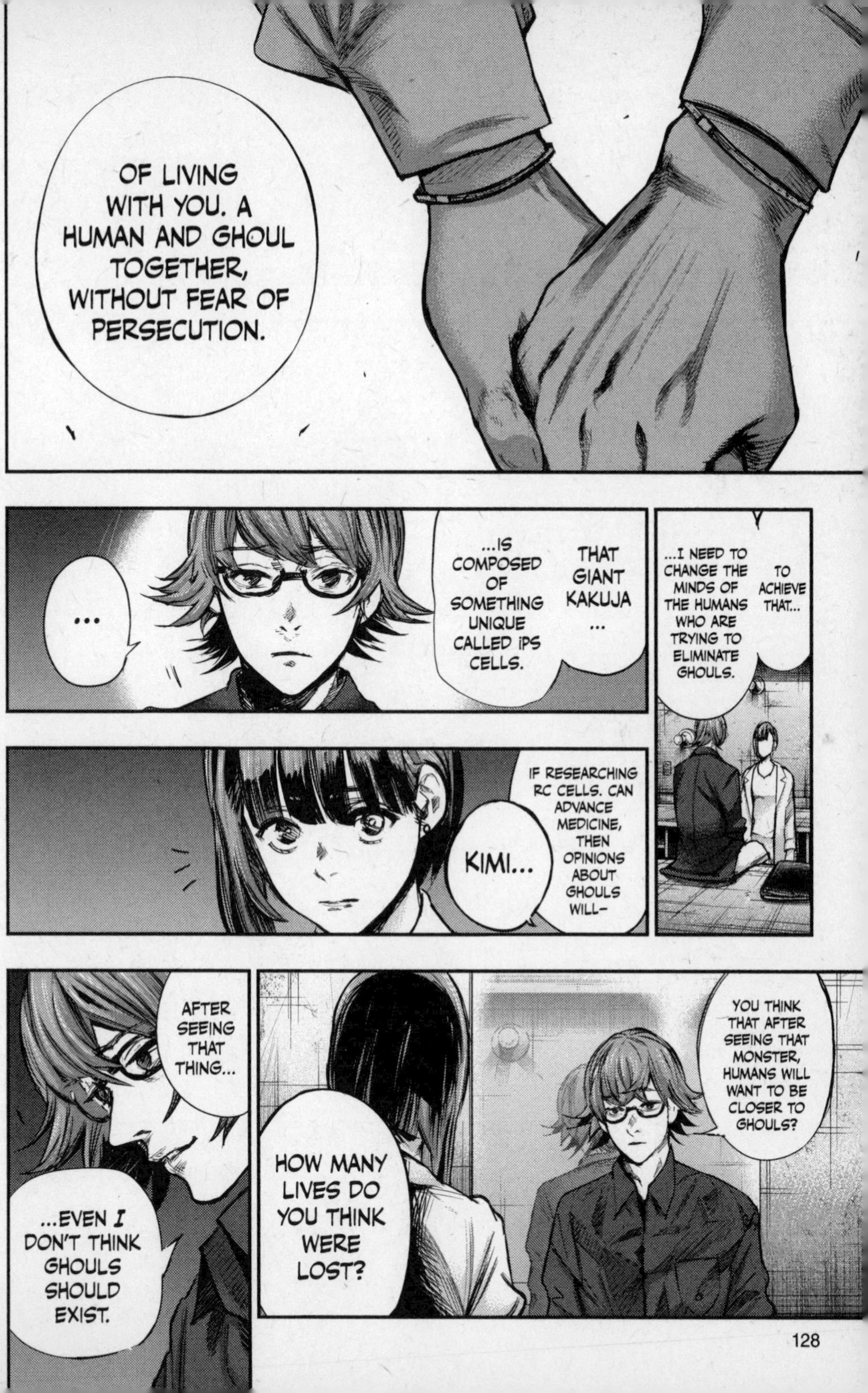
OF LIVING WITH YOU. A HUMAN AND GHOUL TOGETHER, WITHOUT FEAR OF PERSECUTION.
TO ACHIEVE THAT...
...I NEED TO CHANGE THE MINDS OF THE HUMANS WHO ARE TRYING TO ELIMINATE GHOULS.
THAT GIANT KAKUJA...
...IS COMPOSED OF SOMETHING UNIQUE CALLED iPS CELLS.
...
IF RESEARCHING RC CELLS. CAN ADVANCE MEDICINE, THEN OPINIONS ABOUT GHOULS WILL–
KIMI...
YOU THINK THAT AFTER SEEING THAT MONSTER, HUMANS WILL WANT TO BE CLOSER TO GHOULS?
HOW MANY LIVES DO YOU THINK WERE LOST?
AFTER SEEING THAT THING...
...EVEN *I* DON'T THINK GHOULS SHOULD EXIST.

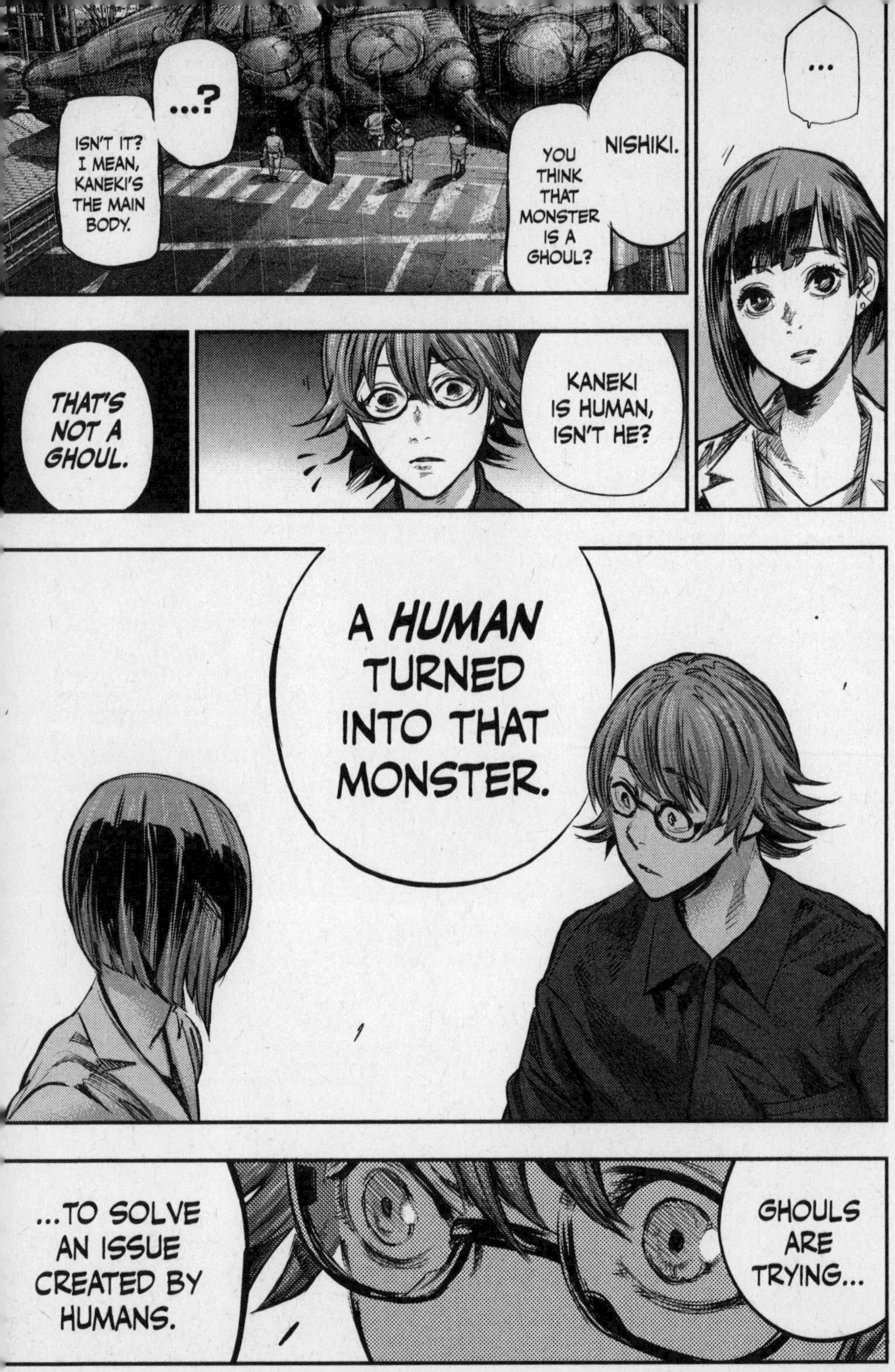
...
NISHIKI.
YOU THINK THAT MONSTER IS A GHOUL?
...?
ISN'T IT? I MEAN, KANEKI'S THE MAIN BODY.
KANEKI IS HUMAN, ISN'T HE?
THAT'S NOT A GHOUL.
A HUMAN TURNED INTO THAT MONSTER.
GHOULS ARE TRYING...
...TO SOLVE AN ISSUE CREATED BY HUMANS.

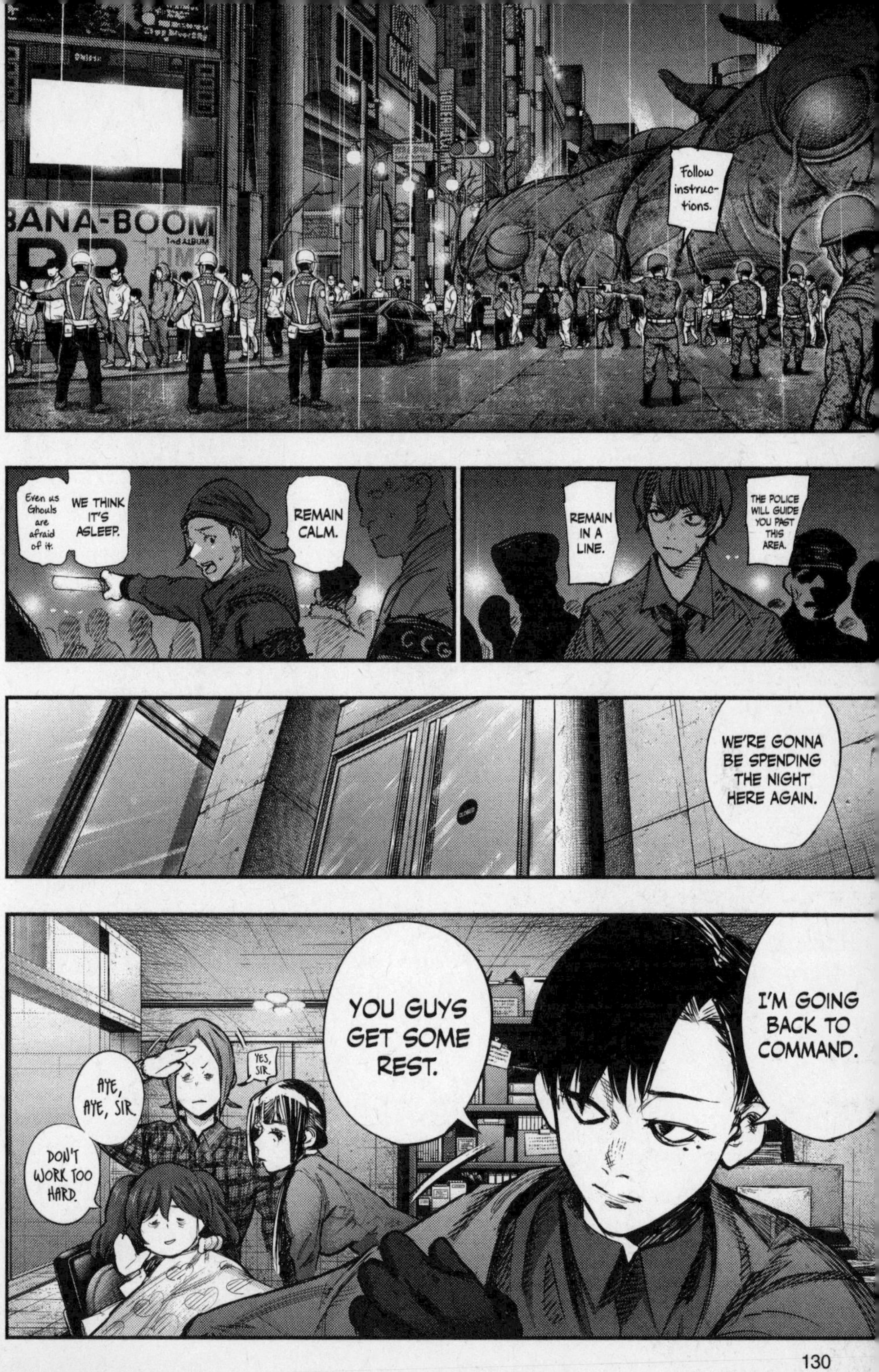
BANA-BOOM
Follow instructions.
THE POLICE WILL GUIDE YOU PAST THIS AREA.
REMAIN IN A LINE.
REMAIN CALM.
WE THINK IT'S ASLEEP.
Even us Ghouls are afraid of it.
WE'RE GONNA BE SPENDING THE NIGHT HERE AGAIN.
I'M GOING BACK TO COMMAND.
YOU GUYS GET SOME REST.
YES, SIR.
AYE, AYE, SIR.
DON'T WORK TOO HARD.

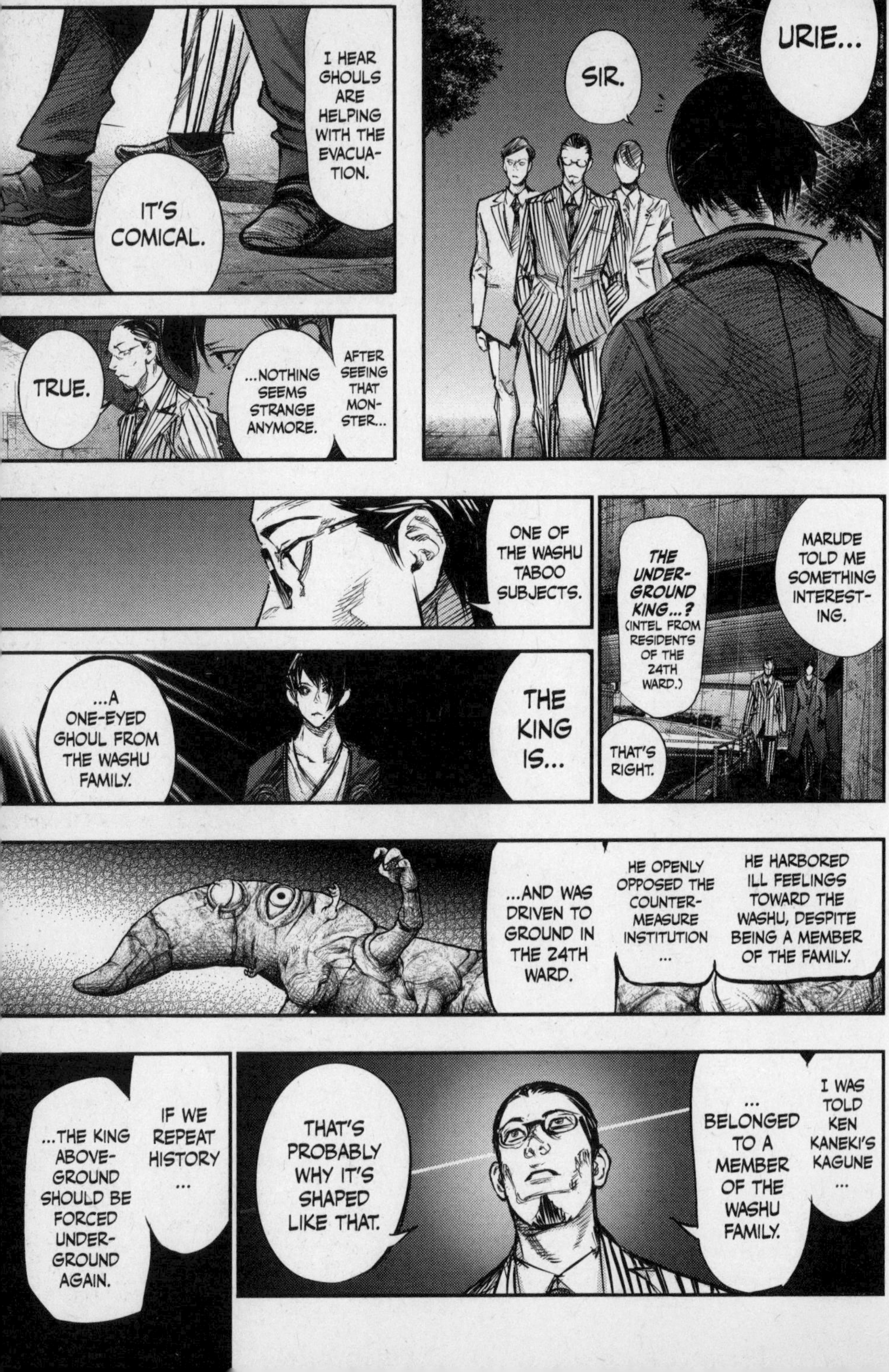
URIE...
SIR.
I HEAR GHOULS ARE HELPING WITH THE EVACUATION.
IT'S COMICAL.
AFTER SEEING THAT MONSTER...
...NOTHING SEEMS STRANGE ANYMORE.
TRUE.
MARUDE TOLD ME SOMETHING INTERESTING.
THE UNDERGROUND KING...? (INTEL FROM RESIDENTS OF THE 24TH WARD.)
THAT'S RIGHT.
ONE OF THE WASHU TABOO SUBJECTS.
THE KING IS...
...A ONE-EYED GHOUL FROM THE WASHU FAMILY.
HE HARBORED ILL FEELINGS TOWARD THE WASHU, DESPITE BEING A MEMBER OF THE FAMILY.
HE OPENLY OPPOSED THE COUNTERMEASURE INSTITUTION...
...AND WAS DRIVEN TO GROUND IN THE 24TH WARD.
I WAS TOLD KEN KANEKI'S KAGUNE...
...BELONGED TO A MEMBER OF THE WASHU FAMILY.
THAT'S PROBABLY WHY IT'S SHAPED LIKE THAT.
IF WE REPEAT HISTORY...
...THE KING ABOVEGROUND SHOULD BE FORCED UNDERGROUND AGAIN.

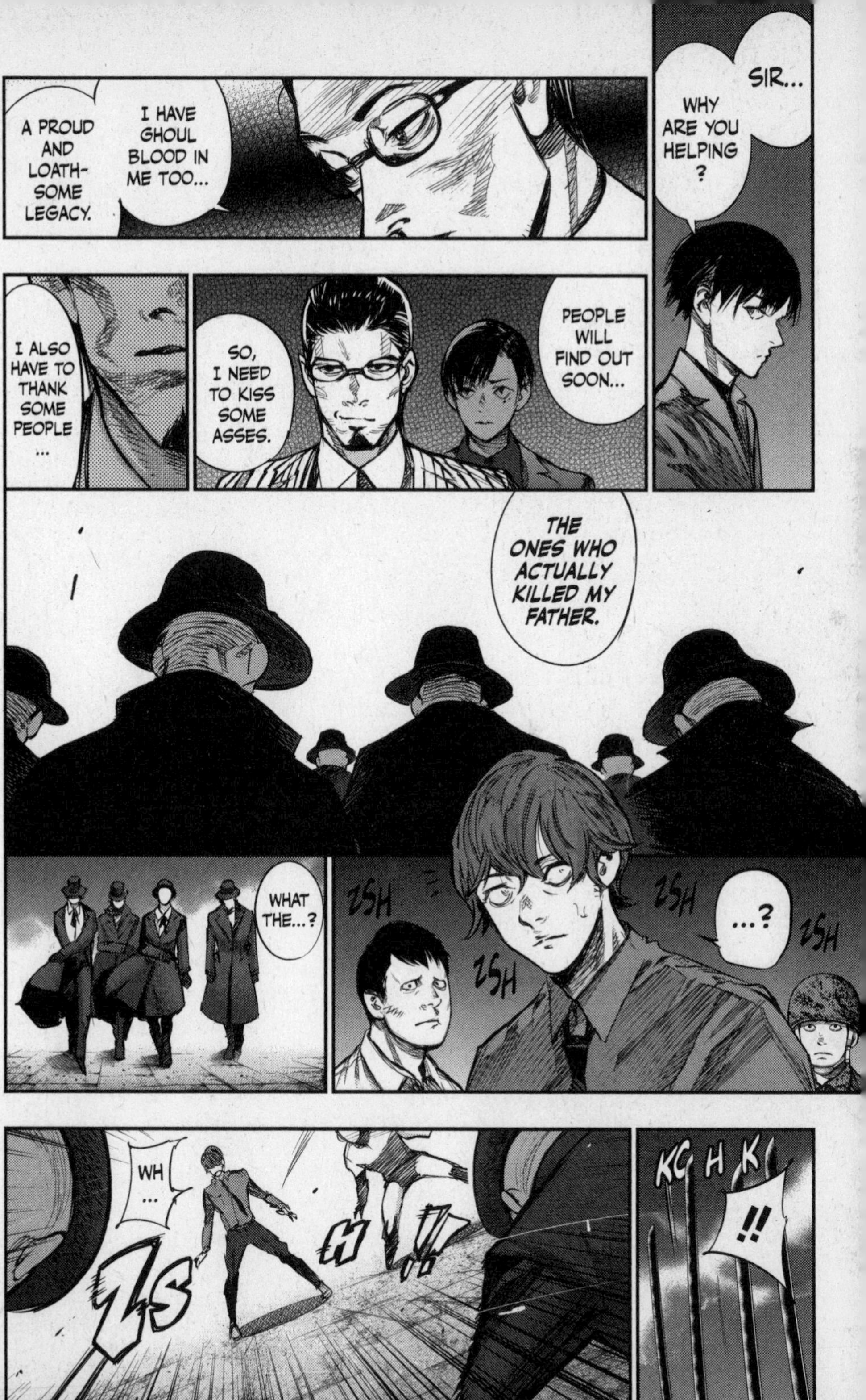
SIR...
WHY ARE YOU HELPING?
I HAVE GHOUL BLOOD IN ME TOO...
A PROUD AND LOATH-SOME LEGACY.
PEOPLE WILL FIND OUT SOON...
SO, I NEED TO KISS SOME ASSES.
I ALSO HAVE TO THANK SOME PEOPLE...
THE ONES WHO ACTUALLY KILLED MY FATHER.
ZSH
...?
ZSH
ZSH
ZSH
WHAT THE...?
KCHK
!!
WH...
ZS

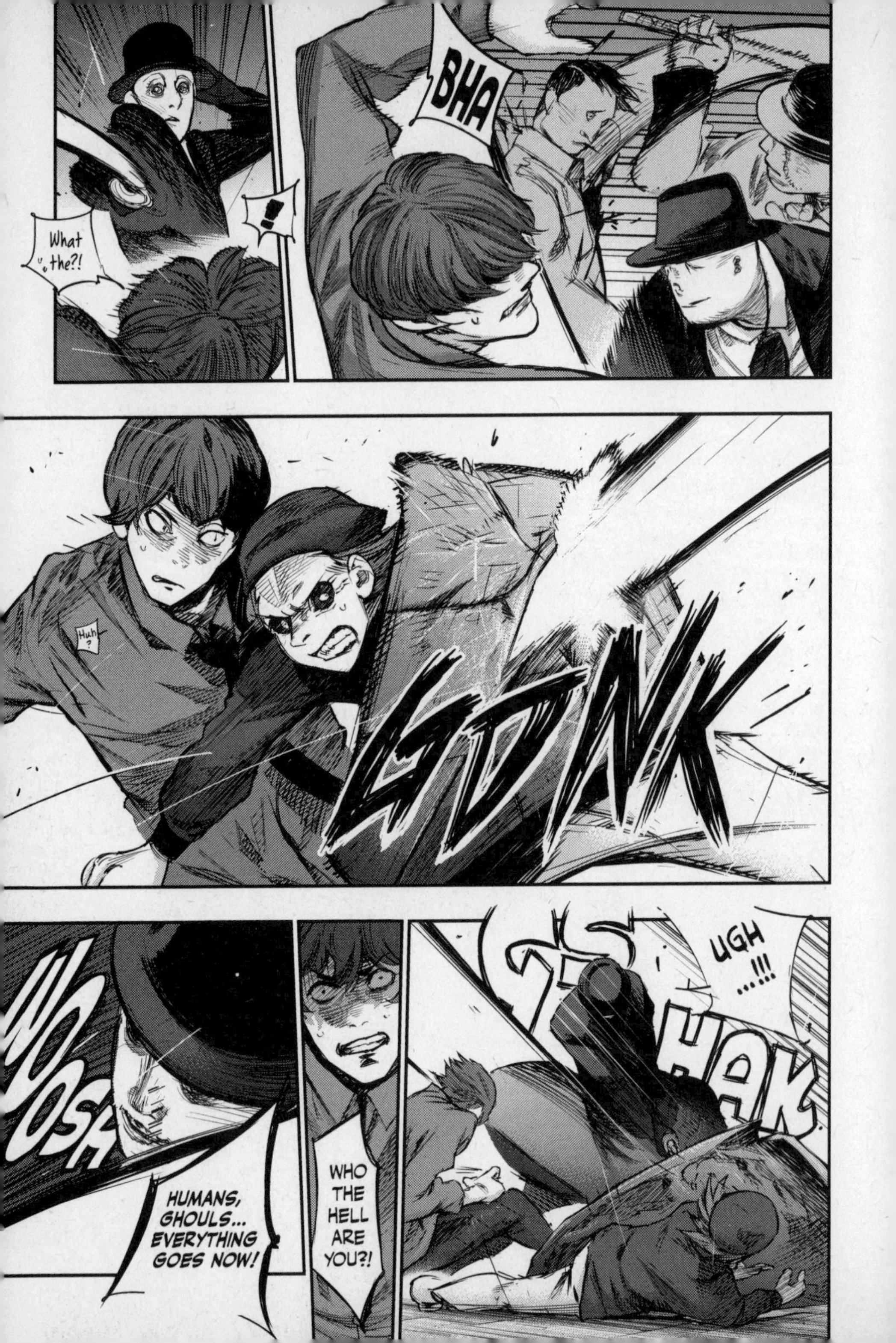
BHA
!
What the?!
Huh?
GDINK
UGH ...!!!
WHO THE HELL ARE YOU?!
HUMANS, GHOULS... EVERYTHING GOES NOW!

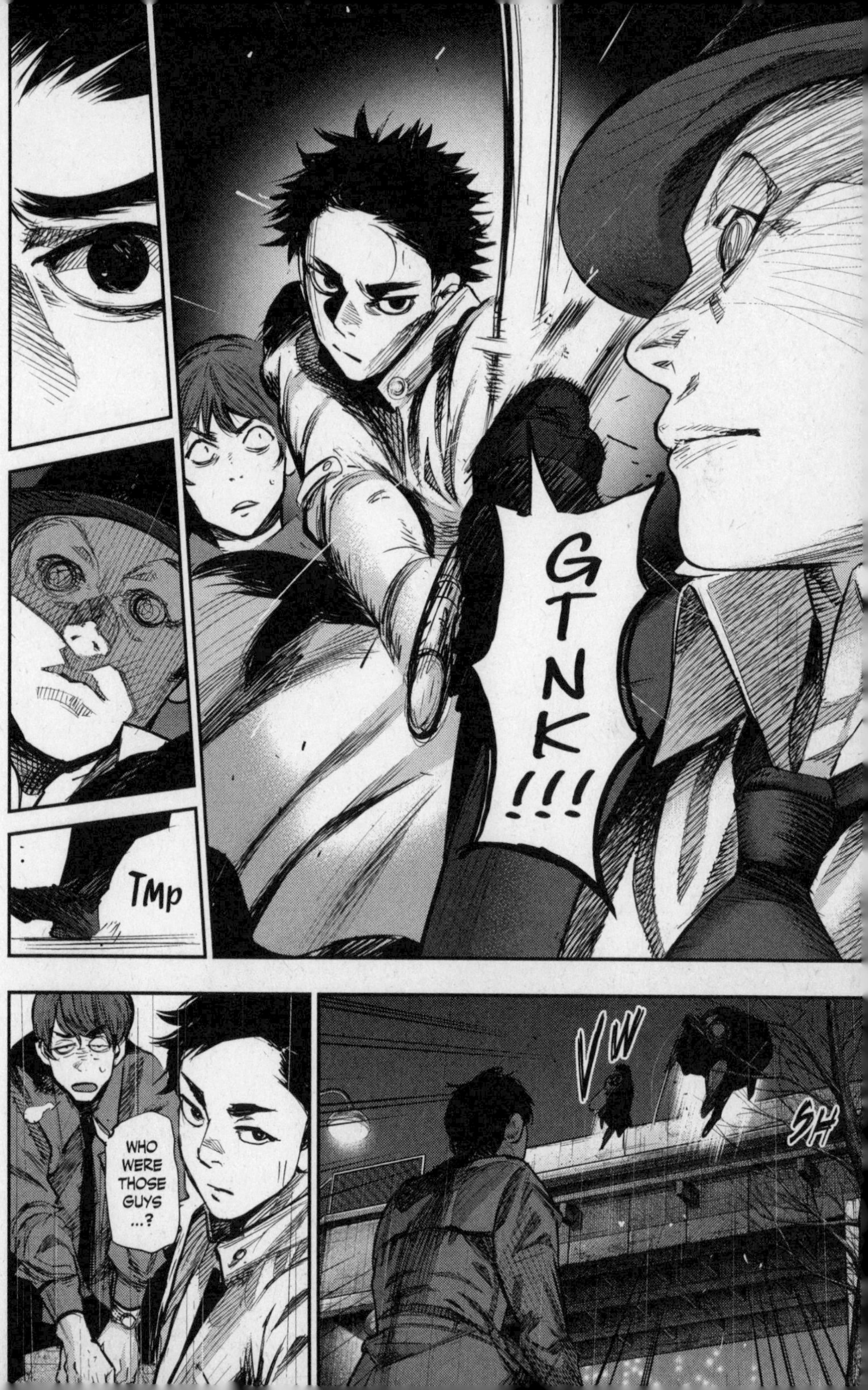
GTNK!!!
TMp
VW
SH
WHO WERE THOSE GUYS ...?

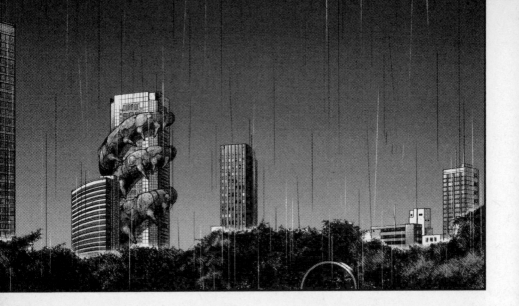

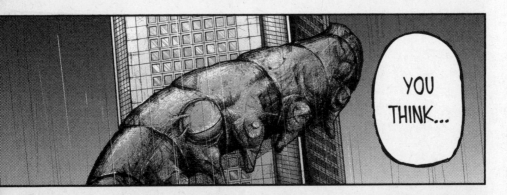

YOU THINK...

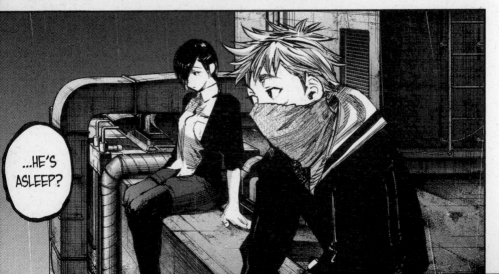

...HE'S ASLEEP?

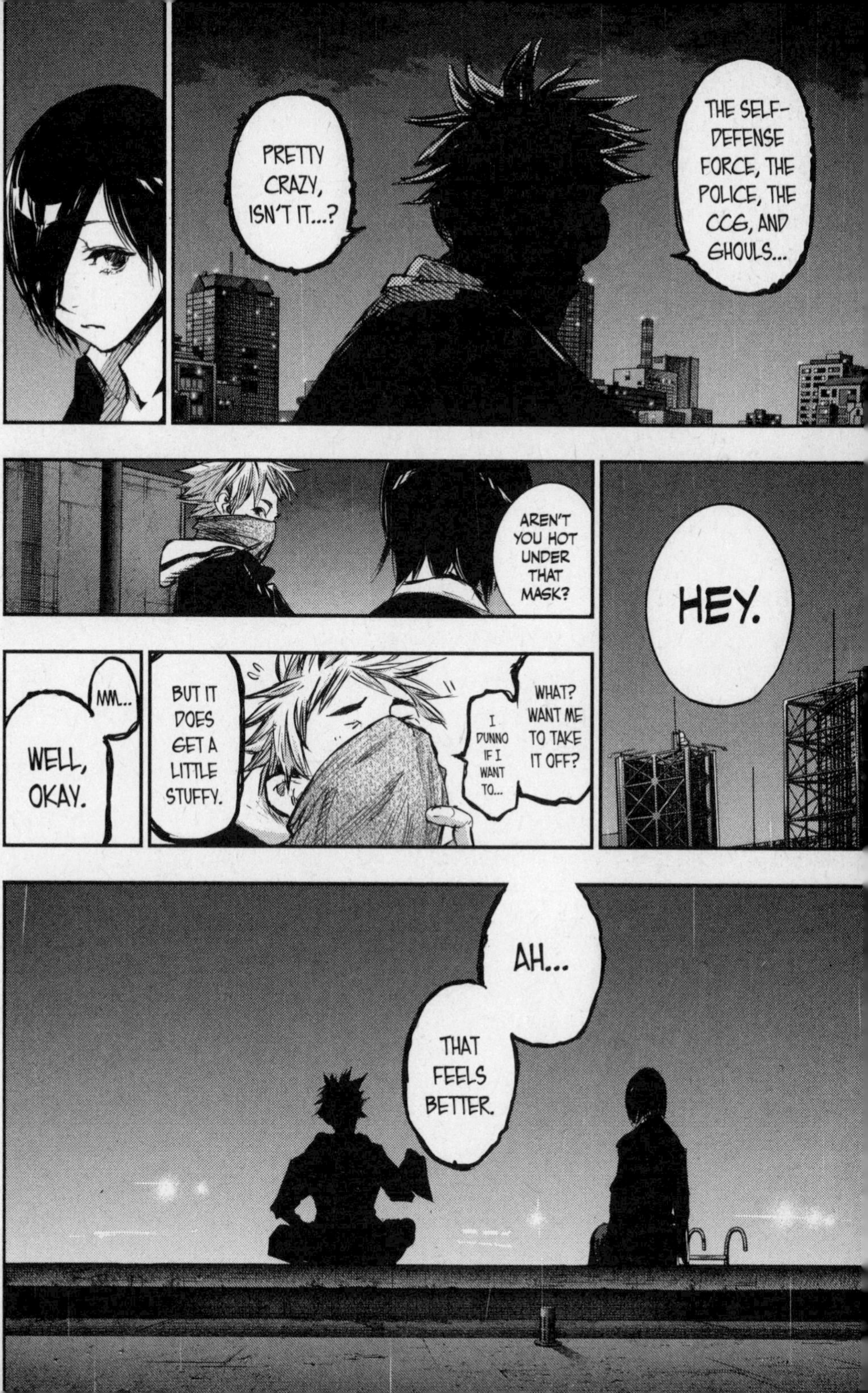
THE SELF-DEFENSE FORCE, THE POLICE, THE CCG, AND GHOULS...
PRETTY CRAZY, ISN'T IT...?
HEY.
AREN'T YOU HOT UNDER THAT MASK?
WHAT? WANT ME TO TAKE IT OFF?
I DUNNO IF I WANT TO...
BUT IT DOES GET A LITTLE STUFFY.
MM...
WELL, OKAY.
AH...
THAT FEELS BETTER.

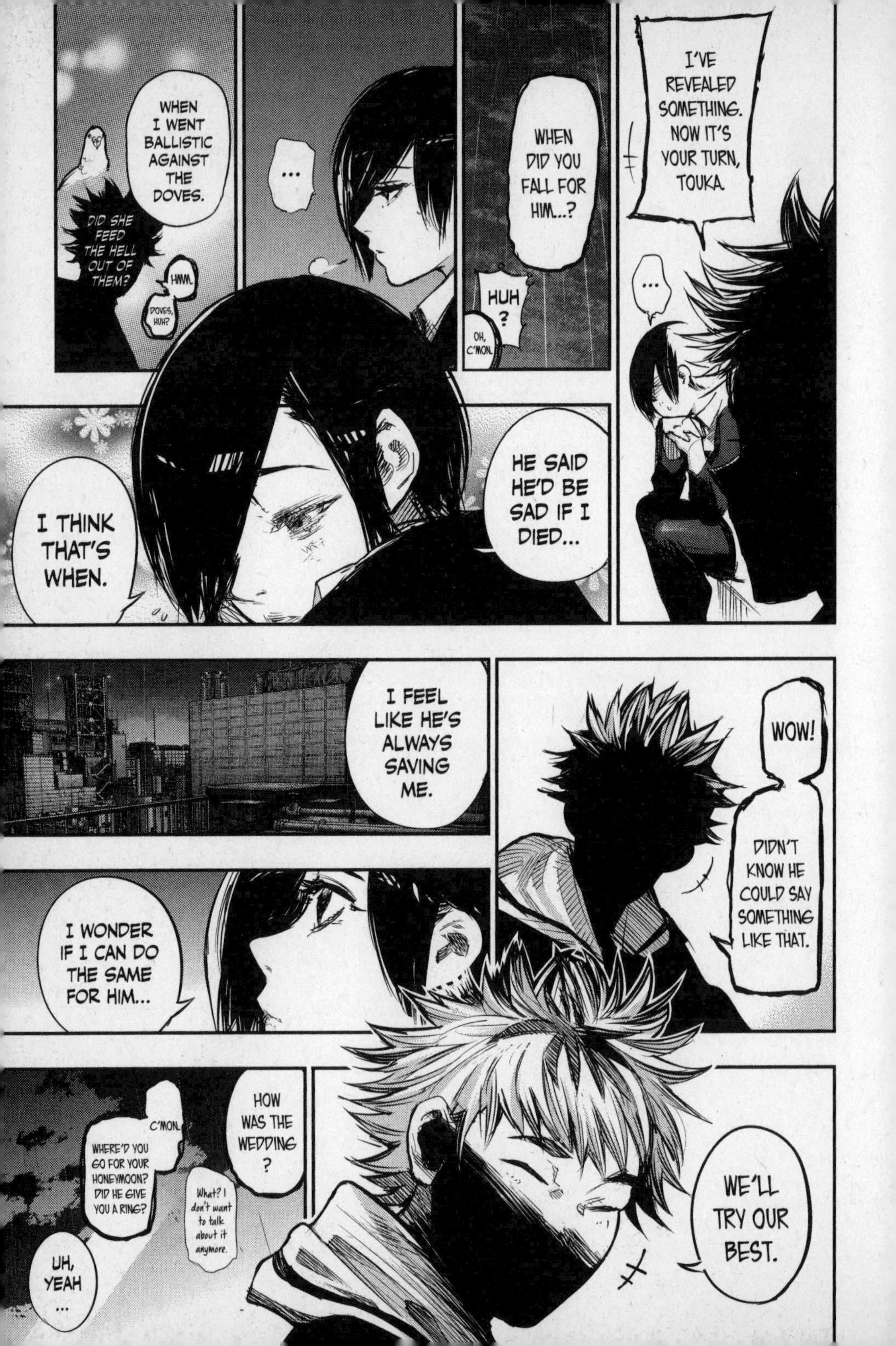
I'VE REVEALED SOMETHING. NOW IT'S YOUR TURN, TOUKA.
...
WHEN DID YOU FALL FOR HIM...?
HUH?
OH, C'MON.
...
WHEN I WENT BALLISTIC AGAINST THE DOVES.
HMM.
DOVES, HUH?
DID SHE FEED THE HELL OUT OF THEM?
HE SAID HE'D BE SAD IF I DIED...
I THINK THAT'S WHEN.
WOW!
DIDN'T KNOW HE COULD SAY SOMETHING LIKE THAT.
I FEEL LIKE HE'S ALWAYS SAVING ME.
I WONDER IF I CAN DO THE SAME FOR HIM...
WE'LL TRY OUR BEST.
HOW WAS THE WEDDING?
What? I don't want to talk about it anymore.
C'MON.
WHERE'D YOU GO FOR YOUR HONEYMOON? DID HE GIVE YOU A RING?
UH, YEAH...

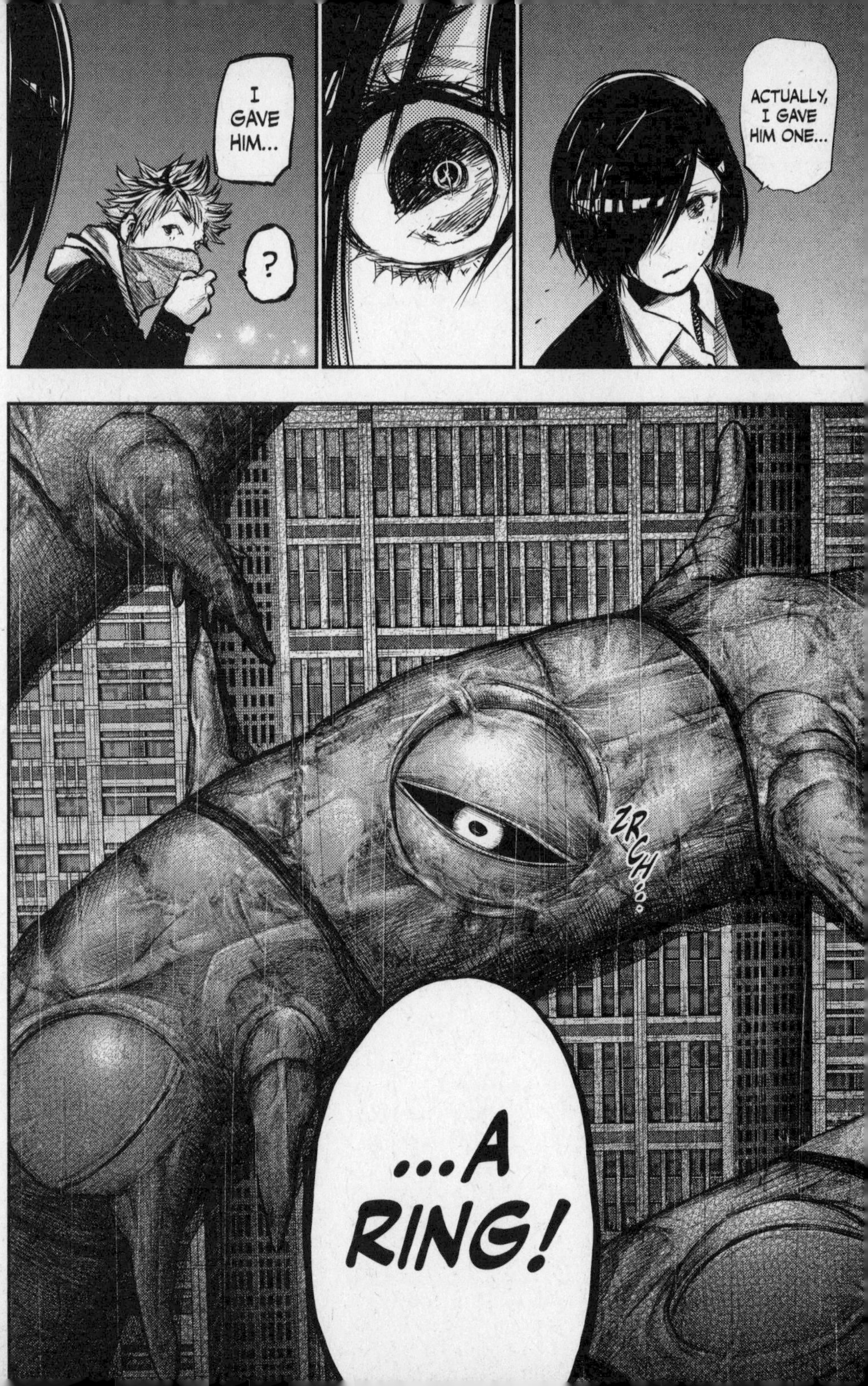
ACTUALLY, I GAVE HIM ONE...
I GAVE HIM...
?
ZRCH...
...A RING!

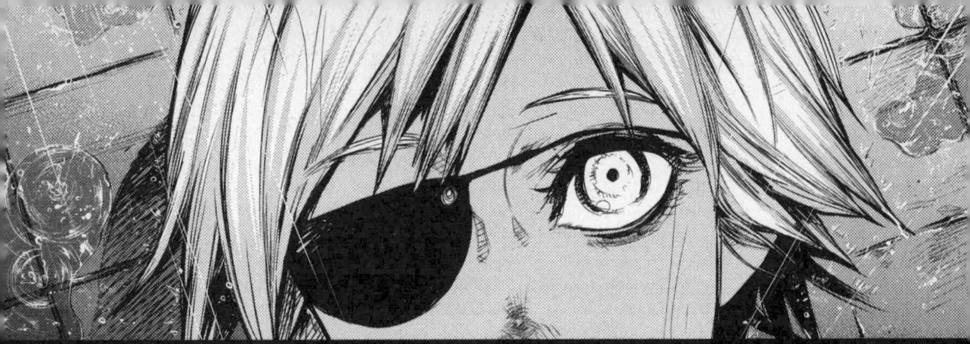

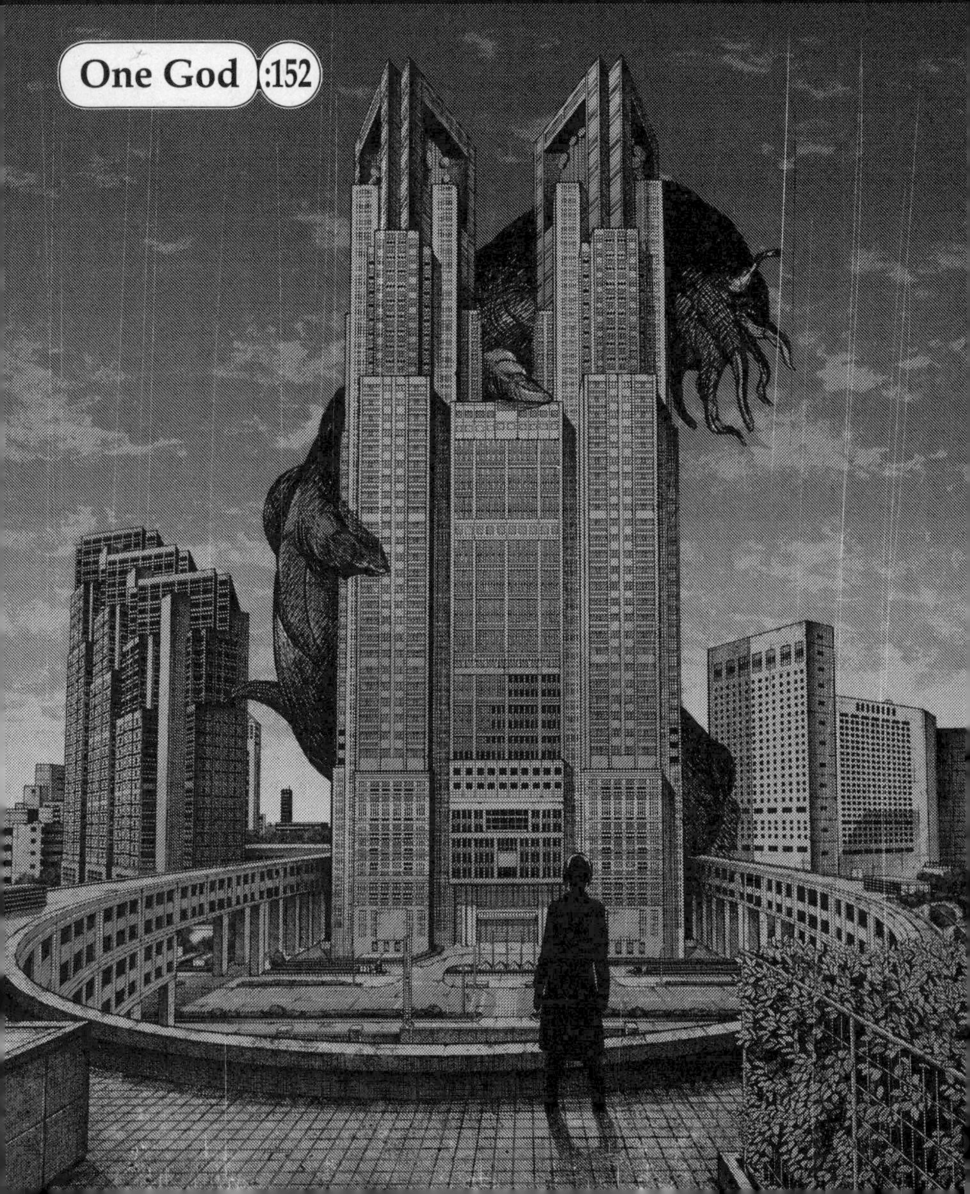
One God :152

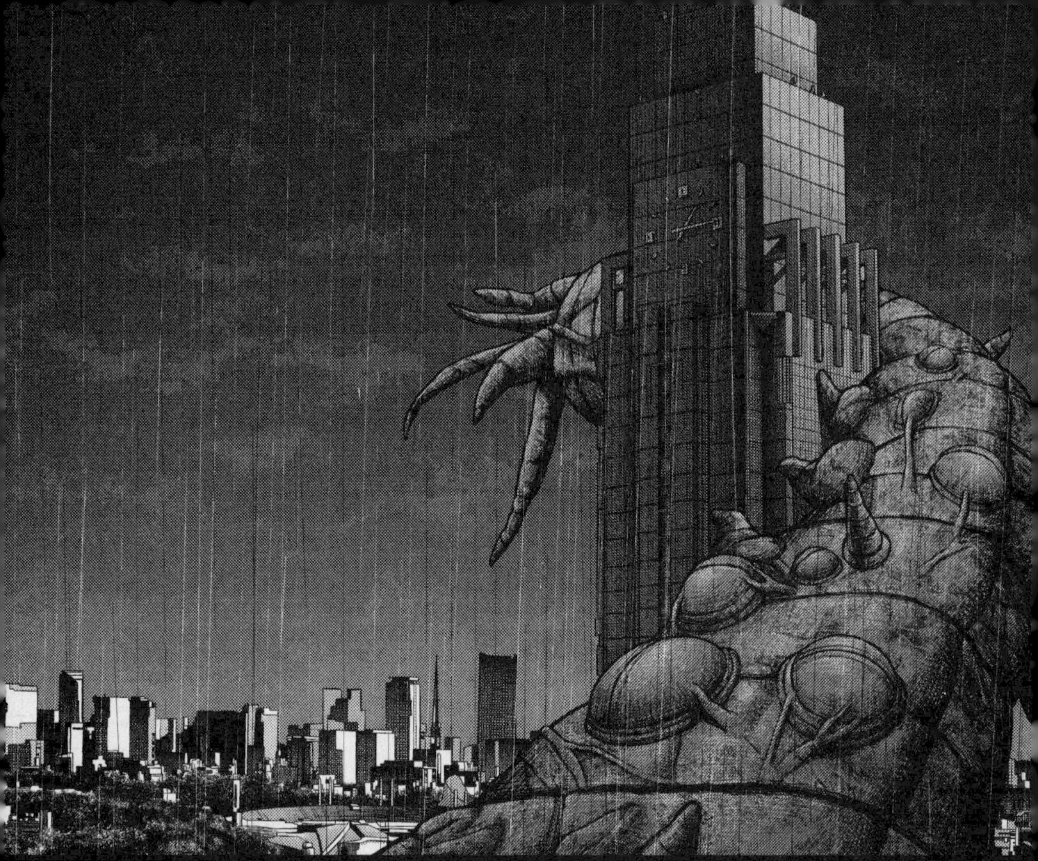

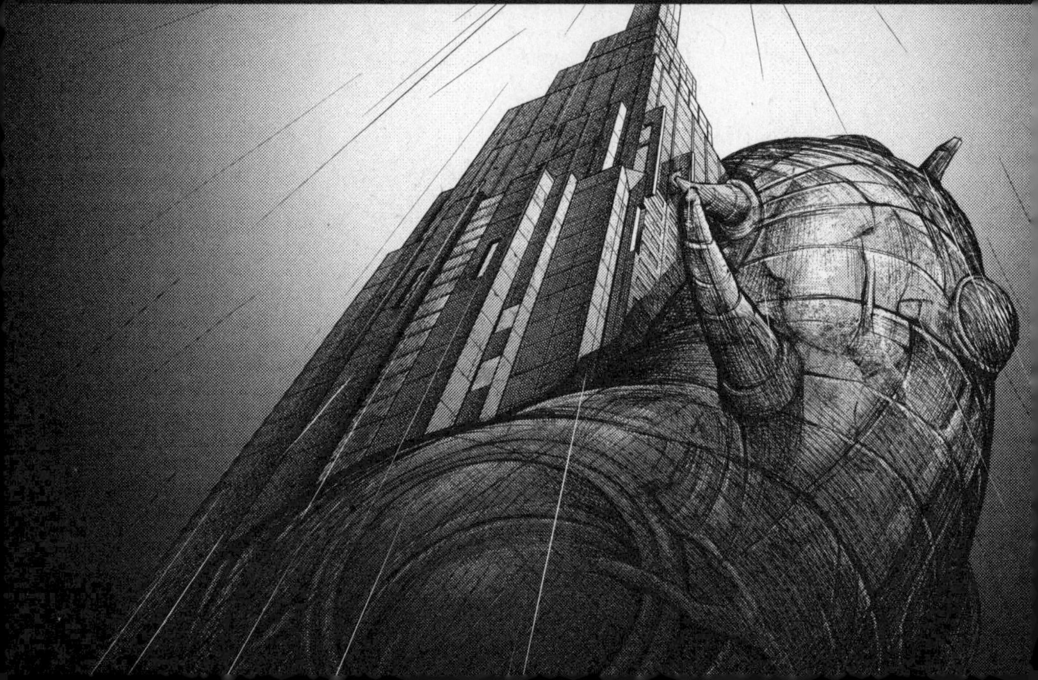

TOKYO WANZU
A RING...?

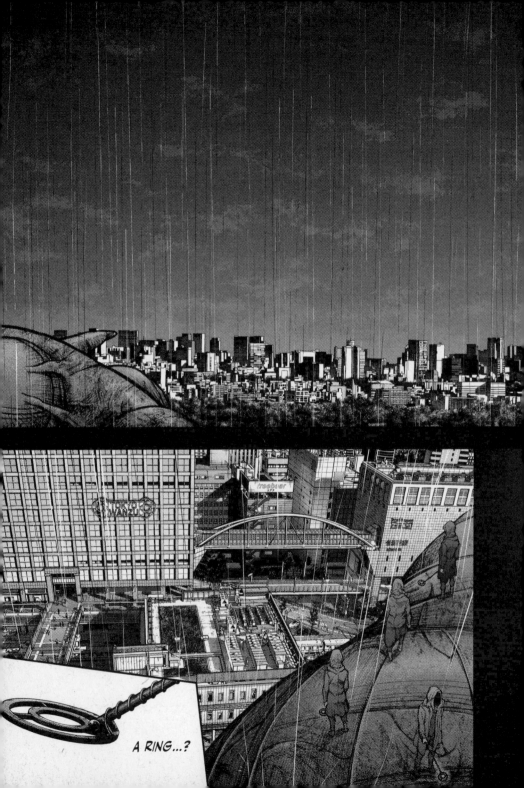

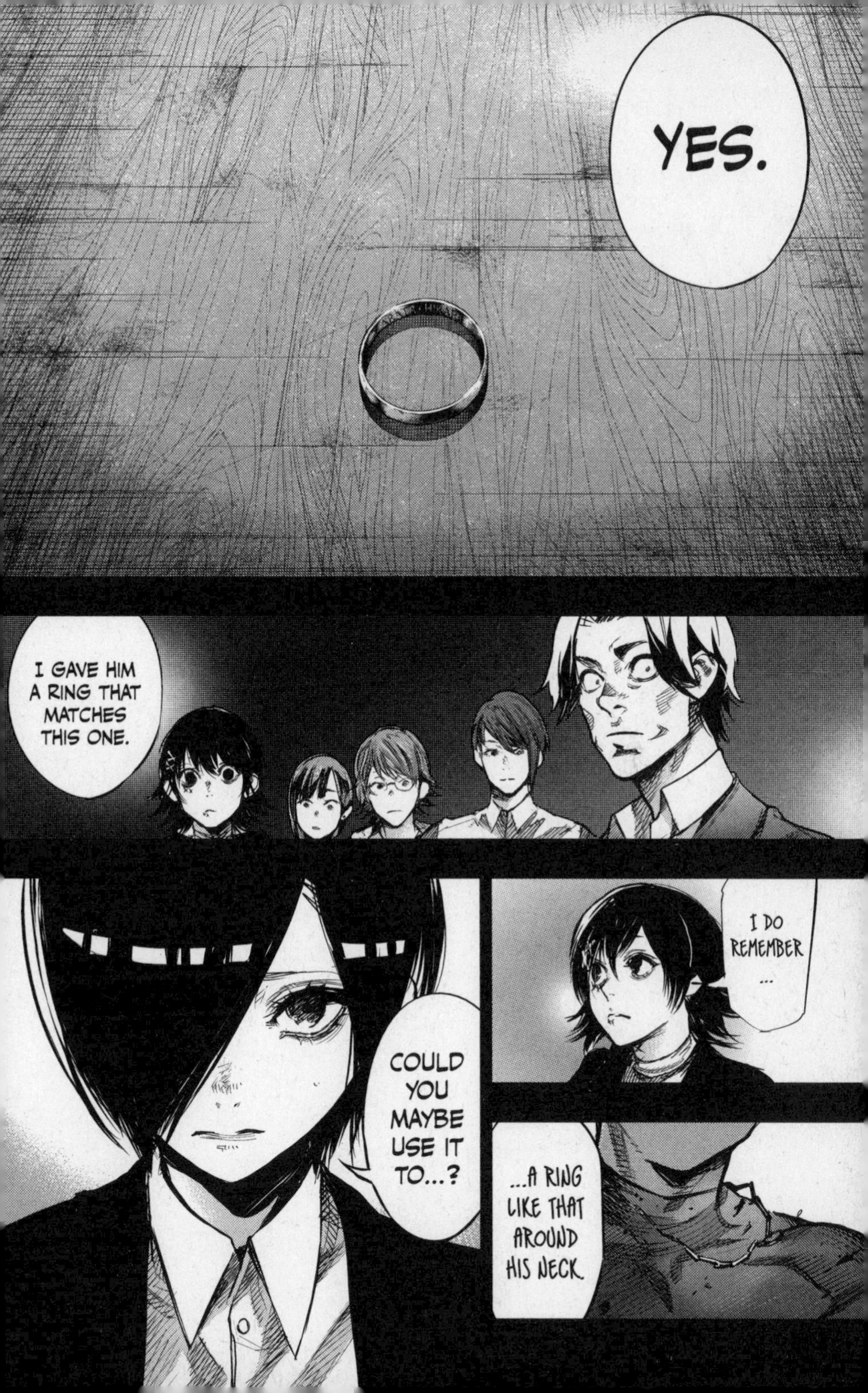
YES.
I GAVE HIM A RING THAT MATCHES THIS ONE.
I DO REMEMBER ...
...A RING LIKE THAT AROUND HIS NECK.
COULD YOU MAYBE USE IT TO...?

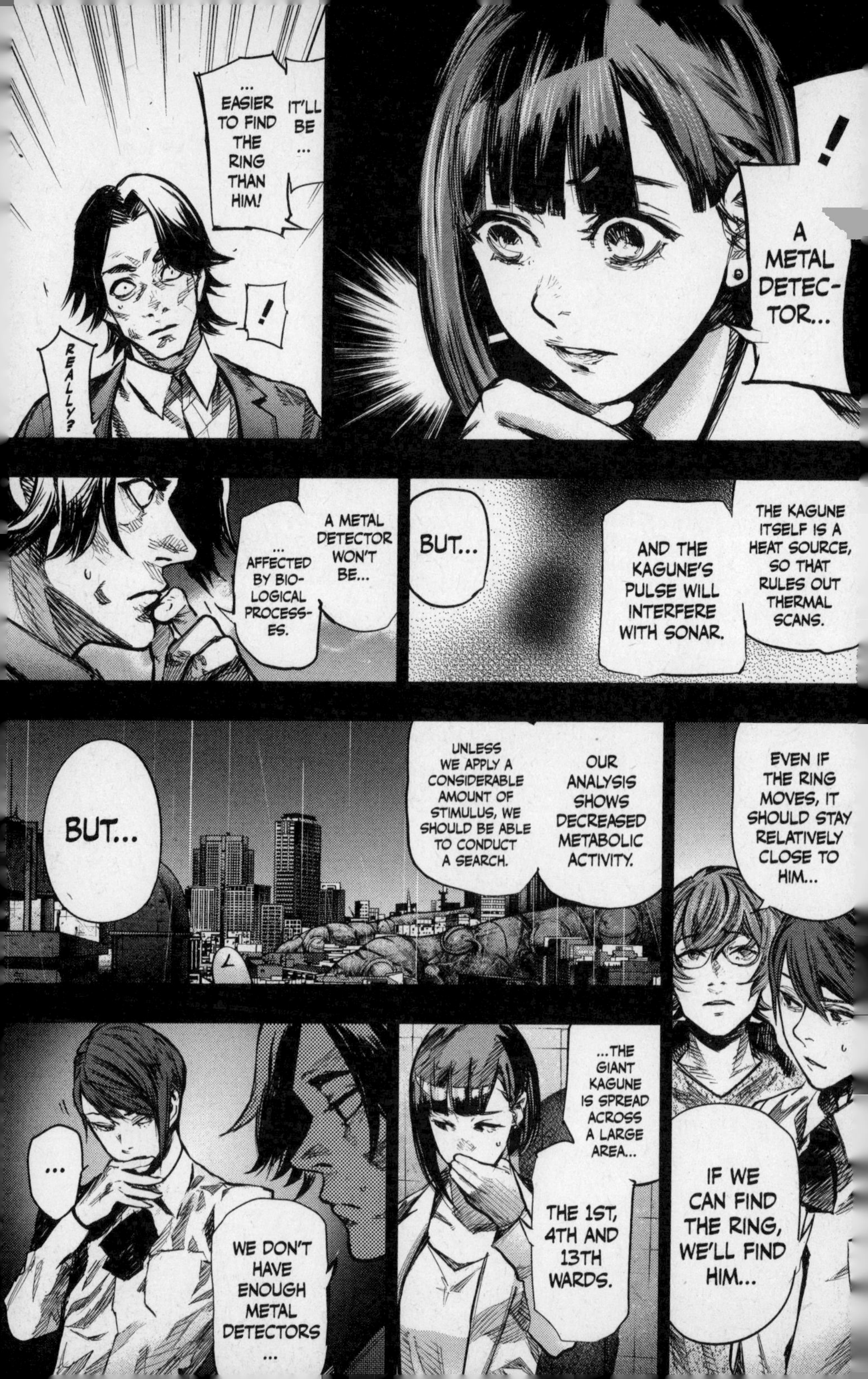
!
A METAL DETECTOR...
IT'LL BE ...
... EASIER TO FIND THE RING THAN HIM!
!
REALLY?
THE KAGUNE ITSELF IS A HEAT SOURCE, SO THAT RULES OUT THERMAL SCANS.
AND THE KAGUNE'S PULSE WILL INTERFERE WITH SONAR.
BUT...
A METAL DETECTOR WON'T BE...
... AFFECTED BY BIOLOGICAL PROCESSES.
EVEN IF THE RING MOVES, IT SHOULD STAY RELATIVELY CLOSE TO HIM...
IF WE CAN FIND THE RING, WE'LL FIND HIM...
OUR ANALYSIS SHOWS DECREASED METABOLIC ACTIVITY.
UNLESS WE APPLY A CONSIDERABLE AMOUNT OF STIMULUS, WE SHOULD BE ABLE TO CONDUCT A SEARCH.
BUT...
...THE GIANT KAGUNE IS SPREAD ACROSS A LARGE AREA...
THE 1ST, 4TH AND 13TH WARDS.
WE DON'T HAVE ENOUGH METAL DETECTORS ...
...

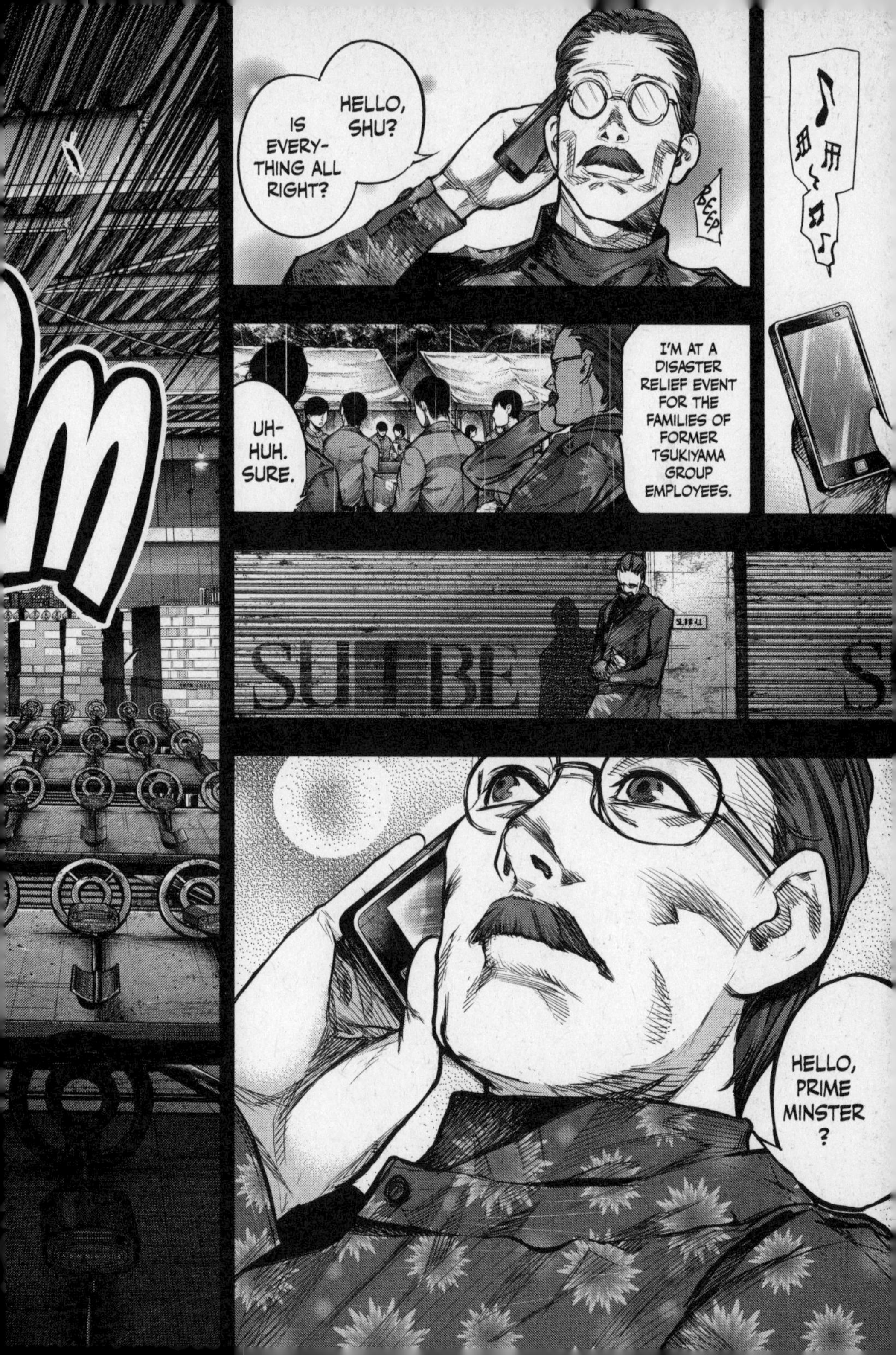
BEEP
HELLO, SHU? IS EVERYTHING ALL RIGHT?
I'M AT A DISASTER RELIEF EVENT FOR THE FAMILIES OF FORMER TSUKIYAMA GROUP EMPLOYEES.
UH-HUH. SURE.
HELLO, PRIME MINSTER ?

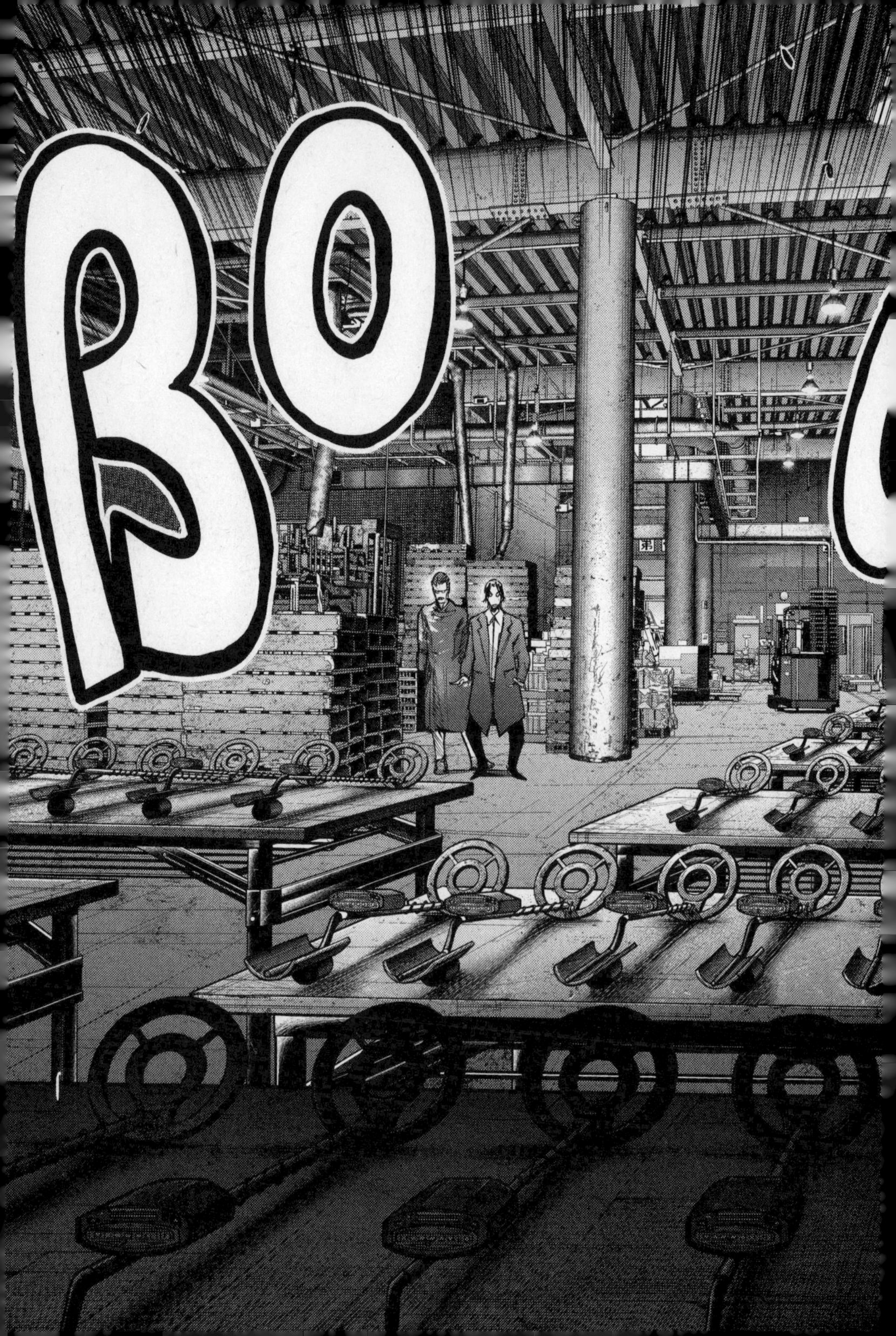
BO

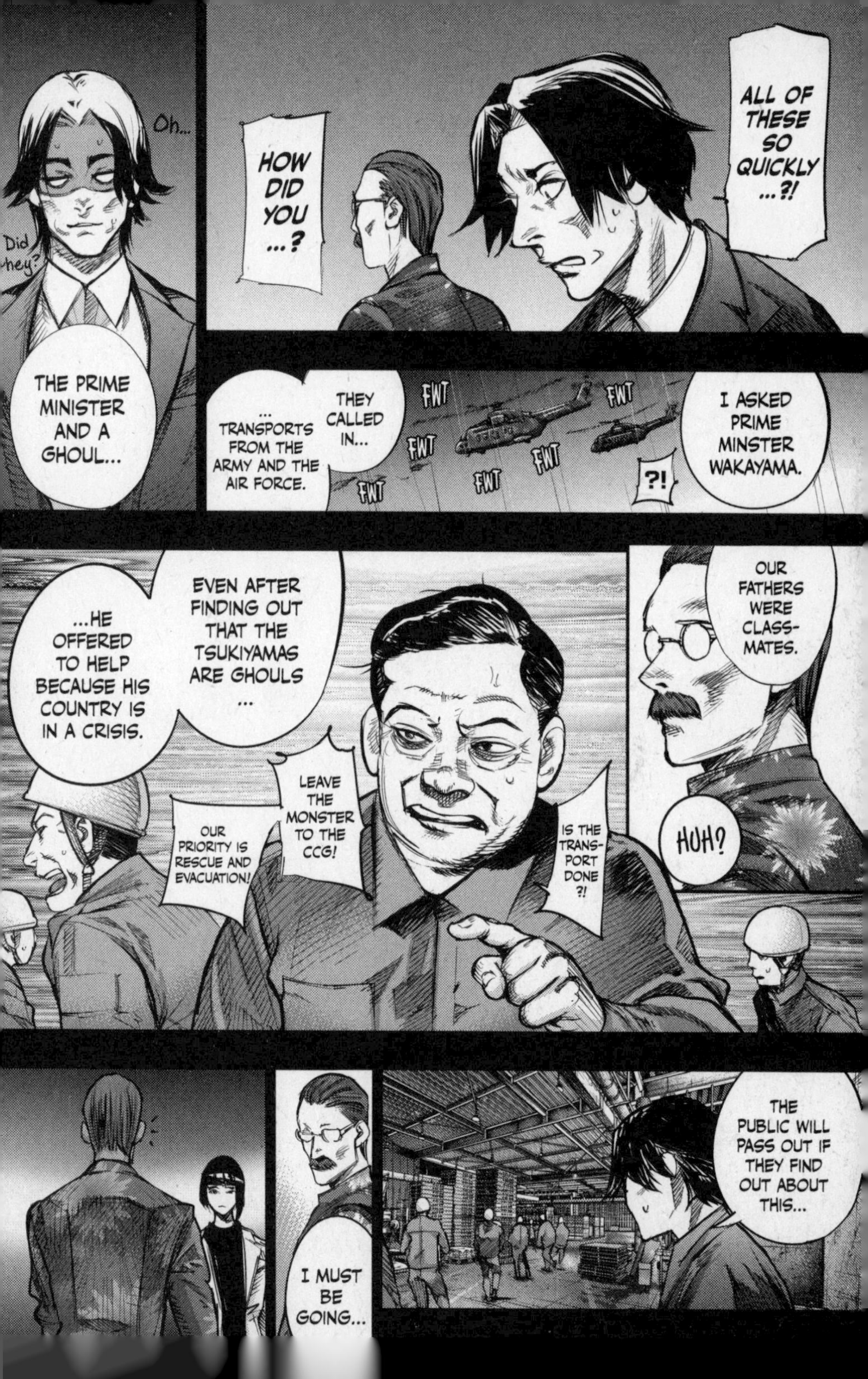
ALL OF THESE SO QUICKLY ...?!
HOW DID YOU ...?
I ASKED PRIME MINSTER WAKAYAMA.
?!
FWT
FWT
FWT
FWT
FWT
FWT
THEY CALLED IN...
... TRANSPORTS FROM THE ARMY AND THE AIR FORCE.
Oh...
Did they?
THE PRIME MINISTER AND A GHOUL...
OUR FATHERS WERE CLASS-MATES.
HUH?
EVEN AFTER FINDING OUT THAT THE TSUKIYAMAS ARE GHOULS ...
...HE OFFERED TO HELP BECAUSE HIS COUNTRY IS IN A CRISIS.
IS THE TRANS-PORT DONE ?!
LEAVE THE MONSTER TO THE CCG!
OUR PRIORITY IS RESCUE AND EVACUATION!
THE PUBLIC WILL PASS OUT IF THEY FIND OUT ABOUT THIS...
I MUST BE GOING...

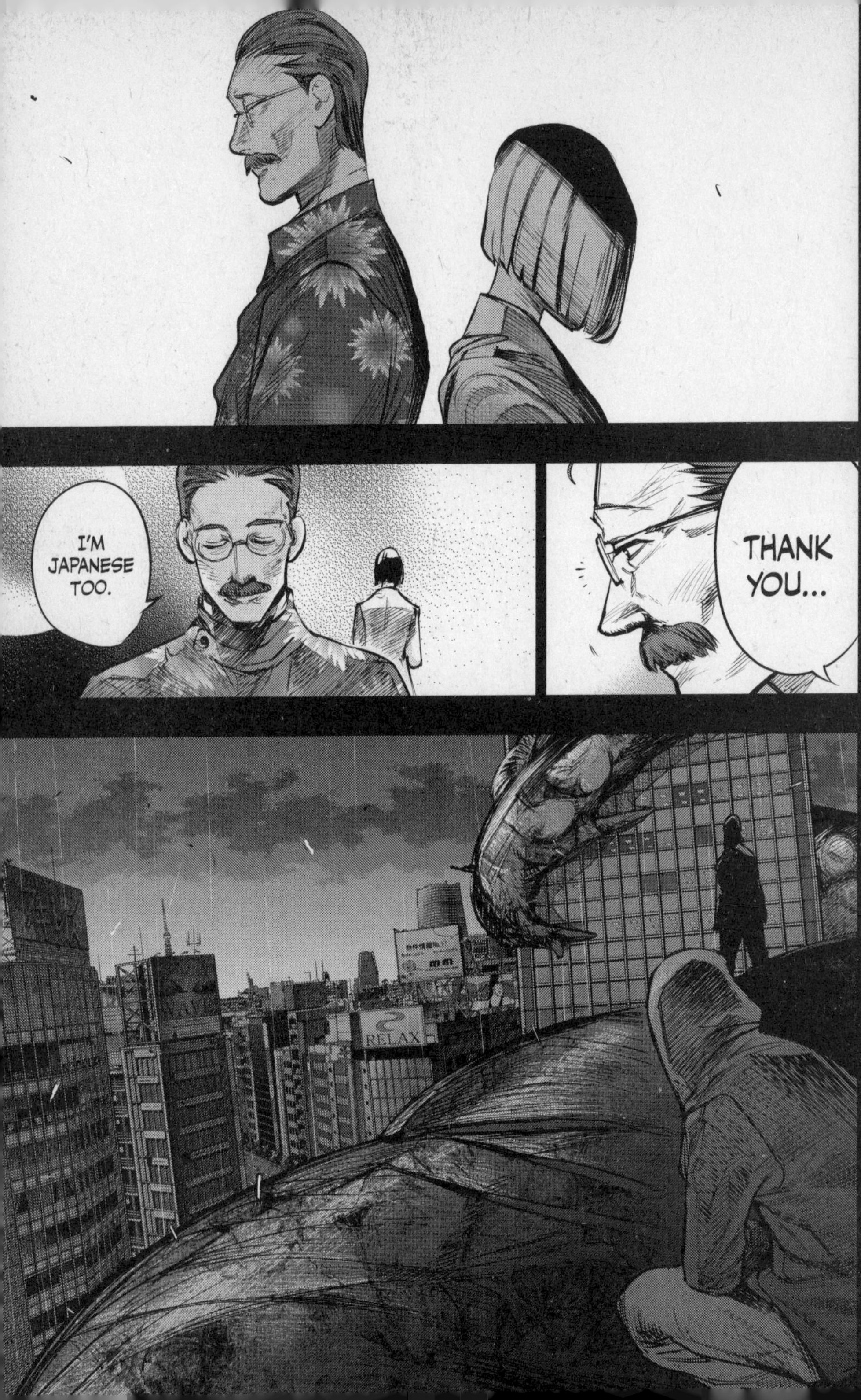
THANK YOU...
I'M JAPANESE TOO.

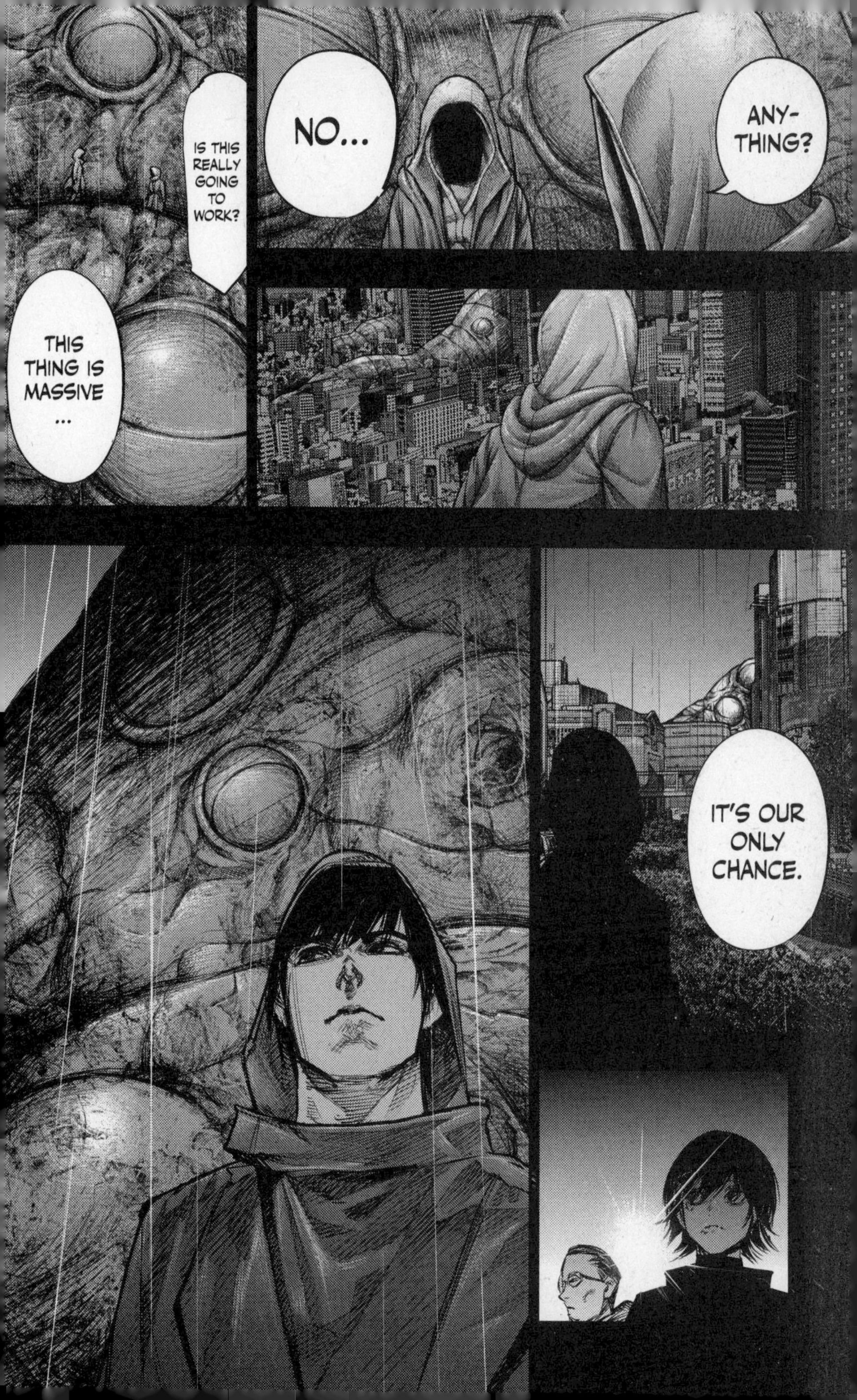
ANY-THING?
NO...
IS THIS REALLY GOING TO WORK?
THIS THING IS MASSIVE ...
IT'S OUR ONLY CHANCE.

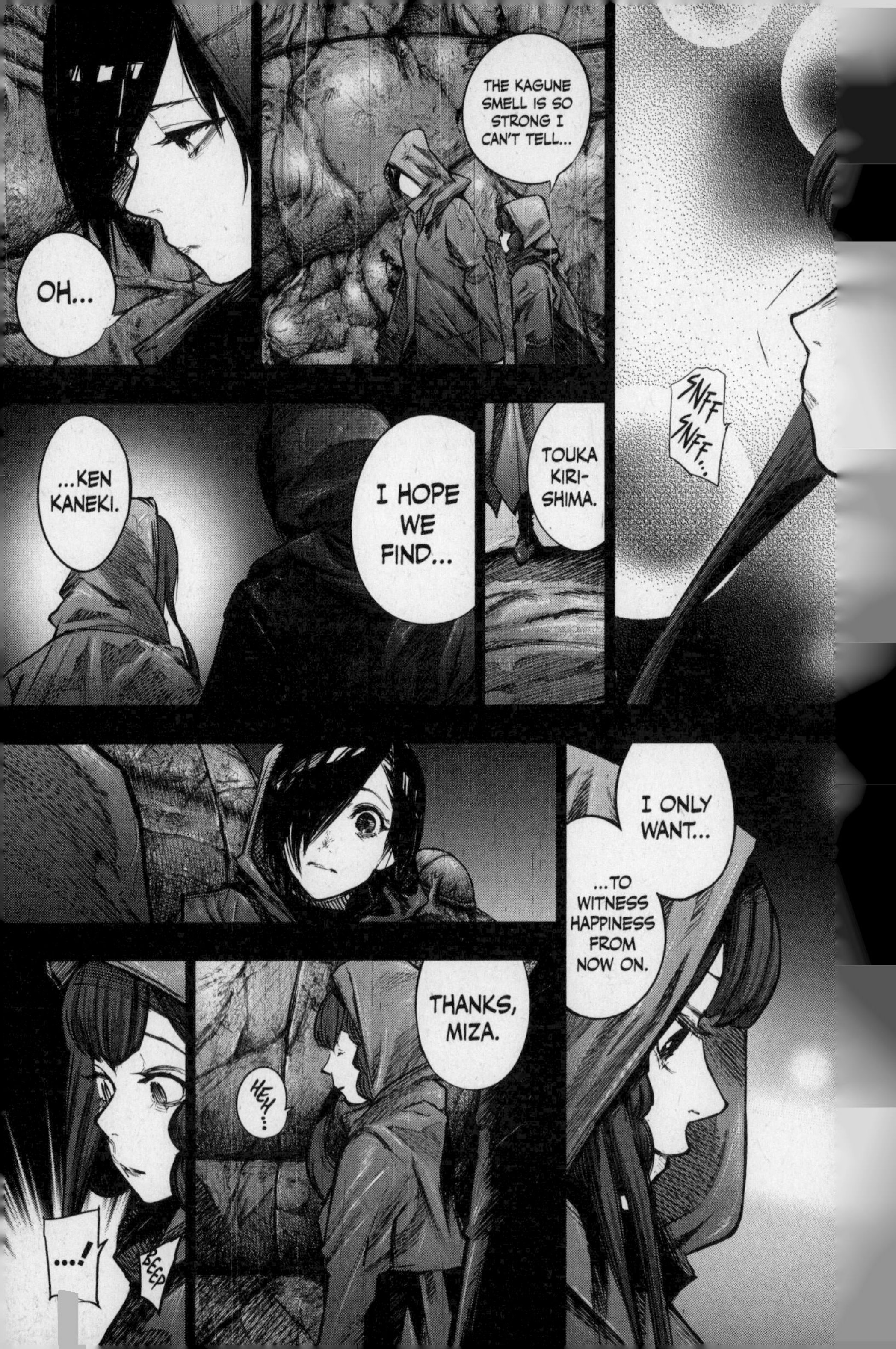
SNFF SNFF...
THE KAGUNE SMELL IS SO STRONG I CAN'T TELL...
OH...
TOUKA KIRI-SHIMA.
I HOPE WE FIND...
...KEN KANEKI.
I ONLY WANT...
...TO WITNESS HAPPINESS FROM NOW ON.
THANKS, MIZA.
HEH...
...!
BEEP

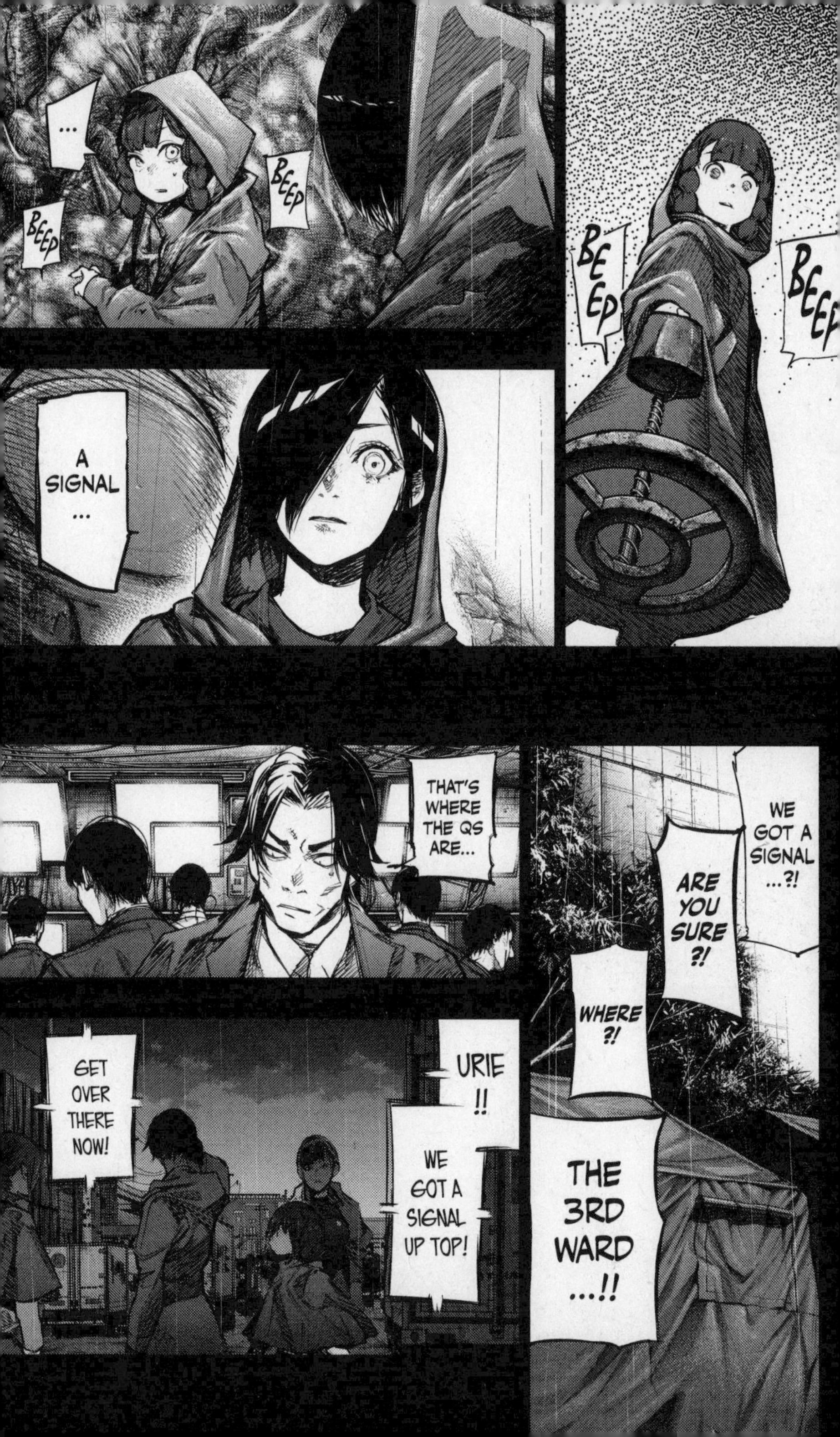
BEEP
BEEP
...
BEEP
BEEP
A SIGNAL ...
WE GOT A SIGNAL ...?!
ARE YOU SURE ?!
WHERE ?!
THE 3RD WARD ...!!
THAT'S WHERE THE QS ARE...
URIE !!
WE GOT A SIGNAL UP TOP!
GET OVER THERE NOW!

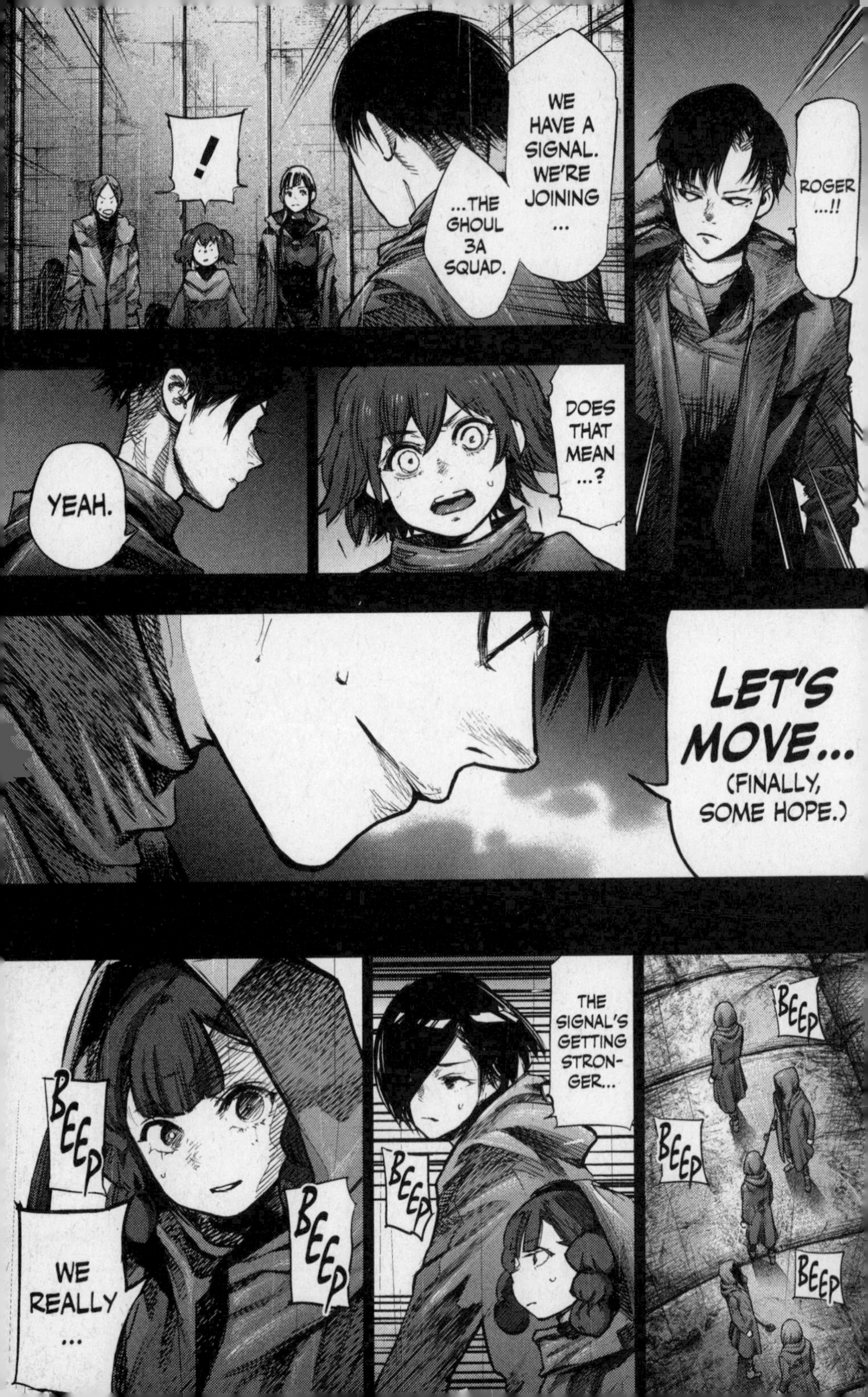
ROGER ...!!
WE HAVE A SIGNAL. WE'RE JOINING ...
...THE GHOUL 3A SQUAD.
!
DOES THAT MEAN ...?
YEAH.
LET'S MOVE...
(FINALLY, SOME HOPE.)
BEEP
BEEP
BEEP
THE SIGNAL'S GETTING STRONGER...
BEEP
BEEP
BEEP
WE REALLY ...

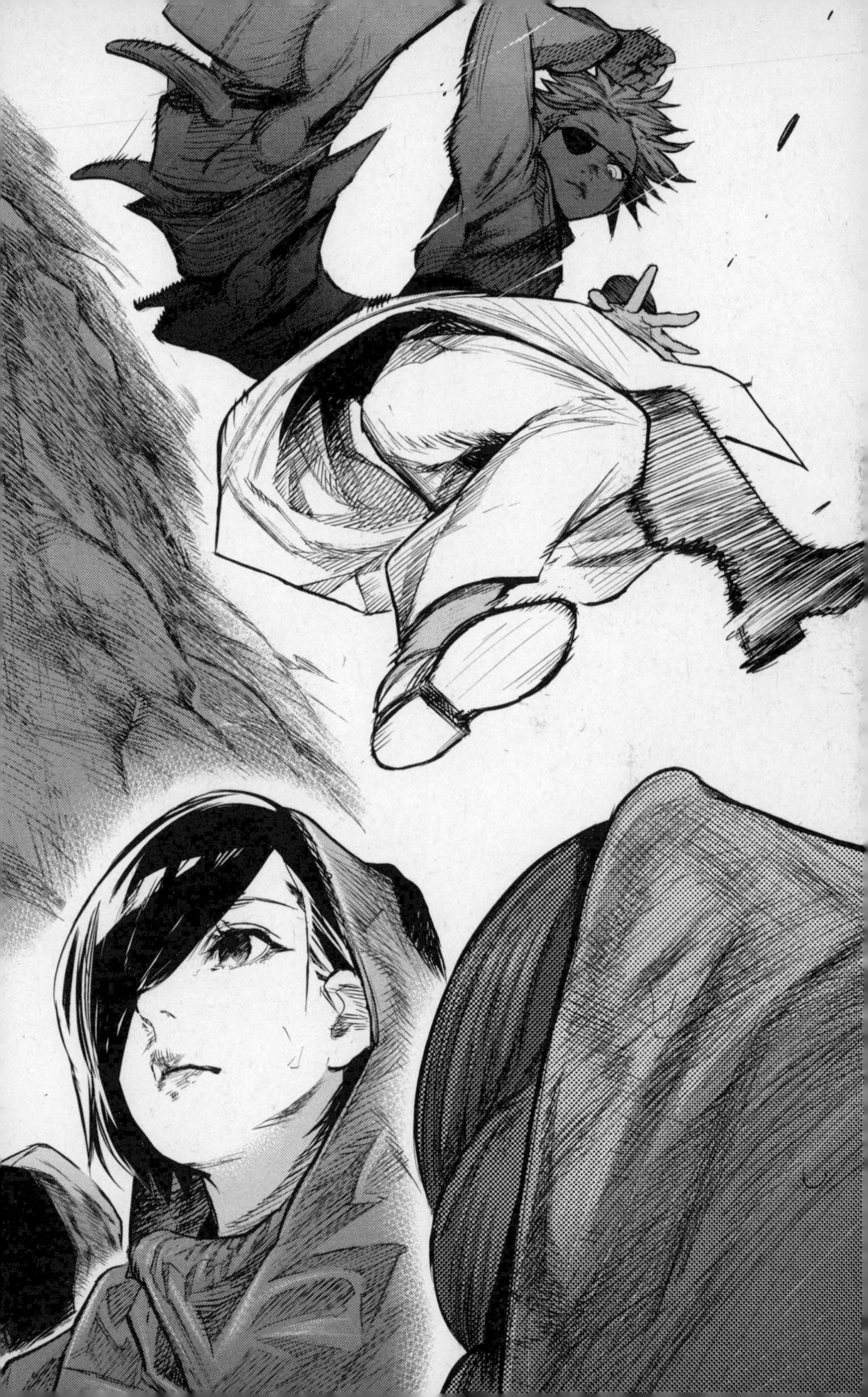

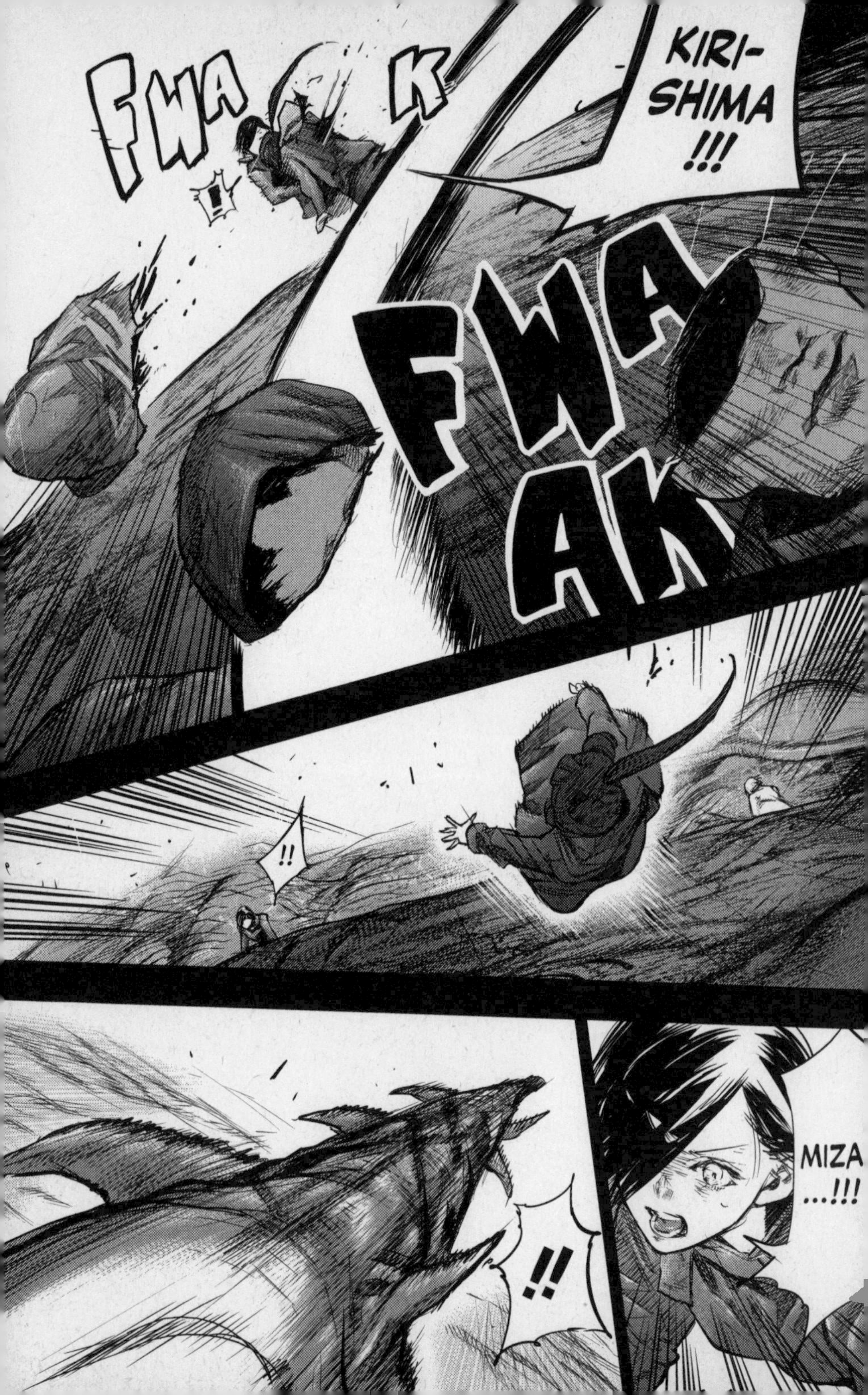
KIRI-SHIMA !!!
FWA AK
FWA K
!
!!
MIZA ...!!!
!!

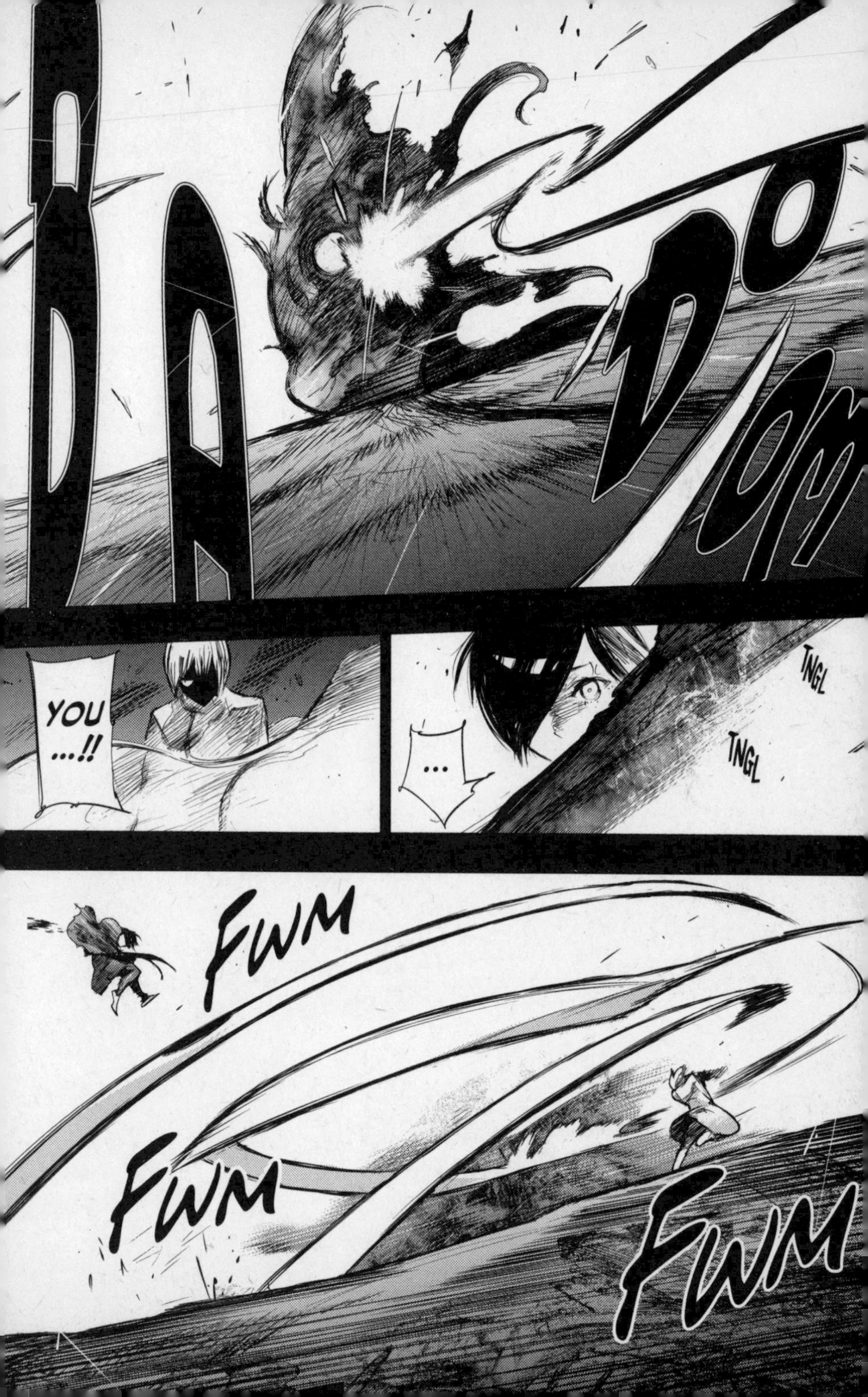
BADOOM
TNGL
TNGL
...
YOU ...!!
FWM
FWM
FWM

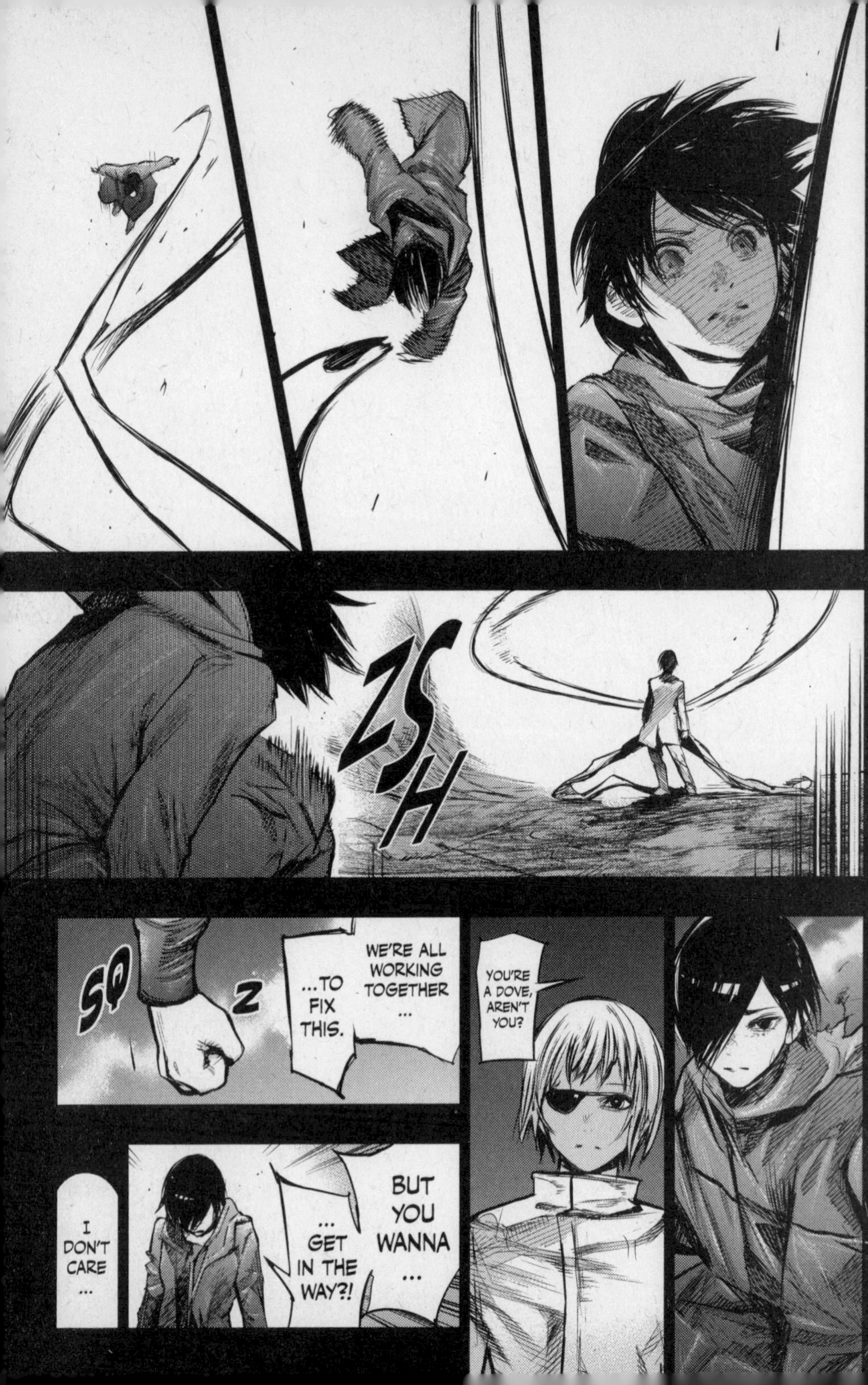
ZSH
YOU'RE A DOVE, AREN'T YOU?
WE'RE ALL WORKING TOGETHER...
...TO FIX THIS.
SQZ
BUT YOU WANNA...
...GET IN THE WAY?!
I DON'T CARE...

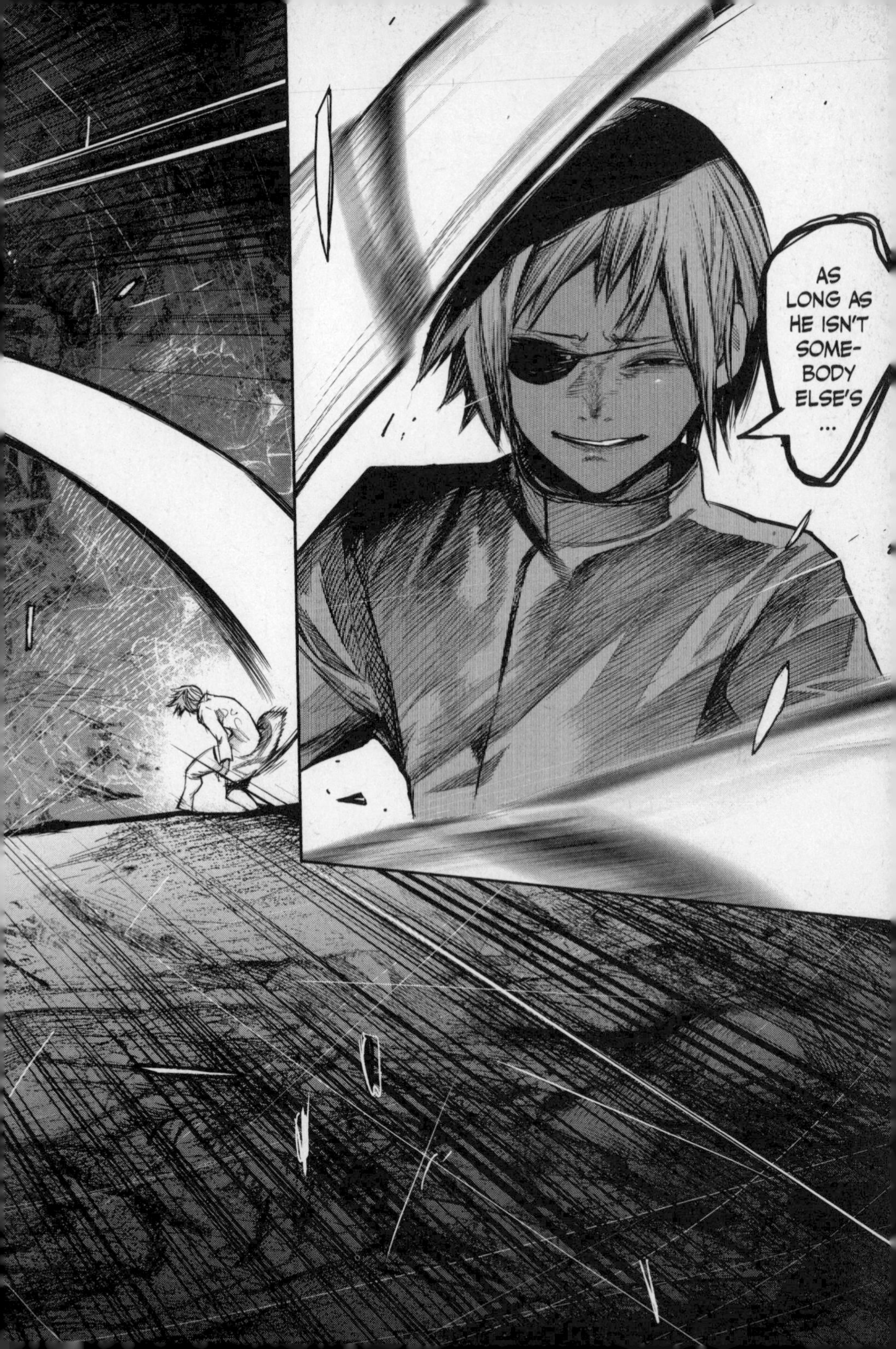
AS LONG AS HE ISN'T SOME-BODY ELSE'S ...

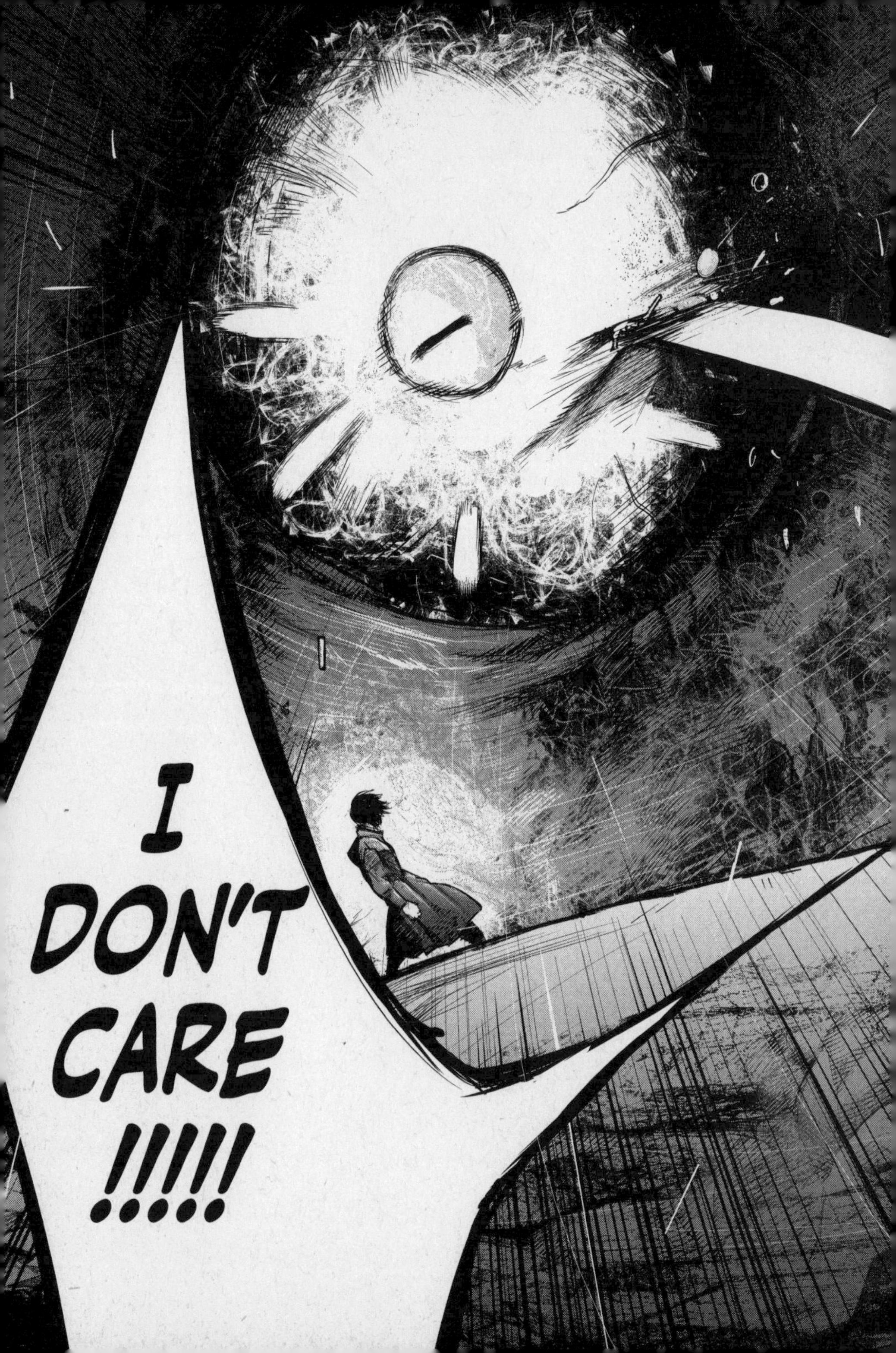
I DON'T CARE !!!!!

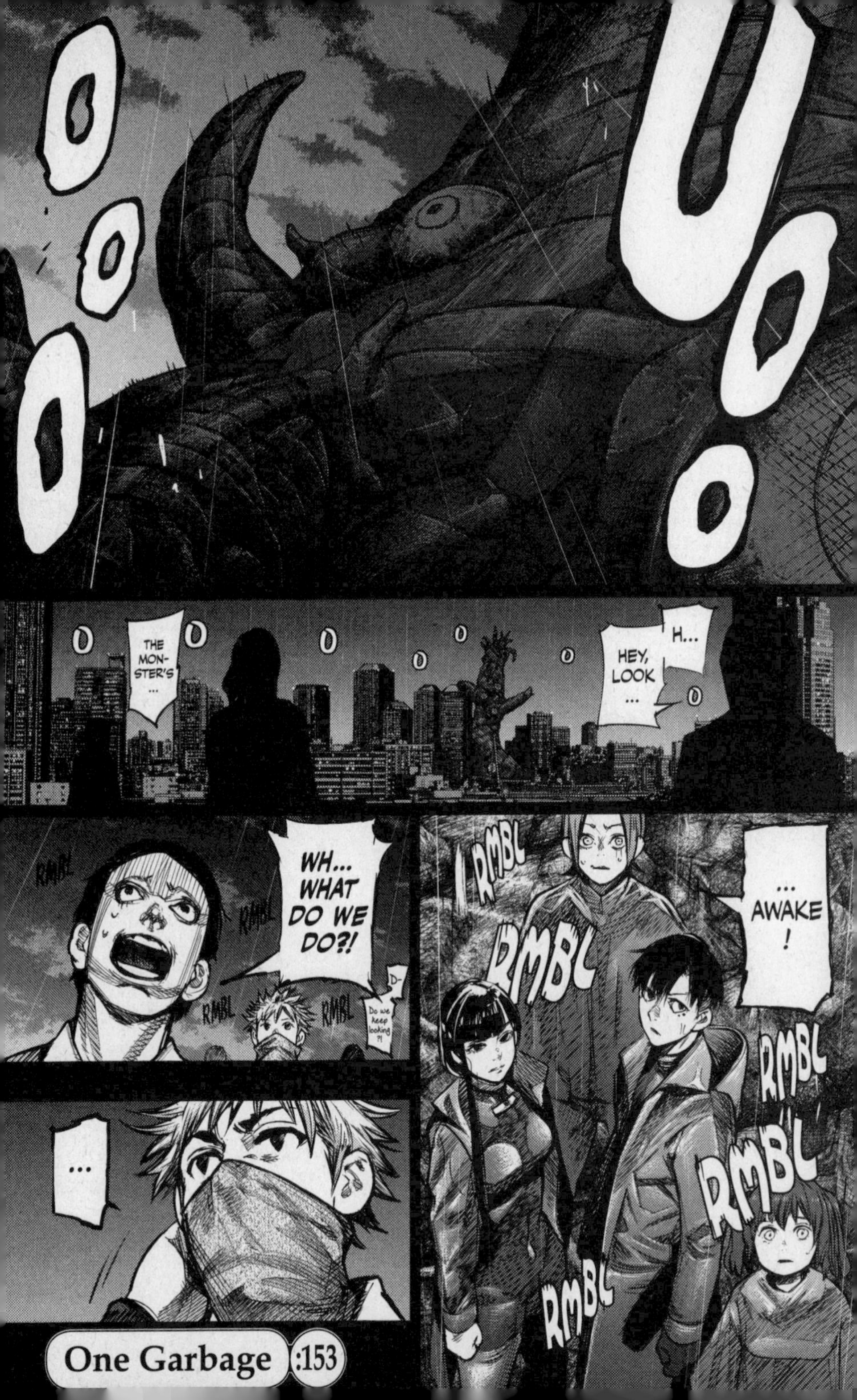
UOOOO
OOOO
H...
HEY, LOOK ...
O
O
O
O
O
THE MONSTER'S ...
O
RMBL
RMBL
... AWAKE!
RMBL
RMBL
RMBL
RMBL
WH... WHAT DO WE DO?!
RMBL
RMBL
D-
Do we keep looking?!
RMBL
...

One Garbage :153

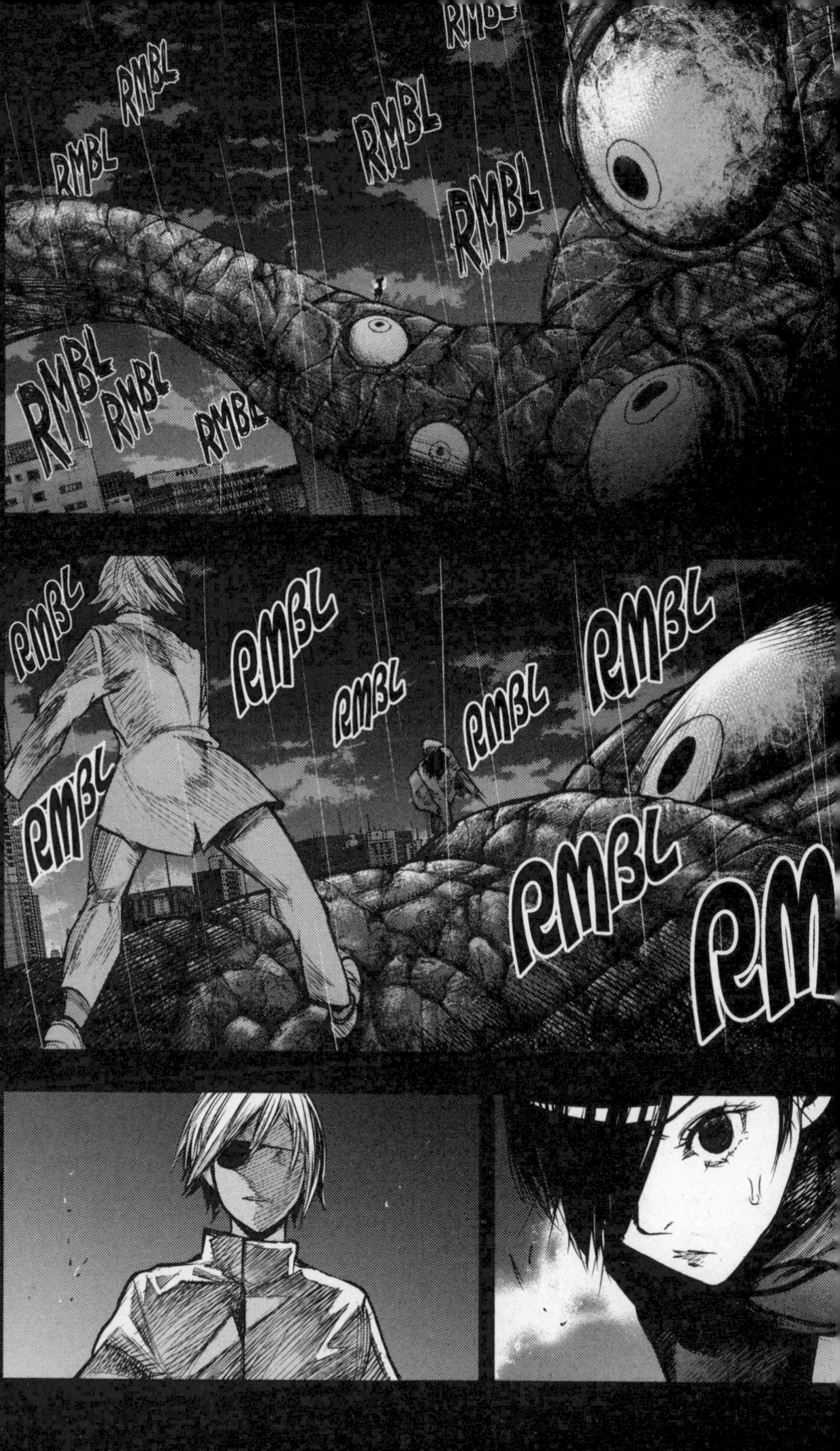
RMBL
RMBL
RMBL
RMBL
RMBL
RMBL
RMBL
RMBL
RMBL
RMBL
RMBL
RMBL
RMBL
RMBL
RMBL
RMBL

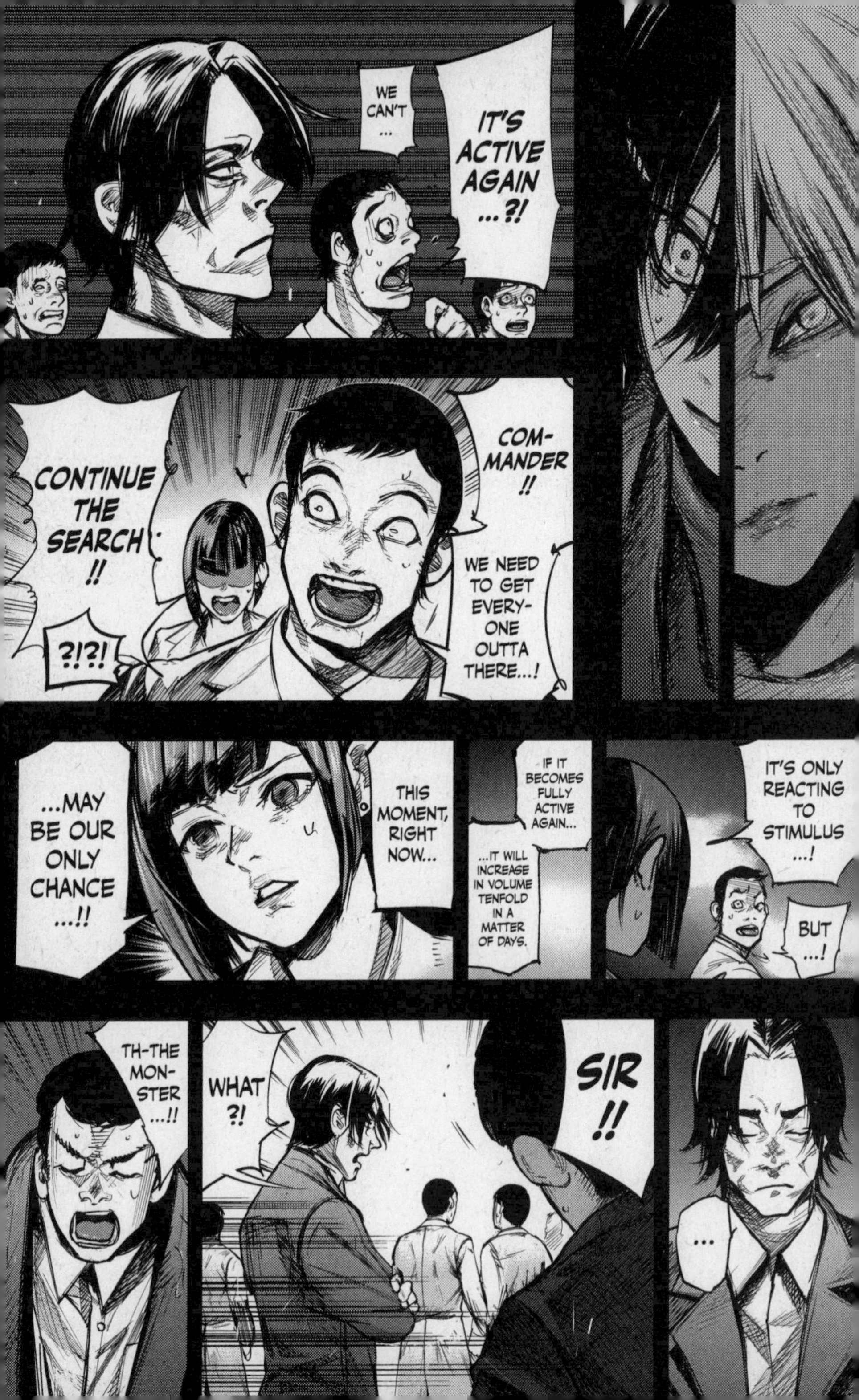
IT'S ACTIVE AGAIN...?!
WE CAN'T...
COM-MANDER!!
WE NEED TO GET EVERY-ONE OUTTA THERE...!
CONTINUE THE SEARCH!!
?!?!
IT'S ONLY REACTING TO STIMULUS...!
BUT...!
IF IT BECOMES FULLY ACTIVE AGAIN...
...IT WILL INCREASE IN VOLUME TENFOLD IN A MATTER OF DAYS.
THIS MOMENT, RIGHT NOW...
...MAY BE OUR ONLY CHANCE...!!
...
SIR!!
WHAT?!
TH-THE MON-STER...!!

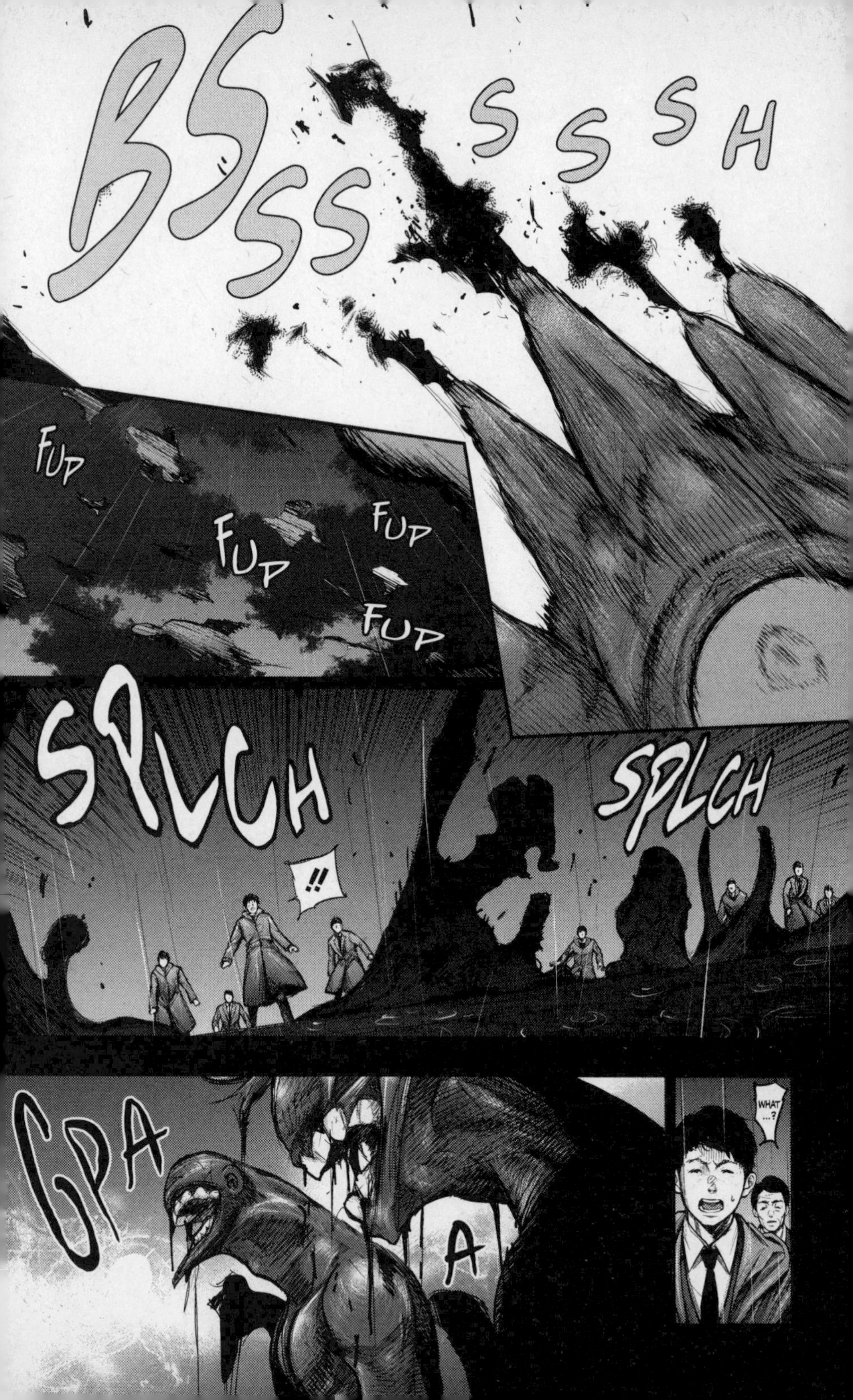
BSSSSSSH
FUP
FUP
FUP
FUP
SPLCH
SPLCH
!!
WHAT ...?
GPA
A

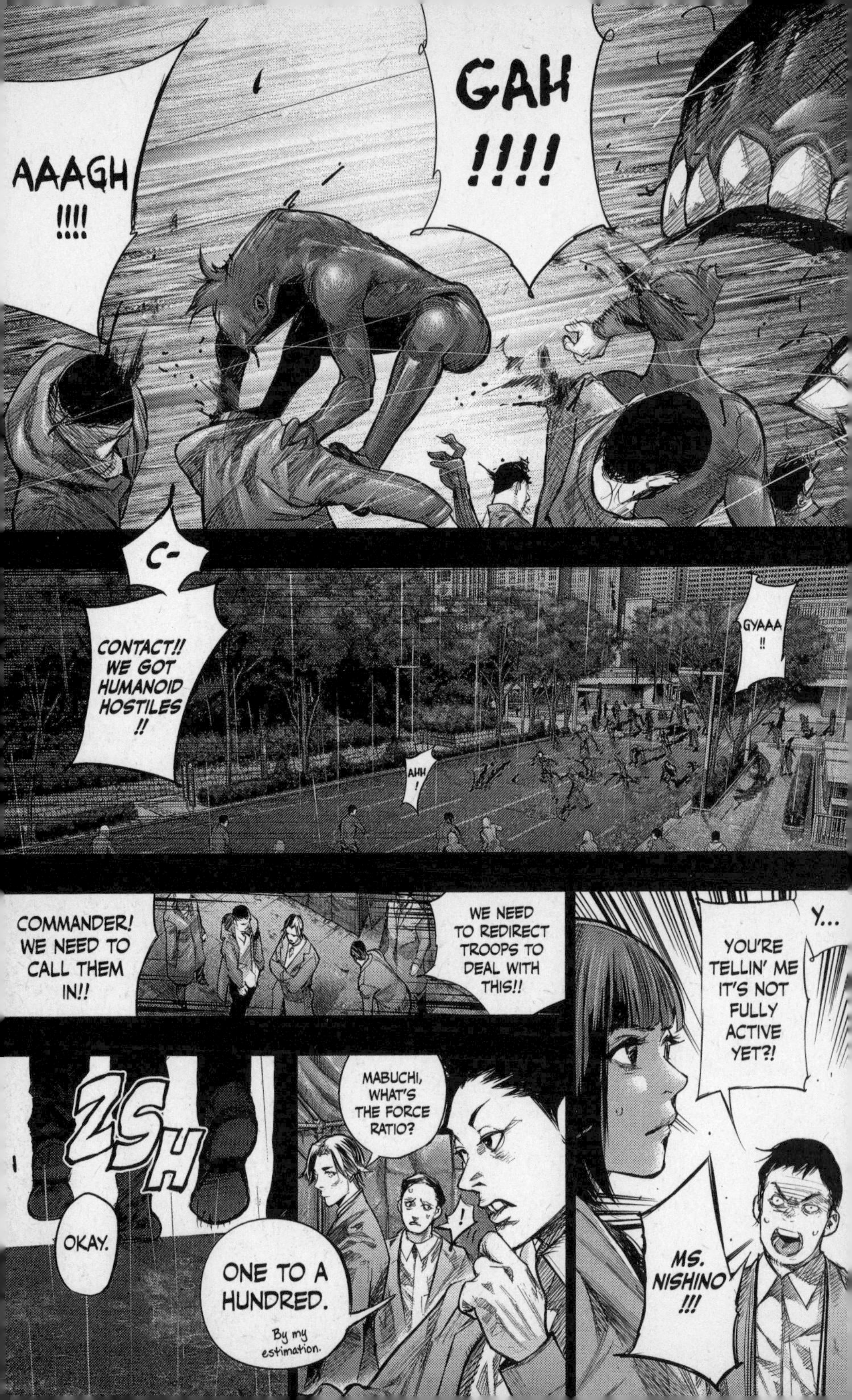
GAH!!!!
AAAGH!!!!
GYAAA!!
C-
CONTACT!! WE GOT HUMANOID HOSTILES!!
AHH!
Y...
YOU'RE TELLIN' ME IT'S NOT FULLY ACTIVE YET?!
MS. NISHINO!!!
WE NEED TO REDIRECT TROOPS TO DEAL WITH THIS!!
COMMANDER! WE NEED TO CALL THEM IN!!
MABUCHI, WHAT'S THE FORCE RATIO?
!
ONE TO A HUNDRED.
By my estimation.
ZSH
OKAY.

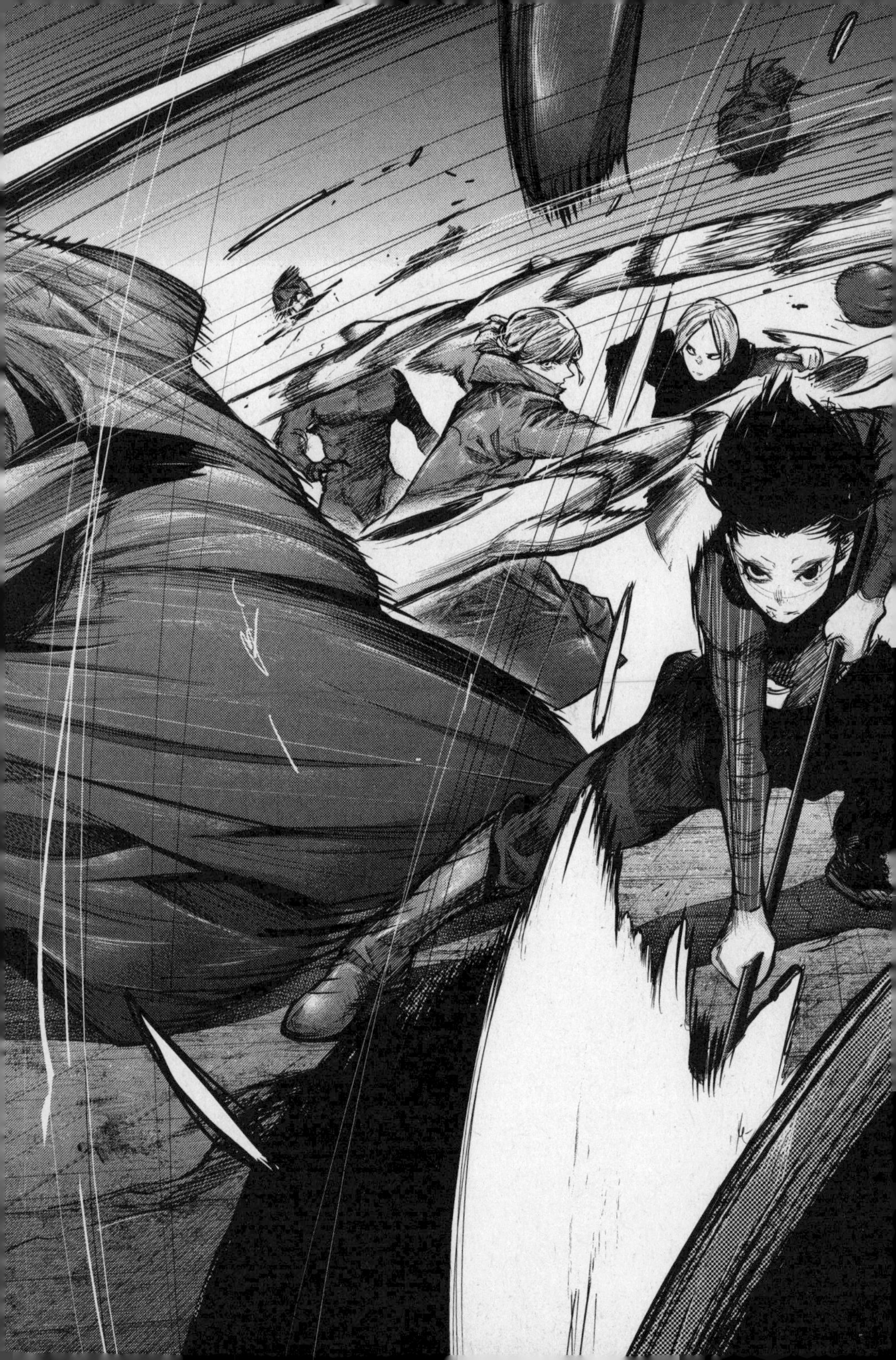

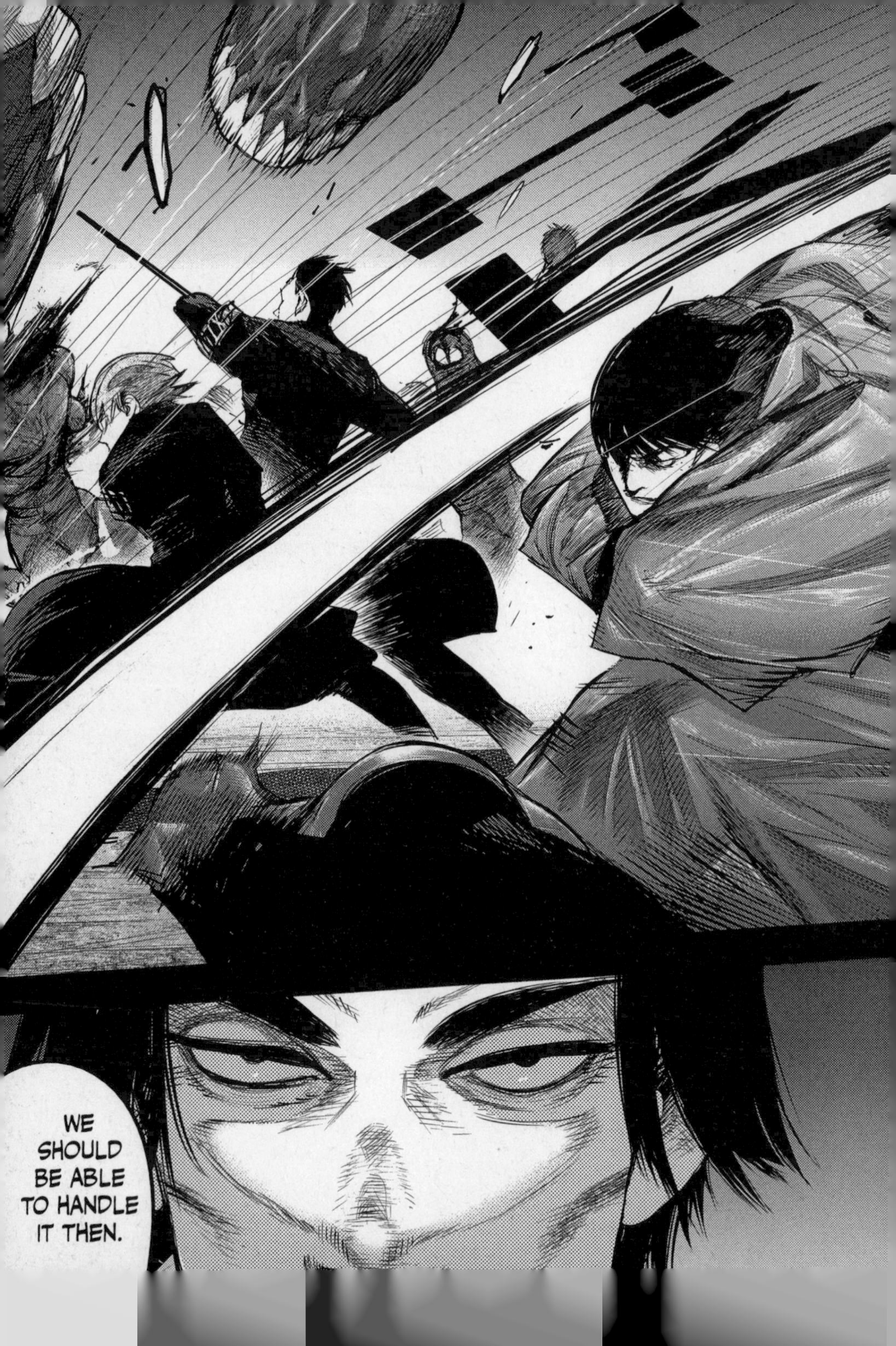
WE SHOULD BE ABLE TO HANDLE IT THEN.

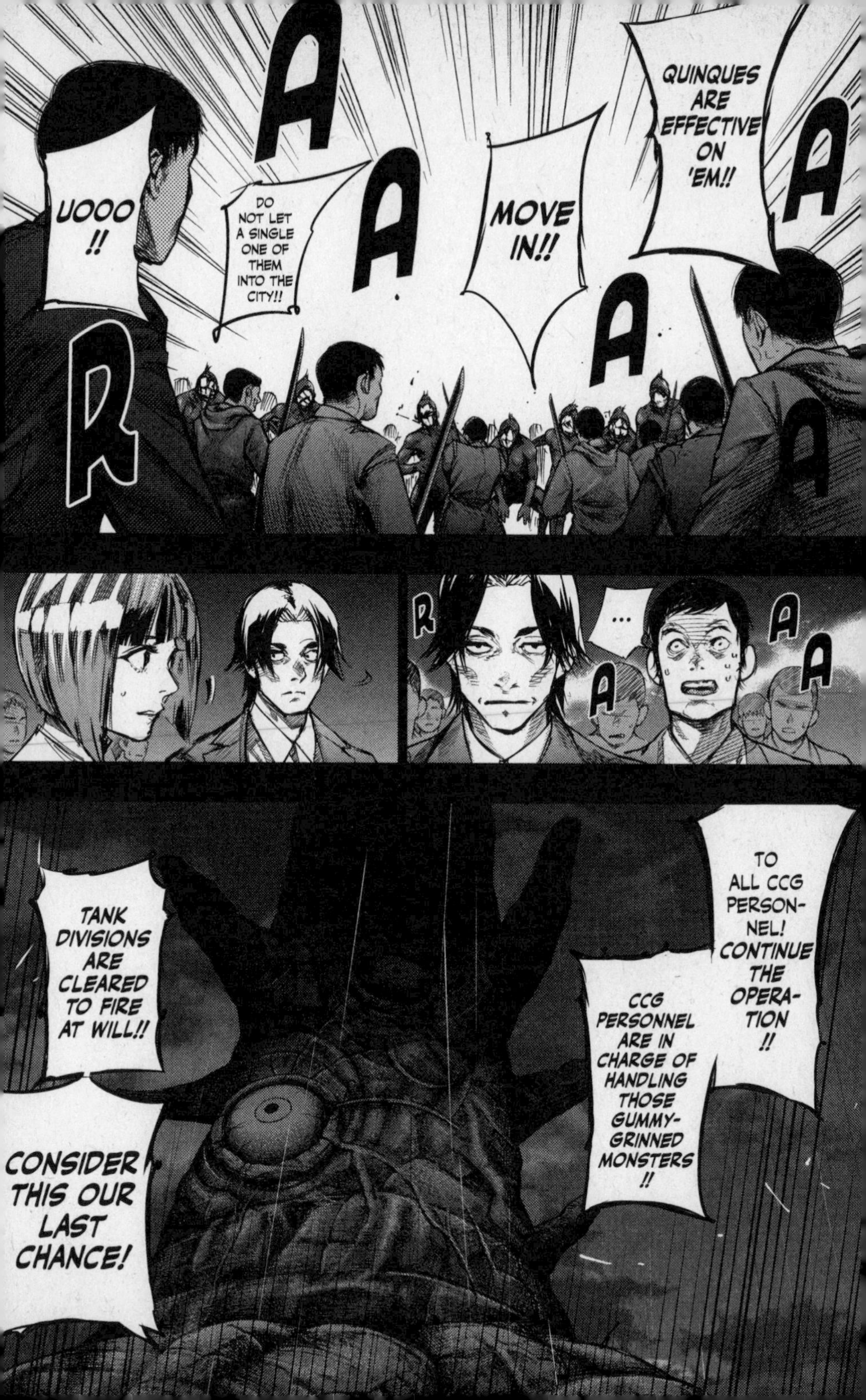
A
QUINQUES ARE EFFECTIVE ON 'EM!!
A
A
MOVE IN!!
A
A
DO NOT LET A SINGLE ONE OF THEM INTO THE CITY!!
A
UOOO!!
R
A
A
...
A
R
TO ALL CCG PERSON-NEL! CONTINUE THE OPERA-TION!!
CCG PERSONNEL ARE IN CHARGE OF HANDLING THOSE GUMMY-GRINNED MONSTERS!!
TANK DIVISIONS ARE CLEARED TO FIRE AT WILL!!
CONSIDER THIS OUR LAST CHANCE!

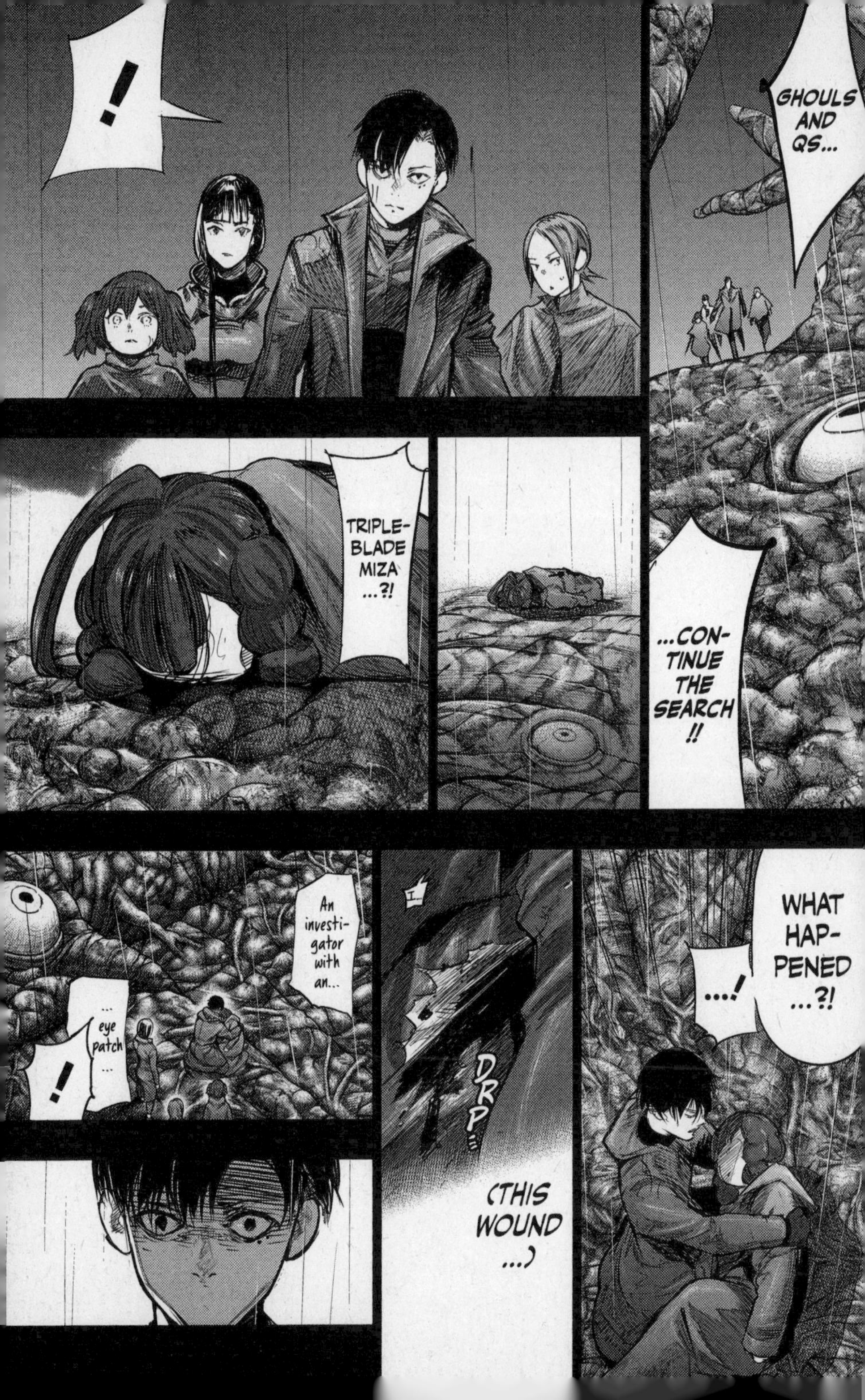
GHOULS AND QS...
...CONTINUE THE SEARCH!!
!
TRIPLE-BLADE MIZA...?!
WHAT HAPPENED...?!
...!
I...
DRP...
(THIS WOUND...)
An investigator with an...
...eye patch...
!

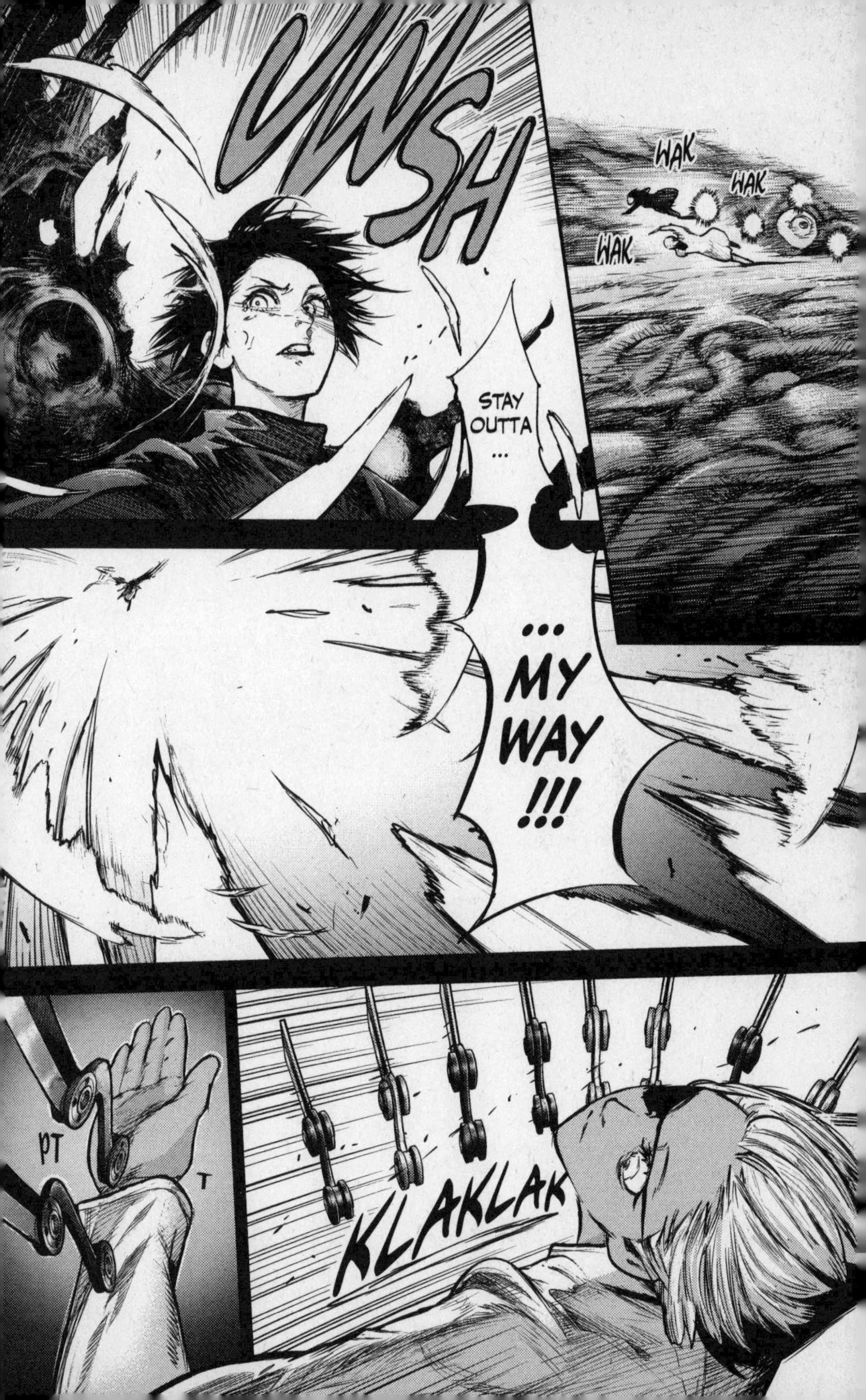
WAK
WAK
WAK
VWSH
STAY OUTTA ...
... MY WAY !!!
KLAKLAK
PT

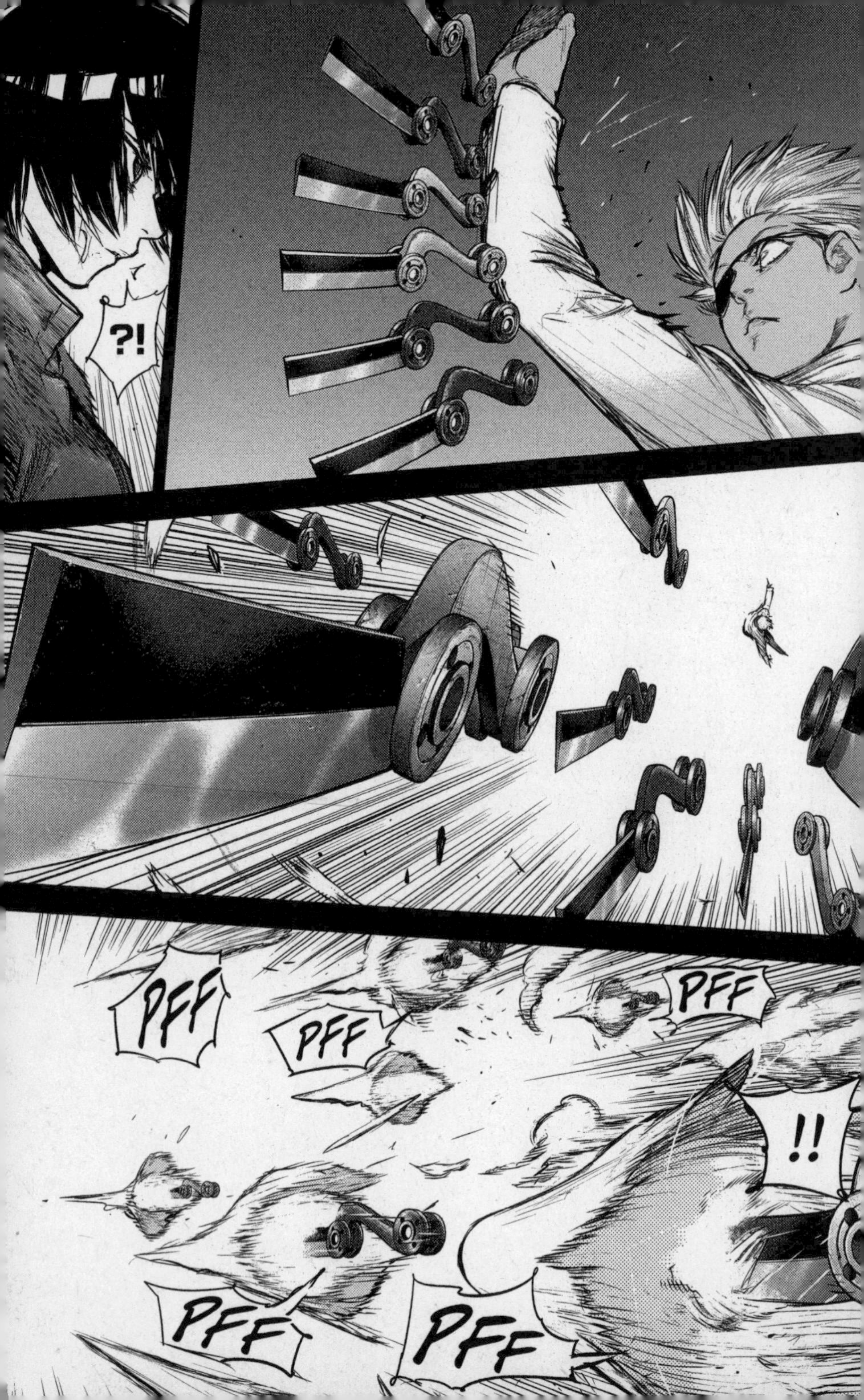
?!
PFF
!!
PFF
PFF
PFF
PFF

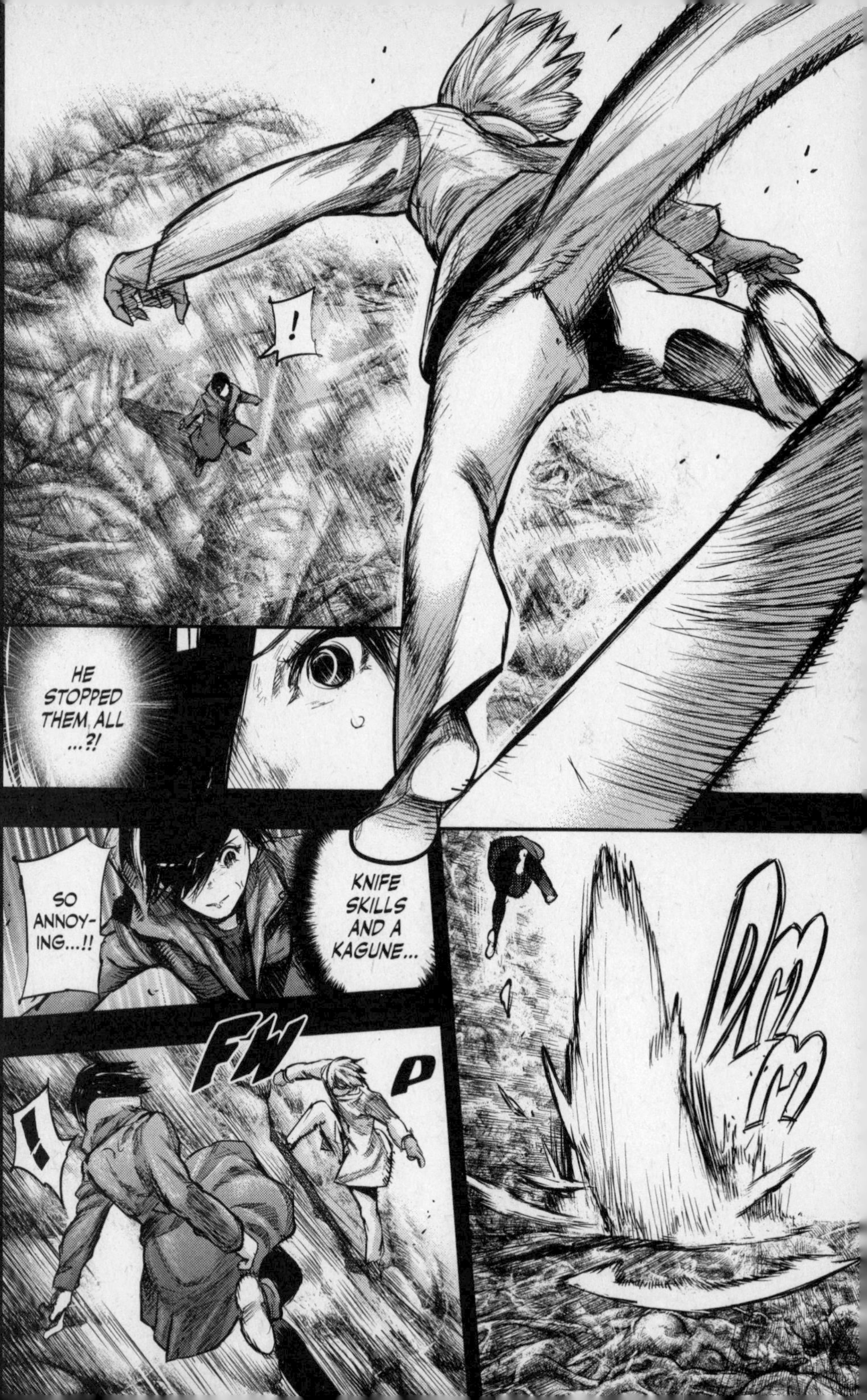

!
HE STOPPED THEM ALL ...?!
KNIFE SKILLS AND A KAGUNE...
SO ANNOY-ING...!!
FW P
!

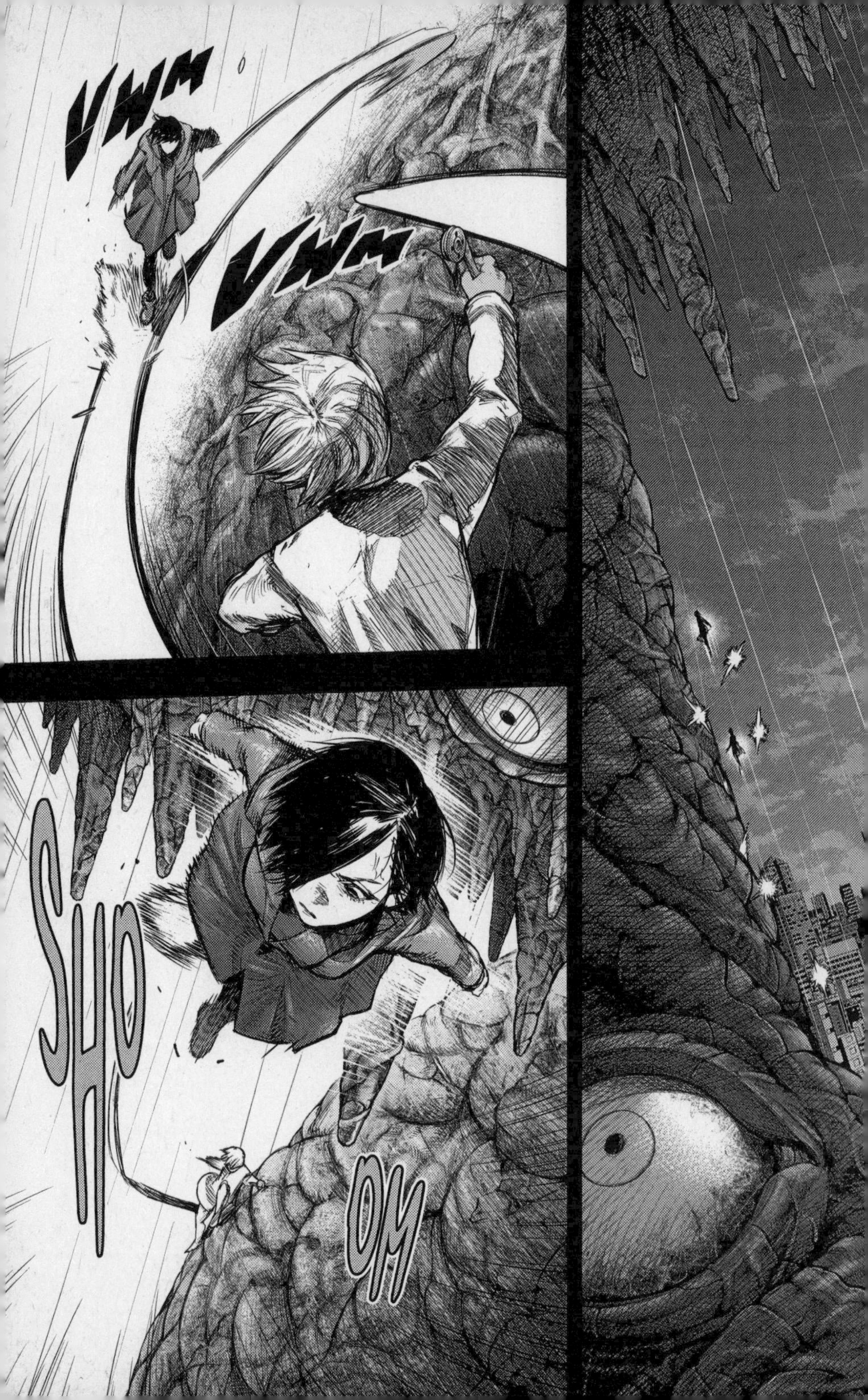
VWM
VWM
SHO
OM

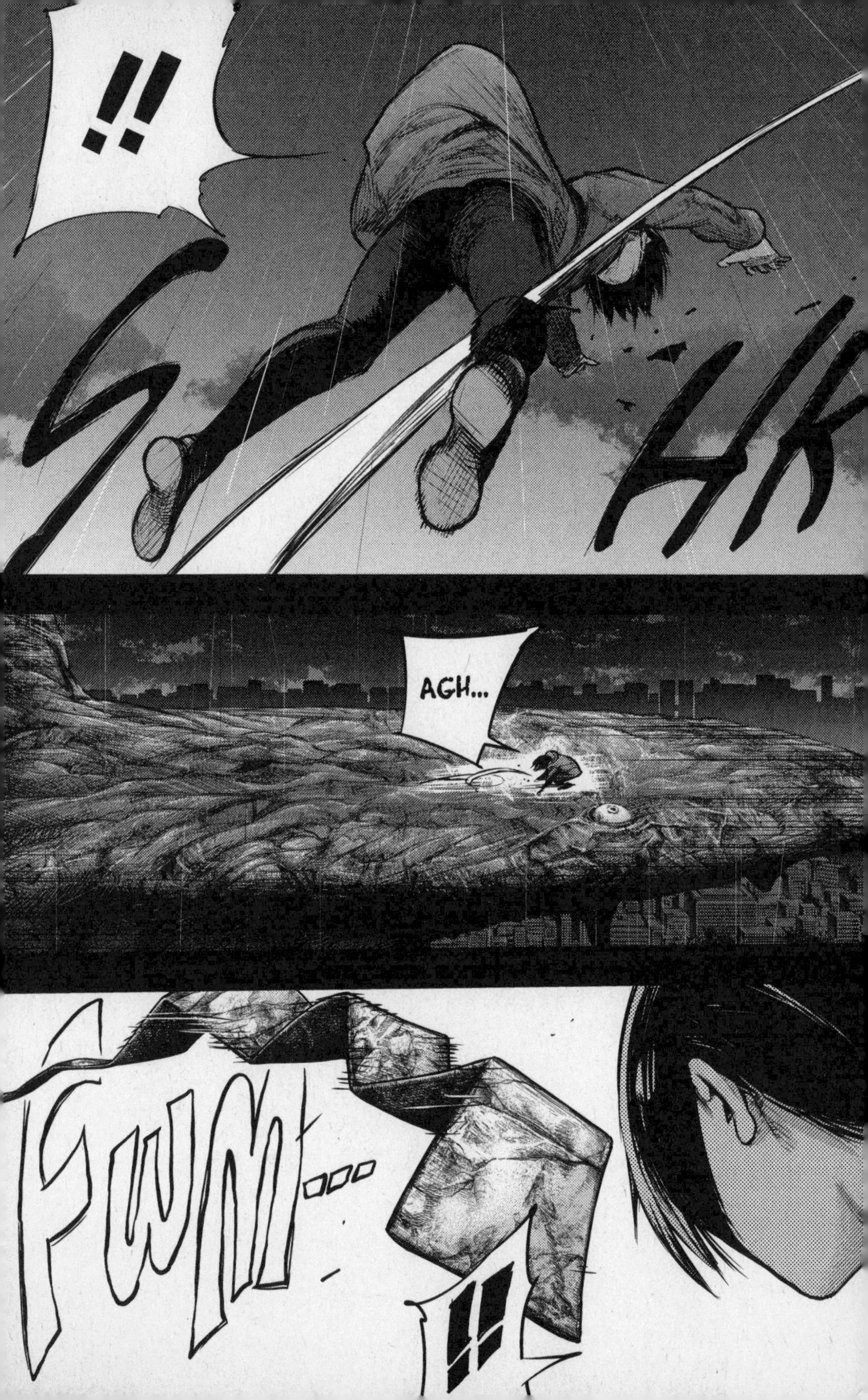
!!
SHK
AGH...
FWM...
!!

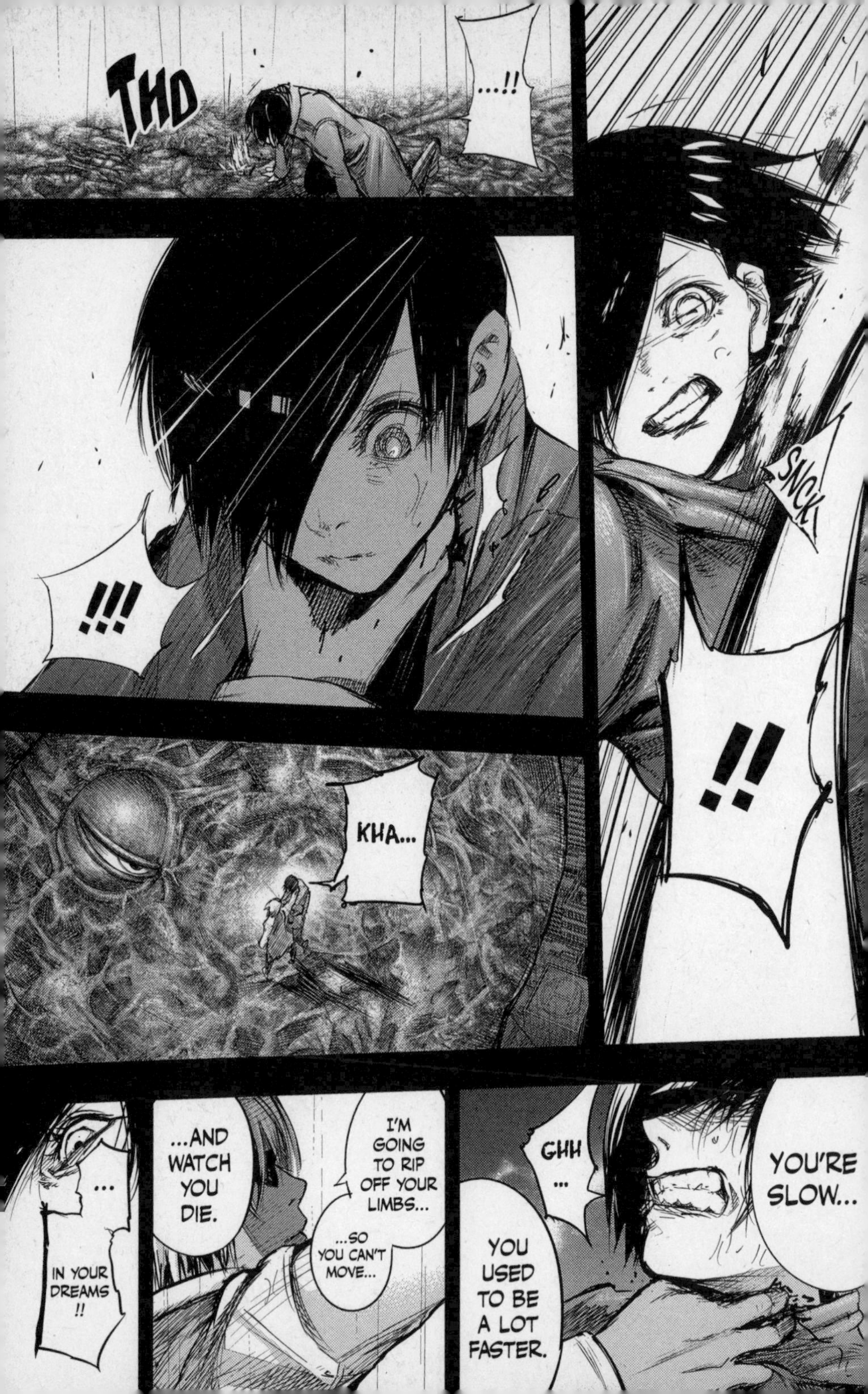
SNCK
!!
THD
...!!
!!!
KHA...
YOU'RE SLOW...
GHH ...
YOU USED TO BE A LOT FASTER.
I'M GOING TO RIP OFF YOUR LIMBS...
...SO YOU CAN'T MOVE...
...AND WATCH YOU DIE.
...
IN YOUR DREAMS !!

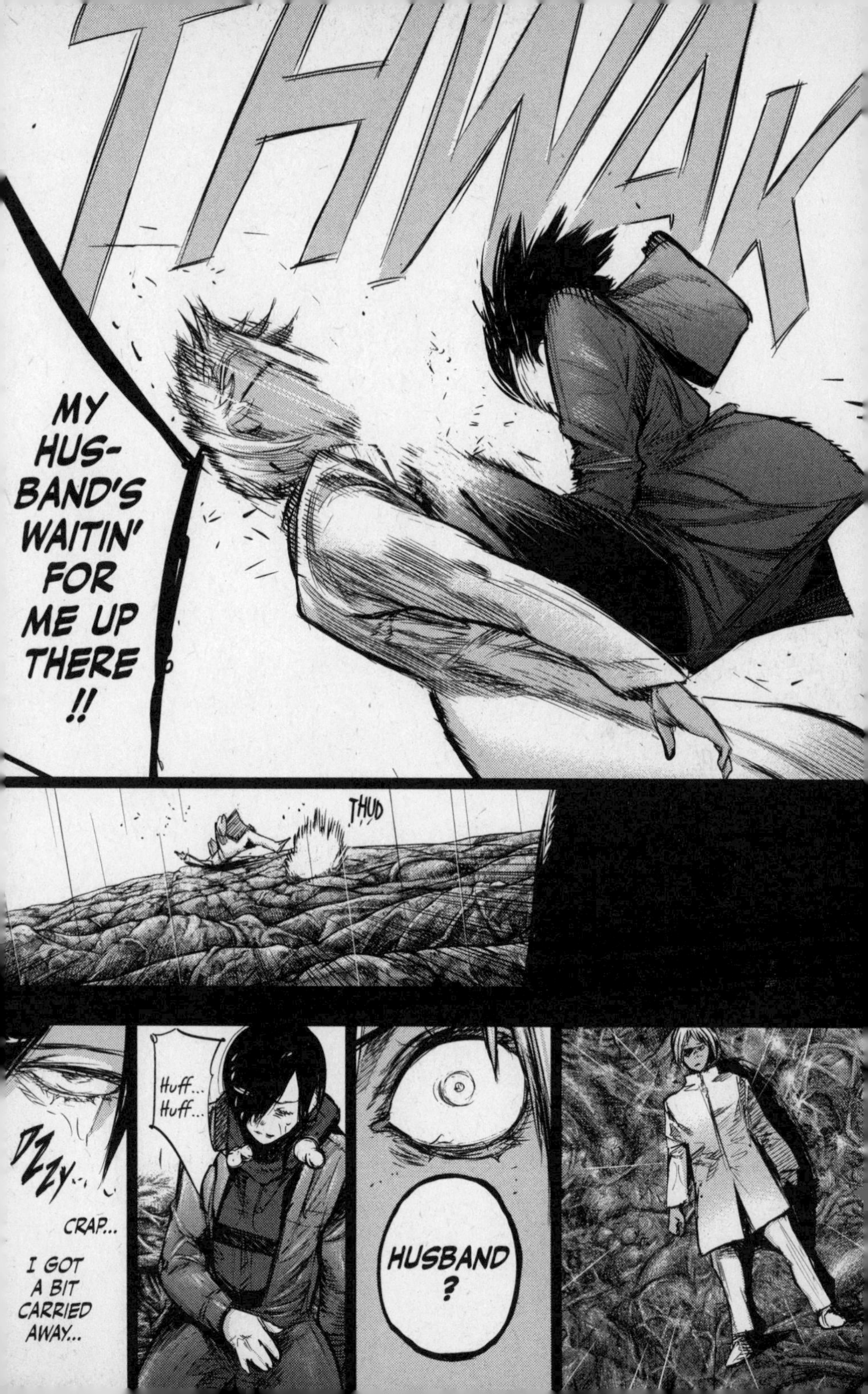
THWAK
MY HUSBAND'S WAITIN' FOR ME UP THERE!!
THUD
HUSBAND?
Huff... Huff...
DIZZY...
CRAP...
I GOT A BIT CARRIED AWAY...

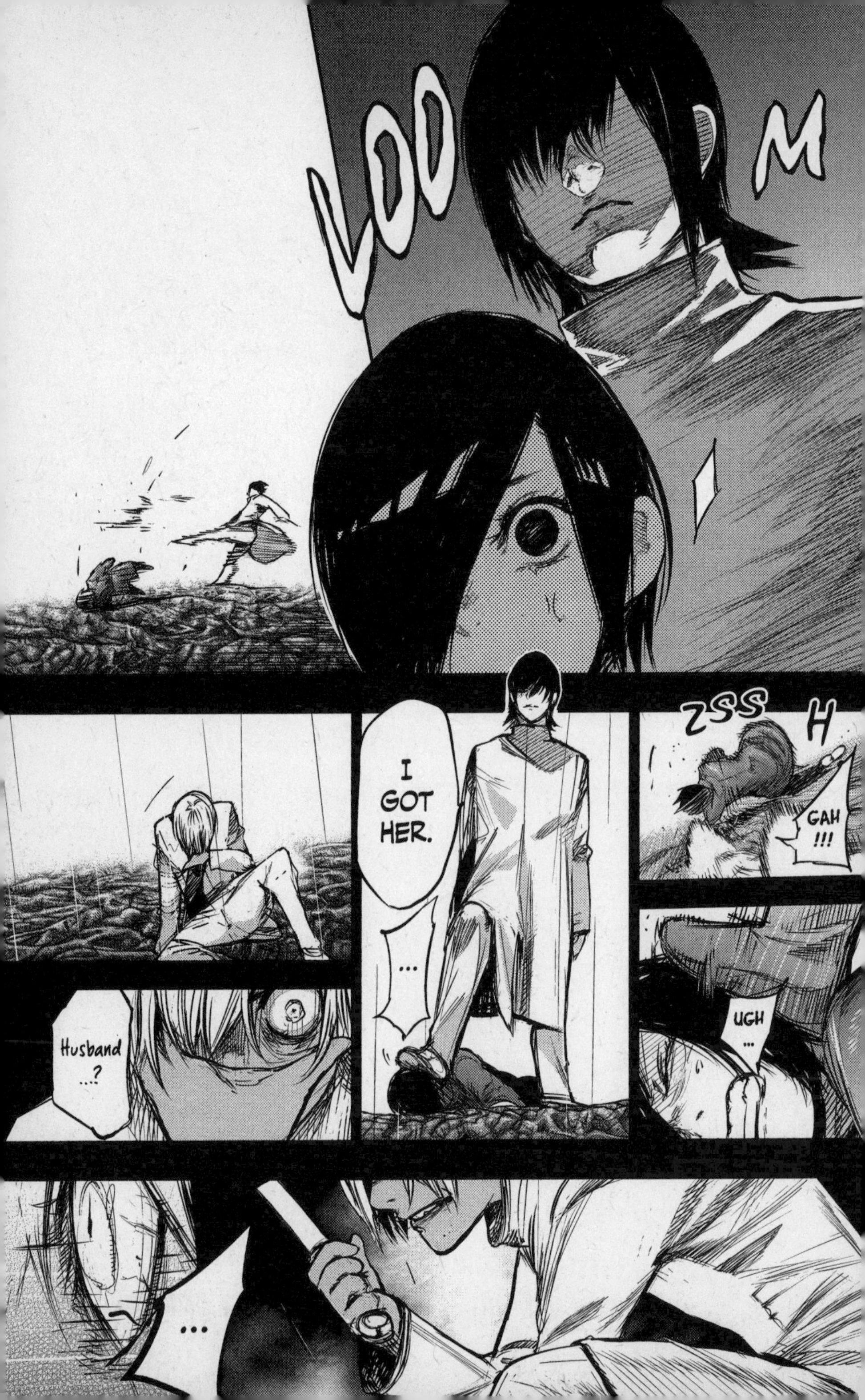
LOOM
ZSSH
GAH!!!
UGH ...
I GOT HER.
...
Husband ...?
...

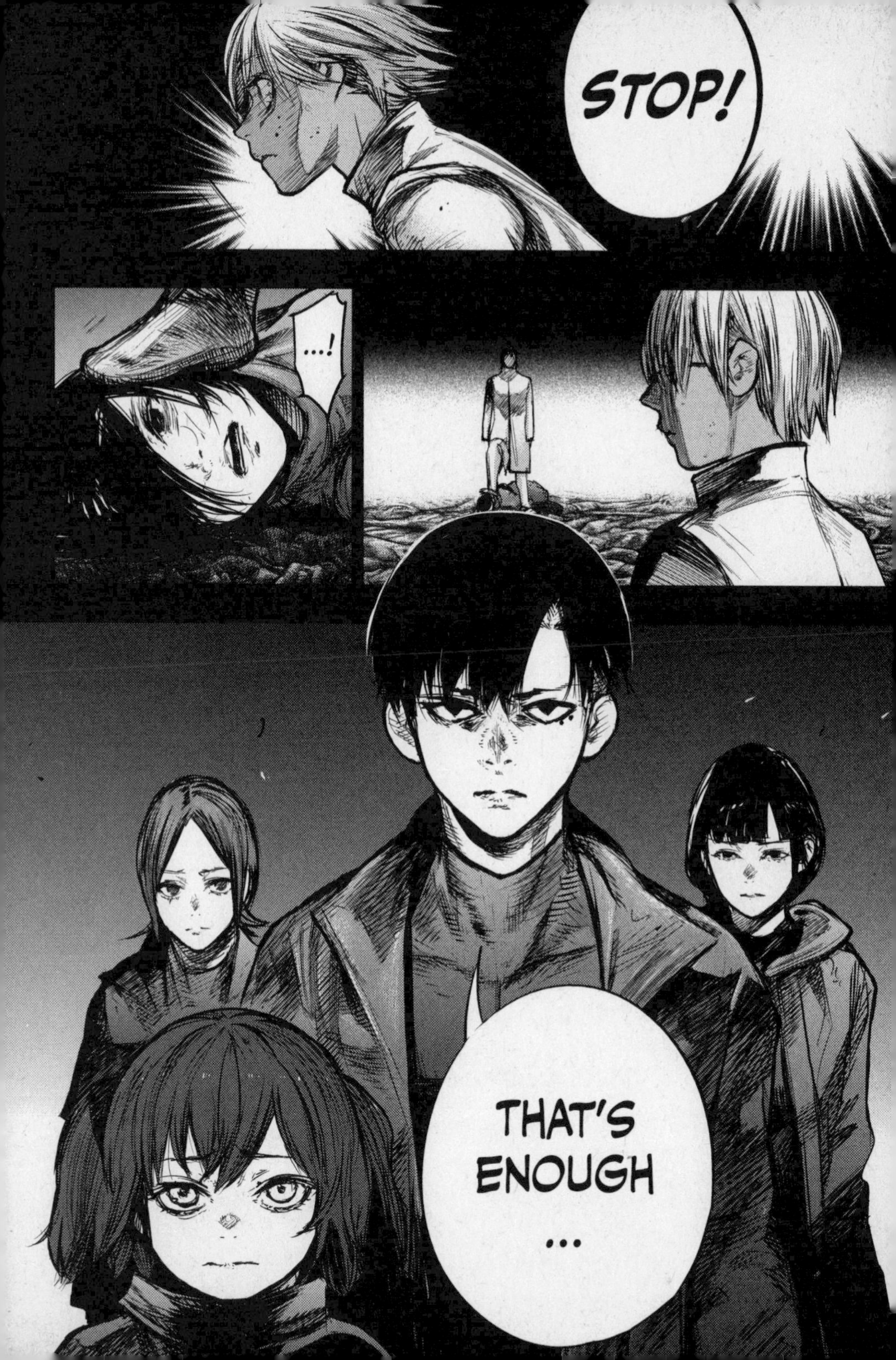
STOP!
...!
THAT'S ENOUGH ...

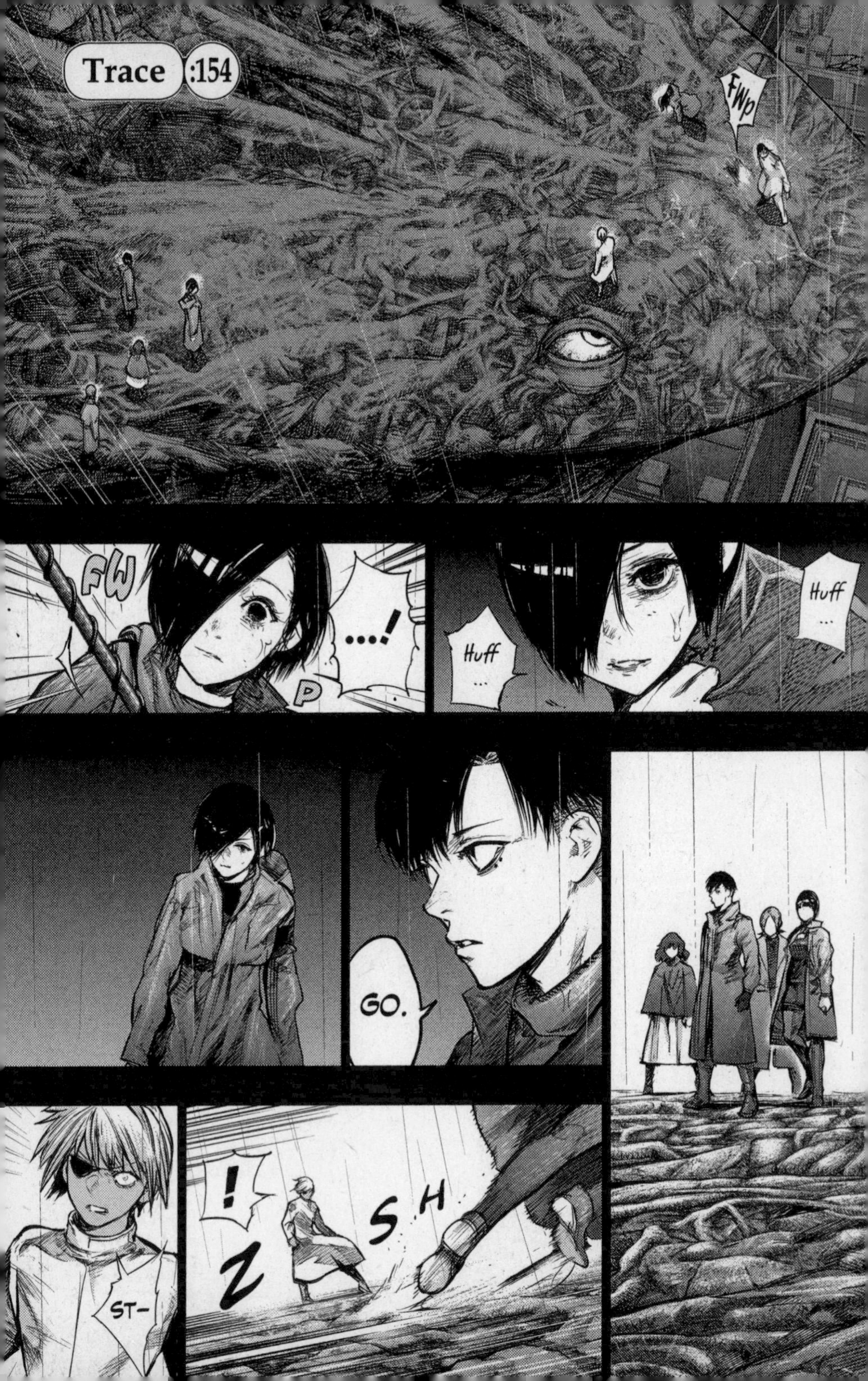
Trace :154
FWp
Huff ...
Huff ...
FW
...!
P
GO.
!
SH
Z
ST-

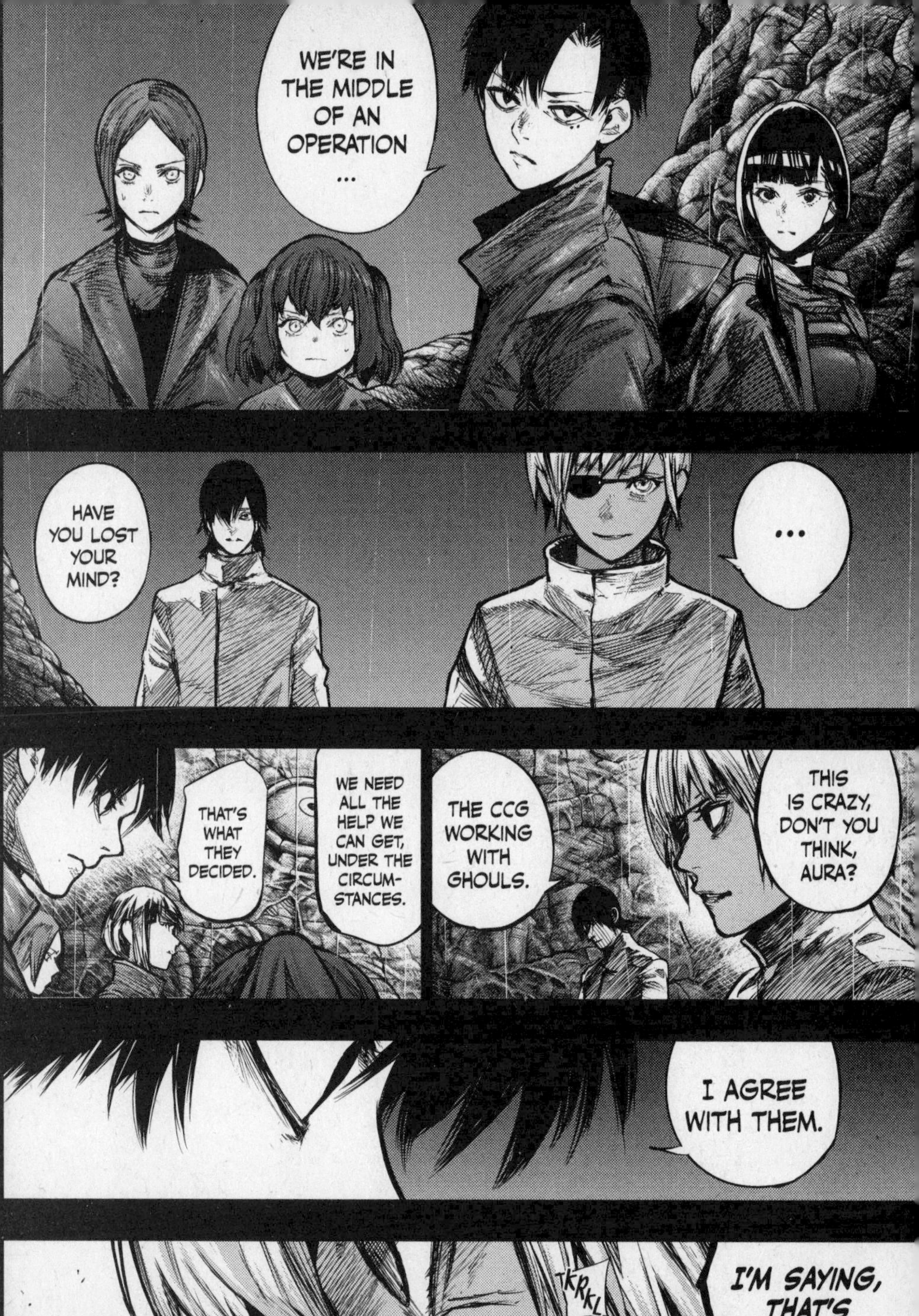
WE'RE IN THE MIDDLE OF AN OPERATION ...
...
HAVE YOU LOST YOUR MIND?
THIS IS CRAZY, DON'T YOU THINK, AURA?
THE CCG WORKING WITH GHOULS.
WE NEED ALL THE HELP WE CAN GET, UNDER THE CIRCUMSTANCES.
THAT'S WHAT THEY DECIDED.
I AGREE WITH THEM.
I'M SAYING, THAT'S WHAT'S...
TKRKL
KRKL

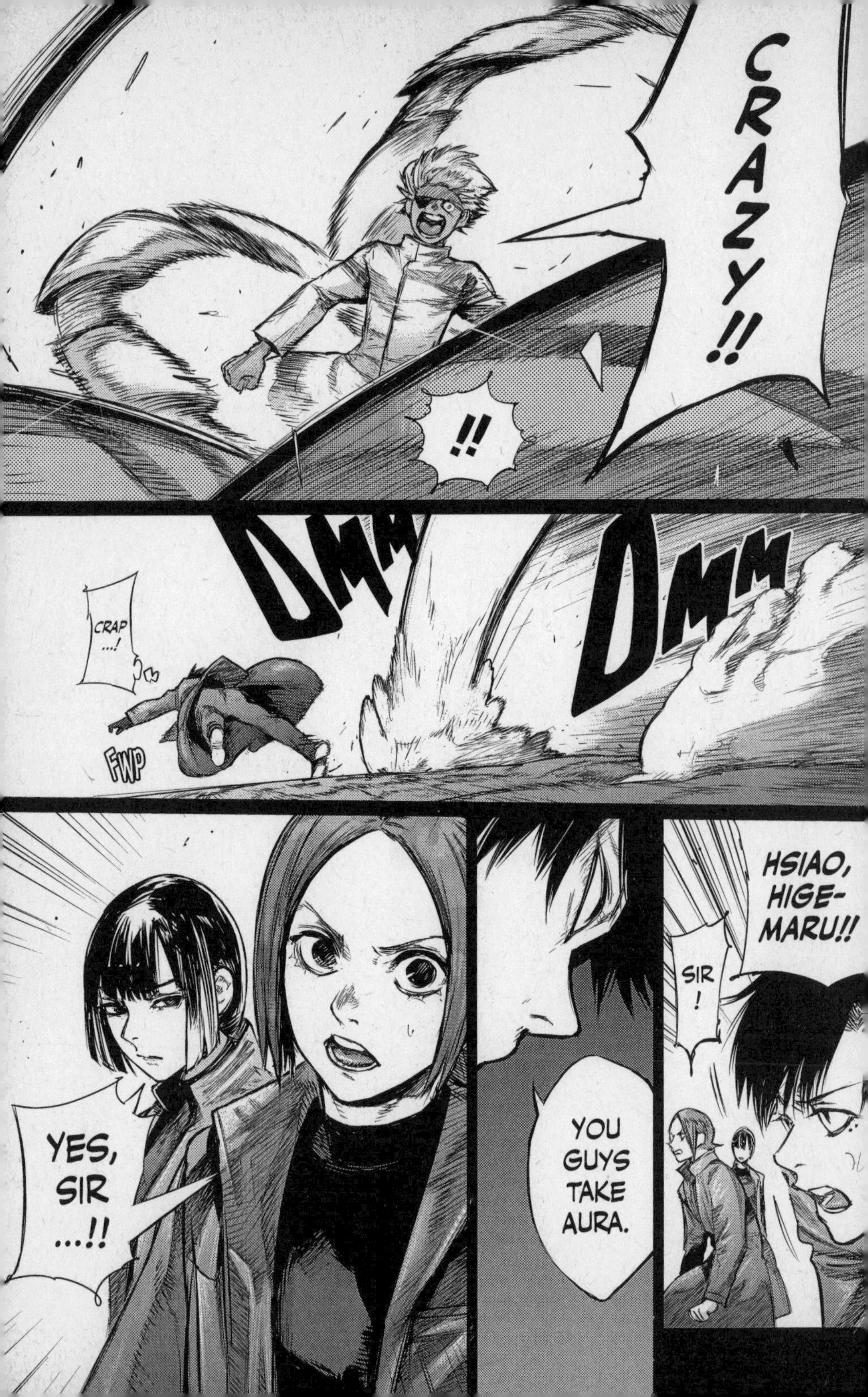
CRAZY!!
!!
DMM
DMM
CRAP...!
FWP
HSIAO, HIGE-MARU!!
SIR!
YOU GUYS TAKE AURA.
YES, SIR...!!

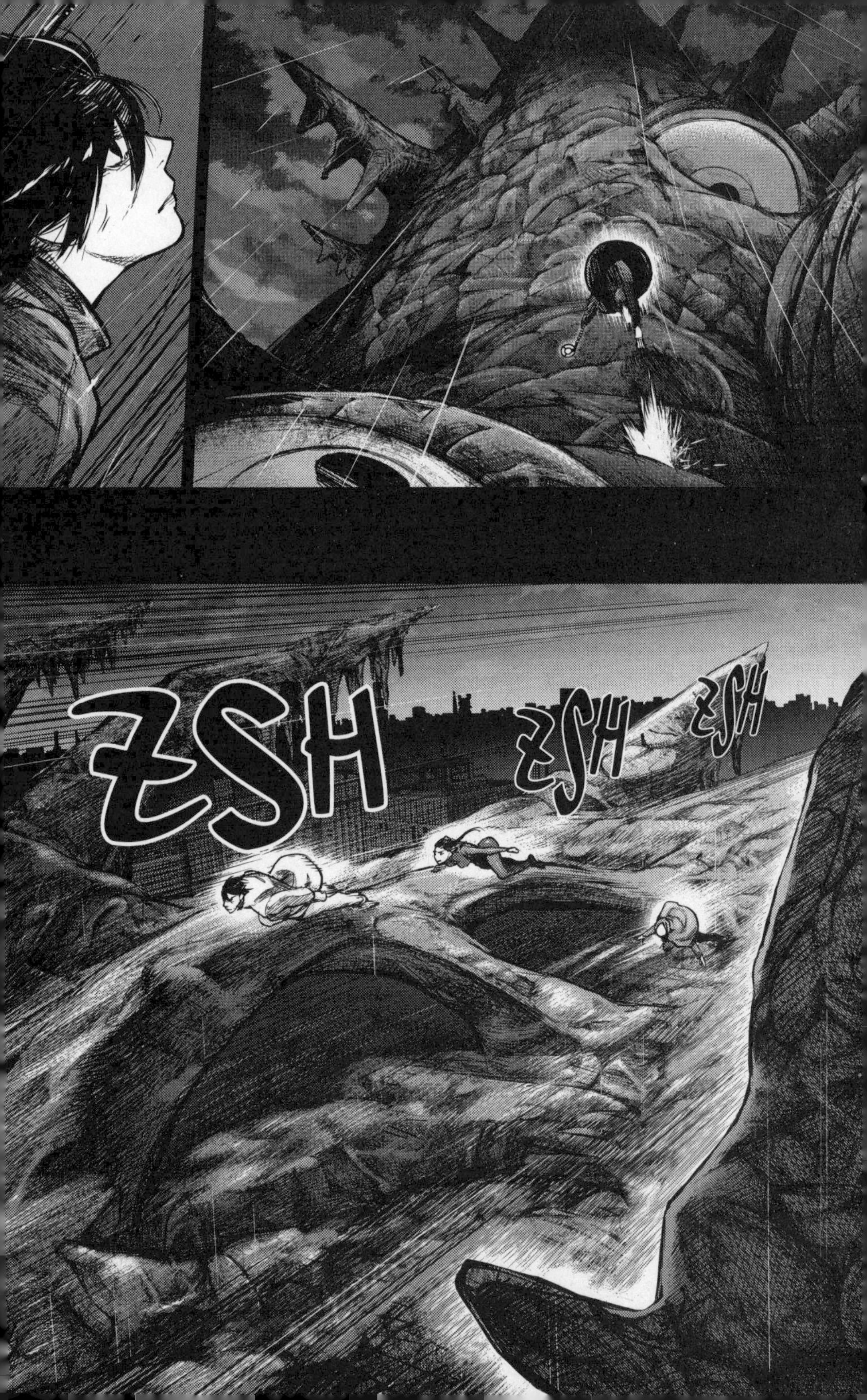
ZSH
ZSH
ZSH

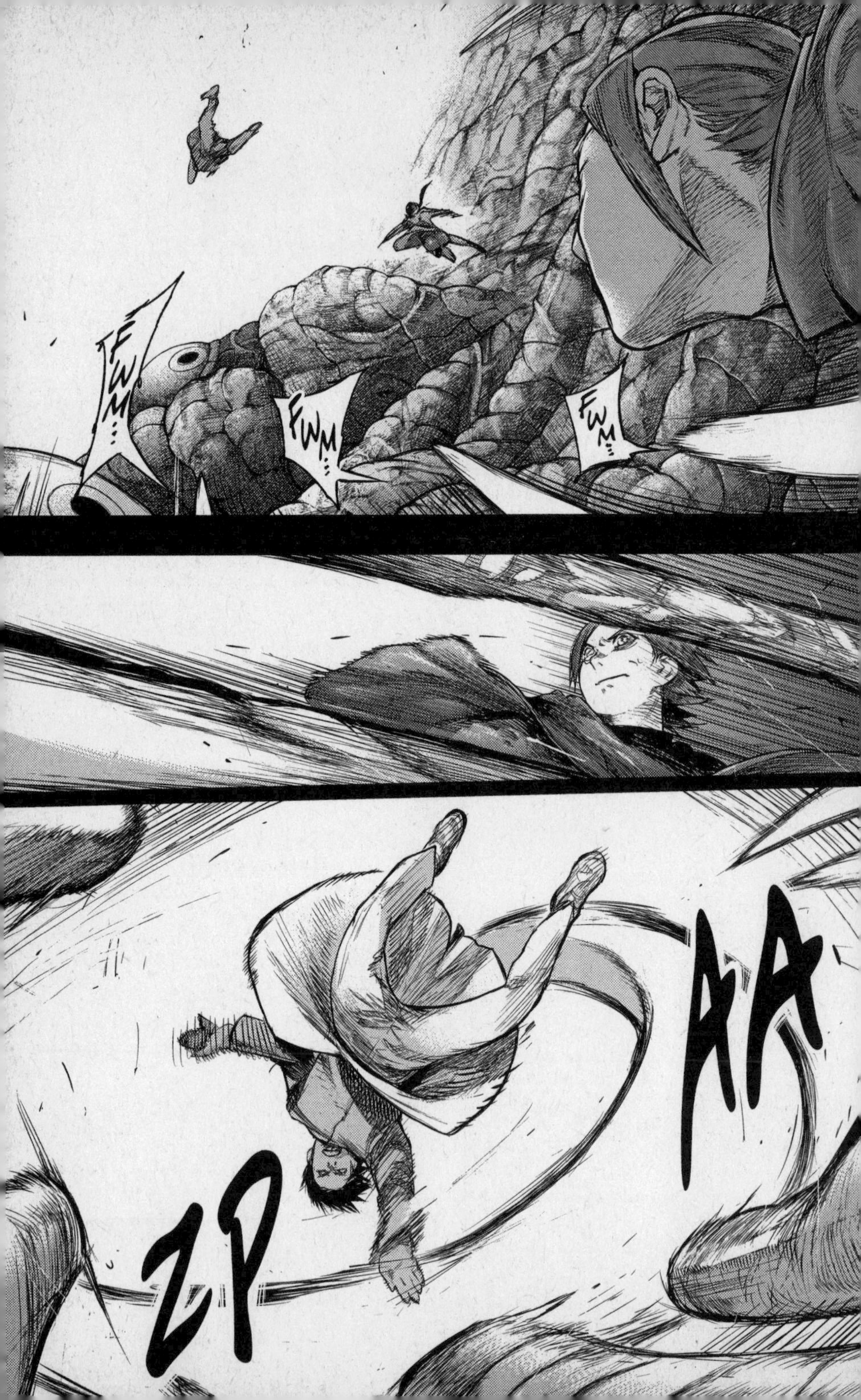
FWM...
FWM...
FWM...
AA
ZP

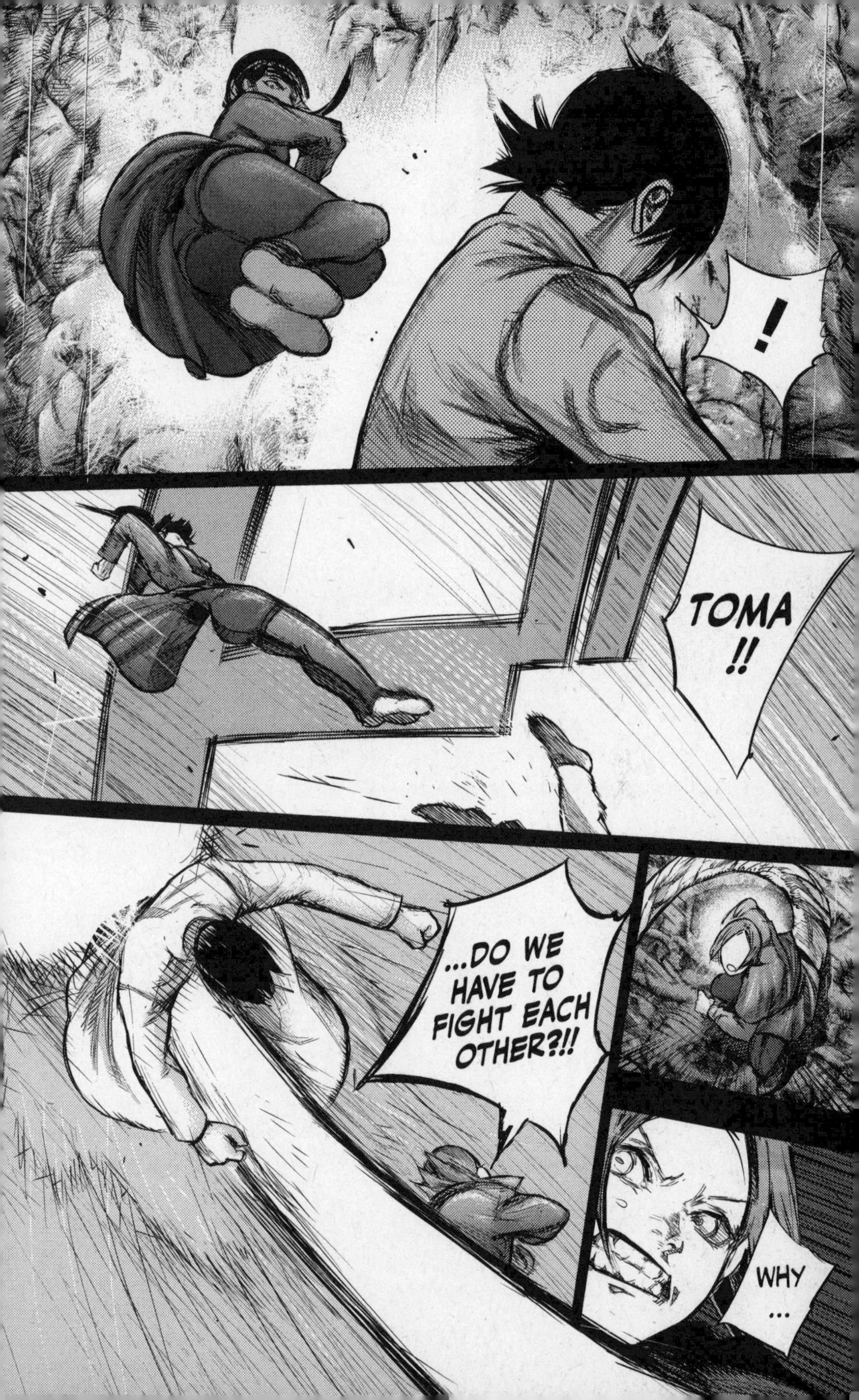
!
TOMA !!
WHY ...
...DO WE HAVE TO FIGHT EACH OTHER?!!

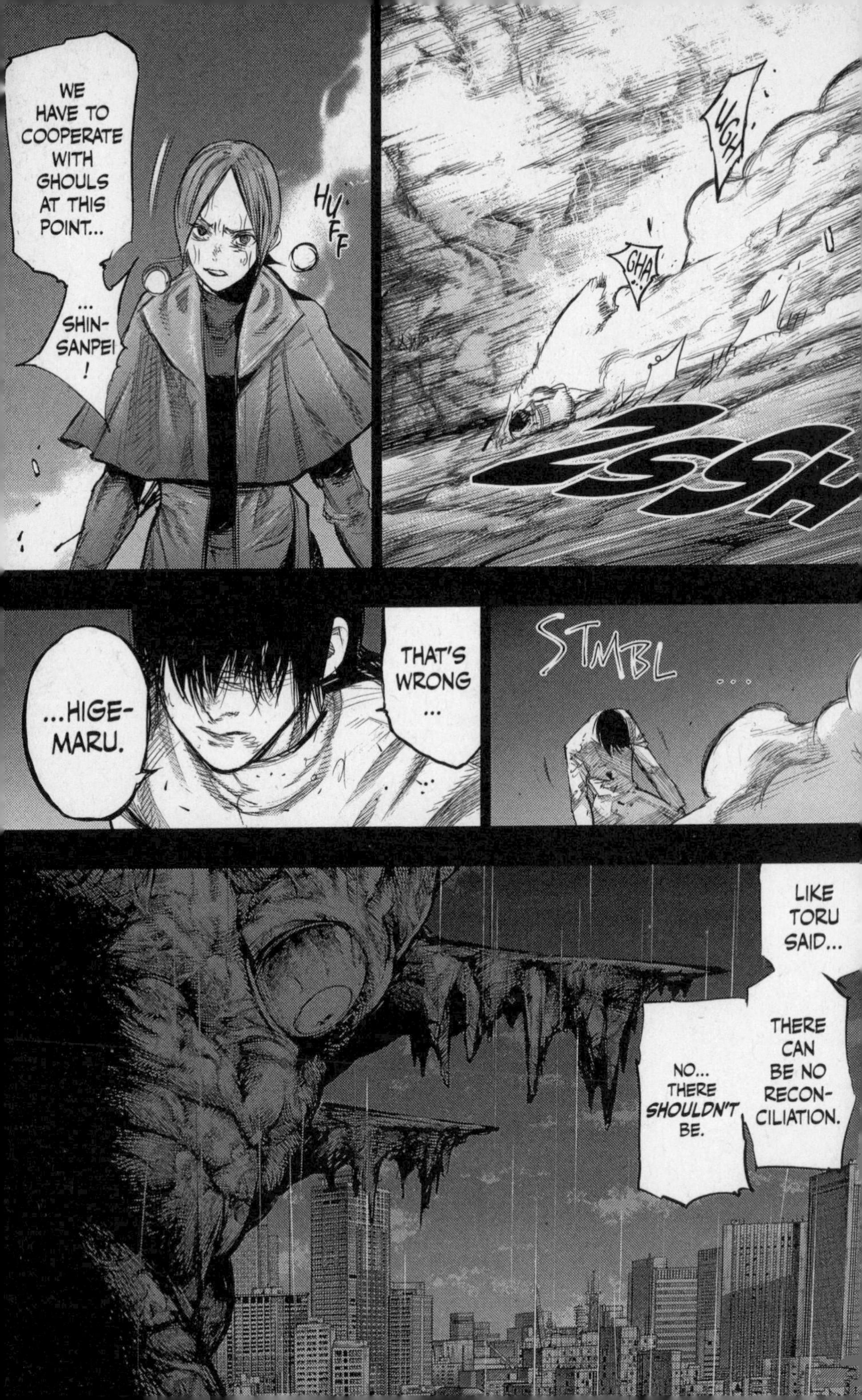
UGH
GHA...
WE HAVE TO COOPERATE WITH GHOULS AT THIS POINT...
HUFF
...SHIN-SANPEI!
STMBL
...
THAT'S WRONG...
...HIGE-MARU.
LIKE TORU SAID...
THERE CAN BE NO RECONCILIATION.
NO... THERE *SHOULDN'T* BE.

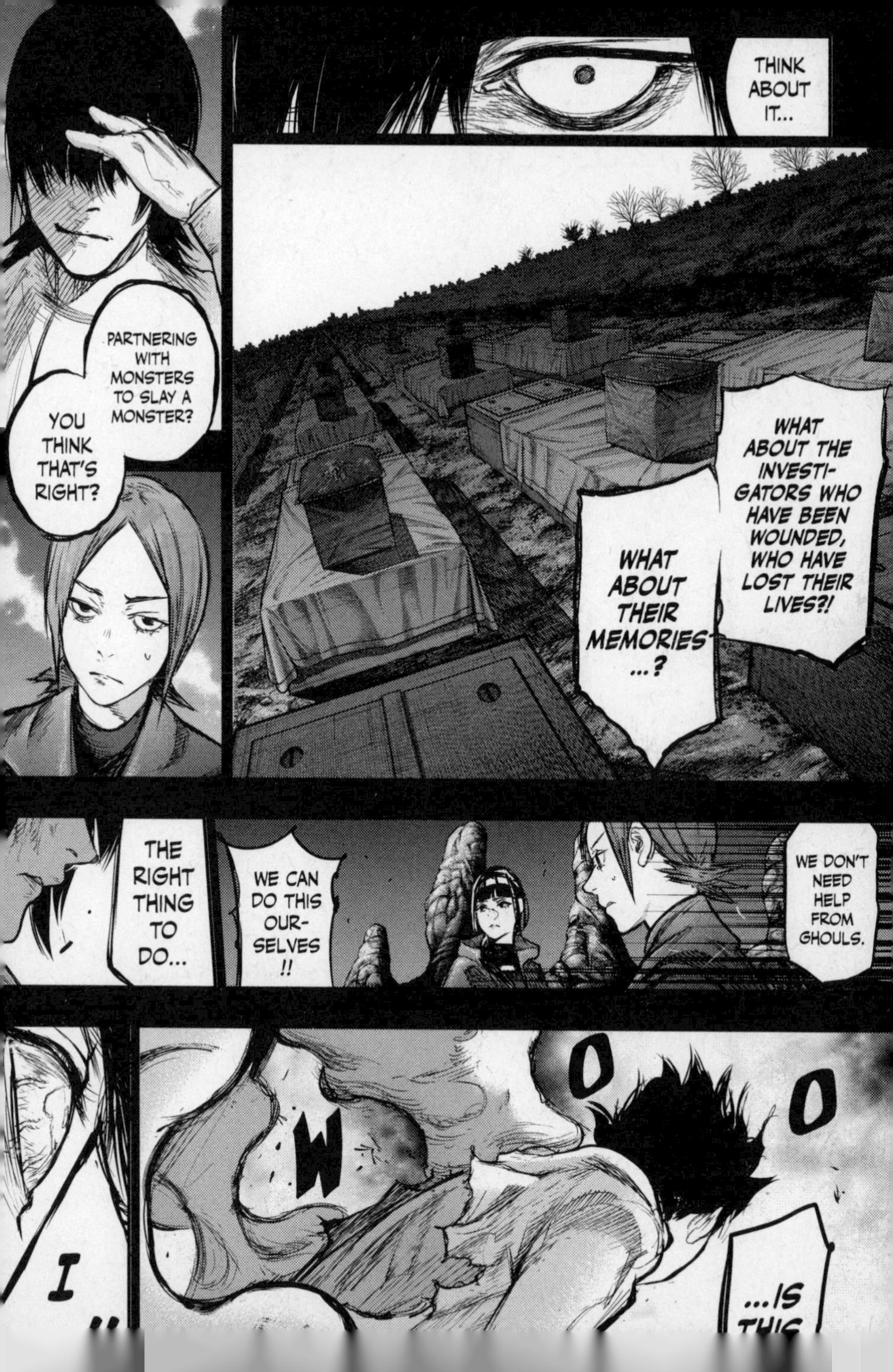
THINK ABOUT IT...
WHAT ABOUT THE INVESTIGATORS WHO HAVE BEEN WOUNDED, WHO HAVE LOST THEIR LIVES?!
WHAT ABOUT THEIR MEMORIES...?
PARTNERING WITH MONSTERS TO SLAY A MONSTER?
YOU THINK THAT'S RIGHT?
WE DON'T NEED HELP FROM GHOULS.
WE CAN DO THIS OURSELVES!!
THE RIGHT THING TO DO...
...IS
O
O
W
I

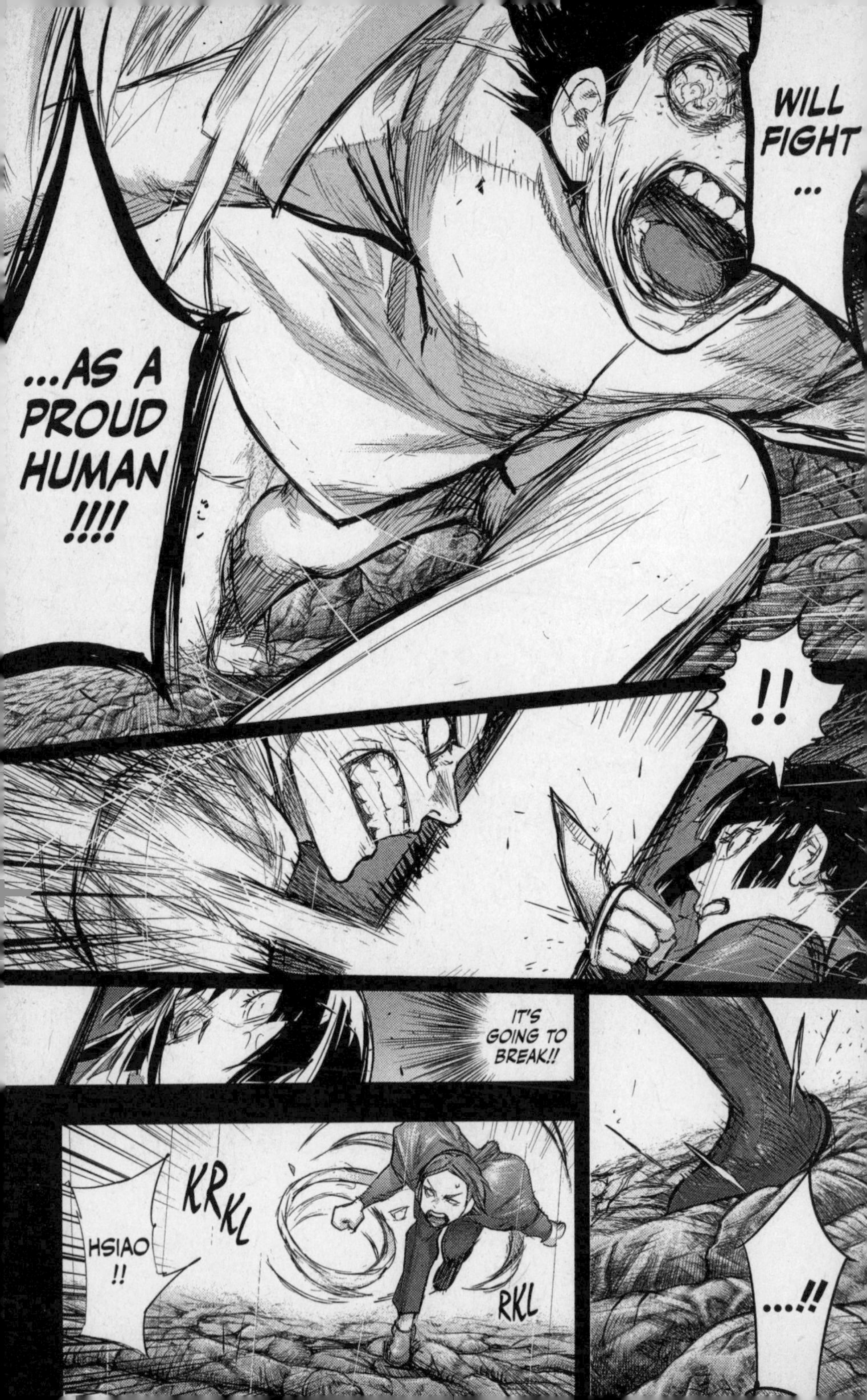
WILL FIGHT ...
...AS A PROUD HUMAN !!!!
!!
...!!
IT'S GOING TO BREAK!!
KRKL
HSIAO !!
RKL

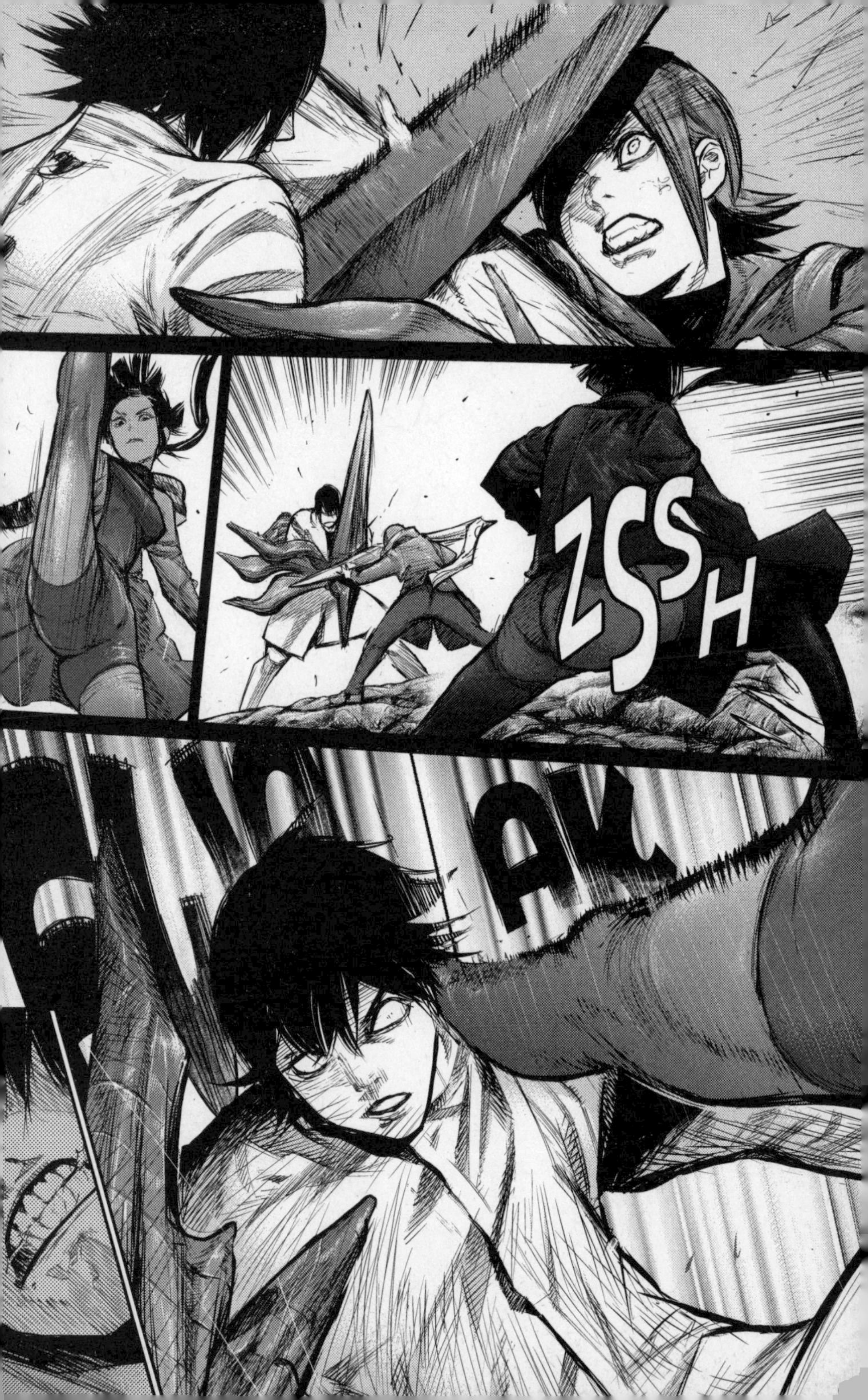
ZSSH

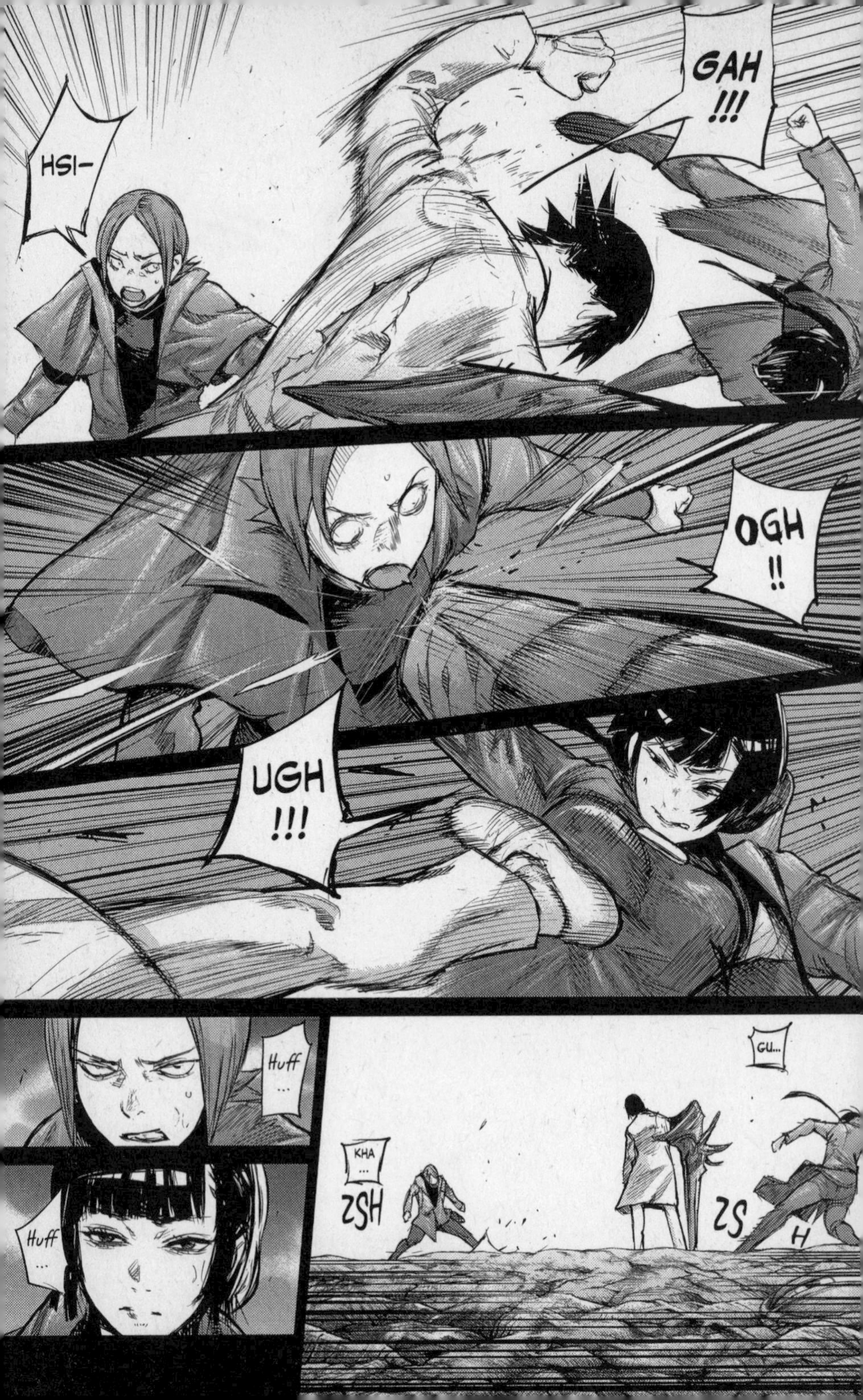
GAH!!!
HSI-
OGH!!
UGH!!!
GU...
ZSH
KHA...
ZSH
Huff...
Huff...

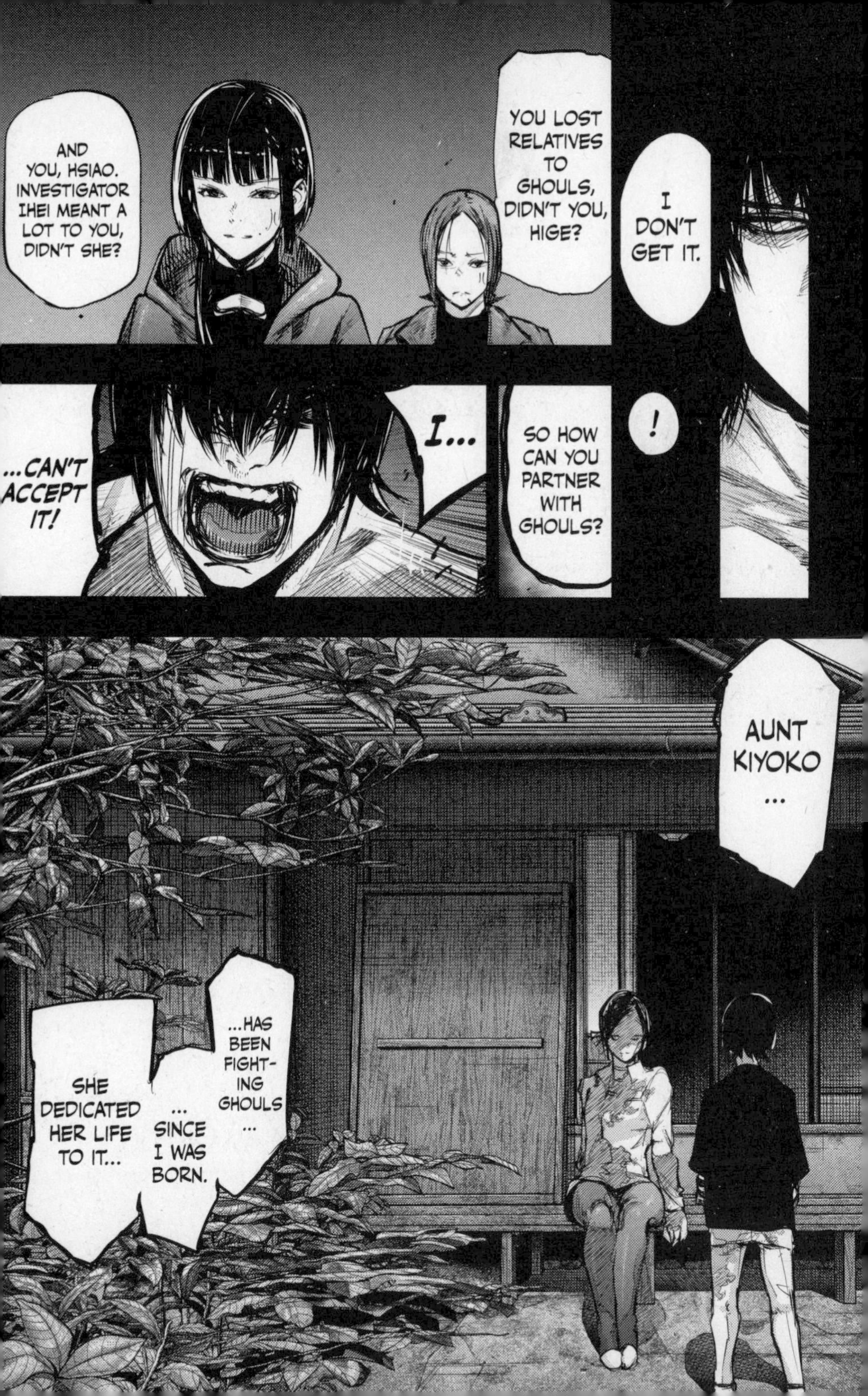
I DON'T GET IT.
!
YOU LOST RELATIVES TO GHOULS, DIDN'T YOU, HIGE?
AND YOU, HSIAO. INVESTIGATOR IHEI MEANT A LOT TO YOU, DIDN'T SHE?
SO HOW CAN YOU PARTNER WITH GHOULS?
I...
...CAN'T ACCEPT IT!
AUNT KIYOKO ...
...HAS BEEN FIGHT-ING GHOULS ...
... SINCE I WAS BORN.
SHE DEDICATED HER LIFE TO IT...

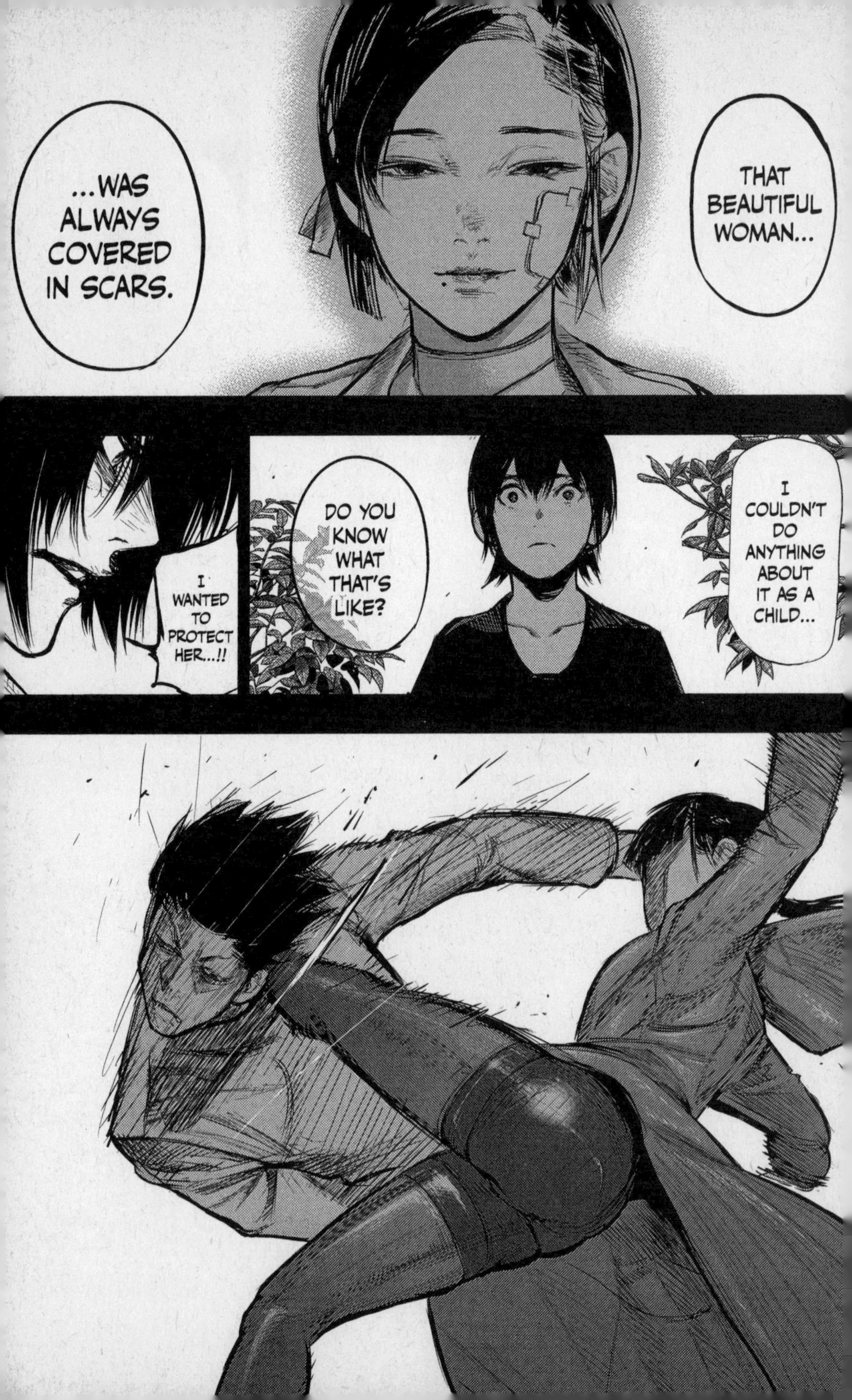
THAT BEAUTIFUL WOMAN...
...WAS ALWAYS COVERED IN SCARS.
I COULDN'T DO ANYTHING ABOUT IT AS A CHILD...
DO YOU KNOW WHAT THAT'S LIKE?
I WANTED TO PROTECT HER...!!

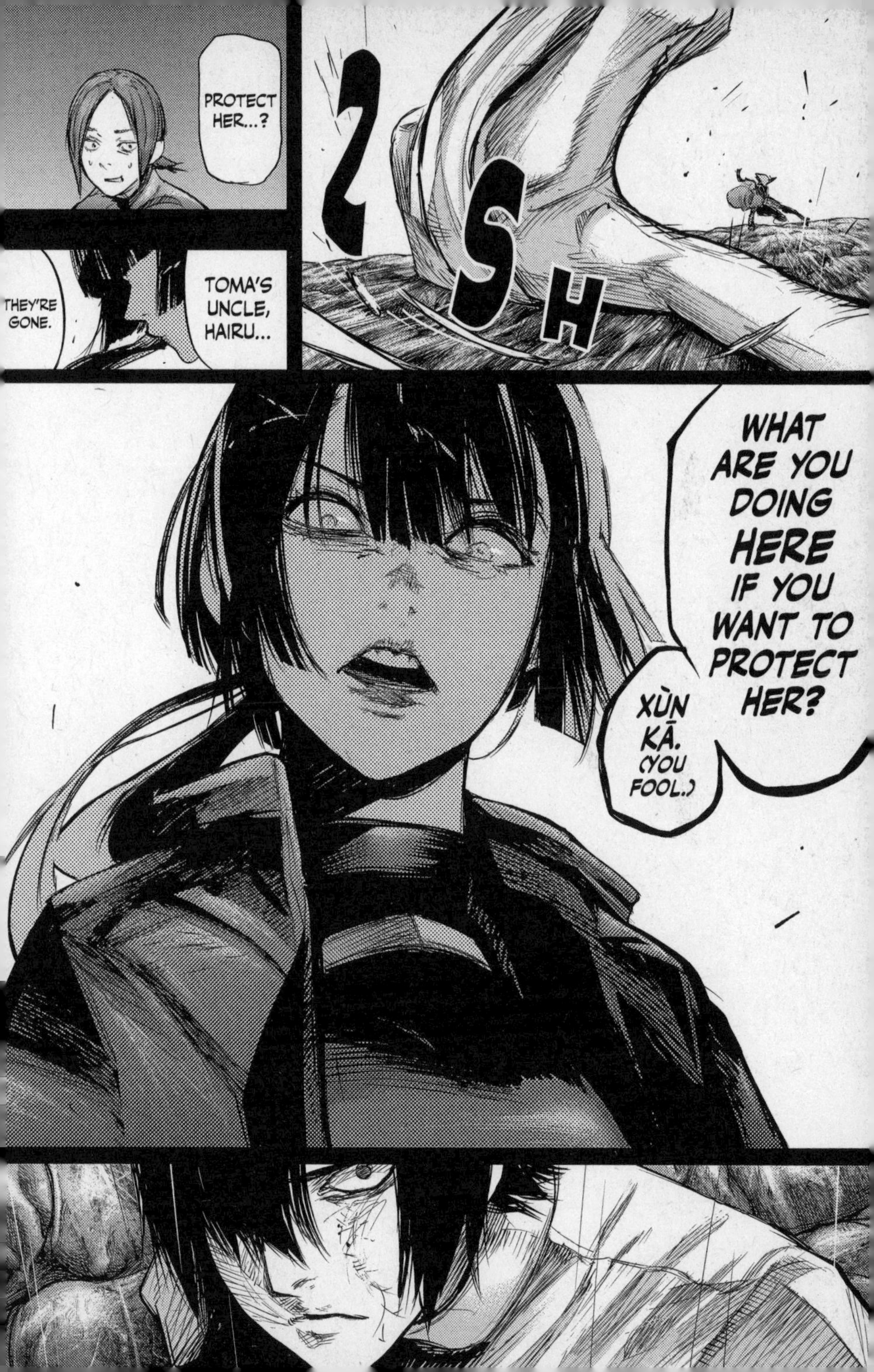
ZSH
PROTECT HER...?
TOMA'S UNCLE, HAIRU...
THEY'RE GONE.
WHAT ARE YOU DOING HERE IF YOU WANT TO PROTECT HER?
XÙN KĀ. (YOU FOOL.)

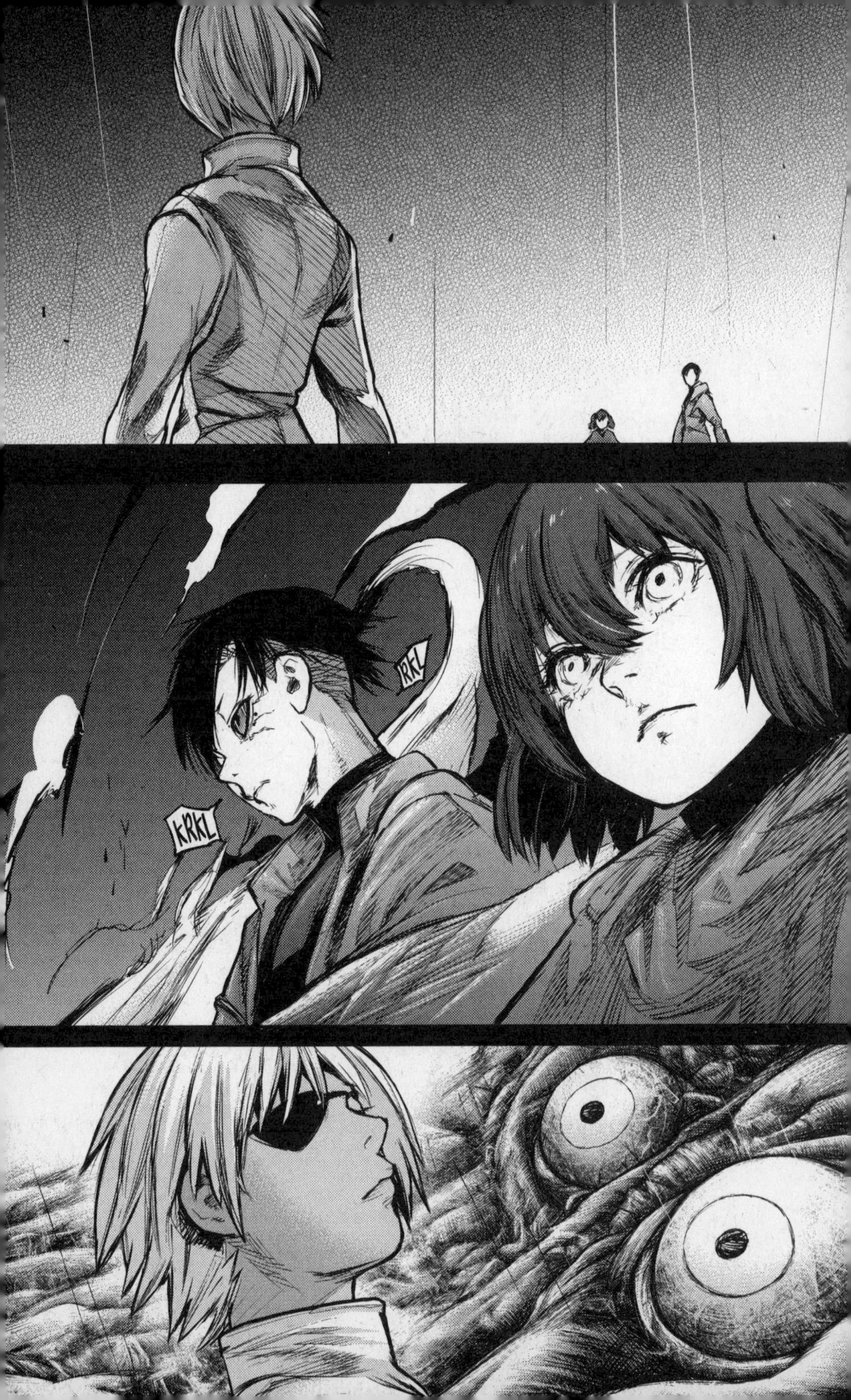
RKL
KRKL

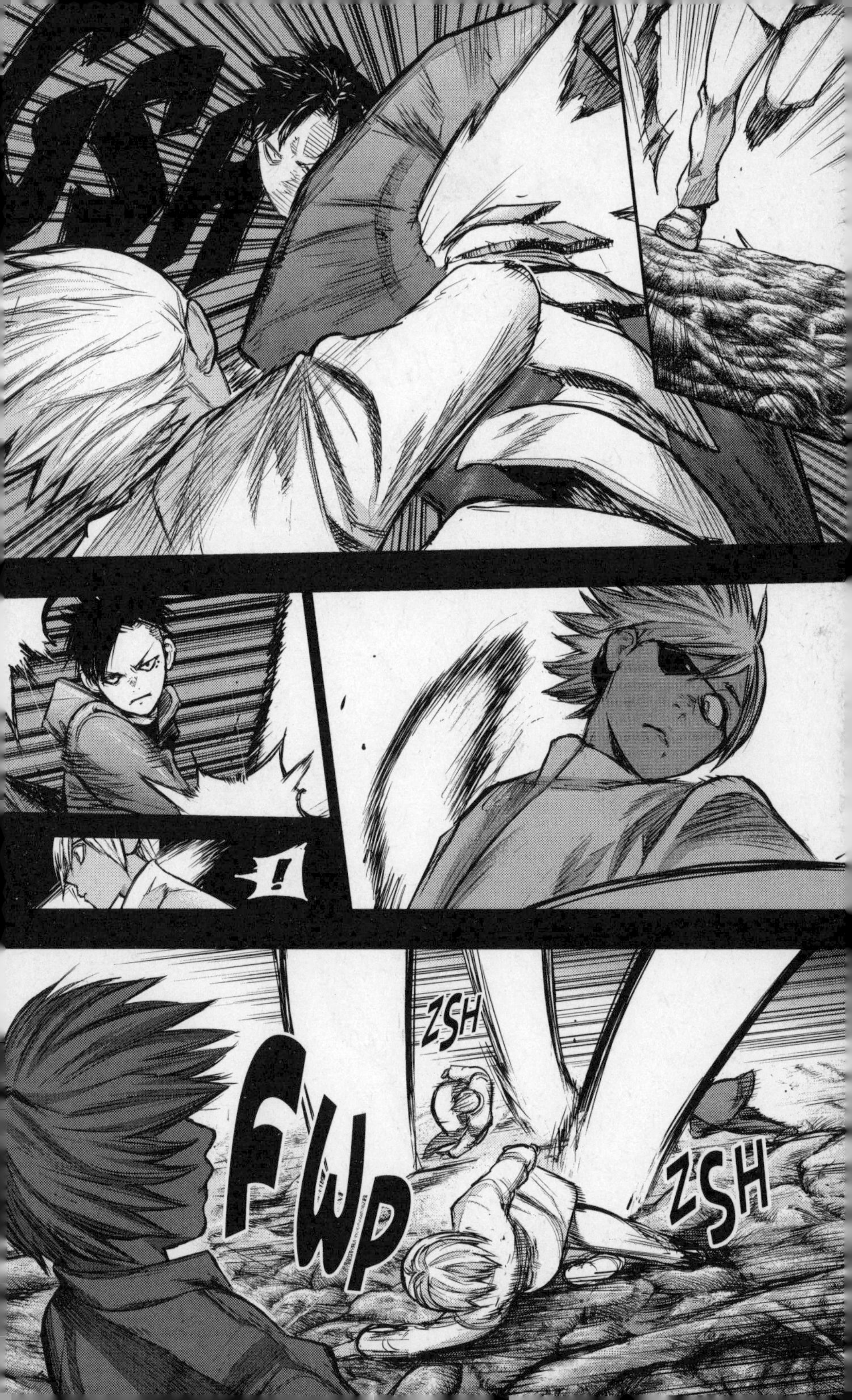
!
ZSH
ZSH
FWP

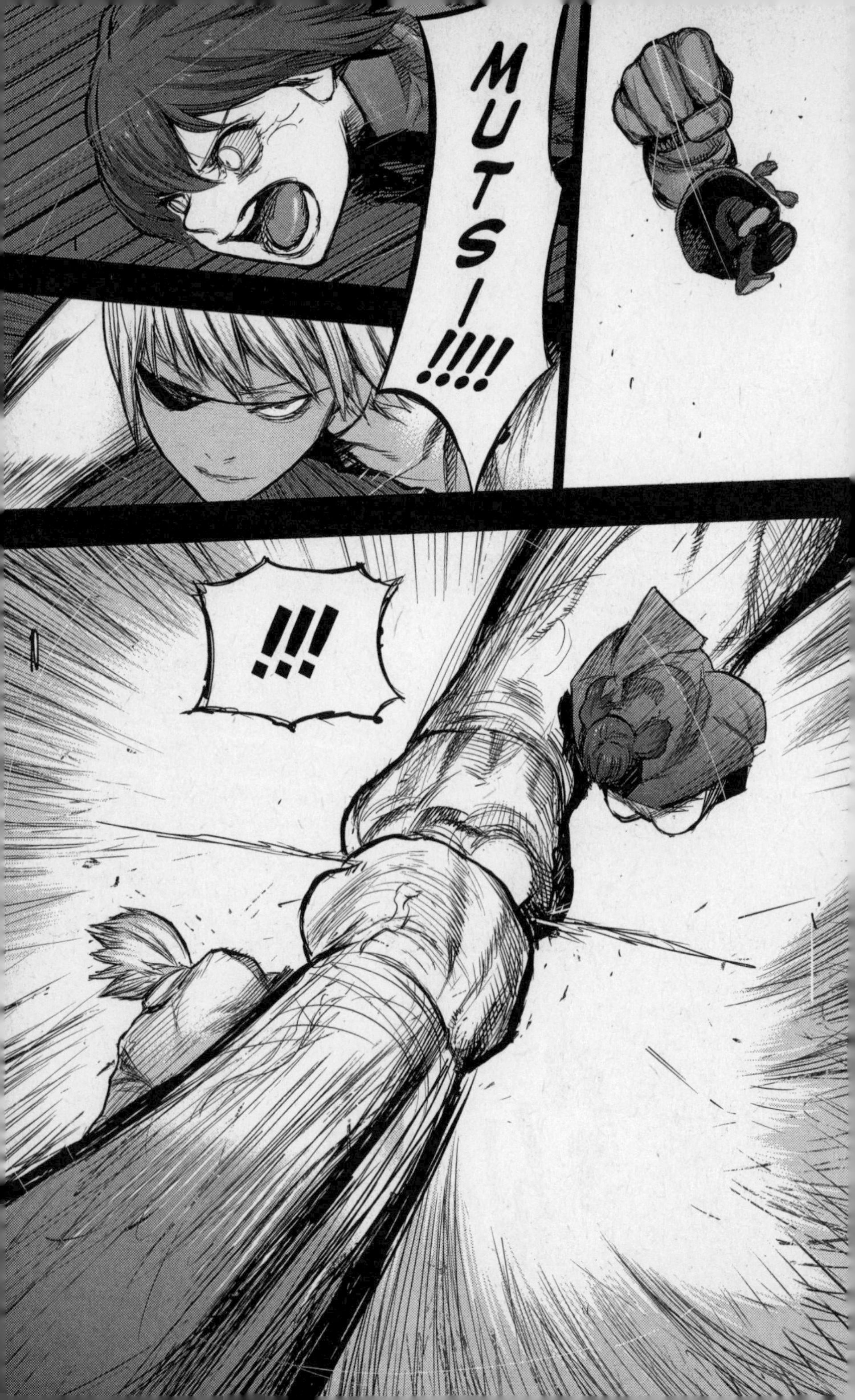

MUTSUKI!!!!
!!!

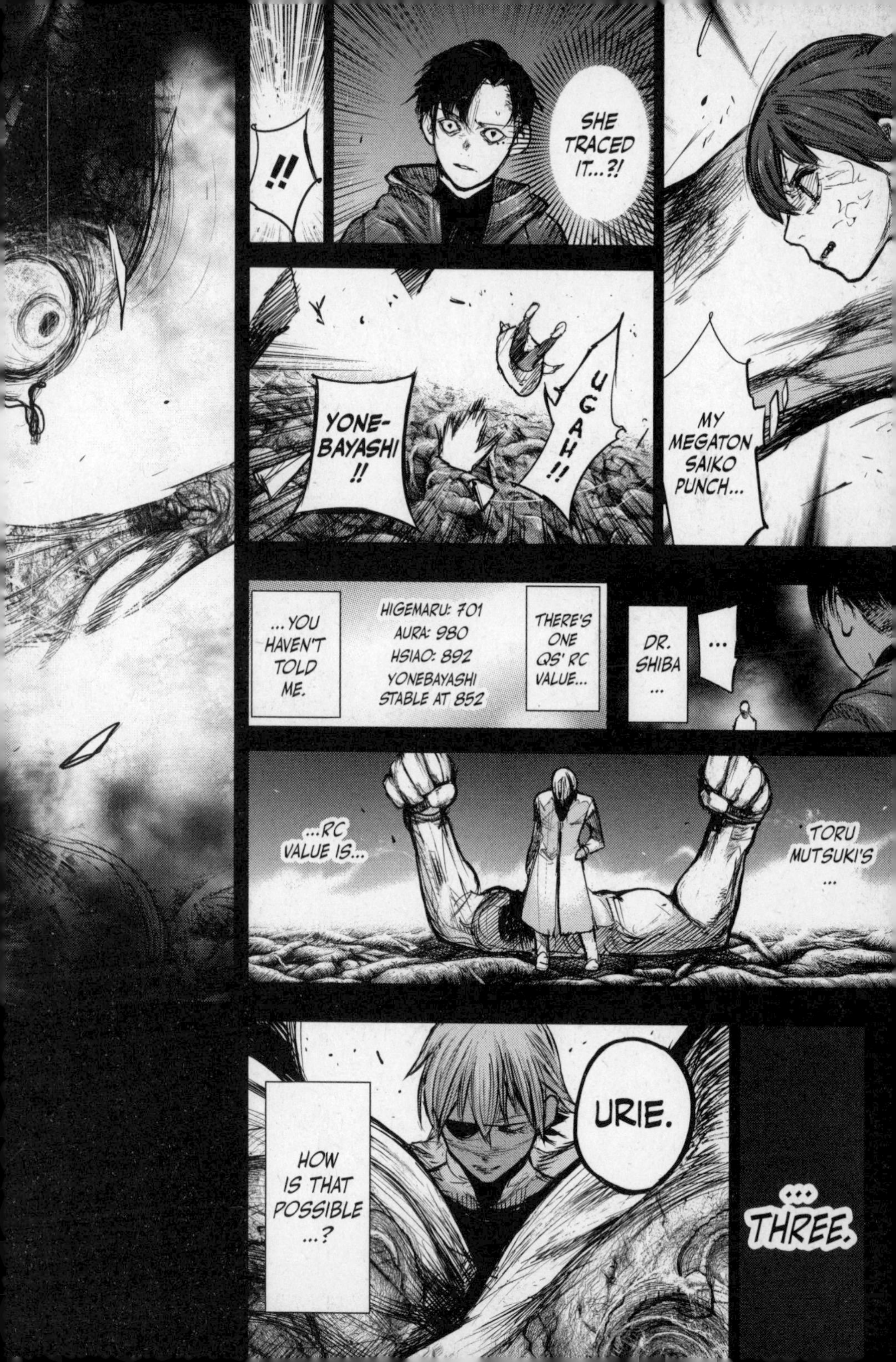
MY MEGATON SAIKO PUNCH...
SHE TRACED IT...?!
!!
UGAH!!
YONE-BAYASHI!!
...
DR. SHIBA ...
THERE'S ONE QS' RC VALUE...
HIGEMARU: 701
AURA: 980
HSIAO: 892
YONEBAYASHI STABLE AT 852
...YOU HAVEN'T TOLD ME.
TORU MUTSUKI'S ...
...RC VALUE IS...
...THREE.
URIE.
HOW IS THAT POSSIBLE ...?

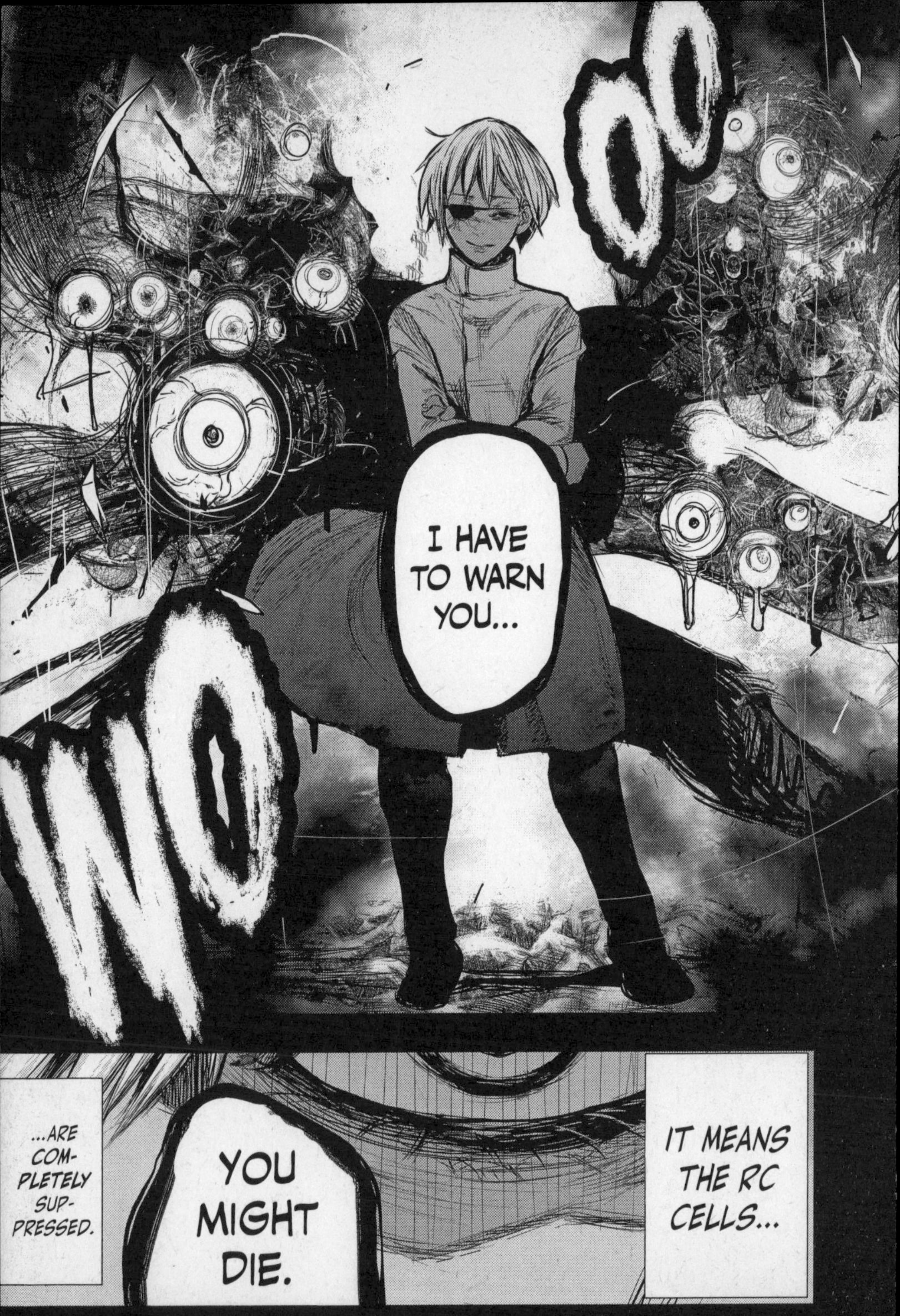
I HAVE TO WARN YOU...
IT MEANS THE RC CELLS...
YOU MIGHT DIE.
...ARE COMPLETELY SUPPRESSED.

To be continued in *Tokyo Ghoul:re* vol. 15

I Know All About It!

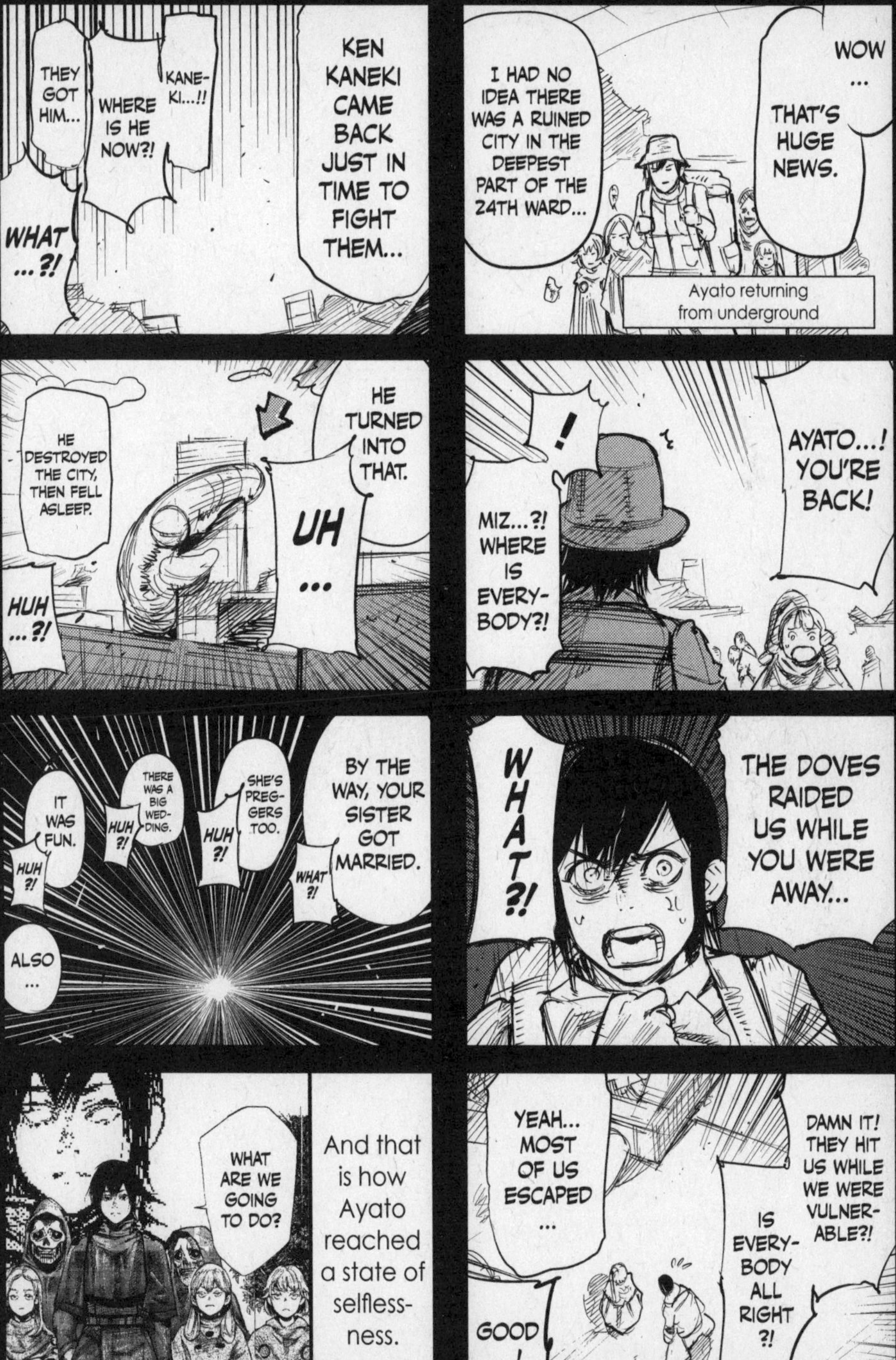
WOW ... THAT'S HUGE NEWS.
I HAD NO IDEA THERE WAS A RUINED CITY IN THE DEEPEST PART OF THE 24TH WARD...
Ayato returning from underground
AYATO...! YOU'RE BACK!
!
MIZ...?! WHERE IS EVERYBODY?!
THE DOVES RAIDED US WHILE YOU WERE AWAY...
WHAT?!
DAMN IT! THEY HIT US WHILE WE WERE VULNERABLE?!
IS EVERYBODY ALL RIGHT?!
YEAH... MOST OF US ESCAPED ...
GOOD ...!
KEN KANEKI CAME BACK JUST IN TIME TO FIGHT THEM...
KANEKI...!!
WHERE IS HE NOW?!
THEY GOT HIM...
WHAT ...?!
HE TURNED INTO THAT.
UH ...
HE DESTROYED THE CITY, THEN FELL ASLEEP.
HUH ...?!
BY THE WAY, YOUR SISTER GOT MARRIED.
WHAT ?!
SHE'S PREGGERS TOO.
HUH ?!
THERE WAS A BIG WEDDING.
HUH ?!
IT WAS FUN.
HUH ?!
ALSO ...
And that is how Ayato reached a state of selflessness.
WHAT ARE WE GOING TO DO?

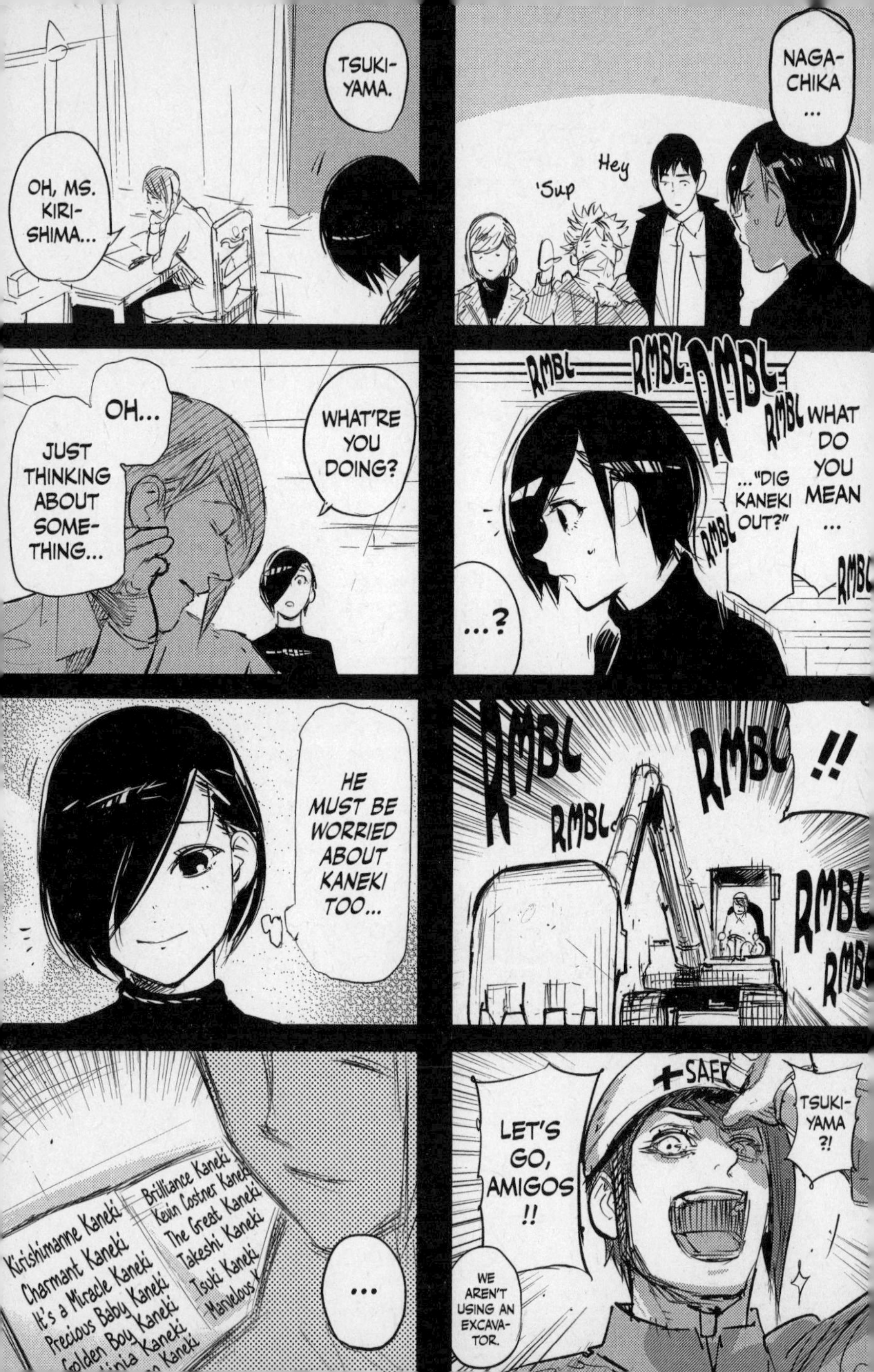
NAGA-CHIKA...
Hey
'Sup
TSUKI-YAMA.
OH, MS. KIRI-SHIMA...
RMBL RMBL RMBL RMBL RMBL RMBL
WHAT DO YOU MEAN...
..."DIG KANEKI OUT?"
...?
WHAT'RE YOU DOING?
OH...
JUST THINKING ABOUT SOME-THING...
RMBL RMBL RMBL!! RMBL RMBL RMBL
HE MUST BE WORRIED ABOUT KANEKI TOO...
TSUKI-YAMA?!
LET'S GO, AMIGOS!!
WE AREN'T USING AN EXCAVA-TOR.
Brilliance Kaneki
Kevin Costner Kaneki
The Great Kaneki
Takeshi Kaneki
Tsuki Kaneki
Kirishimanne Kaneki
Charmant Kaneki
It's a Miracle Kaneki
Precious Baby Kaneki
Golden Boy Kaneki
...

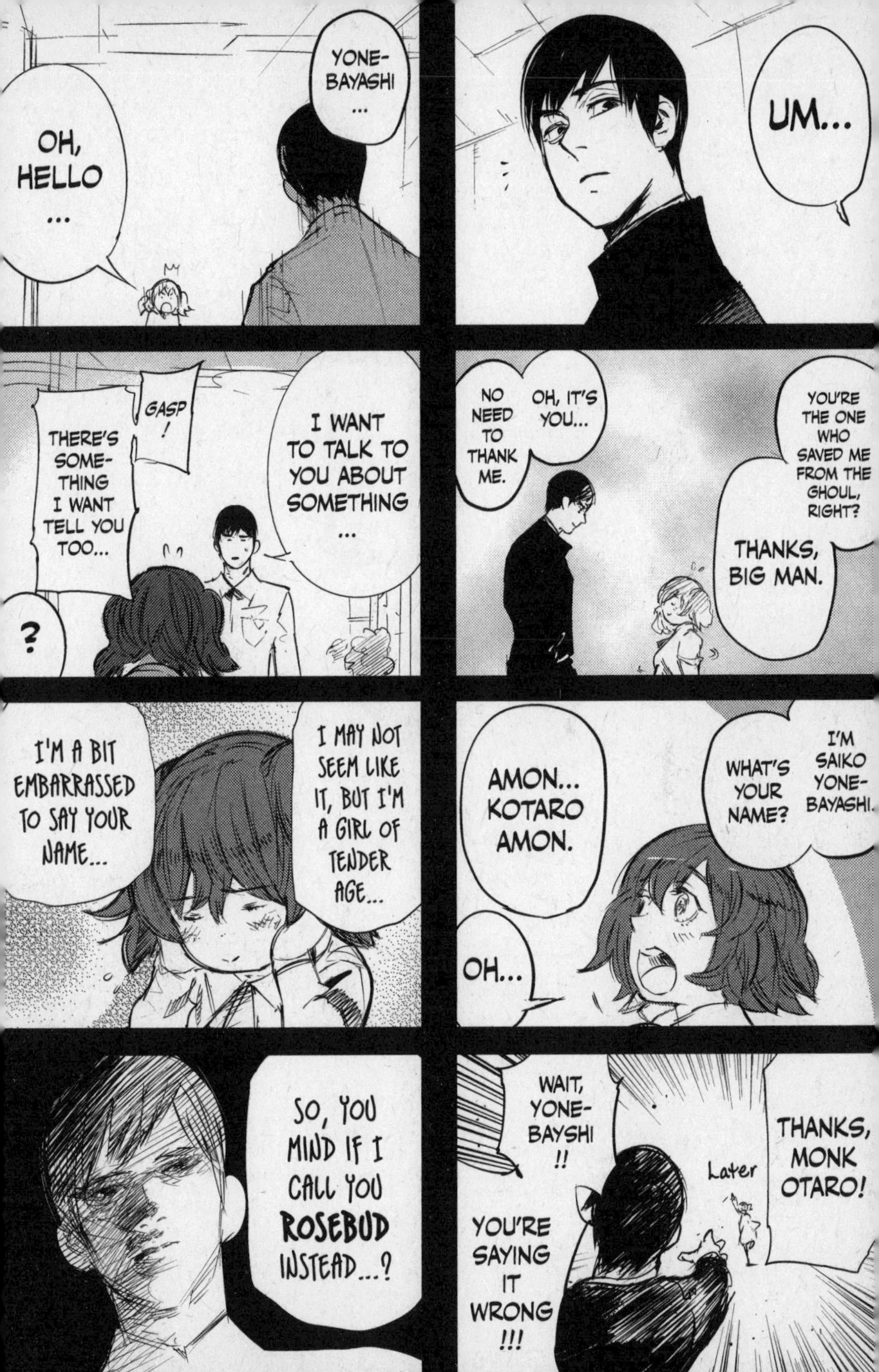
UM...
YONE-BAYASHI ...
OH, HELLO ...
YOU'RE THE ONE WHO SAVED ME FROM THE GHOUL, RIGHT?
THANKS, BIG MAN.
OH, IT'S YOU...
NO NEED TO THANK ME.
I WANT TO TALK TO YOU ABOUT SOMETHING ...
GASP !
THERE'S SOME-THING I WANT TELL YOU TOO...
?
I'M SAIKO YONE-BAYASHI.
WHAT'S YOUR NAME?
AMON... KOTARO AMON.
OH...
I MAY NOT SEEM LIKE IT, BUT I'M A GIRL OF TENDER AGE...
I'M A BIT EMBARRASSED TO SAY YOUR NAME...
THANKS, MONK OTARO!
Later
WAIT, YONE-BAYSHI !!
YOU'RE SAYING IT WRONG !!!
SO, YOU MIND IF I CALL YOU ROSEBUD INSTEAD...?

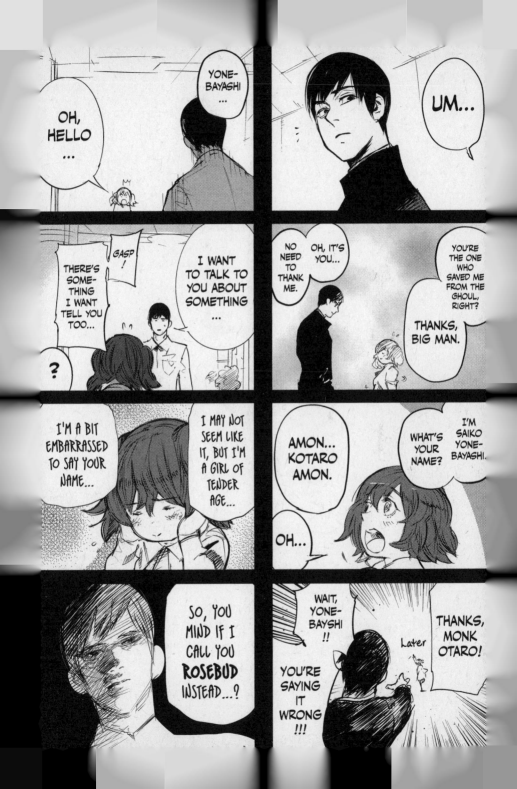

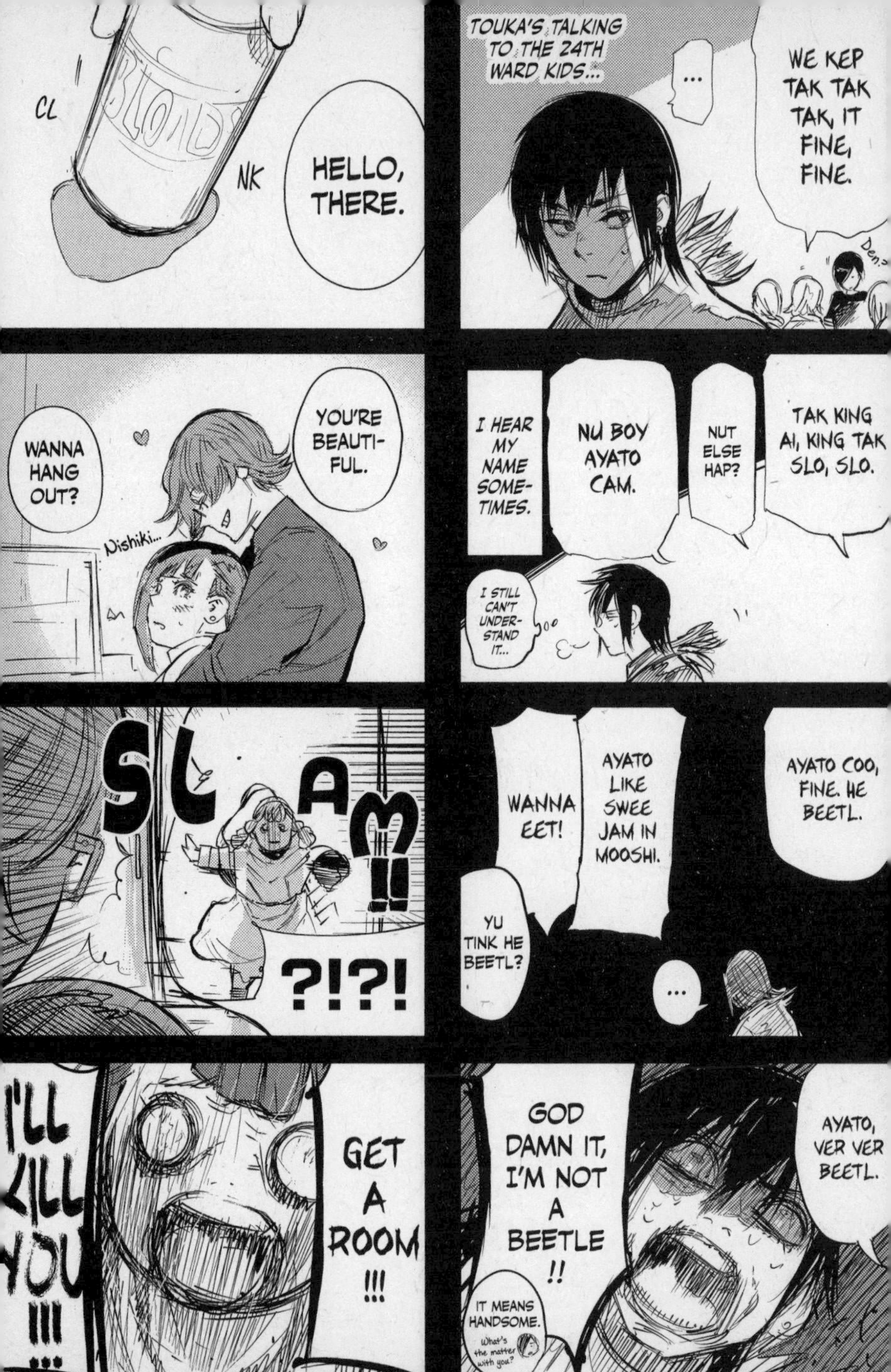
TOUKA'S TALKING TO THE 24TH WARD KIDS...
...
WE KEP TAK TAK TAK, IT FINE, FINE.
Den?
CL
NK
HELLO, THERE.
TAK KING AI, KING TAK SLO, SLO.
NUT ELSE HAP?
NU BOY AYATO CAM.
I HEAR MY NAME SOME-TIMES.
I STILL CAN'T UNDER-STAND IT...
YOU'RE BEAUTI-FUL.
WANNA HANG OUT?
Nishiki...
AYATO COO, FINE. HE BEETL.
AYATO LIKE SWEE JAM IN MOOSHI.
WANNA EET!
YU TINK HE BEETL?
...
SLAM!!
?!?!
AYATO, VER VER BEETL.
GOD DAMN IT, I'M NOT A BEETLE!!
IT MEANS HANDSOME.
What's the matter with you?
GET A ROOM!!!
I'LL KILL YOU!!!

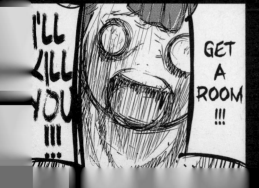

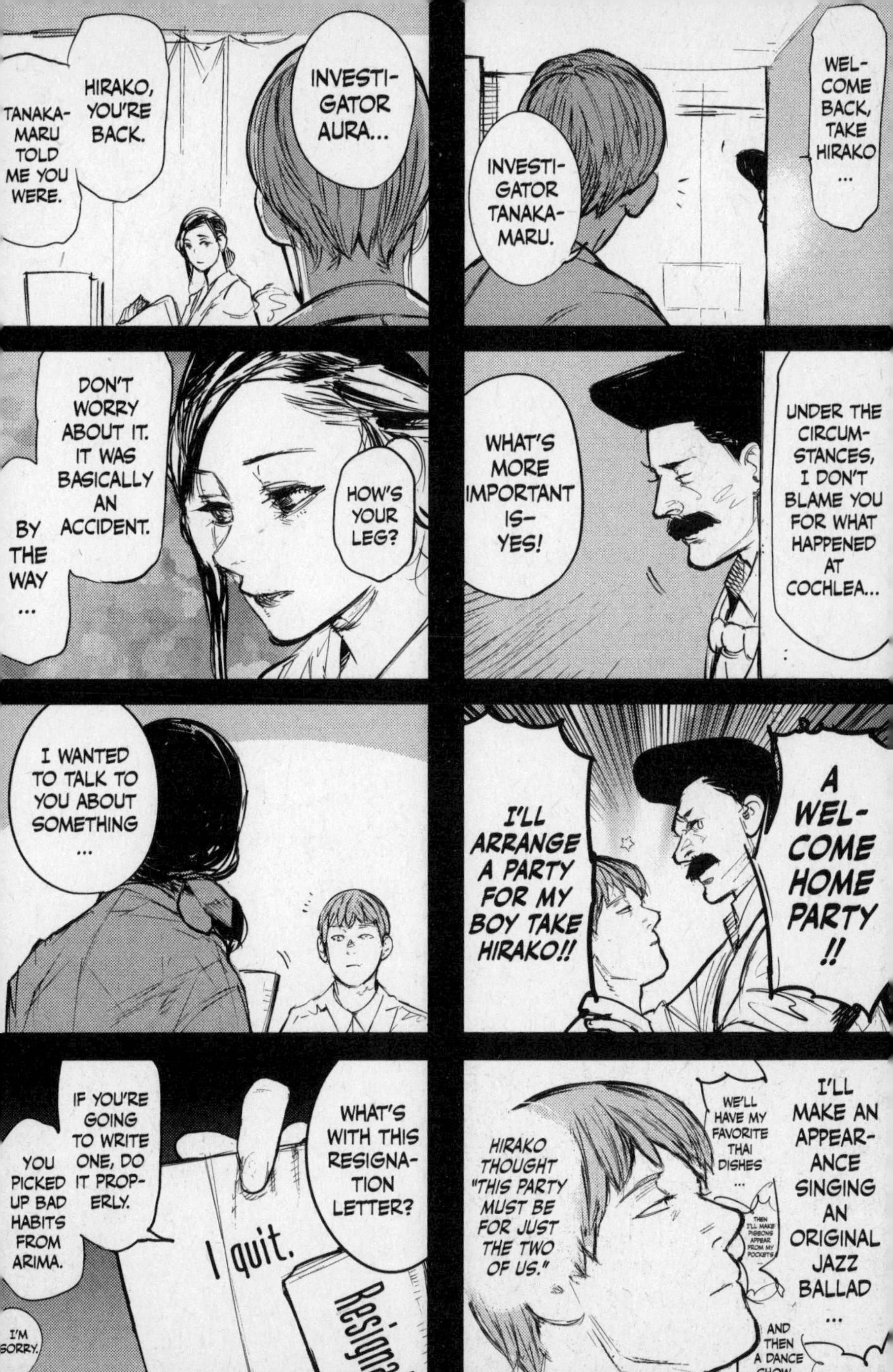
WEL-COME BACK, TAKE HIRAKO...
INVESTI-GATOR TANAKA-MARU.
INVESTI-GATOR AURA...
HIRAKO, YOU'RE BACK.
TANAKA-MARU TOLD ME YOU WERE.
UNDER THE CIRCUM-STANCES, I DON'T BLAME YOU FOR WHAT HAPPENED AT COCHLEA...
WHAT'S MORE IMPORTANT IS— YES!
HOW'S YOUR LEG?
DON'T WORRY ABOUT IT. IT WAS BASICALLY AN ACCIDENT.
BY THE WAY...
A WEL-COME HOME PARTY!!
I'LL ARRANGE A PARTY FOR MY BOY TAKE HIRAKO!!
I WANTED TO TALK TO YOU ABOUT SOMETHING...
I'LL MAKE AN APPEAR-ANCE SINGING AN ORIGINAL JAZZ BALLAD...
WE'LL HAVE MY FAVORITE THAI DISHES...
THEN I'LL MAKE PIGEONS APPEAR FROM MY POCKETS...
AND THEN A DANCE SHOW...
HIRAKO THOUGHT "THIS PARTY MUST BE FOR JUST THE TWO OF US."
WHAT'S WITH THIS RESIGNA-TION LETTER?
I quit.
Resignat
IF YOU'RE GOING TO WRITE ONE, DO IT PROP-ERLY.
YOU PICKED UP BAD HABITS FROM ARIMA.
I'M SORRY.

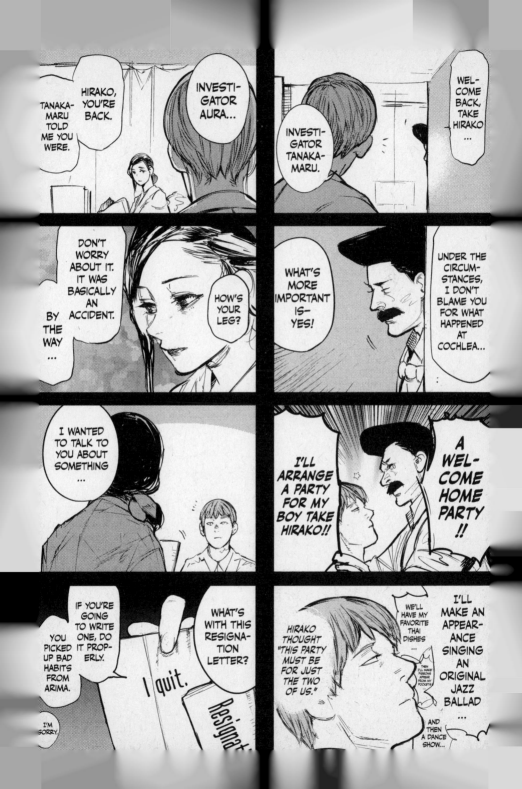

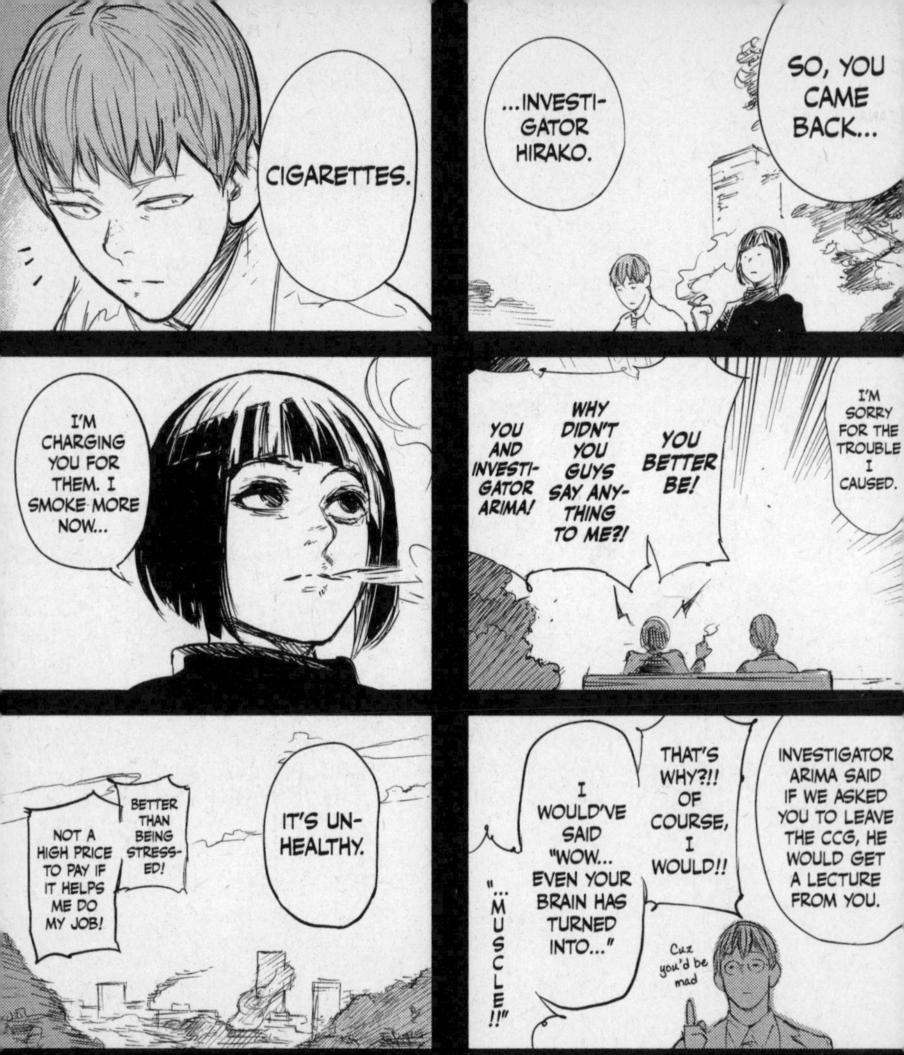
SO, YOU CAME BACK...
...INVESTI-GATOR HIRAKO.
CIGARETTES.
I'M SORRY FOR THE TROUBLE I CAUSED.
YOU BETTER BE!
WHY DIDN'T YOU GUYS SAY ANY-THING TO ME?!
YOU AND INVESTI-GATOR ARIMA!
I'M CHARGING YOU FOR THEM. I SMOKE MORE NOW...
INVESTIGATOR ARIMA SAID IF WE ASKED YOU TO LEAVE THE CCG, HE WOULD GET A LECTURE FROM YOU.
THAT'S WHY?!! OF COURSE, I WOULD!!
I WOULD'VE SAID "WOW... EVEN YOUR BRAIN HAS TURNED INTO..."
"...MUSCLE!!"
Cuz you'd be mad
IT'S UN-HEALTHY.
BETTER THAN BEING STRESS-ED!
NOT A HIGH PRICE TO PAY IF IT HELPS ME DO MY JOB!

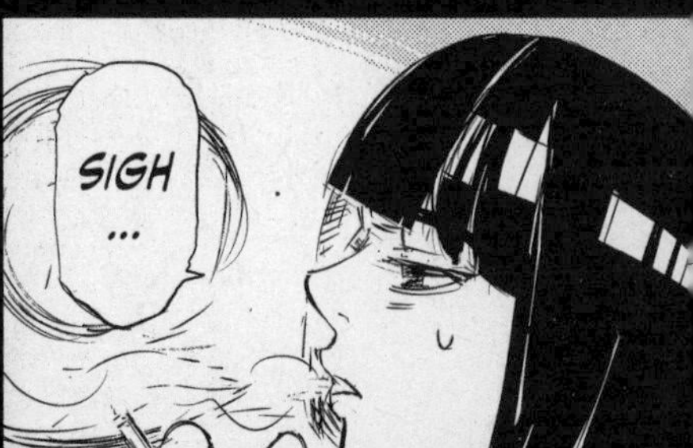
SIGH ...

Staff
Kiyotaka Aihara
Nina
Ippo Yaguchi
Akikukni Nakao
Nomaguchi
Abe

Comic Design
Hideaki Shimada (L.S.D.)
Magazine Design
Miyuki Takaoka (POCKET)
Photography
Wataru Tanaka
Editor
Junpei Matsuo

Volume 15 is out Feb. 2020

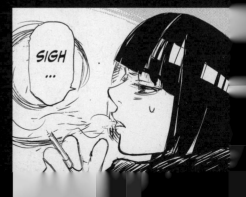

● Akihiro Kano
嘉納 明博 （かのう あきひろ）

Graduated Teiho University Medical School
Chief Researcher at GFG
CCG Medical Examiner
Former researcher at Kano General Hospital

● Blood type: A ● Height/weight: 178cm/72kg

Born into a family of health-care providers. His father took over
a hospital that had been run by his family for three generations.

Enrolled in Teiho University Medical School to pursue medicine
like his father. Graduated with excellent grades.

Joined the Ghoul Research Society in college.

Moved to Germany upon graduation to work at the GFG
(Ghoul Forschung Gesellschaft). Worked for three years
in Adam Gehner's lab, researching cell differentiation and
high-order structures of Rc cells.

Joined the CCG upon his return to Japan, where he assisted
as a doctor in Kakuho removal and Quinque application.

While at the CCG he was secretly invited to join the Hakubi
Group, a Washu-supervised team specializing in certain
Ghoul-related research. Quit the CCG after leaving the group.

After leaving the CCG, he took over Kano General Hospital.
Met Nimura Furuta while conducting independent research.

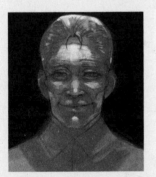

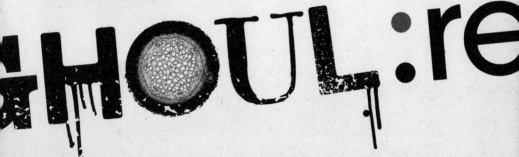

SUI ISHIDA is the author
of the immensely popular
Tokyo Ghoul and several
Tokyo Ghoul one-shots,
including one that won
second place in the *Weekly
Young Jump* 113th Grand
Prix award in 2010. *Tokyo
Ghoul:re* is the sequel to
Tokyo Ghoul.

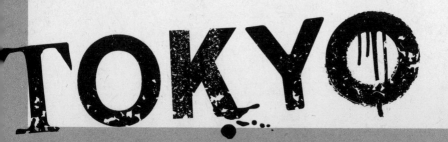

TOKYO GHOUL:re

VOLUME 14
VIZ SIGNATURE EDITION

Story and art by
SUI ISHIDA

First published in Japan in 2014 by SHUEISHA Inc., Tokyo.
English translation rights arranged by SHUEISHA Inc.

Translation Joe Yamazaki
Touch-Up Art & Lettering Vanessa Satone
Design Shawn Carrico
Editor Pancha Diaz

Printed in the U.S.A.

Published by VIZ Media, LLC
P.O. Box 77010
San Francisco, CA 94107

10 9 8 7 6 5 4 3 2 1
First printing, December 2019

VIZ MEDIA
viz.com

VIZ SIGNATURE
vizsignature.com

RATED T+ OLDER TEEN
ratings.viz.com

PARENTAL ADVISORY
TOKYO GHOUL: RE is rated T+ for Older Teen and is recommended for ages 16 and up. This volume contains violence.

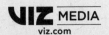

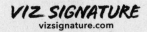

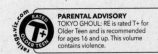

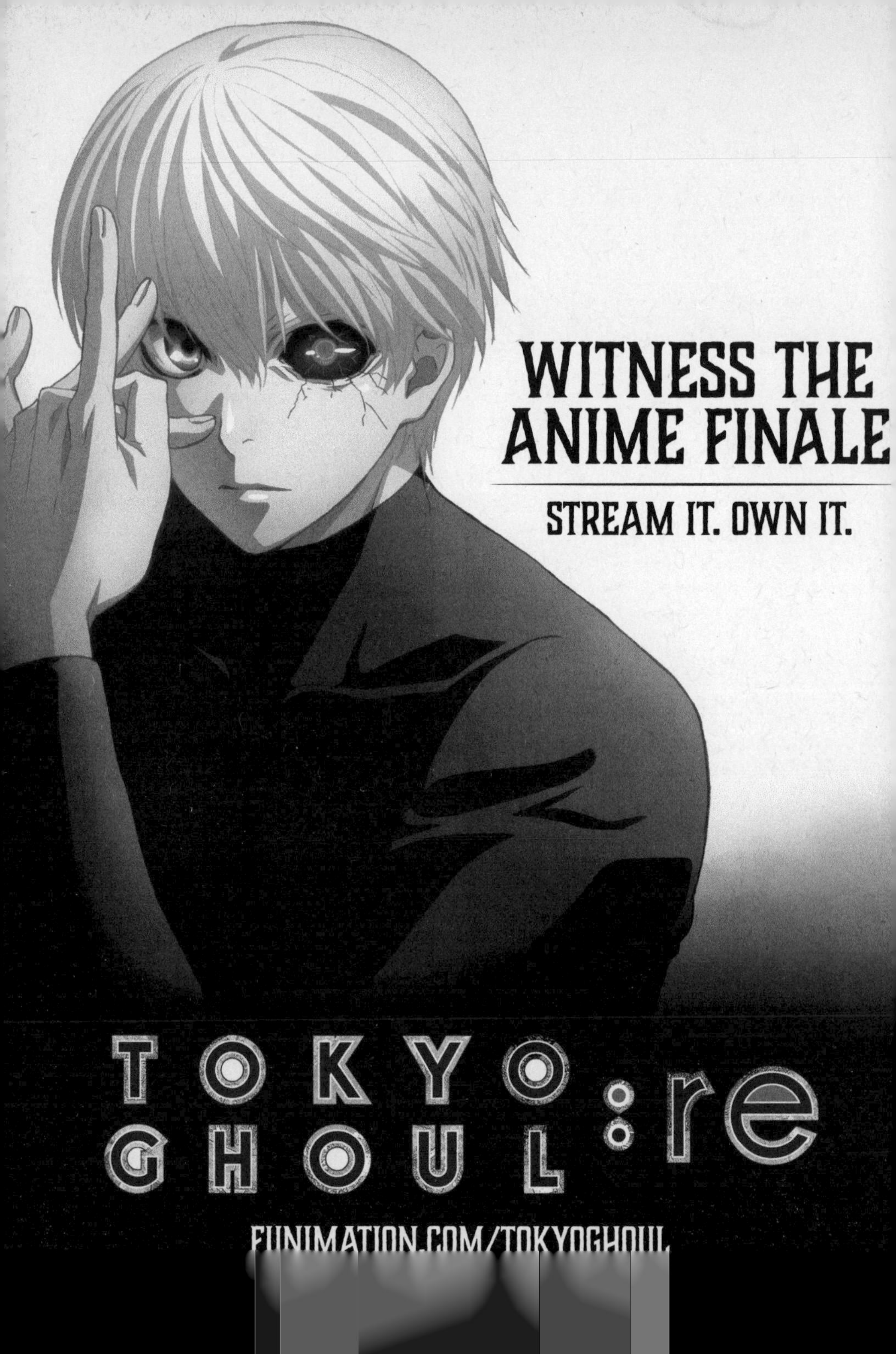
WITNESS THE ANIME FINALE
STREAM IT. OWN IT.
TOKYO GHOUL:re
FUNIMATION.COM/TOKYOGHOUL

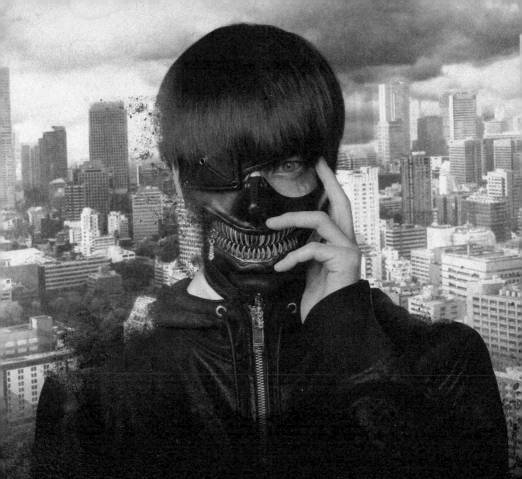

Tokyo Ghoul

YOU'VE READ THE MANGA
NOW WATCH THE
LIVE-ACTION MOVIE!

OWN IT NOW ON BLU-RAY, DVD & DIGITAL HD

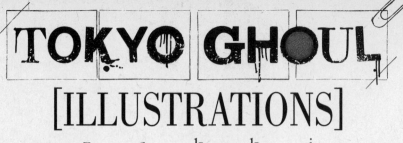

TOKYO GHOUL
[ILLUSTRATIONS]
z a k k i

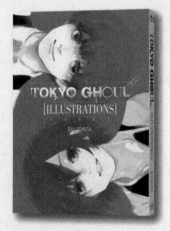

Tokyo Ghoul Illustrations: zakki features artwork and behind-the-scenes notes, commentary and ruminations from ***Tokyo Ghoul*** creator Sui Ishida. Discover the creative process that brought the hit manga to life, in gloriously ghoulish full color.

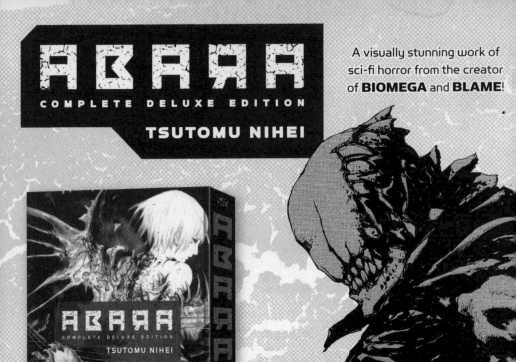

ABARA
COMPLETE DELUXE EDITION
TSUTOMU NIHEI

A visually stunning work of sci-fi horror from the creator of **BIOMEGA** and **BLAME**!

A vast city lies under the shadow of colossal, ancient tombs, the identity of their builders lost to time. In the streets of the city something is preying on the inhabitants, something that moves faster than the human eye can see and leaves unimaginable horror in its wake.

Tsutomu Nihei's dazzling, harrowing dystopian thriller is presented here in a single-volume hardcover edition featuring full-color pages and foldout illustrations. This volume also includes the early short story "Digimortal."

TOKYO GHOUL:re

This is the last page.
TOKYO GHOUL:re reads right to left.